THIRD EDITION

COMPOSITION AND GRAMMAR

FOR HCC BY HCC

HCC EDITORIAL BOARD

Hillsborough Community College: Dale Mabry Campus
ATTN: Dr. Jenifer Paquette (DHUM 303)
4001 W. Tampa Bay Blvd.
Tampa, FL 33614
Email: enctextbookhcc@gmail.com

Textbook Editorial Board

Dr. Jenifer Paquette—Editor
Phillip Chamberlin
Laura Mita
Michelle Sanders

Contributors

Dr. Benjamin Barrett, Jana Bielecki, Dr. Dexter Brock, Molly Brown-Fuller, Lorenzo Carswell, Phillip Chamberlin, Christina Connor, Ed Coursey, Dr. Tim Curran, Dr. Angela Eward-Mangione, Natalia Fiore, John Frank, Dr. Charity Freeman, Dr. Robert Funk, Judith Gaspar, Dr. Richard Gaspar, Dr. Barbara Goldstein, Kenneth Hawkins, Dr. Suzanne Lynch, Rocky Marcus, Laura Mita, Dr. Judith Nolasco, Dr. Jenifer Paquette, Doug Peterson, Carol Reid, Jeffrey Rubinstein, Valerie Saad, Michelle Sanders, Melissa Steinhardt, Angela Tartaglia, Alex Tavares, Dr. Raymond Vince

Student samples used with permission.

All images fall under Creative Commons License and are pulled from several sources including ShutterStock, Pixabay, and similar resources.

Accomplishing Innovation Press

Accomplishing Innovation Press
1497 Main St. Suite 169
Dunedin, FL 34698
accomplishinginnovationpress.com
AccomplishingInnovationPress@gmail.com

Library of Congress Control Number: 2022936480

Paperback ISBN-13: 978-1-64450-596-0
Hardcover ISBN-13: 978-1-64450-632-5
Ebook ISBN-13: 978-1-64450-597-7

Acknowledgements

First Edition

Creating a textbook is a tremendous endeavor. This particular text would not exist without the heroic efforts of the Editorial Board and the contributors, so I would like to acknowledge each of them with a hearty thank you for putting together a quality product for our students. You are all amazing for making this idea a reality.

A very special thank you goes out to Phil Chamberlin for reading and re-reading endless drafts, creating literally dozens of exercises, and toning down my exclamation points; to Michelle Sanders for tirelessly working to get student quizzes together, for finding great student samples, and for adding depth and insight to formerly weak sections; to Laura Mita for sharing her tech knowledge and spending countless hours on Google docs; to Benjamin Barrett and John Frank for coordinating a companion reader for this textbook; to Ed Coursey for the best argument chapter I've seen in a composition textbook; to Jana Bielecki for her detailed comments that made the book so much better; to Maribeth Mobley for catching the little things we kept missing; to Angela Eward-Mangione for providing another set of eyes; to Melissa Steinhardt for writing all of the missing chapters when we needed them; to Suzanne Lynch and Valerie Saad for the initial conversation that raised the possibility of a faculty-created textbook; and to Rebecca Todd and Dustin Lemke, the best hallmates ever, for giving perspective whenever I got lost in the weeds.

An English textbook is not complete without samples, so I would like to thank all of the students who shared their work with us: Asma Abdallah, Sabrina Arocha, Nia Baptiste-Dena, Shae Barhonovich, Xye Borg, Tiffany Brown, Wesley Bryan, Krista Byrd, Rachel Carter, James Curry, Laura Dilts, Markie Gourley, Kelly Gutierrez, Amber Imeh, Jared Kleinkopf, Andrew Koplin, Alia Machin, Kelsey Means, Jo Neuman, Luigi Garcia Otero, Jessica Oswald, Kristina Piloto, Peggy Reyes, Jasmine Rolph, Alex Rose, Tabitha Saletri, Riley Schmidt, Laura Vasquez, and Andrea Waters. This textbook would not be what it is without your contributions.

Another important part of a textbook is artwork. I thank the nameless artists who shared their work with the world so that we could enjoy it here. Finally, I would like to thank Patchanit Srivinach for her pencil drawing of the DTEC building.

Dr. Jenifer Paquette—Editor
15 June 2018

Second Edition

Revising this textbook for the second edition has been an epic undertaking that would not have been possible without the help of so many others.

Thanks to the contributors, new and returning, who volunteered their time and expertise to this project time and again, especially Jana Bielecki, Christina Connor, Ed Coursey, Dr. Tim Curran, Dr. Angela Eward-Mangione, Kenneth Hawkins, Carol Reid, and Valerie Saad.

Insane levels of special thanks to Phillip Chamberlin, Laura Mita, and Michelle Sanders, without whom this revision would never have been finished on time—or anywhere near this level of quality. I could not have asked for a better team to work on this project. You guys rock. Seriously.

Dr. Jenifer Paquette—Editor
26 April 2021

Third Edition

Thanks yet again to Phil Chamberlin, Laura Mita, and Michelle Sanders. Best. Team. Ever.

Dr. Jenifer Paquette—Editor
18 May 2022

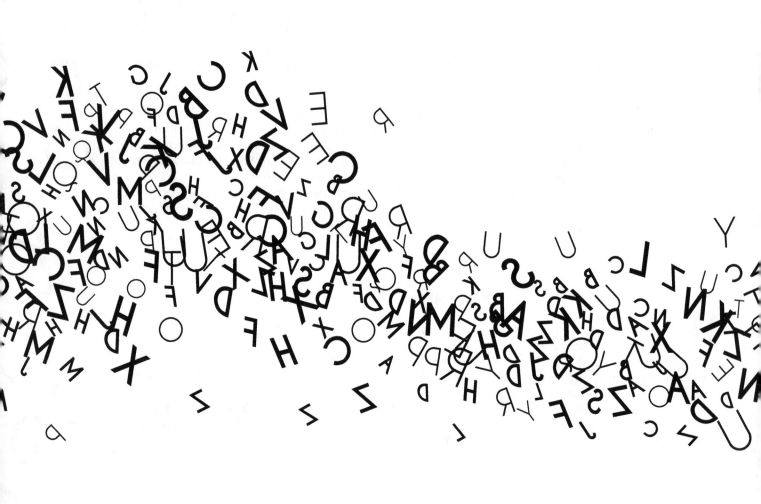

TABLE OF CONTENTS

Part Five: Research

Chapter 20

Chapter 21

Chapter 22

Chapter 23

Chapter 24

Chapter 25

Editing Symbols

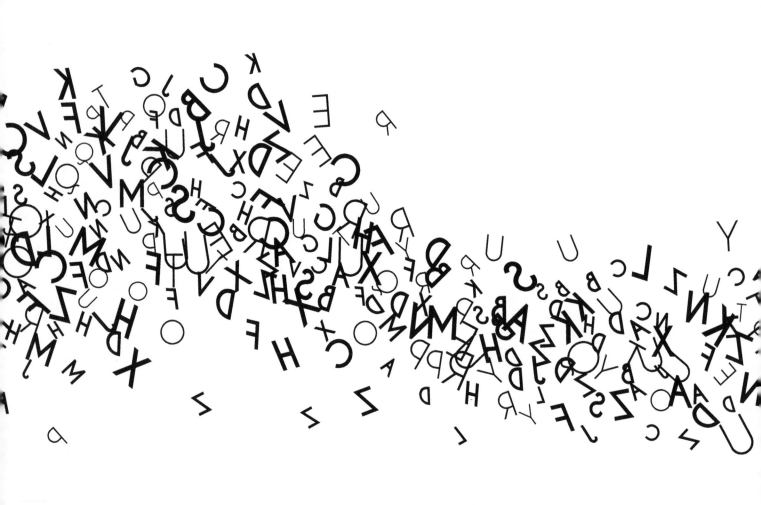

PART ONE

Reading Techniques

OVERVIEW

Good writers are always good readers, so it only makes sense to begin by reading the written word before you try to write words of your own.

A few things to know before we begin:

- Reading is more than scanning your eyes over the little marks on the page. Reading is an active process.

- Reading well-written words will help you craft your own well-written words—not because you copy them, but because while reading, you internalize the rhythm of the language, and when it is your turn to compose words, you can call on that knowledge to write words that follow the same rhythm.

A note on the structure of this section:

- Part One begins with an explanation of common reading techniques, offering strategies like previewing, annotating, and summarizing to help you become a more active reader.

- Part One continues with reflective techniques like self-questioning and synthesis.

Chapter 1

ACTIVE READING TECHNIQUES

It's easy to get lost when you are reading. Sometimes, you may find yourself re-reading the same paragraph over and over again. One way to avoid this waste of time and energy is to read actively the first time (instead of buckling down and focusing during the last few moments before the due date or the test).

There are some useful strategies that you can use to stay active when reading:

- Previewing

- Annotating

- Summarizing

When reading, don't let yourself become a passive receiver of words. You aren't standing in the shower letting the words run over you—on the contrary, you are doing what is known as active reading. You are consciously taking in each word and sentence, comprehending the idea (or looking up unknown words and using context clues). Touch the page with your hand, run a finger underneath each line, keep yourself actively engaged in the reading process. If you find yourself drifting away from the content, start again.

1.1 Previewing

Before you read, take a moment to preview the text. Look at the length and decide how long it will take you to get through it—or how much time you plan to devote to this project at this moment. Look over the table of contents, section and subsection headings, and anything in bold. Is this a textbook? Check the chapter ending for review questions. Get a sense of what you are in for before you dig in and start reading. This is called **previewing**.

Look at the **title**—What does this make you think about? Is there a subtitle?

Consider the **publication information**—Who wrote it? Where and when did it appear? How does that information affect what you are reading?

Assess your **expectations**—What do you expect from this reading? What ideas are you looking for here?

Length—How long is this reading? How fast do you read? Do the math and if necessary, set up a reading schedule.

Now that you know what to expect, it's time to get to it. Read.

Sample Preview[1]

The following is an example of mental notes a reader might make when previewing a text:

Topic: Florida Man

Author: I don't recognize Alex Rose, but I trust Hawkeye News

Publication date: March 2015

Expectations: Definition of concept/examples/casual tone

Length: 7 paragraphs, roughly 1 page, no headers or section breaks

_____

[1] Image shows page layout of essay (find complete essay in Chapter 12.5)

Florida Man: The man, the myth, the legend

hawkeyenews.net/commentary/2015/03/30/florida-man-the-man-the-myth-the-legend/

Alex Rose

He's drunk, high, rich, poor, black, and white. He has no respect for the law or himself. His favorite drink is orange juice with meth. He's robbed stores and kidnapped and murdered. He's a citizen, a football player, a lawyer, governor, and a constant pervert. He's your neighbor, your brother, father, uncle and sometimes you. He is Florida Man and there's a little bit of him in all of us.

Florida Man is not one person, but the conglomerate of all Florida residents. No one is safe from him because he is everywhere and everyone, at least in Florida. He has Twitter, Instagram, and Facebook accounts. He even has a new beer made by Cigar City Brewing Company. Combined, he has killed every animal in the state, and eaten most of them, including humans. The only creature to elude Florida Man is the Skunk Ape, and it can't run forever.

The rest of the nation knows that Florida is crazy. Scientists have blamed the fact that we don't have winter. We get to spend more time outside and get in more trouble. But that doesn't account for the sheer insanity and volume of the incidents. It could be because of Florida Man's easy access to guns and unwillingness to learn gun safety. Or maybe his fondness of meth and alcohol drives him to rob. I say it is because Florida Man is in us all, and only in Florida can he exercise his full potential.

Web results for other states bring similar men of this caliber. Georgia Man lives in a similar way, as does Arizona Man, but they do not match Florida Man's track record. Florida gives too many opportunities for insanity to take over. We have swamps, farms, forests, big cities, small towns, and at most three hills. Florida Man is confined by the sea on three sides and has nowhere to go but crazy.

But our state's special brand of insanity has not missed the fairer sex. Florida Woman is also on the prowl, stabbing, shooting, and crashing her car with the same ferocity as her male counterpart. If anything, Florida Woman is more of a threat due to her close proximity to babies. Leaving a child in the care of Florida Woman is inadvisable to anyone but Florida Man.

Taking a look back at some of Florida Man's more famous exploits, we see that he is a talented and determined individual. Florida Man buried his cat, and fought to keep ownership of it when it clawed its way out of the ground five days later. Florida Man shot a teenager, was set free, and continues to assault people. Florida Man ate a guy's face while on bath salts. Florida Man hunts alligators for food and pythons for fun. Florida Woman had an affair with a fourteen year old student and mostly got away with it. Florida Woman killed her baby and walked on lesser charges.

As we reflect on our state's pride and glory, it makes it hard to wonder why anyone would live in Florida in the first place. Maybe we just never left. Or maybe we can't resist the allure of 90 degree, 90% humidity and the constant risk of hurricanes. But really, Florida isn't a state of the nation, it's a state of mind, and no amount of distance will free us from our madness.

Sample Essay: Florida Man

1.2 ANNOTATING

You should always read with a writing tool in hand: a pen, pencil, highlighter, or whatever works for you. A pile of sticky notes is useful if the idea of writing in the book is upsetting to you. If reading on a screen, use the digital annotation tools available (i.e. underlining, highlighting, text boxes, sticky notes, etc.). Whatever method you employ, take notes as you read. Highlight important ideas, underline key points, and jot down questions or ideas that you have while reading. The more you annotate a text, the more likely you are to remember what you've read. This also makes it easier to go back and study later since you don't have to swim through a sea of words—you can just scan your notes and highlighted bits. Annotating a text makes studying more effective.

The more you physically engage with the text, the more information you will retain for later.

Florida Man: The man, the myth, the legend

hawkeyenews.net/commentary/2015/03/30/florida-man-the-man-the-myth-the-legend/

Alex Rose

He's drunk, high, rich, poor, black, and white. He has no respect for the law or himself. His favorite drink is orange juice with meth. He's robbed stores and kidnapped and murdered. He's a citizen, a football player, a lawyer, governor, and a constant pervert. He's your neighbor, your brother, father, uncle and sometimes you. He is Florida Man and there's a little bit of him in all of us.   **Thesis?**

What is it?

Florida Man is not one person, but the conglomerate of all Florida residents. No one is safe from him because he is everywhere and everyone, at least in Florida. He has Twitter, Instagram, and Facebook accounts. He even has a new beer made by Cigar City Brewing Company. Combined, he has killed every animal in the state, and eaten most of them, including humans. The only creature to elude Florida Man is the Skunk Ape, and it can't run forever. **HA!**

#Stereotype

The rest of the nation knows that Florida is crazy. Scientists have blamed the fact that we don't have winter. We get to spend more time outside and get in more trouble. But that doesn't account for the sheer insanity and volume of the incidents. It could be because of Florida Man's easy access to guns and unwillingness to learn gun safety. Or maybe his fondness of meth and alcohol drives him to rob. I say it is because Florida Man is in us all, and only in Florida can he exercise his full potential.

Web results for other states bring similar men of this caliber. Georgia Man lives in a similar way, as does Arizona Man, but they do not match Florida Man's track record. Florida gives too many opportunities for insanity to take over. We have swamps, farms, forests, big cities, small towns, and at most three hills. Florida Man is confined by the sea on three sides and has nowhere to go but crazy. **Repeated**

Comparison

But our state's special brand of insanity has not missed the fairer sex. Florida Woman is also on the prowl, stabbing, shooting, and crashing her car with the same ferocity as her male counterpart. If anything, Florida Woman is more of a threat due to her close proximity to babies. Leaving a child in the care of Florida Woman is inadvisable to anyone but Florida Man.

Details

Taking a look back at some of Florida Man's more famous exploits, we see that he is a talented and determined individual. Florida Man buried his cat, and fought to keep ownership of it when it clawed its way out of the ground five days later. Florida Man shot a teenager, was set free, and continues to assault people. Florida Man ate a guy's face while on bath salts. Florida Man hunts alligators for food and pythons for fun. Florida Woman had an affair with a fourteen year old student and mostly got away with it. Florida Woman killed her baby and walked on lesser charges.

TONE

As we reflect on our state's pride and glory, it makes it hard to wonder why anyone would live in Florida in the first place. Maybe we just never left. Or maybe we can't resist the allure of 90 degree, 90% humidity and the constant risk of hurricanes. But really, Florida isn't a state of the nation, it's a state of mind, and no amount of distance will free us from our madness.

SAMPLE ANNOTATION[1]

See how the essay to the left has been annotated by a reader who was clearly engaged with the text:

- Main ideas are underlined to make them stand out.

- Questions and ideas are jotted around the text.

- Phrases that stood out are enclosed in a box or emphasized.

- A brief overview of the main ideas is at the bottom.

---

[1]   Image shows annotated essay with notes and underlined phrases

Annotated Sample Essay

1.3 SUMMARIZING

It has happened to everyone: You begin to read a chapter. You read all of the words. You know the information. You stop reading, turn aside, and do another activity for a few moments. You return to the book, certain you are ready to move on to the next chapter, but cannot recall anything you've just read. It's gone, wandered out of your brain while you weren't looking.

How can you retain the information? After you've finished reading, as soon as you are done, take a minute to summarize what you've read. Even a few sentences will do the trick—just enough to capture the general gist of the reading. In your own words, write a summary on a sticky note, in a notebook, or even in the margins of the book; you can also use your phone or whatever device makes sense to you. Record the main idea and supporting details, and save your summary to look over later, like before a test or final exam.

> ## SAMPLE SUMMARY
>
> Florida Man is a "conglomerate of all Florida residents." He is crazy but "in us all." He is joined by Georgia Man and Arizona Man, but they ultimately lose in comparison. Florida Woman is another unique creature, a suitable mate only for Florida Man. A list of exploits may make Floridians question their life choices, but Florida "isn't a state of the nation, it's a state of mind."
>
> **Point of view:** We Floridians
>
> **Audience:** Non-Floridians as an explanation/ Floridians as a reminder

Florida Man: The man, the myth, the legend

hawkeyenews.net /commentary/2015/03/30/florida-man-the-man-the-myth-the-legend/

Alex Rose

He's drunk, high, rich, poor, black, and white. He has no respect for the law or himself. His favorite drink is orange juice with meth. He's robbed stores and kidnapped and murdered. He's a citizen, a football player, a lawyer, governor, and a constant pervert. He's your neighbor, your brother, father, uncle and sometimes you. He is Florida Man and there's a little bit of him in all of us.   Thesis?

What is it?
Florida Man is not one person, but the conglomerate of all Florida residents. No one is safe from him because he is everywhere and everyone, at least in Florida. He has Twitter, Instagram, and Facebook accounts. He even has a new beer made by Cigar City Brewing Company. Combined, he has killed every animal in the state, and eaten most of them, including humans. The only creature to elude Florida Man is the Skunk Ape, and it can't run forever.   HA!

#Stereotype
The rest of the nation knows that Florida is crazy. Scientists have blamed the fact that we don't have winter. We get to spend more time outside and get in more trouble. But that doesn't account for the sheer insanity and volume of the incidents. It could be because of Florida Man's easy access to guns and unwillingness to learn gun safety. Or maybe his fondness of meth and alcohol drives him to rob. I say it is because Florida Man is in us all, and only in Florida can he exercise his full potential.

Web results for other states bring similar men of this caliber. Georgia Man lives in a similar way, as does Arizona Man, but they do not match Florida Man's track record. Florida gives too many opportunities for insanity to take over. We have swamps, farms, forests, big cities, small towns, and at most three hills. Florida Man is confined by the sea on three sides and has nowhere to go but crazy.   Repeated   Comparison

But our state's special brand of insanity has not missed the fairer sex. Florida Woman is also on the prowl, stabbing, shooting, and crashing her car with the same ferocity as her male counterpart. If anything, Florida Woman is more of a threat due to her close proximity to babies. Leaving a child in the care of Florida Woman is inadvisable to anyone but Florida Man.

Details
Taking a look back at some of Florida Man's more famous exploits, we see that he is a talented and determined individual. Florida Man buried his cat, and fought to keep ownership of it when it clawed its way out of the ground five days later. Florida Man shot a teenager, was set free, and continues to assault people. Florida Man ate a guy's face while on bath salts. Florida Man hunts alligators for food and pythons for fun. Florida Woman had an affair with a fourteen year old student and mostly got away with it. Florida Woman killed her baby and walked on lesser charges.

TONE
As we reflect on our state's pride and glory, it makes it hard to wonder why anyone would live in Florida in the first place. Maybe we just never left. Or maybe we can't resist the allure of 90 degree, 90% humidity and the constant risk of hurricanes. But really, Florida isn't a state of the nation, it's a state of mind, and no amount of distance will free us from our madness.

Annotated Sample Essay

SHOULD YOU ALWAYS DO ALL OF THIS WHEN READING?

These techniques will help you actively read material that is challenging, but sometimes, you will read something that isn't hard—and actually grabs your interest. If this is the case, great! Just read it; you will probably remember the information because you care about the topic already. Even so, you should still take notes or write a summary, but you probably won't find it as difficult to stay focused if the topic is something you want to learn about.

Try these methods. Find out what works best for you.

WHAT ELSE SHOULD YOU DO WHILE READING?

- **Define new words**—Not sure what that word means? Look it up. Use your phone. You have access to all the knowledge known to humanity available online. Use it.

- **Ask questions**—What are you thinking about while reading? Jot down related ideas.

- **Identify recurring words and themes**—Do you see a pattern developing in the text? Note it.

- **Cite current events**—How does the text connect to the world around you now?

- **Summarize paragraphs**—As you finish each paragraph, ask yourself what it was about. Stay on target while reading. Pay attention.

- **Categorize information**—As you learn new information while reading, try to place the knowledge into specific categories to help you remember it.

- **Draw pictures**—Do you like to doodle? Put your pen to work. Draw pictures that connect to the information you are reading while you read.

IN-CLASS EXERCISE

Read the article below and practice using the active reading techniques mentioned in this chapter, such as previewing, annotating, and summarizing. After marking the text, try to answer these questions:

1. In previewing the article (i.e. looking at original publication and date), what do you think is the purpose of this article?

2. What is the general point in each paragraph? Create a brief phrase or summary to indicate each paragraph's main idea. Write it next to the paragraph (annotate!).

3. What is the main point of the entire article? Review all your annotations and create a one sentence summary of the article.

This article appeared in the Fall 2013 (Vol. 5 Issue 3) of *A Bird's Eye View,* a Dale Mabry Campus newsletter for faculty and staff.

A New Face at Dale Mabry by Michelle Sanders

Although Dean Jim Wysong is new to the administration team, he has a rich history of involvement with Hillsborough Community College that makes him a familiar face to many. Beginning in 1988 as a full-time temporary physical science instructor at the Brandon campus, he then progressed to a tenure track position and later to program manager. Throughout his time, Dean Wysong has served on numerous committees, from longest co-chair of the General Education Committee, to a member of the Tenure Committee, to Vice President of FUSA, just to name a few.

Over the last twenty-five years, Dean Wysong has experienced and participated in the evolution of HCC. He remembers, as an inaugural faculty member at the Brandon campus, teaching on card tables with metal folding chairs. He shared that all the campuses have grown not only in number of students, but also in appearance, as is evidenced by the transformation of Dale Mabry campus through the Beautification Program. In addition, Dean Wysong believes these changes helped enhance the collegial atmosphere of our college.

When he asked about his vision for HCC, Dean Wysong shared the philosophy his mentor, Lon Brown, instilled in him: to provide a top quality education for our students, which is no different from the education they would receive at a four-year university. He believes passionately in this and is proud of the success our students experience when they continue their education at a university.

In addition to providing students quality education, Dean Wysong loves working at HCC because he has the good fortune of working with outstanding colleagues, several of which encouraged him to take this position as interim Dean. He appreciates the warm welcome he has received at Dale Mabry as well as his freshly painted office!

In addition to his contributions to our college, during some summers, Dean Wysong also leads University of Texas faculty development trips and courses to Iceland to study the myriad of volcanic landforms and geothermal features in that region. Studying geology and geography are personal interests of his, as well as taking his family on unusual vacations like exploring active volcanoes and traveling in submarines.

When he has free time, Dean Wysong enjoys flying. Having a father who worked in an aviation business, he started flying at a young age. On his 16th birthday, he earned his private pilot license and made his first solo flight. Wysong has many fond memories of flying, and he still loves flying in his favorite plane, the Cessna 172.

Hopefully, those of you who do not already have the privilege of knowing our new dean will have an opportunity to meet him and discover the experience and wisdom he has to offer.

EXERCISES

ACTIVE READING TECHNIQUES EXERCISE 1A

Prepare, read, and respond to Suzanne Berne's "Where Nothing Says Everything" (originally published in *The New York Times* on April 21, 2002).

Apply the active reading techniques of previewing, annotating, and summarizing to your reading of Berne's essay. Draft a paragraph describing each phase of your reading process.

- **Previewing:** As you preview the work, consider the title and publication information. Assess your expectations, note the length of the essay, and estimate the time needed to complete the reading.

- **Annotating:** While you read, annotate using whatever method works best for you (pen and paper or digital tools). Highlight and/or underline key concepts and jot down any questions that pop up as you are reading. Pause to look up any words you do not know. Note any major points or quotes that really stuck out or left an impression on you.

- **Summarizing:** When you finish reading, draft a brief summary of the work. Use your own words to describe the main points and supporting details.

ACTIVE READING TECHNIQUES EXERCISE 1B

Choose an article on a topic that interests you. Take a moment to preview the text before you begin. As you read, annotate the article: jot down ideas and questions and underline key phrases. After you finish, take a moment to summarize the gist of the article in your own words.

ACTIVE READING TECHNIQUES EXERCISE 1C

Choose an article on the same topic you read about for Exercise 1B. Take a moment to preview the text before you begin. Then, read the article, taking notes and recording ideas and questions as you read. Write down any new words you encounter.

After you are finished, re-read the sections that you found particularly intriguing. Write down two quotes from the article that could be useful if you were writing a paper about this topic.

Now, paraphrase the main ideas of the article in your own words.

ACTIVE READING TECHNIQUES EXERCISE 1D

Choose another article on the same topic you read about for Exercise 1B and 1C. Preview first and annotate as you read. Then, illustrate the main ideas. Draw pictures that connect to the ideas as you read. Draw pictures that connect to the bigger concepts in the text.

ACTIVE READING TECHNIQUES EXERCISE 1E

Review the notes you made for each of the articles you read in Exercise 1B, 1C, and 1D. Use the information you learned to write a paper about your topic. Be sure to differentiate between your ideas and those you learned from the sources, giving appropriate credit when needed. (See Part Five for more information about research and citing sources.)

Chapter 2

READING COMPREHENSION TECHNIQUES

Reading comprehension is more than simply understanding the meaning of individual words. It is also comprehending the larger concepts that the words, sentences, paragraphs, and even complete chapters are expressing. While it is helpful to understand the definition of a specific word, putting that word in context is essential for a complete understanding of any text. Fortunately, there are several strategies to help you increase your reading comprehension, skills that will help you not only in your academic pursuits but also in your career—and life in general.

2.1 ASKING QUESTIONS

Ask yourself questions before reading, while reading, and after reading any informational text:

- What is the significance of the topic or title of the piece?
- What can I learn from the book cover and visuals throughout?
- What can I learn from the table of contents?
- What can I learn from the headings and subheadings?
- What did I just read about?
- How can I explain what I just read to someone else?

2.2 BUILDING BACKGROUND KNOWLEDGE

When sitting down to read, think about everything you already know. We all have various educational experiences not only in the classroom but also in life. When confronting new reading material, take a moment to recall your previous knowledge about the topic.

- What did I learn about this in high school?
- What have I heard on the news?
- How do my friends and family feel about this topic?
- What are my personal feelings?
- How willing am I to challenge some of my preconceived notions?

You may want to jot down some ideas about what you already know and set up your expectations for this new material.

2.3 Determining the Importance

Not every single detail in the text is critical to comprehension—although that doesn't mean you should skip them. You should read through the information carefully because even seemingly insignificant details could prove to be important later. Investigate the text thoroughly to extract the most important information. Your previewing strategies can be helpful, so remember that the book cover, table of contents, and subheadings can all help you determine the importance of ideas. Similarly, words or phrases that textbooks highlight or place in bold font are often the most important ideas.

2.4 Synthesizing Information

Sometimes it is necessary to combine different ideas, often from multiple sources, for a more sophisticated understanding of the topic. This process is called synthesis. In order to synthesize ideas, you must understand each concept individually as well as how they all work together.

For instance, you may be asked to use the information from a video, a lecture, and a group assignment to create one single essay. In short, you are connecting information from several sources to create a unified product.

2.5 Visualizing Images

When reading new material, it may be helpful to picture images in your mind. This process is called visualizing. This strategy helps you to imagine the writer's description of what is happening in the text. It also helps you stay focused while reading dense sections of text. Have you ever found your mind wandering away from the words on the page? Try picturing the scene and imagining the details to understand what the writer is telling you about. This technique will encourage active reading and help you remember what you have read.

However, it's important not to go overboard when visualizing. You should be able to imagine the scene, but you don't need to break down each word, phrase, sentence, and paragraph. The goal is not to map out every single detail but to stay engaged with the text.

2.6 Re-reading the Text

One of the best ways to comprehend what you've read is to re-read the text. Some readers may feel that a second reading is unnecessary, perhaps even boring; however, it is the single best way to get information you might have missed while reading the text the first time. While re-reading the text, you may come across information that you simply overlooked. Did you finish reading it, but it didn't stay with you? Reading the text again allows for a better understanding each time.

2.7 Thinking Critically

Critical thinking is one of the highest cognitive skills that humans possess. Making a valid argument requires critical thinking based on sound reasoning.

What this means is that you must not only understand the assumptions and conclusions you make; you must also justify them. For example, it is not enough to say that you liked one presidential candidate more than the other. You must justify your reasoning with logical evidence that is specific and verifiable.

A sound argument cannot be made advocating one candidate over the other on the grounds that one is a "good and honest American." By itself, this claim is not enough. You should explain what you mean by "good," you need to qualify your expectations of "honest," and you need to understand the significance of each concept and how it relates to being a better candidate. Simply stating it as a fact, without support, is not enough. In addition, even defining and explaining your terms may not be sufficient if your audience has different values than you do. Consider how subtlety and nuance can affect the complexities of an argument. Ultimately, critical thinking means that you think deeply about your terms and what they mean to different people.

Let's consider another ineffective argument: He makes a good candidate because he works for the average American. Who is the average American? What does it mean to "work" for an American? What specifically has the candidate done? How will his actions benefit his community as a whole?

So, can you argue for one candidate over another? Sure! You just have to think critically about what you are actually arguing. Consider this argument: This candidate has more experience in the field, displays leadership skills, and values creative approaches.

To support your first point, you could begin this argument with a discussion of the candidate's history and experience. Avoid using generalities here; all of your points should be specific, detail-oriented facts. After that, you could move into your next point about leadership skills. You would likely need to give examples of those skills and explain them in such a way that your reader understands why and how those examples are evidence of leadership. Finally, you could explain when and how the candidate has shown a respect of or value for creative approaches, keeping in mind that you would need to clarify what you mean by "creative approaches."

In other words, thinking critically requires that you do not take assumptions for granted and that you recognize assumptions and clarify how and in what way you are working with those assumptions.

EXERCISES

READING COMPREHENSION STRATEGIES EXERCISE 2A
Using the skills covered in Chapters 1 and 2 (Part One), choose a topic that you would like to explore and find an article that satisfies your curiosity on that topic.

> **Self-Questioning/Background Knowledge:** Once you have chosen your article, consider what the text reveals to you and what you already know.

> **Annotate/Determine Importance:** Record the ideas in the text as you find them and categorize them according to importance.

Think about how this article has affected your understanding of the topic. Reflect on the impact of this new knowledge, noting the significance of at least two new things you have learned.

READING COMPREHENSION STRATEGIES EXERCISE 2B
Follow the same steps you completed for Exercise 2A using a different article on the same topic.

> **Annotated/Synthesize:** After reading the second article, take a break and let the ideas settle for a few minutes. Then, identify the ideas in both sources that surprised you.

Why? How does this new information mesh with what you already know?
 If you feel like you didn't learn anything new from your articles, you should find more challenging material.

READING COMPREHENSION STRATEGIES EXERCISE 2C
Now, choose another article on the same topic you explored in Exercise 2A and 2B.

> **Visualize:** While annotating this new article, practice picturing the details as you read.

> **Re-read:** Read all three articles again to ensure that you have captured the main ideas and important details.

> **Summarize:** When you finish reading, draft three individual summaries (one for each work). Use your own words to describe the main points and supporting details.

READING COMPREHENSION STRATEGIES EXERCISE 2D
Use the information you learned from the articles you read for Exercise 2A, 2B, and 2C to write a paper about your topic. Review your notes, annotations, synthesis, and summaries. Be sure to differentiate between your ideas and those you learned from the sources, giving appropriate credit when needed. (See Part Five: Research for more information.)

PART TWO

Writing Process

OVERVIEW

Writing can be both an exploration and a process. It begins with ideas, moves forward through discovery, and ends with a concrete product.

A few things to know before getting started:

- There is no set-in-stone, perfect, magical way to write. Different methods work for different people at different moments in different places. Find what works best for you.

- This section does not require you to write in a specific way. However, it does offer many techniques to find your own writing voice.

A note on the structure of this section:

- Part Two begins with a discussion of the writing situation. It also explains prewriting/planning techniques for finding topics and developing ideas.

- The next section covers outlines, thesis statements, introductions, conclusions, and then the finer points of organization to plan the details.

- Part Two concludes with drafting, revising, and editing.

Chapter 3

WRITING SITUATION

So, you have a writing assignment. You're ready. You know what to do. Or do you?

If you find yourself pausing right now, slightly intimidated by the idea of having to write an entire essay on something you haven't really thought about before, you're in the right place!

Start with something concrete. Right now, there are three things you should consider:

- Purpose
- Context
- Audience

3.1 PURPOSE

Why are you writing this? Well, of course: because it's an assignment and you have to. But beyond that, if you were just writing because you felt compelled to and didn't have to worry about a grade for a class, what would be the goal of your words? Generally, people write to communicate or share some ideas with the reader. Sometimes, there is another goal along with sharing information, for example, to persuade the reader to interpret the information in a specific way or even just to entertain the reader.

There are three general reasons for writing:

- To inform—to tell the reader about a topic

- To persuade—to convince the reader how to think/feel about a topic

- To entertain—to make the reader want to keep reading

Often, these purposes will cross into one another when you are writing—and that's fine! Your writing should be entertaining to read; otherwise, no one will want to read it. Your purpose for academic writing will often depend on the assignment. Always write in the manner suggested by your instructor in this case.

3.2 CONTEXT

Context has to do with the assignment itself and refers to the situation surrounding your writing.

- Is this a school assignment?
  - Essays for a class, or academic writing, have certain guidelines regarding everything from page layout to organization.

- What are the assignment guidelines?
  - What is the topic?
  - Is the audience specified in the instructions, or do you need to decide?
  - Is there a word count requirement?
  - When is it due?

- Where will readers encounter your words?
  - Yes, of course, your instructor will read them. But outside the classroom, where else may your words be effective?
  - For instance, if you are arguing to change a local law, you may already know the context: You want to reach elected officials at a city council meeting. How are laws changed in that community?

Context determines not only what you say but also how you say it and to whom. Always consider the context of a writing assignment before you sit down and start writing.

3.3 Audience

Who will read your paper? The default answer is your instructor, but beyond that, who else may be interested in what you have to say? Please don't say "everyone." There are few things in the world that every single person would want to read, and even if "everyone" is interested, you would not teach every reader using the same methods. For example, the way you would write for children may be very different from the way you would write for adults.

When you speak, you usually take a moment to consider who is listening and adjust your comments accordingly:

- If you're talking to your best friend, your speech will likely be casual, and you don't need to explain in great detail about what happened last night. After all, your friend was probably with you and already knows much about what happened last night, anyway. Therefore, your audience (in this case, your best friend) affects not only your tone but the specific details you decide to include in what you're telling him or her.
- If you're speaking to a co-worker, you might not be so casual, and you may have to explain everything that happened last night because that person wasn't there to witness it.
- If you're talking to your boss, you would definitely watch your tone, and you may not want to mention last night at all.

Considering your audience for an essay is crucial because the same rules apply. What you say and how you say it are determined by who will be reading your words.

For example, what if a student were to compose an essay that presented an argument with one clear goal: to convince her husband to paint their house this weekend? She would probably talk about why it's simply time to just do it, how happy they both will be when it's finished, and how the weather this weekend is perfect for an outside project.

Now, if this student were to use the same topic—"help me paint the house this weekend"—but change her audience from her husband to her brother, she would likely change her tactic a little bit. She would probably keep the perfect weather part, since that always appeals to people working outside, but she would change the other reasons. She may, for example, remind him of the time she helped him put down new floors in his house, and she may promise that pizza and beer would be supplied for the painting party that weekend.

With this new audience, the topic hasn't changed, but the way she approaches the reader has. Her husband lives in the house, so he's likely to respond to the arguments about it being time to paint and feeling better after it's done. Her brother doesn't live in the house, so instead of convincing him that way, she may bring up some leverage ("remember when I helped you?") and offer a bribe (pizza and beer). When thinking about your potential reader, consider the following questions:

- What person or group do you want to reach? What do you know about your audience?
- What assumptions can you make about your reader? What points will your reader respond to?
- What is your relationship with the audience? What is your attitude toward your reader?
- What does your reader already know? What does your reader need background on?
- What opinions or values does the audience already hold on the topic?
- What tone should you use when addressing this reader you have in mind? Why will that tone be more effective?
- How can your essay help your audience focus on aspects they might not have considered or might have even dismissed?
- What kind of response do you want to invoke in your audience?

EXERCISES

WRITING SITUATION EXERCISE 3A

Label the items below as purpose, context, or audience.

Ex: book club members—This would be an example of audience.

Ex: a large corporate meeting—This would be an example of context.

Ex: getting a promotion—This would be an example of purpose.

1. Church leaders
2. Bumper sticker
3. Raising public awareness
4. City council meeting
5. Getting votes for a candidate
6. Fraternity president
7. Passing an ordinance
8. Sales presentation
9. Your friend's father
10. Getting scheduled for better hours at work

WRITING SITUATION EXERCISE 3B

Write a brief response for the following situations.

1. Purpose: To inform
   - Audience: Kindergarten teacher
   - Context: He has been fired.

2. Purpose: To persuade
   - Audience: The city mayor
   - Context: You want the government to support a local community project.

3. Purpose: To entertain/persuade
   - Audience: Your roommate
   - Context: The messy apartment you share needs to be cleaned.

4. Purpose: To inform
   - Audience: Your instructor
   - Context: You will miss class due to sickness.

5. Purpose: To inform/entertain
   - Audience: Your significant other
   - Context: You want to share the hilarious reason why you are late coming home today.

Chapter 4

WRITING AS EXPLORATION

Writing as exploration is a technique that uses writing to figure out what you want to write about. While this may sound contradictory, many writers find it helpful to begin the process of putting words and ideas together as they develop their feelings about the topic. Similar to freewriting (see Ch. 5), this process allows you to begin considering prior knowledge, engaging questions, and challenging assumptions. Exploratory writing gives you the freedom to say what you want to say as you are saying it.

As you grow intellectually and academically, you may begin to see the writing process as an exploration of ideas rather than a mere mechanical task. In other words, good writing is both a process of discovery and a process of creation. Consider letting go of the idea that writing by prescription yields perfection, and embrace the idea of learning as you write. This, however, is not to say that you should write as a stream of consciousness, without direction or plan. Writing as a process of evolution means that you are intimately connected with your words and knowledge of the subject. It means that you are constantly questioning the appropriateness of your language and your ideas. It indicates you are fully aware of writing as a creative process that engages feeling and knowledge simultaneously.

Writing as exploration implies that you might end up at a place you did not expect. It asks that you come to writing with the following questions in mind:

- Where did I get this idea?

- How have my assumptions changed while writing this?

- Why did I say that? Why is this relevant?

- How can I prove the claims that I am making?

- What ideas or feelings do my words carry?

Writing as exploration opens up possibilities of thought, allowing your mind to wander to places you had not anticipated. In doing so, you evaluate your learning while communicating complex ideas with clarity, reason, and precision. Writing as a process of discovery, therefore, asks that you make room for the unexpected in order to allow creation and reason to flourish.

EXERCISES

WRITING AS EXPLORATION EXERCISE 4A

Consider the following topics:

- How can divorce affect children?

- What does it mean to be family?

- How can college be more affordable?

- How can Americans stop school shootings?

- What is the best way to study for a test?

- How can America improve its public school system?

- What is the purpose of art education in schools?

WRITING AS EXPLORATION EXERCISE 4B

In April 2017, a teenager collapsed and died after consuming a large Mountain Dew, a large latte, and an energy drink in a period of two hours. Should there be a limit on the amount of caffeine a person can legally consume? Who should impose this limit and how should it be enforced?

Chapter 5

PLANNING/PREWRITING

All writers struggle, sometimes, to come up with ideas. Professional writers as well as students can face writer's block. Any writer can use one or more prewriting techniques to develop ideas. These techniques can be used at any stage of the writing process, but they are most commonly used to generate ideas before the writing of a substantial rough draft.

The goal of prewriting is to generate as many ideas as possible. At this point in the writing process, quantity is actually more important than quality. Ideas will be selected and refined later, but at this point, exploration is key.

This is time to play the Believing Game.

Believe in yourself and your ideas.

Nothing is stupid.

Nothing is off limits or a waste of time.

Everything is worth writing down— no matter how crazy it may seem.

Often your best ideas are crowded in among the other random thoughts.

Find the gems by writing EVERYTHING on the page.

- Brainstorming
- Clustering
- Freewriting
- Questioning

You may prefer one method over another. Try several and see what works best for you, keeping in mind that your own preferences may change depending on the scope, requirements, and deadlines of the project.

5.1 Brainstorming

Brainstorming is a method of prewriting that usually involves a list of ideas. To begin, you should have a general topic in mind. Then, take about three minutes to list as many ideas as possible that relate to that general topic.

For example, if your general topic is science-based children's shows, your brainstorming may look like this:

<u>Science-based children's shows</u>

Magic School Bus

teaching science is important

how to teach younger audiences

getting kids into STEM

promoting scientific method of inquiry

Sid the Science Kid

Bill Nye the Science Guy

Now this is a working list of ideas that might be pursued in the paper. The focus could be on different kids' shows or reasons for science-based programming.

In-Class Exercise: Brainstorming

Take one minute to brainstorm about the following general topic: childhood moments.

Did you list as many ideas about childhood moments as you could? If so, your list may look like this:

losing front teeth

writing Christmas lists

going to breakfast with my mom on Sundays

falling off my bike in Central Park

going on weekly field trips to the Statue of Liberty, Empire State Building, Museum of Science and History

Notice how the list went from general childhood events to events unique to the writer. Brainstorming starts with a general topic, but more specific ideas will emerge as you write. If you're a writer who has so many ideas for an essay you don't know where to start, try brainstorming. It can help you narrow your focus.

5.2 CLUSTERING

Clustering is similar to brainstorming in that the goal is to generate a list of potential ideas for a paper after having a general topic in mind, but rather than simply writing a list, clustering (also known as bubbling, mapping, mind mapping, etc.) allows you to think in any direction.

Start by writing the general topic in the center of the page, and then write down any related ideas as they come to mind. Branch out one idea into another, into another, into another. As the name implies, cluster concepts together, but don't worry too much about logic or relevance. The goal here is to generate potential ideas.

IN-CLASS EXERCISE: CLUSTERING

Take a moment to cluster about the following topic: effective apology.

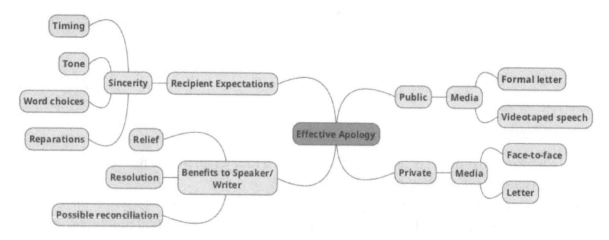

Your clustering may look like this, but it may also look completely different. Every writer will have a different way of approaching the topic. Did you generate some ideas? Great!

5.3 FREEWRITING

Freewriting is the prewriting method used by many last-minute paper writers. When you sit down and just start typing away without doing any planning, that's freewriting. Ideally, you will discover your ideas as you go, narrowing your ideas down by the end of the first page or so, perhaps finding a groove by the middle of page two. That's fine! Getting words down on paper is crucial.

However, the downside to freewriting is significant. Usually, writing begins with a lot of unrelated ideas or words, sort of like clearing your throat before speaking or running the water in a sink in a home that has been vacant for a long time. This excess writing is like the stuff in your throat or the old water in the pipes. You should probably delete the excess at the beginning and start the paper at the place where you figured out what you wanted to say (and where you started to say it).

Yes, of course, it is impossible to forget many essays have word count requirements. However, those first few sentences are rarely gems. They are worth deleting. Just let them go so your good ideas and your honest voice can shine through.

That said, there are a few ways to use freewriting as an effective prewriting method:

A. BASIC FREEWRITING

Sit down and start typing about anything at all for an entire three minutes. Set a timer and don't stop typing. Write every word that comes to mind. If you get stuck or run out of ideas, repeat the last word you just wrote until something else comes to mind. Keep those fingers (or writing implements) moving. It's only three minutes. You can do it!

IN-CLASS EXERCISE: BASIC FREEWRITING

Take three minutes to write whatever you would like. Don't worry about where to start; just look away from the textbook and write.

How did it go? Like the following example, it's possible your freewriting consists of random thoughts and language that is not up to par with the rules of Standard American English.

I'm so tired. I don't wanna be here. FML...I think I left the stove on. My stomach hurts, and I'm hungry. I want some pancakes. I can eat pancakes all day. What the name of that restaurant I had those pumpkin spice pancakes? I'm gonna Google it as soon as I finish this freewriting exercise.

Unless your paper is going to be about pancakes, this freewriting didn't generate many useful ideas. Sometimes that happens, but it is not a reason to avoid freewriting!

B. INVISIBLE FREEWRITING

Look away from your screen, or if you can, turn off your monitor, and start typing for a set time limit—probably three minutes should do it. You won't be tempted to judge yourself (or your typos). This is prewriting—just get the ideas out. You can make them pretty later on after you've decided to keep them.

IN-CLASS EXERCISE: INVISIBLE FREEWRITING

Without looking at what you are typing, take three minutes to write about a problem in your life.

How did it go? Sometimes, not reading as you type can free you from judgmental thoughts and can allow ideas to flow.

C. FOCUSED FREEWRITING

Begin with a word or phrase related to your topic and write for three minutes about that idea. This method works best when you have a general topic in mind but are not sure where to begin. Use this initial idea as a starting point and pour out anything that comes to mind about that topic.

IN-CLASS EXERCISE: FOCUSED FREEWRITING

This time, taking a cue from the Basic Freewriting example above, write for three minutes about the following topic: breakfast.

How did it go? Most likely, you will find that your writing is not as disjointed as your previous freewriting attempt.

Anytime I think of breakfast, I think of my brother and me trying to get our mom to take us out with her on Sunday mornings. She would only take one of us, so I would always try to make sure I was ready before he was. On Saturday nights, I would take a shower and lay my clothes out for the next day, but that plan didn't always work.

Look at how much more cohesive this example is compared to the Basic Freewriting one.

D. FREESTYLING

This term, taken from the rapping technique of saying whatever comes to your mind, refers to speaking your thoughts aloud into a recording device. Have a conversation with yourself. You can focus your freestyle by choosing a general topic (like Breakfast) or just speak whatever you please. Now, go back and listen to your ideas. See what ideas strike you as particularly interesting. Chances are, you may have just found the topic for your next paper.

5.4 QUESTIONING

Another method of prewriting is to answer the classic six questions of journalism:

- Who?
- What?
- Where?
- When?
- How?
- Why?

This method lends itself to certain topics and types of papers—informative essays, narration papers—and it's a useful tool for seeing what you already know about a topic.

Exercises

Planning/Prewriting Exercise 5A

Consider the following thoughts about life:

Raging against life seems such a futile exercise. One might effect a change more easily by raging against an apple. Are muscles built by this isometric exercise in futility? Is "definition" gained? Is life itself supposed to be so impressed by the magnificent "definition" of myself that it will roll over to have its belly scratched? For that matter, how is life treating you, personally?

Do some prewriting to generate ideas for an essay on this topic.

Planning/Prewriting Exercise 5B

If you could have one superpower, what would it be? Do some prewriting to generate ideas for an essay on this topic.

Planning/Prewriting Exercise 5C

Select three of the suggested topics below, and practice a different planning technique for each of these. For example, you could brainstorm for three minutes about music. Then, you might cluster for three minutes on the topic of hobbies. Finally, try freewriting for three minutes about social media. Choose the topics that appeal to you.

- Sports
- Music
- Movies
- Social Media
- School
- Work
- Cooking
- Finances
- Holidays
- Hobbies

OUTLINES

Outlines are a great way to organize the points in your essay and provide an important step in the prewriting process. You can take the main ideas you want to cover in your essay and lay them out in a brief outline that lets you see exactly where each idea belongs. Your outline should address the following elements:

Topic: Position/stance taken in the paper

Thesis Statement: A single declarative statement that addresses the specific purpose of my paper (tells my reader exactly what I am going to talk about). See Ch. 7 for more information.

Audience: Who will be reading this paper?

Purpose: What do I aim to accomplish? (to inform/engage, to persuade, to provide a fresh perspective on an old topic, to pose new questions, to invite discussion/argument, etc.)

Main Points: Specific assertions I make about my topic (taken from my thesis), which I will support with details and examples drawn from outside sources, from the text itself if applicable, and from my interpretation and synthesis of both.

Topic Sentence: Includes a summary statement of the thesis/main idea you have developed in each paragraph; the materials, methods, and strategies you have used to develop and support your thesis; the benefits and importance of this material to the reader, and any follow-up action you desire for the reader to take.

Paragraph: Each paragraph should include the following:

- **General Support:** Broad examples (inclusive: could apply to large groups/categories of people, things, etc.)
- **Specific Examples:** Exclusive/limited (taken from experience and/or research-relative to specific persons, groups, things)
- **Supporting Details:** Circumstances, experiences, etc., directly related to thesis/theme/point development; sources that articulate a similar perspective or aid and enhance the development of your thesis
- **Transition:** Statement to connect current point to the following point; should connect back to your thesis and the development of that thesis

Conclusion: Briefly summarize the pattern of development followed in completing the essay. In other words, in your thesis statement, you have told the audience what you were going to do in your essay, you have done as promised in the body of your essay, and now you conclude by telling them not just what you have done but also how you did it.

6.1 INFORMAL OUTLINES

An informal outline is a visual look at your main points using words, phrases, or complete sentences.

AN INFORMAL OUTLINE

Introduction: I will introduce my topic here.

Main Point: This is my first point. I may list some details underneath it somewhere.

Another Point: This is my second point. I may have some details underneath it, but only if I had details for the first point. Outlines should be parallel in the level of information, even if they are informal.

Another Point: This is my third point. I may add some details here too.

Conclusion: I will have something about how I plan to end the essay here.

IN-CLASS EXERCISE

Using your focused freewriting about breakfast in Chapter 5 as your topic, develop an informal outline.
Introduction: I'm going to talk about how my brother and I used to compete for the chance to go to breakfast with our mom on Sunday. This will lead to discussing the ways we learned about the three different ways our mom could say no.

Point 1: Not now

Point 2: We'll see

Point 3: I'll think about it

Conclusion: What I learned from those outings and my mom's responses

6.2 FORMAL OUTLINES

A formal outline does the same thing as an informal outline, but it uses a specific system of numerals and letters to show the relationships between ideas. A formal outline is much more structured. Using a formal outline is particularly helpful if you have a tendency to veer away from your point. The organization of a formal outline can help you stay focused.

A FORMAL OUTLINE

I. Introduction
    A. Hook
    B. Background information
    C. Thesis
II. First point
    A. Topic sentence
        1. Narrow down sentence
        2. Details
            a. Specific detail
            b. Specific detail
    B. Transition
III. Second point
    A. Topic sentence
        1. Narrow down sentence
        2. Details
            a. Specific detail
            b. Specific detail
    B. Transition

IV. Third point
    A. Topic sentence
        1. Narrow down sentence
        2. Details
            a. Specific detail
            b. Specific detail
    B. Conclusion sentence
V. Conclusion
    A. Sum up main points
    B. Clincher

IN-CLASS EXERCISE

Now give the informal outline you wrote more structure by creating a formal outline.

The following formal outline uses full sentences. Full sentences, however, are not a requirement for a formal outline. Note: The sentences included in a formal outline may not appear in the final essay draft. Unless you change the focus of your paper, however, the organization of the essay will remain the same.

I. Introduction
    A. Hook- Every Sunday, my mother and one of her close friends met for breakfast. (This "Once Upon a Time" hook lets the reader know that it's story time).
    B. Background information- My mother would sometimes buy a small gift for the child who accompanied her to breakfast. Naturally, my brother and I competed for this spot. But my brother and I were often disappointed when our requests were not immediately granted.
    C. Thesis- My brother and I had to learn how to understand and deal with the different ways our mom could say no.

II. Not now
    A. Topic sentence- This alliterative utterance gave us hope.
        1. Grammar
            a) The phrasing pointed towards the possibility of future acquisition
        2. Follow-up
            a) Requests greeted with "not now" needed to be renewed the following week.
                (1) This is the only time my brother and I collaborated. If one of us got a "not now" the previous week, the other would walk away gracefully.

III. We'll see
    A. Topic sentence- This ambiguous response was puzzling.
        1. Grammar
            a) The use of first-person plural suggested objectivity.
        2. Follow-up
            a) There was no need to follow up. Although my brother and I knew what we wanted, there was no way ALL parties were going to reach an equitable agreement.

IV. I'll think about it
    A. Topic sentence- This was, paradoxically, the most honest and deceptive response.
        1. Grammar
            a) The first-person singular made it clear our mother was the sole decision-maker.
        2. Follow-up
            a) Common sense made it clear our single mother, who had to handle the responsibilities of raising five children, had no downtime with which to consider our Sunday requests.

V. Conclusion
    A. Sum up main points-I'm glad my mother never gave a straight answer.
    B. I learned life lessons and, more importantly, how to appreciate my mother.

EXERCISES

OUTLINES EXERCISE 6A

Again, consider these thoughts on life:

> *Raging against life seems such a futile exercise. One might effect a change more easily by raging against an apple. Are muscles built by this isometric exercise in futility? Is "definition" gained? Is life itself supposed to be so impressed by the magnificent "definition" of myself that it will roll over to have its belly scratched? For that matter, how is life treating you, personally?*

You did some prewriting for this topic in the previous chapter. Now it's time to put those ideas together in an outline.

OUTLINES EXERCISE 6B

If you could have one superpower, what would it be?

You did some prewriting for this topic in the previous chapter. Use those ideas to create an outline that illustrates the main points of your essay on this topic.

Chapter 7

THESIS STATEMENT

The thesis statement is the main idea of the essay, usually contained in one sentence in the introduction. An effective thesis statement should not only clearly express the main idea of your essay but also communicate the writer's attitude toward the topic. Thesis statements should always be clearly worded and free of grammatical errors.

Ineffective thesis example: Marriage is supposed to be forever, but many marriages are short-lived.

Readers will know that this essay is going to be about marriage, but they won't know what specific aspect of marriage the paper will focus on. Will it discuss the idea of marriage? The idea of forever? Or will it focus on how marriages are short-lived? Or maybe why they are short-lived? This thesis statement is not focused enough to be effective.

Effective thesis example: While there are many reasons that marriages fail, three of the most common are financial problems, infidelity, and poor communication.

Readers will know right away that this essay will focus on three specific reasons for marriage failure. There is none of the confusion or ambiguity felt in the previous example.

Thesis statements do not appear magically on the page fully intact. They are often the most revised part of your essay--sometimes they grow as you write. In order to craft a thesis statement, you have to ask some questions, engage in observation and critical reflection, and perhaps even research your topic before formulating a position on or response to the issue. Be open to changes as you move through the drafting process. As long as your final thesis matches what you actually say in the paper, it's fine!

7.1 FOUR QUESTIONS YOUR THESIS SHOULD ADDRESS

Your thesis statement should consider the following questions, and most likely in this order, but think of this process as a way to generate a rough draft of a thesis rather than producing a polished thesis statement.

WHO/WHAT?	EXAMPLE
This is the subject of your sentence. Ask yourself, who or what am I talking about in this essay?	Renewable energy sources, like wind and solar,
DOES WHAT?	
This will be your verb. What is it/he/she doing?	create opportunities for a cleaner environment and reduce energy consumption and costs
THROUGH WHAT?	
This is where you list several examples of the ways in which the verb is performed. These examples are the evidence you will expand upon later in your easy and should be presented in the same order.	through new technology and innovation
TO ACCOMPLISH WHAT?	
This is what makes your thesis statement *debatable*. Here, you will explain why the subject performs the action. It is important that this is drawn from the evidence provided and is not exactly the evidence provided. You will come up with this, and you will not find it word for word in the text itself. A reasonable reader should be able to read the text and disagree with you.	which allows Florida homeowners to save money.

Using these four questions as a starting point, you can revise the sentence for clarity and concision:

> Renewable energy sources, like wind and solar, create opportunities for a cleaner environment and reduce energy consumption and costs ~~through new technology and innovation~~ which allows Florida homeowners to save money.

While knowing this phrase is useful for your thought process, it is redundant. Removing it makes the sentence more concise. Also, the "to accomplish what" part needs an addition to address both ideas in the "does what" section.

POLISHED THESIS STATEMENT:

> Renewable energy sources, like wind and solar, create opportunities for a cleaner environment and reduce energy consumption and costs, which allow Floridians to protect nature and save money.

CONSIDER ANOTHER EXAMPLE:

WHO/WHAT?	EXAMPLE
	Peter Jackson's adaptation of *The Hobbit*
DOES WHAT?	
	strategically emphasizes the violent and adventurous elements of Tolkien's original tale
THROUGH WHAT?	
	such as the encounter with Smaug, the significance of Azog, and the Battle of Five Armies
TO ACCOMPLISH WHAT?	
	in order to better fit viewer expectations of action and intrigue. OR in order to better fit in with Jackson's oeuvre. OR in order to create a seamless tonal transition between *The Hobbit* and *The Lord of the Rings*.

Before you do any other writing for your paper, you should establish your thesis statement. Many instructors suggest that you actually write out a "who/what? Does what? Through what? To accomplish what?" chart. If you don't, and you simply write out your argument in sentence form, you may not realize you are missing important elements.

For example, you might think that the following sentence is a complete thesis statement:

"Peter Jackson's adaptation of *The Hobbit* strategically emphasizes the violent and adventurous elements of Tolkien's original tale such as the encounter with Smaug, the significance of Azog, and the Battle of Five Armies and thus are different."

Although the statement seems to be quite long, it doesn't provide enough depth for a satisfying essay. *The Hobbit* films do what? They emphasize different elements than the books? Well, of course. How does that answer do anything debatable or different from the "does what?" question? Just having a difference or similarity does not answer the "to accomplish what?" question, the *agency* question. So, here, your essay would simply list the differences between the book and movie without an anchoring point of argument to tie those details down.

Additionally, if you do not have a someone or something that can choose to *do* things for explicit purposes (an agent) in your who/what category, you will not be able to answer the other thesis questions. For example, if a writer wants to say that "trees represent life in many texts" as a thesis statement, that writer may have a problem.

CONSIDER THIS EXAMPLE:

WHO/WHAT?	Trees
DOES WHAT?	represent the stages of human life
THROUGH WHAT?	through their physical changes in response to the seasons
TO ACCOMPLISH WHAT?	???

You are left with nothing that could make sense in response to the final, most important question of the thesis. Trees can't "purpose" to accomplish anything; they just *are* (that is, they exist), and thus, are not agents, and cannot be the "who/what?" of your thesis statement. However, most of the time, ideas can be transitioned into a proper thesis statement by finding an agent and putting that agent in place of the original "subject" placeholder. You can get to this by asking yourself the question: "who or what uses [insert your original who/what? and does what? answer]?" So, with the example above: "Who or what uses trees to represent the stages of human life?" The answer to this question might begin generally, such as "artists" or "some authors." Obviously, you'll want your final thesis statement to be specific, but getting things in the correct place is more important at first. So, with an (albeit generalized) agent in the "who or what?" you can reformulate the thesis like so:

WHO/WHAT?	Artists and authors
DOES WHAT?	use trees to represent the stages of human life
THROUGH WHAT?/ HOW?	because of the physical changes trees undergo in response to the seasons
TO ACCOMPLISH WHAT? WHY?	in order to add layers of depth and a connection to nature to their depiction of human aging.

IN-CLASS EXERCISE

In Chapters 5 and 6, you completed pre-writing strategies and wrote an outline for an essay that stemmed from a simple idea: breakfast. The sample formal outline in Chapter 6 has a basic thesis statement, but does that thesis statement answer all four questions a thesis statement should address? Take another look:

My brother and I had to learn how to understand and deal with the different ways our mom could say no.

QUESTION	ANSWER	DID THESIS STATEMENT ADDRESS QUESTION?
WHO/WHAT?	My brother and I	Yes
DOES WHAT?	had to learn how to understand and deal with the different ways our mom could say no.	Yes
THROUGH WHAT?	???	No
TO ACCOMPLISH WHAT?	???	No

The thesis statement has to be revised for it to provide a comprehensive summary of the essay. Consider this revision:

Over time, my brother and I managed our frustration by decoding my mother's replies of "not now," "we'll see" and "I'll think about it" to reveal the likelihood of receiving our award for winning our race to Sunday Breakfast.

QUESTION	ANSWER	DID THESIS STATEMENT ADDRESS QUESTION?
WHO/WHAT?	My brother and I	Yes
DOES WHAT?	managed our frustration	Yes
THROUGH WHAT?	by decoding my mother's replies of "not now," "we'll see," and "I'll think about it"	Yes
TO ACCOMPLISH WHAT?	to reveal the likelihood of receiving our award for winning our race to Sunday Breakfast.	Yes

7.2 FOUR CHARACTERISTICS OF AN EFFECTIVE THESIS STATEMENT

1. An effective thesis clearly communicates your essay's main idea. It tells the reader not only what your essay is about but also how you are going to approach the topic. It reflects your purpose.

- **Poor thesis**: All administrators earn a salary of over $80,000.

- **Rewritten thesis**: Earning over $80,000 each year, college administrators are adequately compensated for their time and effort in bringing the college's mission statement to life.

Claim: College administrators are adequately compensated for their time and effort.
Justification/method of discussion: Although $80,000 is a lot of money, bringing the college mission to life is a difficult job.

2. An effective thesis must be carefully worded.

- **Poor thesis**: Our school is filled with many problems.

- **Rewritten thesis**: The real problem in our schools is not the absence of nationwide goals and standards but the absence of resources with which to implement them.

Claim: There is a serious problem in our schools.
Justification/method of discussion: the absence of resources, not the goals

3. An effective thesis should suggest your essay's direction.

- **Poor thesis**: Romance novels have been widely ridiculed in the past.

- **Rewritten thesis**: Once widely ridiculed as escape reading, romance novels are increasingly important as a proving ground for new writers and as a showcase for strong heroines.

Claim: Romance novels are becoming increasingly important.
Justification/method of discussion: They are not what they used to be and have grown in importance because they introduce new writers and new ideas.

4. An effective thesis should be more than a general truth.

- **Poor thesis**: The US currently has no peacetime draft.

- **Rewritten thesis**: The US needs a military draft to improve the quality of the armed forces.

Claim: America needs a draft.
Justification/ method of discussion: to increase the quality of the armed forces

EXERCISES

THESIS STATEMENT EXERCISE 7A

Evaluate the following thesis statements:

1. This paper will discuss the advantages and disadvantages of lifting weights.
2. The new *Star Wars* movie will be the best movie ever released in the history of humankind.
3. Going to college can be very difficult, but it's worth it in the end.
4. Reading good writing will improve your own writing over time.
5. Eating dinner as a family has many great long-lasting effects.

THESIS STATEMENT EXERCISE 7B

Review the following thesis statements and identify each as effective or ineffective. Be prepared to explain your evaluation. Revise ineffective thesis statements.

1. Rihanna is my favorite musical artist.
2. Drinking and driving can be very expensive; it can have mental, physical, and financial consequences.
3. There is an opioid prescription drug epidemic in Florida.
4. Many economists maintain that the current real estate market is favorable for buyers but unfavorable for sellers.
5. Strategies for avoiding procrastination.
6. Consuming a diet composed largely of high-fat foods can lead to health problems such as high-blood pressure, obesity, and heart disease.
7. In an argument, the intent is to sway the audience toward believing or acting in a certain way.
8. YouTube is becoming increasing popular and many people are making a lot of money.
9. The memoir is a genre that documents the past and focuses specifically on the personal experiences of the writer.
10. Women who are victims of domestic violence often suffer from low self-esteem, depression, and/or anxiety.
11. Since my early childhood days of nurturing my pet rabbits and bringing home stray cats, I have known that I wanted to pursue a career in medicine by becoming a pediatric nurse.
12. The "Me Too" movement has empowered women.
13. Old school hip-hop music by artists like Snoop Dogg, DMX, Biggie, and Tupac laid the foundation for much of today's rap music.
14. Nine steps to transforming your relationship with money and achieving financial independence.

THESIS STATEMENT EXERCISE 7C

According to Count Leo Tolstoy, "Happy families are all alike; every unhappy family is unhappy in its own way." Drawing from your own experiences, explain your point of view. Begin by writing three different possible thesis statements.

THESIS STATEMENT EXERCISE 7D

If you could have one superpower, what would it be?

In previous chapters, you did some prewriting and an outline for this topic. Now it's time to write three different thesis statements answering this question.

Chapter 8

INTRODUCTIONS

All essays will have an introduction and a conclusion.

Think about the relationship between your paper and the reader: the reader is essentially leaving the world of his or her thoughts to enter the world of your thoughts. Consider things this way: your reader is alone in a room, just daydreaming. Suddenly you barge in, shouting about something that has nothing to do with anything; that is the effect of an essay that ignores its introduction. On the other hand, imagine another scenario. In this one, instead of barging in, you knock at the door, open it, and say something like, "Excuse me, I hate to bother you, but I've been thinking about something that you might find interesting; could I take a few minutes of your time?" This is a bit more reasonable, right? That is the effect of the introduction.

A good intro can also be viewed as a delivery system for the thesis, and in this regard, your aim is to work up to your main point—the thesis—perhaps by giving an idea of the nature or pattern of the thought that will appear in the essay. The rest of the essay, of course, will provide more depth and detail than the one-sentence thesis could convey.

Finally, a strong introduction lends a certain gravitas to the essay, suggesting that you take the idea of creative non-fiction seriously and that your diligence merits a careful read of the essay.

A few approaches exist for crafting an introduction, some inherently better than others, but each valid depending on the essay's purpose.

8.1. EMOTIONAL APPEAL

These types of introductions engage readers by connecting on a personal level; you are one person talking to another. Emotional appeals establish a connection with the readers before getting down to the business of the essay.

A. A QUESTION

Are motorcycles passé? Are they sort of *over*? I ask as a rider of two-wheel Italian beauties that go very fast, gracefully streamlined subsonic technology from the Ducati factory in Bologna. I own two sport bikes and two racers. I ride racing motorcycles in the street. One of my motorcycles is capable of nearly 200 miles an hour. I write prose about motorcycles. I write *poems* about motorcycles.

Seidel, Frederick. "Is the Era of the Motorcycles Over?"
New York Times, Sunday Review, 6 Nov. 2011, p. 4.

What makes a Christian a real Christian? Is it possible for anyone to know whether a professed Christian is really a follower of Christ? With approximately 39,000 Christian denominations around the world today, it would be nearly impossible for anyone to accurately describe all the different types of Christians that exist, or to know for sure whether they are sincerely following Jesus or not. Fortunately, Jesus Himself was wise enough to give His disciples some clear definitions of what it means to follow Him. For instance, in the Bible, in the book of John, verse 13, chapter 35, Jesus says, "By this everyone will know that you are my disciples, if you love one another." Considering how many Christians judge and condemn other Christians who do not think, behave, or worship as they do, people can see that this lack of love and unity has become a real problem among Christians today. A closer look at a few different types of Christians may help clarify some of the root causes of this problem. Based on their love for Christ and how they practice their faith, Christians across many denominations can be divided into five categories; The Do-Gooders, The Seat Warmers, The Law Abiding Religious, The Church Hoppers, and The Lovers of Christ.

Waters, Andrea. "Do Christians Really Follow Jesus?"
Student Essay, HCC, 2017.

B. AN ANECDOTE

We were sitting in homeroom—this would have been sometime in the late 70's. As was usually the case, our group, like all the groups in the room, had coalesced on a Monday to shake off the weekend and settle into another week of high school routine. One of our group, a smallish kid with longish seventies hair and modish glasses, looked at the rest of us with the wizened stare of a combat veteran. "Saw *Night of the Living Dead* at the midnight show," he said. Of course, this was news for us as in an age before VCR's, let alone Netflix or the internet, when most sophomores didn't have access to the midnight show, the only venue for a notorious movie like *Night*. But we affected nonchalance: "Yeah?" we replied. "Let me tell ya, just the poster alone will scare the crap outta you—but the movie? I didn't even go to sleep Saturday night." Impressed we were. And looking back at that time, despite its quaintness, I can't help but think that the truly frightening movies of days past, even factoring in their lack of special effects, were much more powerfully frightening than the special effects driven movies of today.

Funk, Robert. HCC Instructor, HCC, 2015.

Envision a small girl sitting in the corner of a classroom quietly playing all alone. Another toddler approaches this girl and asks sweetly, "Can I play with you?" This timid girl looks down at her toys, back up at this new potential friend, opens her mouth to respond, but words refuse to leave her. This friendly little child backs away scared and confused as to why this seemingly normal girl could not simply say "Yes." That's a small glimpse into what Destiny faced for the first few years of her life. Unfortunately, a speech impediment was not the only obstacle she had faced. At the young age of eleven, both of her parents passed away due to lingering addictions. With no other options, Destiny was forced to move to a distant, unfamiliar state to live with estranged family members. As a result of all this chaos, she developed memory issues that made exceling in academics that much harder. Despite all of these unfavorable odds, this persistent young scholar managed to go from a mute, introverted child to a respected leader at Colombia University.

Machin, Alia. "Destiny." Student Essay, HCC, 2017.

We took our sons fishing in the spillway next to the dam one moonlit night. In the hush of the night, one hooked a small trout. But when the landed fish screamed aloud, my son fled the scene in horror and hasn't eaten flesh since. While not all people adopt a vegetarian diet out of horror, there are significant reasons to do so and today's consumer will find it easier to do so with more options in grocery stores, restaurants, and cookbooks.

Scott, Theresa. HCC Instructor, HCC, 2019.

C. An Intriguing Perspective

I think we're all mentally ill: those of us outside the asylums only hide it a little better—and maybe not all that much better, after all. We've all known people who talk to themselves, people who sometimes squinch their faces into horrible grimaces when they believe no one is watching, people who have some hysterical fear—of snakes, the dark, the tight place, the long drop . . . and, of course, those final worms and grubs that are waiting so patiently underground.

King, Stephen. "Why We Crave Horror Movies."
Scribd, 2014. Accessed May 2016.

Every time a cork is popped on a bottle of wine, the setting turns into an event. People gather to indulge in the celebration of fellowship between friends, family, and coworkers. From red to white, if a big dinner is being served or just a couple of appetizers, the mood is set by the wine, and it is important that it is enjoyed properly. Professional hospitality can be hard to find in today's society, as food and beverage handling becomes a saturated field for college students and adults alike. When a person goes out to eat and experiences bad service, it is often due to lack of education. With the proper training, anything is possible. A guest's experience can always be enhanced with a personable server who knows what product they are selling and can talk about it fluidly and with passion.

Rolph, Jasmine. "How to Serve a Bottle of Wine." Student Essay, HCC, 2016.

D. An Emphatic Opinion

I'm really angry at the black residents of Ferguson, Mo., where a white police officer shot and killed unarmed black teenager Michael Brown and set off days of protests and disturbances.

Maxwell, Bill. "Why Blacks Need to Vote." *Tampa Bay Times*,
7 Sept. 2014. Accessed 9 Sept. 2014.

E. A Powerful Comparison

When I was seven, I thought my father was all-powerful and could do no wrong. When I was seventeen, I thought he was a jerk.

Scott, Theresa. HCC Instructor, HCC, 2019.

F. A Provocative or Startling Statement

According to the United States Census Bureau, in 2000, the ten largest cities in the U.S. comprised 54% of the total U.S. population.

Scott, Theresa. HCC Instructor, HCC, 2019.

The fact that one in every five teenagers between the ages of thirteen and fifteen smokes calls into question the efficacy of laws prohibiting advertising cigarettes to children.

Scott, Theresa. HCC Instructor, HCC, 2019.

8.2 Logical Appeals

These introductions forego the personal connection with readers and get started right away with the topic.

A. A Statement of Fact

When I go to the movies these days, I sometimes find myself gripped by a very peculiar sort of nostalgia: I miss flesh. I see skin, I see bones, I see many rocklike outcroppings of muscle, but I rarely see, in the angular bodies up there on the screen—either the hard, sculpted ones or the brittle, anorexic ones—anything *extra*; not even a hint of the soft layer of fatty tissue that was once an essential component of the movies' romantic fantasy, the cushion that made encounters between the sexes seem like pleasant, sensual experiences rather than teeth-rattling head-on collisions. The sleek, form-follows-function physiques of today's film stars suggest a world in which power and brutal efficiency are all that matter, in the bedroom no less than in the pitiless, sun-seared arena of *Gladiator*. This may well be an accurate reflection of our anxious time, but it's also mighty depressing. When I come out of the multiplex now, I often feel like the archetypal ninety-eight-pound weakling in the old Charles Atlas ads—like big bullies have been kicking sand in my face for two hours. And that's just the women.

Rafferty, Terrance. "Kate Winslet, Please Save Us." *GQ*, May 2001, p. 107.

Now that is one good introduction—well-written, full of detail—and while it appears to be an opinion, it isn't; instead, it presents facts as the writer has experienced them.

Contrast the above introduction with this much less effective one:

In the world we live in today, smart phones are a necessity. People use them for communicating, researching, directions, entertainment, and many more exciting functions. When there is an invention as massive as the smart phone, competition begins to occur between a few of the larger corporations. . . .

(An anonymous student essay, HCC, 2016)

Well yes, those are facts, but would anyone not be aware of these very general considerations? They are not only obvious but boring. Another and related approach is to begin with a dictionary definition of a common word like "love" or "sin" or "college." Shouldn't we assume that our readers will know what these ordinary words mean—and isn't it insulting to suggest that they might not? These methods reveal a lack of imagination and are little better than no introduction at all.

B. An Example from Research

Kathy, age 32, is a successful lawyer specializing in estate planning; she was top of her class at Yale and is very active, along with her husband, in the alumni club, attending every event that they can. Steven, age 47, is a grocery store manager, has been married for 27 years and has three teenage sons. Eva, age 15, is a high school sophomore, was active last year in cheerleading and the church choir, and, until recently, has considered following in her aunt's footsteps in pursuing law at Yale. All three of these individuals share a secret. All three are being abused – one by her husband, one by his son, and one by her boyfriend. Domestic violence doesn't have a common face of the abused wife anymore. Today, domestic violence is affecting more lives, both male and female, and at a younger age; however, there are signs to watch for and help is available if one knows where to look.

Scott, Theresa. HCC Instructor, HCC, 2019.

8.3 TRADITIONAL APPROACHES

These introductions are classic--and they get the job done, if done well.

A. QUOTATION

This is self-explanatory. Starting an essay with a quote is an age-old tradition. Is it effective? Sometimes. It depends on what you are writing about.

> As Jedi Master Yoda said, "Fear is the path to the Dark Side. Fear leads to anger. Anger leads to hate. Hate leads to suffering." In the *Star Wars* saga, Anakin Skywalker was thought to be the "chosen one" of an ancient Jedi prophecy; he was to bring balance to the Force. Anakin was considered to be one of the strongest Force-sensitive humans in the entire galaxy, but his power and strength could not save him from being corrupted by the Dark Side of the Force. The transition from innocent Anakin Skywalker into the villainous Darth Vader, one of the most tragic tales in all of science fiction, occurred following the progression of Anakin's fear, anger, hatred, and suffering.
>
> Bryan, Wesley. "Requiem for a Skywalker." Student Essay, HCC, 2017.

> Albert Einstein once said, "Any man who can drive safely while kissing a pretty girl is simply not giving the kiss the attention it deserves."
>
> Scott, Theresa. HCC Instructor, HCC, 2019.

> Daniel Webster, creator of the Webster Dictionary, defines friendship as mutual feelings of trust, affection, assistance, and approval between people (207). However, friendship sometimes is knowing when to walk away.
>
> Scott, Theresa. HCC Instructor, HCC, 2019.

B. DEFINITION

Again, this is another standard introductory technique. Does it work? Maybe. Is it always effective? Absolutely not. Ask yourself if there is another more relevant way to begin your essay.

> Love is a many-splendored thing. Love is poetry in motion. Love is a chemical reaction. Love is that thing that keeps you up at night, unable to sleep, desperate to dream. Love is a reason to get out of bed in the morning, wager for a chance to glimpse the beloved. However you define love, no one will debate that love is a powerful force in many people's lives.
>
> Paquette, Jenifer. HCC instructor, HCC, 2017.

Introductions are the way to get readers to continue reading your essay. Use those first few words carefully.

IN-CLASS EXERCISE

Write the introduction for your "breakfast" essay from Chapters 5-7.

You might end up with something like this introduction:

> Every Sunday, my mother and one of her close friends met for breakfast. Since my mother would allow ONE of her children to accompany her, my eldest brother and I would race to get dressed. Whoever was ready first won the seat in the car. The reward for winning was not simply going to a restaurant for breakfast. Oh no! The reward came after breakfast when my mother and her friend walked off their breakfast calories at a department store where my brother or I might discover a new toy, gadget or book (only me) we would want our mom to buy. However, this reward was not guaranteed. My siblings and I were taught not to excessively ask for things when we were out. Repeated cries of "Mommy. Mommy. Gimme. I want, please" and tantrums on the floor were not in our repertoire of childhood behaviors. We could express our interest in ONE item...ONCE. Our "sales pitch" had to be precise, methodical, imbued with consideration and pre-emptive gratefulness. A simple breakfast experience turned into reconnaissance, strategic planning, and a sales pitch. But these pitches often led to (inner) frustration because my mother would never give a straight "Yes" or "No" answer. Over time, my brother and I managed our frustration by decoding my mother's replies of "not now," "we'll see" and "I'll think about it" to reveal the likelihood of receiving our award for winning the race to Sunday Breakfast.
>
> Steinhardt, S. Melissa. HCC Instructor, HCC, 2018.

EXERCISES

INTRODUCTIONS EXERCISE 8A

Read the following introduction. What are its strengths? What are its weaknesses? Revise this introduction to make it stronger.

It's a fat world! Statistics show that many Americans are overweight. It is not surprising that many people are preoccupied with physical fitness. People of all ages are focusing on improving their health through exercise, diet, and a positive attitude.

INTRODUCTIONS EXERCISE 8B

Read the following introduction. What does it do well? How can it be improved?

America is in trouble. The temperature in classrooms, homes, and office buildings is being lowered. Farmers and transportation companies cannot get adequate supplies of fuel to continue normal operations. Electric companies predict serious power shortages in the near future. These are, of course, serious problems, but only symptoms of the real problem of how to make Americans aware that only they can avoid the disastrous petroleum crisis. Indeed, unless the users of petroleum begin conserving fuel immediately, America will experience shortages that will drastically alter the American way of life. True, conservation means changing habits and accepting inconveniences, but if everyone would make three small changes in his or her driving, the impending ecological crisis would be postponed. By eliminating engine warm-up time, by avoiding "jack-rabbit" starts, and by traveling no faster than fifty-five miles per hour, individuals can help conserve rapidly dwindling auto fuel supplies.

Chapter 9

CONCLUSIONS

I f readers leave the world of their thoughts to enter the world of *your* thoughts at the beginning of the essay, so metaphorically are they returning to their world at the essay's conclusion. With this in mind, consider the conclusion of the essay as being a polite send-off on the journey back to the world. In this regard, you are like the good host, who, at the end of a delightful conversation, rises with your guests, walks them to the door, and offers a polite goodbye—instead of just saying, "Well, that's all I have to say—now go home." (Of course, a conclusion is also a signal that the essay is now over, but hopefully the flow of your thoughts has also suggested that!)

9.1 "Big Picture" Conclusions

With these conclusions, you are clearly leading your reader on a path away from your specific discussion. These conclusions tend to work because they in some way reinforce the essay's purpose, that your ideas exist not only unto themselves, but reflect larger social concerns.

A. Draw a Conclusion

Therefore, if you want to gain weight, you must do either of two things: eat more calories (units of heat, therefore energy), or use less through inactivity. If you want to lose weight, you do the reverse: decrease your input of calories or increase the amount of energy you spend. There is no other way. Gaining or losing weight is always a relation between intake and output of potential energy.

> "Student Example: Draw a Straight-forward Example." *Conclusions*. mrstitcombe. weebly.com/uploads/8/7/1/8/8718911/060313intros.txt. Accessed 8 June 2017.

B. Evaluates the Significance

The process which marked the conclusion of the ten-month Constitutional Convention set a symbolic seal on the long process and thus had the effect which many public ceremonies have of making it all seem a real and believable event. In the words of Benjamin Rush, the Philadelphia physician and signer of the Declaration of Independence, "Tis done. We have become a nation."

> "Concluding Techniques." *Writing*. teacher.edmonds.wednet.edu/mhs/streit/.../ ConcludingTechniquesPageOne.pdf. Accessed 8 June 2017.

C. Make a Prediction

Pollution is a major world-wide problem against which many powerful interests are being marshaled. From the private citizens who are concerned with the type of detergent or pesticide they use to the leaders of great nations, all thinking people are involved in the environmental crisis. There is still time for humanity to resolve this problem, as people are creative, inventive, and ambitious. These qualities, which are responsible for precipitating this crisis, will be the very means for humanity's salvation.

> "Conclusions." *StudyLib*. http://studylib.net/doc/7309167/your-conclusion-is-your-opportunity-to-wrap-up-your-essay. Accessed 8 June 2017.

9.2 Artistic Conclusions

With artistic conclusions, you are leading the reader away from the essay's thought with an interesting related but detached idea. Think of this way as dessert after a meal—sort of.

A. Use an Anecdote

At the 50th anniversary of the announcement of the successful vaccine in Ann Arbor, a celebration was held at the University of Michigan. Salk was asked how he wanted to be remembered. He answered, 'I want to be there when a child in the next generation asks his father, "Hey Daddy, what's polio?"'

> Clare, Jini. "Memories of What Life Was Like before the Polio Vaccine." *Daily Herald*, 29 Mar. 2012. www.dailyherald.com/article/20120329/news/703299818/. Accessed 8 June 2017.

B. Use Quotations and Ask Questions

Samuel Johnson defined a patron as "one who looks with unconcern on a man struggling for life in the water, and when he has reached ground encumbers him with help." Shall we be merely patrons of the needy?

Johnson, Samuel. "Letter to the Right Honorable the Earl of Chesterfield."

> 1755. *Prefaces and Prologues*, Vol. XXXIX, The Harvard Classics, P.F. Collier and Son, 1909-14. *Bartleby.com*, 2001, www.bartleby.com/39/. Accessed 27 May 2017.

C. Echo the Introduction

Perhaps the most flamboyant of these artistic conclusions and the one that most obviously closes the essay into a unified work, this paragraph connects the ideas from the introduction to bring the essay back around full circle.

Consider the introduction to "Chauvinist Pigs in Space" by Juliet Lapidos:

> The best fighter pilot in the 1970s television series *Battlestar Galactica* is a cigar-smoking womanizer. The best fighter pilot in the current television series *Battlestar Galactica* is a cigar-smoking woman. This sex change, according to the actor who played the original character, Starbuck, is proof of an insidious feminist agenda: "There was a time—I know I was there—when men were men, women were women," Dirk Benedict wrote in the May 2004 issue of the magazine *Dreamwatch*. "But 40 years of feminism have taken their toll. The war against masculinity has been won." Is Benedict right? Is *Battlestar*—now in its final season—the televised culmination of the feminist movement?

Notice how the conclusion echoes the introduction:

> My hunch is that the gender inequities on *Battlestar* are unintentional; the writers don't sit around inventing new, technologically advanced ways to denigrate women. Yet because the writing staff lives on Planet Earth in 2009, not [in space] in the distant future, chauvinism creeps onto the show. There is something toxic in those vats of resurrecting goo, and even aggressive fighter pilots are not immune to it. So Dirk Benedict can rest assured: Men are still men, and women are still women.

> Lapidos, Juliet. "Chauvinist Pigs in Space." *Slate*, 25 Mar. 2009.

The essay begins with Dirk Benedict's concern about gender roles and questions the depiction of women in *Battlestar Galactica*. The conclusion reiterates the idea that there are some issues with the way women are depicted and ends by answering Benedict's question, so the ideas from the start of the essay reappear at the end.

9.3 "Special Purpose" Conclusions

This last type of conclusion, in middle school and even often in high school, is probably taught as the one and only acceptable type of conclusion: the summary. For college writing, however, this type of conclusion is often unacceptable. For most short papers, you should avoid the summary. After all, if you have written a two- or three-page essay, do you really think you need to summarize the information that your audience has read five minutes ago? If the information was especially dense, you might, but otherwise this conclusion just shows a thoughtless writer. However, as the example suggests, summaries work very well for longer discussions:

A. Emphasize Points in a Summary

The last three chapters have granted that at times language can be confusing, illogical, and infuriating; that it can play tricks on both speaker and listener; that though all human beings belong to the same species, they do not characterize their experience in any mutually intelligible way; that a mere flicker of the eyelids can sometimes belie the most carefully structured and grammatical utterance. In view of all this, can we regard the language game as an honest one? Yes, we can—despite the flaws. The flaws and limitations in language are a reflection of the flaws and limitations in our species; an understanding of these will allow us to function within the boundaries of language with greater freedom and understanding than heretofore.

Farb, Peter. *Word Play: What Happens When People Talk.* Knopf, 1974.

9.4 Ineffective Conclusions

A. Repetition

The following conclusion includes an awkward transition and boring repetition of the topics already listed in the thesis sentence:

In conclusion, the three main reasons that homeowners should choose Florida-friendly landscaping are, as stated in my thesis, water conservation, an environmentally conscious yard and prevention of soil erosion. Perfectly manicured grass lawns are not only outdated, but also toxic. Hopefully, reading this essay has persuaded my audience to make an informed and ethical choice in landscaping their property.

B. Insupportable Claims

This conclusion needs to be revised to avoid making insupportable claims. For example, what if the writer used the word "suggests" instead of the word "proves"?

In sum, there are many reasons to legalize marijuana, but the most important of these is its potential in medicine. In my essay, I pointed out the ways that it has been used to treat illnesses such as diabetes, Parkinson's, cancer, and thyroid disease. This proves that legalizing marijuana would improve the lives of those affected by these illnesses. A vote for marijuana is a vote that might ease the pain of your loved one someday.

C. New Information

The best place for new material and research is not in the conclusion, but in the body of the essay.

> In the final analysis, the topic of free range parenting is a controversial one and has gained momentum in recent months. Detractors should ask themselves if they would be just as quick to judge lenient parents of a higher socioeconomic status as they would judge poor parents with the same parenting styles. Further, recent research from the Firth Institute of Learning shows that second graders who completed homework without parental assistance tended to fare better on tests compared to those who had received help from their parents (736). So, free range parenting styles can even be an asset to young children's academic scores. Although this parenting style is not for everyone, its numerous merits far outweigh the risks.

One final comment here on conclusions, and the most important caveat: No matter what, the conclusion should not provide additional supporting details directly related to your subject. If you do that, you simply haven't written the conclusion; you've added another point to the body of your essay.

In-Class Exercise

Write the conclusion for your "breakfast" essay.

The following conclusion builds on the "Breakfast" writing activities in Chapters 5-7 and the associated introduction in Chapter 8.

> Looking back, I'm glad my mother never gave a straight answer. Her coded replies helped me increase my appreciation for her, as well as my understanding of statistics, probability, and grammar. Through the dense vagueness of her answers, and competition with my brother, I developed clear and effective persuasive techniques and espionage skills. I also learned how to handle triumph and defeat. Sometimes I got what I asked for. Sometimes I didn't. But on some weeks, I got to spend extra time with my mother and devour stacks of pancakes. Not a bad way to spend a Sunday.

Steinhardt, S. Melissa. HCC Instructor, HCC, 2018.

EXERCISES

CONCLUSIONS EXERCISE 9A
Write a brief summary of all of the things your conclusion should accomplish in a paper. Consider all of the different types of conclusions described in this chapter.

CONCLUSIONS EXERCISE 9B
Imagine you have just finished writing an essay about the stress caused by college classes. How would you conclude? Write a possible conclusion for that essay.

CONCLUSIONS EXERCISE 9C
Find a news article on a current event. Imagine that you have just written an essay about that topic. Now, write the final paragraph of that essay that sums up your main points and leaves the reader with something to ponder.

CONCLUSIONS EXERCISE 9D
Look at an essay that you have written. Revise the conclusion.

Chapter 10

ORGANIZATION

Organizing your essay is crucial. Fortunately, there are some things you can do to make your ideas fit together in a way that the reader can follow along. Paying attention to the way you put your essay together can be an encouraging way to start.

Successful organization relies on careful planning. Think about how each of your points is connected to the others. Follow the thesis you establish in the introduction. Use topic sentences to stay focused, and then tie your ideas together with transitions and segues. Next, make sure your paragraphs are unified and coherent so that readers can follow what you want to say.

Some instructors may require that you create the kind of outline described in Chapter 6 of this book. Others may not. In either case, be aware that creating an outline is useful for organizing your ideas within a unified, easy-to-follow structure.

This chapter explores the following topics:

- The Five-Paragraph Essay

- Topic Sentences

- Transitions and Segues

- Unity and Coherence

10.1 THE FIVE-PARAGRAPH ESSAY

This specific type of writing is, to put it mildly, controversial. The five-paragraph essay has been called traditional, outdated, unnecessary, and that deepest of insults for college students—*high school.* But there is a reason why teachers have beaten this pattern into their students' heads all these years: it works. Plus, it's a great place to begin when organizing your ideas for an academic essay. Does this mean you are always limited to five paragraphs? Of course not! But before you can start to play around with the organization of your essay, you have to know the basic structure that readers will expect from you.

A note before getting started: The essay should have a title that reflects the topic. The title should not be a complete sentence. Prepositions, articles, and coordinating conjunctions are not capitalized (except when one is the first word).

Chapter 6 in this book covers outlines. After reviewing Chapter 6, see below for an illustration of how the rules of outlines can be easily applied to the basic structure of a five-paragraph essay:

I. Introduction: The purpose of the introduction is to state the topic, give some brief information about the topic, and state the thesis.

    C.   **Significant statement**: Some refer to the opening sentence of an essay as the attention grabber or opening statement. The purpose of the first sentence is to get the reader's attention in some significant way. There are several ways to grab the reader's attention. Consider these examples:

        1. **Fact or statistic**: Essays that describe a current social problem or scientific issue might begin with an interesting or startling statistic or fact.

        2. **Humorous anecdote**: An anecdote is a brief story used to make a point.

        3. **Rhetorical question**: Asking a provocative question that does not require an answer is an effective way to keep a reader's attention. (See Ch. 8 Introductions)

    D.   **Thesis statement**: Perhaps the most important sentence in the essay, the thesis statement contains the main idea of the essay and states the direction the essay will take. (See Ch. 7 Thesis Statements)

        1. **The three-part thesis**: In five-paragraph essays, the three middle paragraphs draw their topics from the three-part thesis. For example, in an essay on declining manatee populations, the thesis might be:

            a) There are several reasons why manatee populations have declined recently, most significantly, habitat loss, water pollution, and accidents with outboard motors.

II. Body paragraphs: To use the above example, the first body paragraph after the introduction will start with a topic sentence about habitat loss since that was the first item listed in the thesis statement.

    E.   **Topic sentence**: The first sentence of the body paragraph should define and limit the topic of the paragraph.

    F.   **Supporting details and illustrations**: Most of the body paragraph should be facts and specific references to support the topic sentence and the thesis statement. (See Ch. 23 Integrating Sources)

    G.   **Tie-up sentence**: The concluding sentence of a body paragraph should tie up the topic of the paragraph and transition to the next paragraph. Transition sentences that mention the topic of both the preceding and next paragraph give the essay cohesion and smoothness.

III and IV. Body paragraphs: Following the same three steps as previous body paragraph, paragraph III would be about water pollution, and paragraph IV would be about the dangers of human activity to manatees.

V. Conclusion: The conclusion of the essay should not be any less than four sentences. For the essay to be effective and provoke the reader to further thought, it is necessary to restate the thesis but don't repeat it word for word. Remind the reader why this is an important topic or why the topic deserves consideration by the reader. It can be effective to finish the essay with a provocative idea. (See Ch. 9 Conclusions)

SAMPLE PARAGRAPH STRUCTURE

This is my first topic sentence; it narrows down the idea I will focus on in this paragraph. I have now limited the ideas I can discuss in this paragraph and will begin giving some details about that topic and only that topic in a sentence or two. This next sentence explains the details that I have just shared. Now I explain why I shared those details, clarifying how they connect to the main idea of this paragraph. Now I'm getting ready to finish this paragraph, but not before I explain how this point relates to my overall purpose in the paper my thesis statement. Finally, I will end with a transition to my next point.

SAMPLE FIVE-PARAGRAPH ESSAY STRUCTURE

This Is My Title

This is my opening hook it says something clever, funny, or witty to get the reader's attention. This is another sentence that further explains my opening hook. This sentence starts to segue from my hook into my main idea. I may have another sentence while I'm getting to my point. By this time, I have introduced my main idea and will explain the points of my paragraphs in a thesis statement. This is my thesis statement.

This is my first topic sentence; it narrows down the idea I will focus on in this paragraph. I have now limited the ideas I can discuss in this paragraph and will begin giving some details about that topic and only that topic in a sentence or two. This next sentence explains the details that I just shared. Now I explain why I shared those details, clarifying how they connect to the main idea of this paragraph. Now I'm getting ready to finish this paragraph, but not before I explain how this point relates to my overall purpose in the paper my thesis statement. Finally, I will end with a transition to my next point.

I may begin this new paragraph with a transition to connect this idea to the previous one. This second sentence is my new topic sentence, where I will limit the idea I will discuss in this paragraph. The following sentences will narrow my topic, give details, explain those details, and then conclude this point. I will repeat this process in the next paragraph for my third point.

Now that I've made all of my points, I'm ready to conclude my paper. I will probably mention all of the points I made in my paragraphs so far. I will remind readers how those points relate to my overall thesis. When I'm finished with that, I will end with a snappy clincher that connects all of my ideas.

EXERCISE

FIVE-PARAGRAPH ESSAY WRITING EXERCISE 10.1A

Consider the following prompts for a five-paragraph essay:

- According to Søren Kierkegaard in *Either/Or*, "If you marry, you will regret it; if you do not marry, you will also regret it." Do you regret it?

- The famous cry of Woodstock (the first Woodstock) was "Sex, drugs, and rock-n-roll!" Since sex and drugs can kill, rock-n-roll had better be . . . really great. Is it? (Thanks to the late-but-still-great Frank Zappa and Abbie Hoffman for this topic.)

- If you could plot the course your life will take, what would you accomplish?

10.2 Topic Sentences

The topic sentence is the main idea of your paragraph. It is often the first sentence, but it can appear later. An effective topic sentence performs the double duty of letting the reader know what to expect while focusing on one idea at a time.

Generally speaking, a paragraph is limited to the following parts:

- Topic Sentence
  This is often the paragraph's first sentence, and it explains the main point of the paragraph.
- Narrow Down Sentence
  This sentence narrows down your main idea to the specific aspect you will discuss in the paragraph.
- Example Sentence
  This sentence gives an example or illustrates the specific aspect of the main idea you are discussing in the paragraph. (This is where you put the evidence for the point you are making.)
- Explanation Sentence
  This sentence explains the example you have just used. Don't assume that the examples speak for themselves—they don't! Why did you share this detail with the reader? Explain the connection.
- Conclusion Sentence
  This sentence sums up the main idea of the paragraph. Sometimes it may also contain a transition or segue that connects this paragraph's idea back to the overall thesis and hints at the main idea of the next paragraph.

Let's say you're writing a paper about the recession in 2008. You've already got your thesis.

Thesis Statement: The Great Recession of 2008 caused many Fortune 500 companies to fail and unemployment and foreclosures to rise. Many Americans who were once optimistic about their retirement security found themselves facing an uncertain future.

Topic sentence: Under the resulting economic conditions, many corporations either downsized, outsourced, or shut down operations altogether, leaving a growing class of unemployed Americans uncertain about where they would find themselves at retirement age.

Details: It became difficult, if not impossible, for American workers to compete or even survive in a market where US employers (1) increasingly outsourced to third-world countries where they could get labor at a fraction of the cost of US labor, (2) downsized operations and laid off employees with little or no advance warning, or (3) filed bankruptcy and totally shut down operations.

Topic sentence: Rising unemployment rates and a dismal job market contributed to the increasing uncertainty that many newly unemployed and displaced Americans faced as a result of the 2008 economic downturn.

Details: American found themselves (1) unemployed or underemployed with (2) fewer job opportunities as (3) major companies closed or downsized. As a result, Americans lost health insurance, a sustainable paycheck, and a sense of purpose.

Topic sentence: With the loss of employment and ballooning mortgage rates, foreclosures escalated, leaving many Americans uncertain about the future of their homes.

Details: Americans had to deal with (1) subprime rates, (2) declining home values, and (3) unsympathetic lenders while attempting to retain their homestead: the one remaining vestige of the American Dream.

EXERCISE

TOPIC SENTENCES EXERCISE 10.2A

Choose an essay that you have written. Underline the topic sentences for each body paragraph. Revise each paragraph to follow the topic sentences you have used.

10.3 TRANSITIONS AND SEGUES

Transitions are words that connect the main ideas in your essay to one another. They may be as simple as *however, next, on the other hand*, or *furthermore*. If you are using an entire sentence to connect your ideas to one another, that's a segue—a logical path from one idea to the next.

A. TRANSITIONAL WORDS AND EXPRESSIONS BETWEEN SENTENCES

Do you have friends or family who are excellent storytellers? If so, notice the way that they maintain their listeners' interest by signaling when a change is about to happen in the story:

Ten minutes before my job interview, I noticed the first set of blotchy hives on my forearms.

In the above example, the use of a transition helps to show tension and provide chronological order in the sentence. Without these cues, the audience might not have a sense of how events connect to each other. You can create the same interest in your own audience when you use transitions in your essay.

When it is time to revise your draft, consider reading it aloud to a friend, a classmate, or even your dog. The goal for this process is simply to listen for ways that your reasoning can be clearer and your ideas more fluent. Begin by printing the essay as a paper copy and reading it uninterrupted but with pen in hand. After you have finished, ask yourself: Do your sentences connect in ways that show your intended message to the audience? If not, circle the problem areas. Consider adding a transitional word or expression to strengthen the connections you are trying to make.

NARRATION	At first, Two hours later, Finally
CAUSE AND EFFECT	Therefore, Thus, As a result
COMPARISON	Likewise, In like manner, Similarly
CONTRAST	Conversely, In contrast, On the other hand
DESCRIPTION	On the left side, Surrounding the stage, Above the audience
EXAMPLE	For instance, As an example, To illustrate further
PROCESS	After, Before, While

Examples of Transitional Phrases:

Process: After securing your vehicle...
Comparison: The striking similarities between both countries also include...
Description: Other beautiful beaches within driving distance include...
Cause and Effect: This restriction also led to...
Contrast: Unlike 4G technology ...
Narration: Later that morning...

B. Transitions Between Paragraphs

Segues are sentences that bridge the gap in subjects from one paragraph in your essay to the next. As an example of why they are useful, think about how jarring it is when a friend suddenly changes the subject during a conversation. In the same way, paragraphs that end abruptly and then switch to a different topic can leave readers feeling confused. You can avoid this mistake by adding a sentence at the end of your paragraph that links that paragraph's topic to the next one:

> Phishing attacks are a kind of email meant to trick you into providing your account credentials to criminals. **Not only do the attacks allow criminals into your bank accounts, but they are also hard to detect.**
>
> The people who craft these emails go through great lengths to make sure their website looks just like the bank's. They even go so far as to link directly to portions of the bank's actual site to make their own fake site look as authentic as possible.

The sentence in bold above shows readers the connection between paragraphs, explaining how phishing works and why people are fooled by it. It makes a smooth transition in the essay.

(For more information on transition words, see Ch. 14.7 Conjunctive Adverbs).

EXERCISES

TRANSITIONS AND SEGUES EXERCISE 10.3A

Make the following sentence groups flow more smoothly by adding transitions as appropriate:

1. The painting depicts a chaotic scene. Baying dogs appear in pursuit of their prey. Our attention is then drawn to hunters, who approach in crouched positions. The wild boar seems to have gained a safe distance. A careful hare hides in tall grasses. *(Hint: Use time transitions that indicate the order in which each step takes place. Combine sentences for conciseness.)*

2. I could see the accident scene from my bedroom window. The driver was yelling. Another car was parked. A police car was parked. A police officer was taking notes. A witness was on his phone. A passenger sat on the sidewalk. Broken glass littered the pavement. *(Hint: Use spatial transitions that show where each person or thing might be in relation to each other person or thing.)*

3. Open your refrigerator. Locate the filter. Remove the old filter. Open the packaging of your new filter. Install it carefully. Make sure the arrows line up. Close the door. Enjoy your fresh water. *(Hint: Use time transitions that indicate the order in which each step takes place.)*

4. I've always enjoyed certain household chores. Doing dishes can be relaxing. Vacuuming can be meditative. One could say I enjoy indoor chores much more than outdoor chores. *(Hint: Use transitions that clarify or announce examples.)*

5. My sister loves her dance lessons. I enjoy practicing the piano. My sister loves to cook her favorite dishes on the stove. I love to bake. Our tastes are different, yet similar. *(Hint: Use transitions that indicate comparison between ideas.)*

6. Not only do the two actors contrast in terms of the way they perform their dialogue, but also they differ in their portrayal of the character's despondency. For example, ____Will Smith uses wry humor to chide the dog who is his sole companion into eating breakfast, Vincent Price demonstrates the same loneliness by agonizing over the decision to let a zombie woman into his empty home. Will Smith shows the doctor as a man who is affable with store mannequins as a preservation of his sanity, but he quakes at night when zombies roam the streets. _____, Vincent Price's Robert is developed through close-ups of his expressive reactions to the Gothic horror around him. Both are talented actors who move audiences to sympathize with Robert. *(Hint: Add the appropriate transitions in the blanks)*

7. Identify a segue used in the above paragraph.

TRANSITIONS AND SEGUES EXERCISE 10.3B

Using either the vocabulary provided or your own ideas, choose transitional words or phrases that complete the following sentences:

Moments after I arrived, Likewise, However, While, Because, As a result, Whereas, Yet, Consequently, Similarly, On the other hand, Nevertheless, Thus, Therefore, Also, In contrast

1. _____ many people blame millennials for the nation's problem with accidents caused by texting, future research may show people of all ages are to blame.
2. _____ campus safety is a priority, additional security officers are needed.
3. The college handbook is meant to be a style reference; _____, the purpose of the reader is to give examples of successful essays of different types.
4. The fire alarm sounded in the middle of class; _____, students were not able to complete their tests.
5. The midterm exam has 50 questions and is of moderate difficulty; _____, the final exam has fewer than 60 questions and is easy to pass if you have read the material.
6. The train began to pull away _____.
7. We studied Fitzgerald's novels; _____, we did not read any of his short stories.
8. I left my car window open; _____, all of my textbooks are soaked.
9. My biology textbook was cheap at only $25 because it was used; _____, I paid over $100 for my algebra book.
10. My commute to campus is only fifteen minutes; _____, rush hour traffic turns the drive into a half hour.
11. My psychology instructor has a warm manner and seems approachable; _____, my algebra professor encourages students to visit him for conferences. ____, they each use humor to make their lectures more interesting.
12. Look at the sentences in question 11 above. The writer wants to write her next paragraph about the differences in the two instructors' attitudes about attendance. Which of the following sentences would make a good segue after the sentences in question 11?

   A. Also, both are understanding about occasional absences.
   B. Likewise, both instructors abhor tardiness.
   C. Although they have much in common, their attendance policies are very dissimilar.

10.4 Unity and Coherence

Paragraphs need to be unified and coherent for readers to truly understand your meaning.

Paragraph unity: Do all of the ideas in your sentences go together and point toward one specific overall idea? If so, the paragraph is unified.

Paragraph coherence: Are all of the ideas in your paragraph comprehensible to the reader? If so, the paragraph is coherent.

A. How can I improve my paragraph unity?

Paragraphs need to stay focused on one topic. A good way to make sure you are staying focused is to have a solid topic sentence—a sentence that explains what the paragraph will discuss—and be sure to add only those details or examples that relate directly to that topic.

> The film industry releases more sequels than original movies these days. From the Marvel comic book adaptations to the seventh installment of the latest horror series, Hollywood seems determined to run a franchise into the ground rather than take a chance on something new. Instead of meeting new characters, moviegoers learn more about Captain America in *The Winter Soldier*, and they follow the ongoing story of Thor and Loki in *Thor: The Dark World*. Even the horror industry seems to be losing creativity—apparently the four *Paranormal Activity* movies need yet another sequel. Remember the hype around the *Star Wars* prequels many years ago? Science fiction movies often have prequels that fans love to see. Moviegoers are ready for something new in theatres; hopefully, the producers in Hollywood will realize that the age of the sequel is coming to an end.

In this example, the sentences are related to one common idea: movie sequels. The first few sentences focus on this idea—right up to the two sentences about *Star Wars* and science fiction prequels. Though they contain interesting information, these points do not fit the main idea of the paragraph, and they disrupt the paragraph's unity. The writer should move them to another point in a new paragraph (about prequels or maybe science fiction movies, depending on the focus of the paper) or get rid of them entirely.

One thought to keep in mind when writing is that not all sentences are sacred. Feel free to cut the words that don't fit your purpose—even if you lower your word count in the process. Having enough words isn't the most important thing; having the *right* words is crucial.

B. How can I improve my paragraph coherence?

Paragraphs should be comprehensible to your reader. Remember the purpose of your essay, review your thesis, and establish your topic sentence. When revising for comprehension, make sure that the ideas you are trying to convey are clear to your reader.

In the following passage, a student makes an ingenious connection between "The Artist of the Beautiful," a short story by Nathaniel Hawthorne, and certain aspects of modern theoretical physics. The selection, the first paragraph of which is the essay's introduction, exemplifies coherence (and unity) both within and between paragraphs.

> Revolutionary scientific experiments conducted in the 20th century have proven the existence of subatomic particles. The idea of a quantum world, however, was explored as early as the mid-19th century—and in quite different contexts than one might expect. Nathaniel Hawthorne's analysis of "spiritualized mechanism" in his short story "The Artist of the Beautiful" prefigured certain elements of modern theoretical physics. It is true that String Theory and the dual-slit experiment took their current form over a century after Hawthorne, but such highly sophisticated discoveries do not happen overnight. Rather, they are emergent: They emerge slowly and over long periods of time with a great many influences driving the process both consciously and unconsciously. Hawthorne's forward-thinking aesthetic theory paves the way for modern theoretical physics by exploring the spaces between philosophy and science. Through the spiritualization of the mechanical butterfly, the central image in "The Artist of the Beautiful," Hawthorne invites readers to imagine how the visible and invisible worlds might be intertwined and to reimagine their conception of time itself.

19th-century avant-garde ideas like Hawthorne's gain in depth and meaning in light of 20th-century scientific discoveries. In this way, the complex feelings of Owen Warland, the story's troubled hero, can be understood. Owen's intuition that the invisible realm exists within the visible world has been validated by String Theory, which was developed in the 1990s. The theory states that quarks, which aggregate to form protons and neutrons, are made of one-dimensional, vibrating strings made exclusively of energy. When the strings interact, a fulcrum of energy is created, a space of pure energy; in other words, the "vibrational amplitude" of two waves interacting with each other add up. In similar fashion, Owen can feel Annie's presence before he sees her, he is "weighted down" by Peter Hovenden's "evil spirit," and he is burdened by the sight of the "monstrous and unnatural" steam-engine. His feelings, like the vibrating strings, compound and gain in energy as a consequence. Owen's empathic nature provides valuable insight into the mystery of quantum mechanics, inviting the reader to think about his or her own connection to the natural and spiritual world.

This paragraph has one main idea and reinforces that concept throughout, building on the comparison (string theory and the short story) with details to illustrate the point.

By contrast, the following paragraph is not coherent. The student attempts to discuss the issue of domestic violence. The paragraph wanders aimlessly from topic to topic, meandering without purpose or direction until it ends abruptly and arbitrarily, leaving the reader disoriented and unsure of what he or she has just read. The sign-posts and transitions are unclear, the language is vague, and the claims contradict one another. In other words, it is an incoherent mess.

One reason for my belief is that many children who have grown up with physical violence have problems during their childhood and during adulthood many of them slip into drugs or even depression, but in some cases, the children are fine and understand the error, but that's still not the case. Furthermore, children who experience violence during their childhood must be violent in the future. A child who suffers from physical violence can have serious mental problems and problems that can put her future at risk. Children are not victims just because they witness violence between their parents, but because they live in violence. They are victims of psychological violence, sometimes also physical, and they grow up believing that violence is a pattern of normal relationships between adults, but it doesn't mean that they will be violent in the future. Children affected by violence by their parents may suffer from insomnia, lack of concentration and poor school performance, enuresis, night terrors, lack of appetite, anger, depression, stress, anxiety, among others.

This paragraph is about one general topic (violence and children), but it moves all over the place without any direction or focus.

Focus on keeping ideas unified and coherent in your writing.

EXERCISES

UNITY EXERCISE 10.4A

Revise the following paragraph to show greater unity:

As impressive as modern video games may be, I feel nostalgia for the classics of the 1980s. Early Atari 2600 games, for all their blocky graphics and beeping sound effects, were often fast-paced and used their simplicity to their advantage. Atari's *Ms. Pacman* gave players at home all the joys of the arcade game without having to spend countless quarters for an evening of entertainment. Likewise, Nintendo's *Super Mario Bros.*, which revolutionized the gaming industry, continues to be fun to this day. *Metroid*, one of the classic platform-jumping games, holds up well alongside modern-day shooters in terms of sheer excitement. Notably, early fighting games began to arouse controversy among certain parenting groups. I think some of these concerns are misguided. While it's probably a bad idea to let a toddler play a nightmare-inducing splatter-fest, I remain unconvinced that violent video games are psychologically unhealthy for older children. At any rate, people will still have a chance to enjoy these vintage games as long as thrift stores, eBay, and retro re-releases exist.

COHERENCE EXERCISE 10.4B

Revise the following paragraph to show greater coherence:

I've had many bad part-time jobs. I enjoyed teaching guitar lessons. My students were eager and friendly. Some students chose to learn guitar and looked forward to their lessons. Some students didn't have any choice. They didn't practice. They enjoyed our time together. A young student gave me a thank-you card that I have. I wish I had time to go back to teaching. My life is busy.

STUDENT SAMPLES

All student samples have been preserved in the form in which they were submitted in class; thus, they contain some errors. After all, papers are never truly done; they are just due.

STUDENT SAMPLE: FIVE-PARAGRAPH ESSAY

Markie Gourley
Professor Chamberlin
ENC 1101
March 2017

How to Change a Dirty Diaper

When someone you know has a baby, you can almost guarantee there will be times when you will be in for a world of surprises, sticky, stinky, messy surprises. One of the most reoccurring and extending surprising messes will be a soiled diaper. It is important because if you do not change the diaper, it can lead to diaper rash or other unneeded health concerns that can be avoided by simply changing the diaper. First we will prepare our supplies, clean the baby, and then re-diaper and redress the baby. Every child's dirty diaper will be different due to age, diet, and digestive system, but today I will teach you an almost fool proof way to not only clean the infant's messy diaper but also keep you and your surroundings clean regardless of the level of mess.

When changing a dirty diaper, the first thing you need is the dirty diaper itself. When waiting for this to happen, you need to keep a look out for warning signs. You may hear grunting, observe a face turning red and the infant may even deterring eye contact. These are all signs of a dirty diaper in process. Once you believe that the diaper is dirty, you will need to confirm your suspicions. There are many ways to do this. You can observe the look of the diaper; it may be bulging or sagging. If you cannot tell by the look, you can tell by taking a gander inside or (more disgustingly) by the scent. Once you have a confirmed soiled diaper, the next steps are gathering your supplies, removing the infant's bottom clothing and getting prepared to change.

Before you change the diaper, you will need to place the infant on a changing table or another surface that is flat and safe so that the infant will not fall or roll off while you are changing them. Make sure to never leave the infant unattended. First you will need to remove the bottom half of the infant's clothes. This may include just removing pants or shorts, unbuttoning the infant's onesie or doing both. It all depends on how the infant is dressed. Once the shorts are removed, you will need to assess the level of mess in the diaper. Look for any visual signs that can indicate what level of mess you are dealing with. It can range from very miniscule to a complete blow out. In a normal occasion, you will need to acquire a few wipes, a new clean diaper, possibly baby diaper cream, and some quick reflexes in case of a squirmy infant. I also prefer to use a scented disposable diaper bag for an odor-free clean up. Once you have all of your required supplies you may need to give yourself a pep talk to prepare you for whatever may be in the diaper; this step is completely optional but always a good way to start the cleaning phase. Start to prep yourself by remembering that it is only a dirty diaper and once you clean it then the seemingly scary task will be over. Simple enough? Then let's get started!

Once you are ready, you will need remove the Velcro straps and pull the diaper away from the infant but do not removed the diaper completely from under the baby. Grab both of the infant's feet with one hand and fold the diaper in half, you can now rest the infant's rear end on top of the folded diaper. This will be used as a safe guard from further expanding the mess and having it get on the surface beneath the infant. While still holding the infants feet, you can grab a wipe to start cleaning. The most effective way I have found is to wipe from front to back creating clean rows. Repeat this step until the infant's bottom is completely clean. Now place the soiled diaper aside and slide a new clean diaper under the infant's bottom. If you happen to observe any redness, now would be the time to apply diaper cream to the irritated area. If you do not, skip this skep and move ahead to fastening the diaper.

Now pull the front of the diaper to the front of the infant. Grab the side Velcro straps and fasten them tightly (but not too tightly) to the front of the diaper. You will want the right and left straps to meet in the middle to ensure maximum security and avoid sliding. Your messy infant is now clean and ready to be redressed! Just as you undressed the infant, you can now redress them. After you place the infant in a safe and secure location you can dispose of the soiled diaper. Depending on if you used a scented disposable diaper bag, you can place it in your indoor garbage can. If you did not, you can opt to place it into your outdoor garbage can to minimize any odors that may happen. If you follow all of these steps in changing an infant's dirty diaper, you will have a high success rate of having a mess-free way of changing an infant.

QUESTIONS FOR CONSIDERATION

What is the essay's thesis?

Explain some of the strengths of this essay.

Identify specific ways this essay could be improved. Consider the essay's focus, organization, development, style, and grammar.

Chapter 11

DRAFTING, REVISING, AND EDITING

11.1 DRAFTING

After you've done some prewriting, you should have your main ideas in mind and a working thesis ready to go. Start with those! Sometimes it's easier to write after your main ideas are already down on paper.

There are no set rules that determine how you draft your paper. What makes sense for you? What works best? You won't know until you've tried a variety of methods. Here are some popular ways to write your paper:

1. Just start typing. Begin with your name. Type the title. Introduce your topic, add your thesis, and you are off and running. The downside to this method is that you need to know your thesis—and you need to know how you plan to begin your essay. Sometimes, it's hard to write an introduction because you don't know what you are going to say (if this is the case, you should try some prewriting to generate working ideas).

2. If you don't know what to say at first (introductions can be intimidating!), no worries. Just think of your first point. What are you going to write about? Start there. Talk about that specific idea, give some examples, and then, when you get into a writing groove, add a transition and segue to your next point. Once you start writing, it gets easier. Don't let the idea of an introduction block your writing. You can always go back and add the introduction after you are done with your main points.

3. Sometimes, you just have an idea and you start typing. Words flow. Life is good. But then you finish the third page, and it's time to go back and see what you've written (a good idea if you're writing something you want other people to read!). You have some interesting things to say, but to be honest, you don't really get to your ideas until the top of the second page. Yes, this can be difficult, but sometimes, you need to cut words. But wait—what about the word count? Yes, you're likely aiming for a word count, and every word is precious when you are struggling, but it just doesn't make sense to keep words that have nothing to do with your topic just for the sake of hitting a word count. Just do it. Delete everything that comes before the sentence where you actually figured out what you were trying to say and start from there. Add more details. Give more explanations. Perhaps add another point to your overall essay—but don't keep the gunk at the beginning just because it came out first.

11.2 REVISING

Congratulations! You've finished your draft.

This is *not* the time to call it done, hit print, and go to bed. Now, it's time to revise your paper. Revising means that you look over the ideas in your paper and make sure they make sense.

This *is* the time to walk away for a few minutes. Get up, stretch, take a break—it doesn't matter what you do, but take a moment away from the screen where your essay is staring back at you. Walking away for a moment allows your brain to reset, so that when you return, you won't see what you *wanted* to write, but what you *actually* wrote.

Have you ever written a paper, printed it, and then gotten to class, only to re-read your first sentence with horror? Why is that word missing? How did you misspell that word? What happened? You probably didn't take a break, so your brain read what you thought you wrote instead of what you actually wrote. Take a break to avoid this problem.

When you are done doing whatever it is you just did for a moment, come back to your essay and re-read it. Yes, re-read the entire thing from the beginning and ask yourself the following questions:

- Did I do the assignment? (In other words, did I actually address the writing prompt?)
- Does this paper make sense?
- Did I introduce my topic properly? Do I have a thesis statement in the introduction?
- Did I follow the thesis statement?
- Do my points follow a logical organization?
- Are my points connected by transitions?
- Do my paragraphs follow their topic sentences?
- Do I have a conclusion that answers the "So what?" question?
- If applicable, do I have my references cited properly?

Now you've revised for the Big Picture items. Please don't start nitpicking and editing your paper for spelling or punctuation at this point. You'll have a chance to do that kind of proofreading later. Right now, your goal is to look at the entire paper holistically—in its entirety—to make sure it makes sense for your purpose.

> Put it before them briefly so they will read it, clearly so they will appreciate it, picturesquely so they will remember it, and above all, accurately so they will be guided by its light.
>
> **Joseph Pulitzer (1847-1911)**

EXERCISE

REVISING EXERCISE 11.2A

When you are finished with your draft, take a break for a moment. When you are ready to work again, sit down and ask yourself these questions for revision:

1. Did you do the assignment? Review the guidelines and make sure you have followed them.
2. Have you properly introduced your topic in the first paragraph? Do you have extra information that doesn't belong there? What should you add/remove?
3. Do you have a thesis statement? What is it? Underline it. Make sure that you have some specific main points.
4. Did you follow your thesis statement? Look over each one of your paragraphs. The main ideas in each should correspond to the points you stated in your thesis. Create a mini outline of your main points and check it against your thesis statement.
5. Do you have topic sentences? Check the first sentence of each paragraph. Did you follow your topic sentences? Read the entire paragraph. Does everything you mention relate to the topic you started with?
6. Do you have transitions? Review your connections between each idea. Circle or underline them in your paper to see where they are.
7. Did you sum up your main points in a conclusion? Did you end with a clincher?

If the answer to any of these questions is "no," please revise your paper until the answer is "yes!"

11.3 EDITING

Now you are ready for the details. Editing means that it's time to look over your paper for those pesky grammatical, mechanical, and stylistic issues. Ask yourself the following questions:

EDITING FOR GRAMMAR

- Do my sentences make sense? Try reading your paper backwards sentence by sentence. Find the last sentence. Read from the capital letter at the start to the punctuation at the end. Does that sentence make sense as a sentence, by itself? If not, fix it. If so, move backwards to the previous sentence. Yes, this is time-consuming. Yes, this is worth it.

- Did you use the right word? Check for misused words (they're/their, etc.), homonyms (accept/except, etc.), and typos. (See Ch. 17.7 Commonly Confused Words)

- Did you use the right verb? Review your verbs for number (singular/plural) and tense (past/present/future) consistency. Avoid weak verbs like "to be" (replace "She is walking" with "She walked" to focus on action in your sentences). This includes words like *is, am, are, was, were,* etc. (See Ch. 14.2 Verbs and Ch. 17.1 Verb Errors)

- Did you use the proper pronouns throughout for your point of view? If using first-person point of view, did you use I/me or we/us? Did you use "you" and if so, who is the "you" you refer to (the writer/reader/someone else)? If you use third-person point of view, were you consistent in number (he/she/it or they)? (See Ch. 14.6 Pronouns and Ch. 17.2 Pronoun Problems)

- Look at your modifiers (really, mostly, just, almost, etc.) and decide if you *really* need to use them (see what I did there?) or if the sentence would be stronger without them. (See Ch. 14.4 Adverbs and Ch. 15.4 Modifiers)

EDITING FOR PUNCTUATION

- Check the punctuation at the end of each sentence. Ask yourself, is that where the end punctuation belongs? Is it the correct mark? (See Ch. 16.1 End Punctuation)

- Check every comma and ask yourself why it is there. What rule does that comma follow? If you can't find the rule, you don't need the comma. (See Ch. 16.2 Commas)

- Check those other marks of punctuation that get lost in the shuffle: apostrophes, hyphens, dashes, colons, quotation marks. Make sure they are where they belong. (See Punctuation Chapters 16.3-16.9)

EDITING FOR STYLE

- Read your paper out loud. How does it sound? Are you stumbling over certain phrases? You may want to edit those parts.

- Check your sentence structure. Do you use the same sentence structure throughout (subject-verb-object). Repetitive sentence structure can make your ideas seem monotonous. Vary the way you design your sentences. (See Ch. 15 Sentence Structure)

- Check your word usage. Did you find the right tone for your purpose, context, and audience? (See Ch. 18.3 Diction and Ch. 18.5 Tone)

- Is the paper interesting to you? How can you make it interesting for the reader?

EXERCISE

EDITING EXERCISE 11.3A

Review your draft for the following grammatical issues. It may be helpful to use Word's Track Changes features so you can keep a record of how your essay progresses from draft to final version.

1. Begin with Word's Spelling and Grammar Check. This won't catch everything, but it's a great place to start! This feature will underline misspelled words, comma splices, run-ons, and other common errors. (You can customize your grammar check in Word settings, so it focuses on the issues you choose--google this for more information!).
2. Check your sentence variety. Do your sentences follow the same format (subject-verb-object)? Underline the subjects and verbs of each sentence and make sure they don't appear in the same place in every sentence.
3. Review your verbs for number (singular/plural) and tense (past/present/future) to make sure you have the right word. Then, identify your passive verbs (is, was, were, etc.). If possible, replace these weaker verbs with active verbs.
4. Review your modifiers and decide if you *really* need them (see what I did there?).
5. Locate all of your pronouns and check them for person (1st, 2nd, 3rd) and number (singular/plural).
6. Review each punctuation mark and make sure you are using it properly.

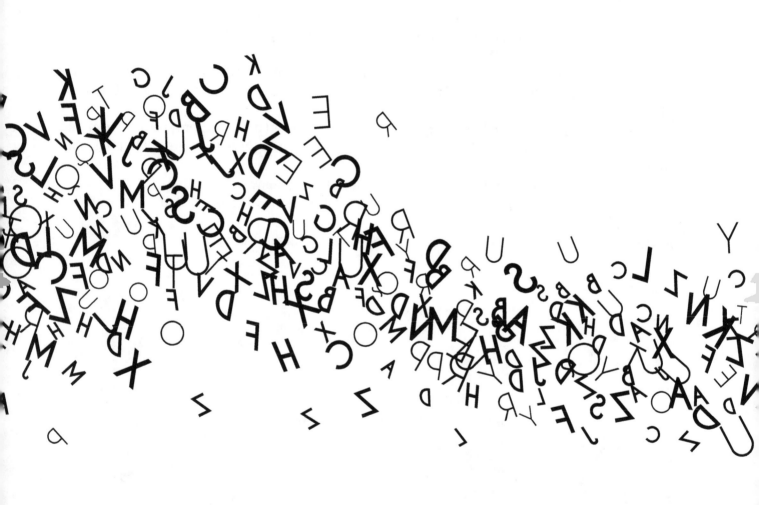

PART THREE

Types of Writing

OVERVIEW

A few things to know before beginning:

- The rhetorical modes may overlap in a single essay; that is, you may use more than one mode in an essay: a narrative essay that also persuades the readers.

- This part includes the types of writing you may encounter in your college classes; this is by no means an exhaustive list of all types of writing.

A note on the structure of this section:

- Part Three begins with an overview of the rhetorical modes of writing. It includes student samples and outlines for each writing style.

- The final section covers additional types of writing: academic writing, essay exams, business writing, public writing, and journals.

Chapter 12

WRITING MODES

This chapter introduces the different modes of writing:

- Narration
- Description
- Exemplification
- Definition
- Classification and Division
- Process
- Compare and Contrast
- Cause and Effect
- Argument

Each section contains an explanation, student samples, and writing prompts.
The Argument section discusses rhetorical appeals, classic models, and logical fallacies.

12.1 NARRATION

A narration paper tells a story. It should be something specific with a beginning, middle, and end, typically told in chronological order, though with the freedom to offer flashbacks and flashforwards as necessary. Readers should feel as if they have gotten the entire picture in a narration paper. Scenes should be described using detailed language and perhaps dialogue. Just like any other story, a narrative requires specific elements like characters, setting, and plot.

Most importantly, a narrative essay should have a point. In academic writing, you are writing for an audience. Therefore, your story should have a purpose. If you were writing for yourself, you would have a journal or diary entry, not an academic essay. Your story should be an example of the greater point that you are trying to make. Your thesis statement in a narrative is, essentially, the moral or lesson of your story. This is how the narration rhetorical mode connects to the exemplification mode. A narrative essay is, quite simply, an extended exemplification essay. Instead of providing multiple examples to demonstrate a generalization, however, you are focusing on a specific event in your life that gave you specific insight. While your readers may not have had the same experience you are sharing, they can connect with you because they can connect to the general point.

While you may not have ever had to playfully compete with a sibling for a chance to go to breakfast (like the sample outlines in Chapter 6), you most likely have had a moment in your life when someone said something that had more meaning behind the words they stated. You may recognize the process you underwent trying to figure out that meaning within the essay.

In narrative writing, you can describe a scene as if you were there (like a scene in a movie), or you can summarize the events after the fact.

Remember that narration essays describe a single event from start to finish. Rather than a description about why you love fishing, a narrative essay will describe a specific fishing trip.

The purpose of a narrative is to tell a story.

KEY ELEMENTS OF A PERSONAL NARRATIVE

A. TELL YOUR STORY WELL
Most narratives set up a situation that needs to be resolved. That need for resolution makes readers want to keep reading. For example, you might write about a challenge you've overcome.

B. PROVIDE VIVID DETAIL
The details you use when describing something can help readers imagine places, people, and events; dialogue can help them hear what is being said. Details bring a narrative to life by giving readers images of the sights, sounds, smells, tastes, and textures of the world in which your story takes place.

C. GIVE AN INDICATION OF THE NARRATIVE'S SIGNIFICANCE
Ask yourself some challenging questions:

- Why should readers care about this story?

- Why does it matter to them?

- What do you want readers to take away from your story?

Be sure to keep your readers in mind as you write.

D. BE INTENTIONAL WITH ORGANIZATION
- Chronologically (from beginning to end)

- Beginning in the middle (*In Medias Res*—Latin for "in the middle of things") or end, and revealing past events with flashbacks or important information through dialogue or narration

- Snapshots of different events, told out of order to coincide with main points in thesis

STUDENT SAMPLES

All student samples have been preserved in the form in which they were submitted in class; thus, they contain some errors. After all, papers are never truly done; they are just due.

STUDENT SAMPLE: NARRATIVE ESSAY

Jessica Oswald
Professor Tartaglia
ENC 1101-93109
26 January 2017

Past the Limits

I sat on the living room couch and stared out the sliding glass door. The afternoon sun lit up the trees, turning their leaves a beautiful shade of light green, and beyond them I could faintly see the outline of a mountain. This was the first time I had ever left the South and I had never seen scenery like that before. My father and I were spending the summer visiting my cousin, Cathy, out in Colorado Springs. So far, the trip had been pleasant, but we had only arrived a couple of days previously. My father and Cathy were both avid hikers who enjoyed the outdoors; I preferred being indoors and reading or playing video games. It's safe to say that I was not very prepared for this trip; I would come to find out that I truly had no idea what was in store for me that day.

It was mid-afternoon by the time we arrived in Manitou Springs and made our way to the trailhead. I gazed in silent horror at the looming incline. I couldn't believe what I had been roped into doing. We were supposed to be on vacation! Vacations are meant to be a reprieve from the difficulties of everyday life; they are relaxing and leisurely. A day filled with tedious //hiking was the opposite of what I had in mind. I wanted to spend my time strolling through picturesque downtowns, riding a trolley up the side of a mountain, or strolling through dense forests, rife with ecological diversity and wildlife. Cathy, her boyfriend, Terry, and my father tried to encourage me, yet my preteen angst could not be abated. They had told me beforehand just how steep the trail was, but seeing it in person was vastly different from what I had imagined. Briefly, I considered just turning around and walking back to the car. The choice was three against one; I would never get my way, so I reluctantly soldiered on. We trudged up the mountain on a trail that seemed more like an endless staircase. The only positive aspect was the weather, which was absolutely beautiful. As we climbed higher and higher, we had a panoramic view of the surrounding mountains and the valley down below. It took us less than an hour to ascend the trail, yet it seemed to last an eternity to me. As I gazed down at where we had started, I felt exhausted and exhilarated. The town we had come from looked so tiny now; the buildings were transformed to mere specks scattered around the base of the mountain. The weather was changing, too. Dark clouds were rolling in. We didn't linger long and made our way to the Barr trail, which would take us back down the mountain.

The Barr trail was six miles long and we knew we wouldn't make it down before the rain started. Adrenaline coursed through me and propelled me forward; I ran faster than I thought possible while deftly maneuvering around large rocks and tree roots. We felt the light sprinkling of rain a couple of miles into our journey, so we picked up our pace despite the steep slope of the trail and the uneven terrain. The wisest course of action would have been to slow down, but I didn't want to. I was too driven and too invigorated to slow down. I felt like I was flying! This proved to be a mistake, as I soon discovered when my foot slid and I was catapulted forward. My palms and knees skidded across the rocky ground and I was completely mortified. I clumsily gathered my dignity, picked out the pebbles that were embedded in my skin, and resumed my pace. I considered slowing down or taking a break to catch my breath, but I had resolve; I wasn't going to stop for any reason. Blood was dripping down my legs and I didn't care; the rain was heavy enough to wash it away now. Lightning soon accompanied the rain, which was like nothing I had ever experienced before; thunder shook the mountains and I felt my whole body vibrate with each mighty clap. We were soaking wet and cold, so we found a rocky overhang and took shelter from the relentless downpour. This wasn't the most comfortable shelter; I had to crouch down low to fit. We were glad to have found it, nonetheless.

This wasn't how we planned our day to be. In fact, we had checked the weather before we left, and it was supposed to be a lovely day. Truth be told, I didn't mind the storm. I knew that it could be dangerous, especially considering the lightning, but I had never been on an adventure like this before. I knew that this would be an experience I would never forget. At the beginning of the trip, I never could have imagined that I was capable of a hike like this. Now, I felt like I could accomplish anything. For the first time in my life, I felt truly strong. My body was aching, bloody, and bruised. I was soaking wet and splashed all over with mud, yet I can't remember a time in my life where I felt more awake and alive. The storm seemed to be over as quickly as it began and we made our way down the trail again. As it turns out, we weren't very far from the end.

Despite my initial reluctance to go on this hike, I was glad I had done it. I consider it a life changing experience that taught me about pushing myself past the limits of what I thought I was capable of. I found confidence in myself and my abilities, and discovered what is now a lifelong passion of mine: hiking.

STUDENT SAMPLE: NARRATIVE ESSAY

Krista Byrd
Professor Gaspar
Triad Magazine
26 October 2013

Waiting No More

She picks up her guitar and closes her eyes. Breathe. One, two, three. Open. She flashes her bright smile at the crowd as they hold their breath in anticipation for the first note.

For many people, pursuing their dream of singing is a fantasy. Many of us have already given up on our dreams, or are becoming weary enough to seriously reconsider chasing them with such abandon. To Melissa Brethauer, 24, and a former HCC student from Riverview, Florida, using her talent and chasing her dream was the only path she could imagine pursuing.

Brethauer is not your typical 24 year old. She drives a motorcycle, has a college education, recorded her debut album "Waiting" at 19, has played historical venues like the House of Blues on the Las Vegas strip, and has toured and played music festivals across the southeast United States.

Most people just want to know how she did it. How did she find time, resources, energy to pursue her passion and her degree? How, in a world full of 'No!' did she find her 'Yes'? "Life takes us down so many unexpected paths and anything can happen, so I stay most encouraged by taking things one day at a time," she said.

The Riverview native started singing when she was three, and grew a serious interest in instruments at seven. She knew that she was meant to be a musician from that point on. In high school, she amazed her classmates, winning talent shows, and playing at the local talent competition, Brandon Idol.

After high school, when most of her peers were trying to pick a major more serious than "Under Water Basket Weaving", she was not only pursuing her bachelor's degree, but was also writing music and producing her debut album with the help of her music management team at Now Hear This. "We [Now Hear This] began working together in 2006, and I give much credit to Now Hear This for most of the opportunities I've had to expand my music endeavors," she said. There was no more waiting for Brethauer, and she jumped into the studio as soon as she could.

This was a lot of work for someone fresh out of high school. The high demands of her music career and her college career were constantly fighting for her attention. "There are so many challenges in this business, but for me, the biggest challenge has been finding a healthy balance with my music life and my social and working life," she said. She adds, "My college years (full-time) were especially tough because I had to make a lot of sacrifices. When I wasn't working my part-time job or in class, I was traveling playing shows. More often than not, I had to spend my free time, or make time if I didn't have any, in between music events writing papers and studying for exams. Somehow I managed to still graduate with my bachelors within four years and with a decent GPA." Her family and friends have been a big support and inspiration during all of the time she has spent working toward her goal. She is recently married, and has a wonderful support system.

As much work as being a musician is, Melissa has found time to enjoy incredibly rewarding moments. The title song on her debut album made it to the top 50 in in MusicTampaBay.com's Top 100 Songs of 2009. She is also ranked in the top 15 on ReverbNation in Atlanta for her genre. She has made numerous television appearances, and even completed a radio interview in New York with Blues Hall of Famer, Sonny Rock.

Radio shows, TV interviews, and charts are not the reason she loves to sing, however. It is performing that gives her a rush unlike any talk show or news program. "I remember playing in downtown Nashville one night and John Legend and John Rich (from Big and Rich) happened to be in the crowd listening!" she exclaimed. "Playing in front of people never gets old to me. Even though I've done it hundreds of times, I still get nervous from time to time."

For Brethuaer, the sky's the limit. She is working on her sophomore album and continuing to write her own music. "'Waiting' was a great learning experience for me. I now have a much better sense of both my musical identity and what I expect of the recording process than I did at age 19. The vision I have for my next album is more of a folky, stripped-down and acoustic feel," she said.

What does the future have in store for Brethuaer? She predicts, "In five years, as long as I'm still challenging myself as a musician and pursuing some music opportunities, I will be happy."

STUDENT SAMPLE: NARRATIVE ESSAY

Tabitha Saletri
Professor Angela Tartaglia
ENC-1101-14282
August 27, 2018

The First Time

You could have had me one day sooner, in a tent near the Chasshowitzka River. Did you know? Cold though it was, I wanted you rather badly, and was prepared to immediately doff my clothing, should the opportunity present itself. To my dismay, it didn't, you being a new creature in my world–a feminist with a strong respect for boundaries, though I was delighted with the night-long cuddle. I look back on the wounded and cautious woman I was that night, completely unaware of the bright, new beginnings I was about to step into with you by my side, and though you are with me only in my memories now, I am still in awe of the gorgeous, far-reaching, technicolor changes in me and in my little world, and the precious two years of companionship that got their start with the events that followed.

The next day dawned as cold as the one before. I woke, cozy and deliciously cocooned with you, and thought with contentment of our previous night's conversation over charred hotdogs and a crackling fire. Over the weeks we had been seeing each other we hadn't shied away from the more serious details of our histories, but that night had been a significant deepening of the trust and understanding we had been developing, and I was hopeful. I was also excited about the fact that we shared a number of varied interests, including time spent away from civilization, in the great outdoors, especially on or in the water, which was why we had decided on this short adventure, which would be refreshing for us both. As chilly as it was, it took us some time to pack up and get down to the water, where you put in your oarboard, and I my rented canoe. But once we got moving, thoughts of the cold went away, as the tranquility of the newly-minted morning, and the joy of companionship filled my soul. We wandered down the river together, and explored some of the narrower ways off of it, soaking in the beauty of the bright blue sky, crisp air, calm water, and the song of life that surrounded us. It had been far too long since I had done anything like this, and sharing the reconnection of a missing piece of myself settled me into a familiarity with you that felt like the product of years, rather than the weeks we actually had.

The first time I went into the river, trying to get under a branch in which bees had collected, it was startling and unnerving, thoughts of gators that might be nearby as I stood in the murky shallows in the forefront of my mind. But I recovered quickly, and managed to blindly put my hand right down on my months-old phone in its waterproof case, and get myself back in the boat with your help. I breathed a sigh of relief, with both the gators and the expense of the phone in mind. The second time I went into the river, on our way back to the dock, was on purpose, as

I had just watched my phone slide off my lap into the water when I tried to reorient myself for a better photo. The water was much clearer here, and still only about waist deep, so I thought I would easily be able to spot it. Unfortunately, the bottom of the river was covered in grass, so I could've been on top of it, and not seen it. As we searched fruitlessly, my dismay grew, and the sinking feeling of resignation settled into my stomach, along with the feeling of being a bit lost that can happen in the circumstance of losing one's phone in the age of devices that contain a rather large chunk of important information pertaining to your daily life. This sounds silly, it seemed so to me at the time, but a tiny little piece of me felt that what followed was my reward for managing not to have a meltdown when my phone went in the river and wasn't retrievable, then having refrained from another possible meltdown when I found out, a couple of hours later at the Verizon store, that I didn't have the cell plan I thought I did and how much a new phone would cost me.

You had asked me on other occasions if I wanted to stay overnight. You asked again. I knew I could do so without any pressure from you, because you had already shown utter respect for my boundaries, not that I was going to take any convincing. When we got to your place, I didn't really know how to go about telling you that I wanted you, so I did my best to show you with my enthusiastic kissing and caressing. You still weren't going to make a move in that direction unless I let you know, and you told me how I could do so.

Then began one of the most profound and incredible experiences of my life. You made me feel like a work of art, a treasure, radiant and powerful. From the gasp that escaped your lips when, straddling you and watching your face, I took off my shirt, I immediately saw myself as beautiful in your eyes. Then, rather than getting right to the task at hand, as I expected, you proceeded to explore my entire body with your hands and your lips, and covered me with your kisses. I was so ready for you, that when you finally entered me, it was a revelation. This. This is how it was supposed to be. Passion, and heat, and desire, the most thrilling and deeply fulfilling purpose of skin-connection, all wrapped up together and woven through mind, spirit, and body. So very now and here, to the utter exclusion of all else. And you showed me still more, drawing me several times again to the heights, till I understood what it meant to be limp with satiated desire, and fell asleep with your heart beating in my ear for the first time. When I woke in the night I heard your breathing, and felt the warmth of your skin on mine, and my heart was at peace in the knowledge that, for the moment and probably more to come, I wasn't alone in this corner of the world and, even better, my companion in this hour was also, in a way that began to make a path for you into my heart, a treasure and a work of art.

STUDENT SAMPLE: NARRATIVE ESSAY

Andrew Koplin
Professor Funk
ENC 1101
16 April 2021

A Brush with Death

Often when we think of human beings as a species, we tend to put ourselves at the top of the foodchain. For most of my life I've agreed with that statement but after a thrilling encounter with a true apex predator, a black bear in the rugged woods of northern Minnesota. I have since doubted if we really are as we say "at the top of the food chain".

My story starts on a chilly 35 degree day in late September of 2016. I had just been woken up by a friend we were hunting with that day, we woke up early around 4 am that morning, all of us shuffling around rubbing the remaining sleep from our eyes. We all did a quick equipment check for the day, I usually carry a backpack filled with water and red bull and beef jerky, on top of that I made sure my bag had my latex gloves, skinning knife, ammunition for my 45-70, and hand and foot warmers. After that we geared up for the day putting on our camouflage and lacing up our boots. I grabbed my Henry repeater 45/70 a gun I absolutely love with its varnished dark maple wooden stock and matte black barrel. It is a symphony of destruction, especially with the ammunition I use the 45/70 nitro rounds. Each one fires a projectile about the size of your ring finger. It is a devastating round. Capable of reducing a bears head to pink mist with one close range shot. I also carry my Glock 23 chambered in .40 mm on my right thigh, along with two spare magazines on my belt.

At 5 am sharp I left the cabin heading north towards my tree stand, elevated about 25 feet off the ground and strapped to an old white birch tree, I have always loved birch trees that time of the year because the bark peels off almost like a thick piece of paper. As I got within 50 feet of my stand I began my ritual of looking for recent tracks, claw marks on trees and recent bear scat. After that I used my flashlight to find my way to my stand and begin the ascent, being careful not to bump my rifle or gear against the metal rungs.

As I settled in my stand for the day I cracked open a redbull using my jacket sleeve to muffle the sound of it releasing the carbonated pressure. I sat there for the next 45 minutes carefully listening to the sounds of wildlife waking up for the morning, I could hear the deer grunting and moving around looking for their breakfast, the squirrels in the trees, I really hate squirrels while trying to hunt every sound they make sounds like a branch or a twig being stepped on. Its almost as if the squirrels know you are there and just want to mess with you. But as dawn finally broke the familiar surroundings of my stand became clear. To my left I had dense pine trees approximately 30 yards away with some sparse tall grass and fallen trees in between, to the right I had pure forest, nothing but leafless oak and maple trees, a perfect sightline to see what is coming, And to the front an open shooting lane for about 100 yards, at the end and smack in the middle was my bait bucket. If you have never seen a bait bucket before here is what it is, It is quite literally an old oil barrel filled to the brim with things like donuts, candy bars, cereal, pretty much anything sweet. It has a hole in the side about a foot wide and it is used to get bears in the area to feed from this spot, bears really do love donuts and honey.

As the hours passed by I began to think that my day was going to be a bust. So far all I had seen was an 8 point buck, but it was out of season. And a gang of squirrels in the trees behind me cackling like the little crackheads that they are. I was cold and tired from being buffeted by 15 mile an hour winds, and my brain was getting tired of reacting to every branch snap and grass movement from the wind. So far I had not seen anything or heard anything to suggest there was a bear in my area, I checked my watch and saw it was almost 11. My stomache growled at the sight of that and realizing I hadn't eaten since that morning I decided I would give it until 1130 before I went in to get some lunch.

About 5 minutes later I heard more noise and movement from the rear, and unable to turn and see around behind me I assumed it was the squirrels again, and swore to myself when I got down I was going to shoot all of them with my glock. I kept scanning my area using my binoculars trying to ignore the branches breaking behind me. That's when I heard the grunt, or more accurately I would describe it as a deep exhale. It came from just behind me, I immediately froze, I knew that sound and I thought to myself "shit, don't move" I kept cussing in my mind while I tried to figure out my next step. I evaluated my options, my rifle was laying across my lap, a bullet already chambered but it was underneath the safety bar, it would be a lot of movement before I could get it ready, and I didn't want to spook it. It was a tense moment for me as I knew one of two things could happen, either the bear would continue walking past me and I would have a shot, or the worst case scenario would be it catches my scent and decides to climb up and say hello. Bears are notoriously good climbers and 30 feet up a tree for a bear would take seconds.

So I waited for what felt like an eternity, but in reality was probably only a couple of minutes. I waited until I felt the tree start to shake and lean back. The bear had decided it was going to come up the tree and say hello. I analyzed my options, stand up and aim my rifle, pull my glock, or sit still and hope it goes away. I pulled my glock out of its holster just in case, knowing full well that if it got close enough and turned violent there was a good chance I wouldn't even get a round off, or the round itself wouldn't be enough to stop that bear. I sat paralyzed with fear as it began climbing, 20 feet away, 10 feet away, I could hear its breathing now, I looked down and to my right. No more than 5 feet away from me was a fully grown male black bear, I could just see his right paw with his 3 inch claws digging into the tree, and resting on his paw was his head, I was close enough to see that his nose was wet, and he had a scar along his cheek where hair didn't seem to be growing. It had large brown eyes like a dog almost. I could see the massive clouds of hot air he was exhaling. I began to panic and didn't know if I should shoot now or wait longer. The look on the bears face is what made me wait, I looked at him and he just stared back at me, yawning and smelling the air. And in that moment I realized that humans are not the top of the food chain, there are plenty of animals who could easily kill us and eat us without hesitation, but the choice is theirs. In that moment I felt powerless, but I also felt like there was this unspoken agreement between me and the bear, he wouldn't attack me and I wouldn't shoot him. Hunting was a game, and I just lost to a better hunter, a black bear.

We stayed like that for a few minutes each of us just checking the other out. I actually thought about throwing him some beef jerky but before I could make a decision he climbed his way back down leaving huge gashes in the tree trunk. I holstered my glock and took a deep breath as I watched him saunter off into the pines to my left, I watched him the whole way, but he never looked back. And I found in myself a newfound respect for animals, especially the dangerous ones.

When I got back to the cabin I told my friends about the whole situation, and a lot of them asked me why I didn't shoot it, It would have made an amazing trophy I agreed with them on that part, it was a massive bear. But my response to them was that they didn't understand because they weren't there, I believed that the bear had spared my life that day, after talking to the guys we all agreed that as long as we owned that property, the black bear with a scar on its cheek would never be killed unless someone was in immediate danger. I never did see that bear again and often I wonder if I ever will. And that is the story of my brush with death.

QUESTIONS FOR CONSIDERATION

What is each essay's thesis?

Explain some of the strengths of the essays.

Identify specific ways these essays could be improved. Consider each essay's focus, organization, development, style, and grammar.

EXERCISES

NARRATION EXERCISE 12.1A

People say that hindsight is 20/20, which means that it is easy to look at one's past and see what should have been done, what mistakes could have been avoided, and what risks were warranted or unnecessary. Almost all people have had an incident in their past that impacts the decisions they make. This incident or episode may have been incredibly trivial or even mundane, or it may have been devastating, even violent. Regardless of the scale of this incident, it has made a significant impact on how you make decisions as an adult.

Find an episode from your childhood and deliver it through a narrative. Once you have delivered the narrative episode, reflect on its importance in your development as an adult.

INTRODUCTION PARAGRAPH:

Begin with a significance statement (lead) that will engage the reader and present the importance of your topic. Remember, your title is an extension of your lead. You will then need to clearly deliver your points of development. These points of development will become your body paragraphs. The order that you present these points will dictate the order of your paragraphs. Finally, you will include a thesis—not an announcement. Be sure to limit your subject to avoid having too broad of a topic.

BODY PARAGRAPHS:

Begin each body paragraph with a topic sentence that limits the discussion of that paragraph. The number of body paragraphs is determined by the points of development you have for your essay. The first body paragraph(s) will present the narrative episode. Remember, show don't tell—the readers need to be able to see the episode taking place; they do not want to be told what happened. Review the narrative essays provided as examples.

Once you have provided the narrative, you will use the following body paragraph(s) to discuss the impact the narrative has had on your adult life and the decisions you make.

CONCLUSION PARAGRAPH:

Once you are ready to conclude your essay, you will need to be sure that your reader leaves your essay with the most important information provided. It is your last opportunity to be certain the reader is taking away what you wish for him/her to have learned from what you have written. Draw any final connections between your main points of development and recap any of your main ideas.

NARRATION EXERCISE 12.1B

You knew English was a Gordon Rule class, but no one told you that writing was going to be quite this difficult and demanding. As you sit quietly in the shade and savor some of what little free time you have this semester, you notice the ground in front of you begin to shift and crack. There, before your very eyes, Godzilla climbs from the earth. You, of course, must chronicle his destruction of HCC in a 500-word essay.

NARRATION EXERCISE 12.1C

Have you ever hated your job? Compose a narrative essay that focuses on the worst (or hardest) job you've ever had. Be sure to stay focused on a single incident or a series of closely related incidents that best describe how difficult this job actually was.

NARRATION EXERCISE 12.1D

After four years of college, you are celebrating with your first real vacation. You have planned three glorious weeks away from the hustle and bustle of city life before you begin to practice your dream career. Climbing aboard the small Learjet, you can't help but wonder if the other five passengers have also planned vacations like the photographer's vacation you designed. As the plane lifts into clouds, you drift off, dreaming of the week you have planned hiking in the Rockies followed by the two weeks in Hawaii shooting pictures of volcanoes. Coughing wakes you to a smoke-filled cabin, and you realize that the loud noise you thought was a dream is really the pilot screaming. The trees seem to leap at the window, and you remember nothing after that. When you finally come to, the plane has crashed. You have only moments to grab three items and throw yourself out the broken window before the plane explodes. Two weeks later, the rescue team finally finds you. Of course, your old English teacher is leading the expedition. You almost wish that you hadn't been found because, as you know, the first words out of her mouth are: "Write me an essay on how you survived two weeks in the Rockies with only those three items you were able to save from the plane!"

NARRATION EXERCISE 12.1E

Compose a narrative essay that illustrates one personal characteristic of someone you know. Although human beings are complex and have many different traits, be sure you focus on only one characteristic. For example, you likely know somebody who is inspiring, clumsy, funny, bitter, or obsessed with a hobby. Choose one aspect and relate an anecdote that best exemplifies this personal quality.

NARRATION EXERCISE 12.1F

Getting out of bed on a Tuesday has never been fun, but today seems more difficult than usual. Slowly, you stretch. First you stretch an arm, then the other arm, then a leg, then another, then another, then . . . oh, no! Shades of Gregor Samsa! You are a cockroach. Chronicle your day.

NARRATION EXERCISE 12.1G

Consider the picture below. What do you think is happening here? Narrate the events before and/or after this moment.

NARRATION EXERCISE 12.1H

Consider the picture below. What do you think is happening here? Narrate the events before and/or after this moment.

12.2 DESCRIPTION

A description essay describes a scene for the reader. This type of writing emphasizes the five senses to evoke a complete picture with words. The purpose is to leave a dominant impression on the reader. You can create this impression using gestures, striking characteristics, descriptive words, active and vivid verbs, and figures of speech like simile, metaphor, and personification.

A. SENSORY DESCRIPTION

You can also build a complete experience using the five senses.

SIGHT: WHAT CAN BE SEEN?

Descriptive essays often use visual details to paint a picture for readers.

SOUND: WHAT CAN BE HEARD?

Though the essay may be dominated by visual cues, descriptive essays also include audio clues so the readers can imagine what the scene sounds like.

TOUCH: WHAT CAN BE FELT?

Sight and sound are often the focal points of descriptive essays, but you shouldn't neglect the sense of touch. Readers can imagine how it would feel to be touching the things the writer includes.

SMELL: WHAT CAN BE SMELLED?

Smell is often associated with memory, so this is a chance for writers to connect the description to the essay's purpose. Do those cookies smell like grandma's house? Does the scent of sunscreen and saltwater recall childhood vacations at the beach?

TASTE: WHAT CAN BE TASTED?

Taste is often the neglected sense in a descriptive essay—unless the writer specifically talks about food. That doesn't mean you should ignore it, though. If you can, tell the readers what your taste buds encounter.

B. OTHER FEATURES TO CONSIDER

- Duration: How long has this lasted?

- Function: What is it made for? What does it do?

- Condition: How does it look? Has it been well cared for?

- Location: Where is it?

- Importance: How important is it? Why?

- Value: What is the value? Who values it? Why?

Descriptive writing conveys information with or without bias and feeling. Description can be objective (impartial) or subjective (personal), but it is often used to enliven narration, make arguments more powerful, examine effects, and help with compare and contrast discussions.

C. SHOW VS. TELL

Descriptive essays should use sentences that show instead of tell.

A sentence that tells: Writing this chapter was a difficult, draining experience for me.
A sentence that shows: I sweated through all five versions of this chapter: biting my nails until my fingers were raw, twisting out clumps of hair, and generally being obnoxious to friends and family.

A sentence that tells: My former boss behaved unprofessionally.
A sentence that shows: My former boss cursed at his employees, leered at female customers, and wore tattered bowling shirts stained with barbecue sauce.

A sentence that tells: My first apartment was messy.
A sentence that shows: The television in my first apartment was covered in so much dust that it was hard to see the screen. Most of the carpet was concealed by dirty clothes. The shower was so dirty that I could barely remember what color it had been originally.

A sentence that tells: My dog is playful.
A sentence that shows: My dog runs around and brings me a toy every time I walk into the room.

A sentence that tells: My husband is romantic.
A sentence that shows: My husband says "I love you" every day, he gives me back massages without being asked, and he sends me flowers at work for no reason at all.

A sentence that tells: I was successful at my last job.
A sentence that shows: I increased my company's profits by 24% over a six-month period.

A sentence that tells: My uncle has a childish sense of humor.
A sentence that shows: My uncle loves sharing bathroom jokes, creating bad puns, and playing pranks on people.

EXAMPLES OF DESCRIPTIVE PHRASES THAT SHOW:

- A cluttered mind
- A taste of chaos
- Sluggishly walked
- Heavy on my mind
- A notch before unbearable
- Mouth was near-watering

These examples of description create an image in the mind of the readers and leave a dominant impression.

TIPS FOR EFFECTIVE DESCRIPTIVE WRITING

- Look at your subject.
- Imagine your subject.
- Create one dominant impression your readers will take away.
- Use details to expand and elaborate.
- Show your readers what you see, hear, and feel—don't just tell them!
- Let the readers share your experiences and observations.
- Don't just summarize; be specific!

TIPS FOR ORGANIZING DESCRIPTIVE WRITING

- Group details.
- Arrange by consistent point of view.
- Observe steadily as you write.
- Tour your subject.
- Move spatially.

TIPS FOR CREATING A DOMINANT IMPRESSION

- Provide vivid details.
- Integrate figures of speech.
- Use vigorous, specific words.

STUDENT SAMPLES

All student samples have been preserved in the form in which they were submitted in class; thus, they contain some errors. After all, papers are never truly done; they are just due.

STUDENT SAMPLE: DESCRIPTIVE ESSAY

Shae Barhonovich
Professor Sanders
ENC 1101
25 September 2016

Bahamas' Beauty

She awoke to her daily alarm – not the buzzing irritation of the modern world but rather the sound of the warm, salty ocean breeze rushing over the shoreline. As she rose from her slumber she ventured outside. One step out of her dwelling and her feet sink into the warm, white sand that covers the ground as far as the eye can see. The coconut palms scatter the coast. This magical place is known as the Bahamian Islands. Formed by 700 islands, the Bahamas offer one of the only places left on Earth where its beauty is not reworked. This place, unaltered by human life, seems to provide a journey into another world. Its virtue is not only present in the environment, but also in the culture and way of life of the Bahamians. The raw beauty of the Bahama's nature and culture is unlike the rest of the world.

The quintessential beauty of the Bahamas is most easily visible through its nature. The islands are nestled between the Caribbean Sea and Atlantic Ocean. The water surrounding is a rich and wondrous blue. The crystal clear water reflects off the sun causing the surface to glimmer like a diamond. Below the surface lies an entirely different universe. The Bahamas are home to some of the world's most beautiful coral reefs. These reefs are home to thousands of different kinds of marine life. This lively community in the water puts on a magnificent show. The bright colors and various species of plants and animals interact in perfect unison. The underwater current makes the plants dance to the music of the waves. The lobster's antennas play peekaboo beneath the rock barriers. The fish gather in schools creating a pallet of colors. The stingrays' sleek physique allows them to glide over the oceans floor with grace. As the current pushes the waves into the shore the water froths like champagne. The water breaks over the white granules. The sand that covers the shore provides the ground for most of the islands. It is rare to see paved roads. The people of the Bahamas have left its nature untouched, using sand as its foundation. Scattering the perimeter of the island lies magnificent rock formations. These coves are carved out by the exceptional strength of the waves. The water hits with incredible force, sending violent splashes in every direction. A glance up into the ceaseless horizon fills one's eyes with mystery. As the sun sets the sky becomes a painting from above with perfect strokes of color. A midnight purple mixes with a pomegranate pink as they fade into a radiating orange that glows off spectator's eyes. The last colors slip away and the twilight beckons the stars. The stars come out to play; speckling the sky and shinning brighter than a flame. Nights on the island bring upon its own magic. The stars reflect off the ocean's surface, illuminating the world forgotten by the sun. From sunrise to sunset, the Bahamas remain unaltered and more beautiful than a postcard.

As if the enchanting nature of the Bahamas was not enough, the culture of the Bahamas brings about another world. One step onto the island and the journey begins. The Bahamian people embody joy and happiness. They speak in a zesty tongue that makes one's heart smile. An easy going dialect broken from the current world affairs. "What da wybe is?" is heard echoing throughout the islands; asking a fellow mate how they are doing. Beyond the way they speak is the way they live. The Bahamian people relish in every given moment. The islands are filled with contagious smiles and radiating energy. The good vibrations are spread through laughter. People of the Bahamas always extend a hand. Everyone on the island lives together in peaceful harmony. There unison is one of a story tale. An admirable aspect of the Bahamian way of life is the way the locals live off the land. They do not alter or change the nature but rather work alongside it to create tranquility. The sandy streets of the Bahamas are filled with barefoot Bahamians darkened by the sun. The fresh markets provide a local gathering for all the town's residents. Grocery stores are few and far between. The big open-aired warehouses are home to all the local produce. These fresh markets are filled with rows of lushes and vibrant fruits and vegetables all grown locally on the island. Regardless of where one is headed on the island, music can be heard from just about anywhere. From block to block the Bahamian people seem to be drifting along to the music. The soulful tunes of reggae fill the air. The steel drums and bongos accompany each other with a euphoric melody. The people snap their fingers and sway their hips to the beat. No matter what direction one goes on the islands they are sure to find a sunny smile awaiting them.

As the day falls away she soaks in the last bit of sun. Brushing the sand off her feet before she returns home. The sounds of the waves carry her to sleep. Whether it be the nature or the culture, the Bahamas are one of the most natural and beautiful places on earth. The virgin complexion of the Bahamas nature provides a supreme experience. The fixed culture of the Bahamas offers a unique actuality far from one's normal reality. The Bahamas provide an overall package that is unrivaled. It is definitely a bucket list destination that everyone

STUDENT SAMPLE: DESCRIPTIVE ESSAY

Tiffany Brown
Hawkeye Newspaper
17 May 2017

Living Large in Tiny Houses

Would you live in a house that isn't much bigger than some peoples master bedroom? Some are choosing to downsize and live in what are called tiny houses.

The Dale Mabry campus recently hosted a Sustainable Living Expo that featured these homes. Tiny houses are considered sustainable living because they cut down on living expenses and they don't offer much room to over indulge in purchases.

Some of these tiny houses are placed on pieces of property where they have long term residence, while others are moved from location to location, depending on where the resident feels like calling home. You might be thinking "But isn't that called an RV?" Yes, that is true, but RV's are not actual houses. Tiny houses, on the other hand, are actual houses, the only difference being that they are tiny.

Tiny houses typically look like regular houses; however, some tiny houses have themes. The same way some people like to theme their bathroom, or their kitchen, a tiny house can easily follow one continuous theme because of its size.

John and Fin Kernoham live in a themed tiny house, decorated to honor firemen. Fin Kernoham says that the theme of the house help raise awareness of the importance firefighters have in all our lives. She goes on to say that she's used to living in small quarters, growing up with extended family under one small roof, and how it creates more unity among family. Some might cringe at this thought, but Fin Kernoham brings up another benefit of living in a tiny house, it is the fact that she can easily see what her husband is doing.

Still, there are more benefits of tiny house living. Less space means consuming less stuff. Tiny House enthusiasts Kristen Brown, a real estate agent, and her boyfriend J. Johnson, an engineer, came to the expo after watching TV specials about Tiny Houses and becoming fans. Brown mentions how in her line of work, it is not uncommon to see people buying more space than they need. An appeal of tiny house living to her was "not having to fill so much space." Brown also took note of the good vertical space in tiny houses, noting how that was a good fit for her 6'7 boyfriend.

One Tiny House explorer, Cianna Girardin, wondered what type of jobs were available to a person that wanted to live in a tiny house without a permanent piece of property to keep it on. Jeremy Roberts, another small living enthusiast, answered by sharing the options of virtual jobs and those jobs that can be worked as self-employed.

Tiny house living might not be for the faint hearted, or for those that like to collect a lot of things, but tiny house living is a reminder of how people don't really need a lot of space in order to live. Tiny houses also don't take up a lot of resources by using access electricity or water. So, if you're looking for a way to be kinder to the planet, and you're willing and able to downsize, a tiny house just might be the next place you call home.

QUESTIONS FOR CONSIDERATION

What is each essay's thesis?

Explain some of the strengths of the essays.

Identify specific ways these essays could be improved. Consider each essay's focus, organization, development, style, and grammar.

EXERCISES

DESCRIPTION EXERCISE 12.2A

Revise the following "Tell" statements so they become "Show" statements instead.

1. My mother was very strict when I was a child.
2. My refrigerator needs to be cleaned.
3. My sister's driving habits are dangerous.
4. I learned a lot at my last job.
5. The weather was beautiful this morning.
6. I am incredibly busy.
7. He seemed worried.
8. Her front yard had been neglected for a long time.
9. She seemed cheerful.
10. I found him to be intimidating.

DESCRIPTION EXERCISE 12.2B

Consider the following descriptive writing prompts:

- What is the object of your technolust?
- If you had an avatar that embodied "your essential form," what would it look like?
- On a scale of one to ten, how weird are you?
- Life seems to contain a number of obstacles. Describe how you overcame one of life's obstacles.

DESCRIPTION EXERCISE 12.2C

Sit somewhere other than your home or your classroom for thirty minutes. You may choose any location you want: perhaps a restaurant, a park, or a bus stop. Be sure to stay in that location for at least thirty minutes; don't take a walk. What is your overall impression of the scene? Is it cheerful? Relaxing? Depressing? Chaotic? Choose one (and only one) dominant impression and describe the details that best illustrate your overall impression. Stay focused, but use as many of the five senses as you can.

DESCRIPTION EXERCISE 12.2D

Describe something without using one of the dominant senses. For example, describe a painting without sight, or a meal without taste, or a song without sound.

DESCRIPTION EXERCISE 12.2E

Describe something using details other than the traditional five senses. Describe this thing in terms of temperature, pressure, hunger, thirst, direction, time, muscle tension, or any other sensory input you prefer.

DESCRIPTION EXERCISE 12.2F

Describe something without letting readers know what it is. Use descriptive language so that your reader can guess the thing you are describing.

12.3 Exemplification

An exemplification essay makes a point using examples and illustrations. If someone asks you, "Have you been to any good restaurants lately?" you probably wouldn't answer with just a "yes." You would go on to illustrate with examples, including very specific illustrations regarding the food, the prices, and the atmosphere. Likewise, in an essay, the details are the important part. The examples prove your point, persuade your reader, and create interest. They also help prevent ambiguity and misinterpretation.

You may focus your exemplification essay on a topic like these:

The benefits of _____

The disadvantages of _____

Try to choose a topic that involves some critical thinking or creativity. Don't choose a topic that anybody could figure out without your input—like the benefits of owning a car or of being rich.

Sample Outline: Exemplification Essay

Topic: Wright's Deli

Thesis: Wright's Deli is a great place to grab lunch because of its convenient location, comfortable atmosphere, and delicious food.

Point One: Convenient Location

- Right off Dale Mabry
- Near downtown
- Easy parking nearby

Point Two: Comfortable Atmosphere

- Chalkboard menu easy to follow
- Grab and go setup for quick purchases
- Plenty of booths and tables to enjoy food

Point Three: Delicious Food

- Quality supplies for sandwiches and salads
- Delectable cakes and cupcakes
- Wide variety of tea flavors

STUDENT SAMPLES

All student samples have been preserved in the form in which they were submitted in class; thus, they contain some errors. After all, papers are never truly done; they are just due.

STUDENT SAMPLE: EXEMPLIFICATION ESSAY

Wesley Bryan
M. Sanders
ENC 1101
3 October 2016

Requiem for a Skywalker

As Jedi Master Yoda said, "Fear is the path to the Dark Side. Fear leads to anger. Anger leads to hate. Hate leads to suffering." In the Star Wars saga, Anakin Skywalker was thought to be the "chosen one" of an ancient Jedi prophecy; he was to bring balance to the Force. Anakin was considered to be one of the strongest Force-sensitive humans in the entire galaxy, but his power and strength could not save him from being corrupted by the Dark Side of the Force. The transition from innocent Anakin Skywalker into the villainous Darth Vader, one of the most tragic tales in all of science fiction, occurred following the progression of Anakin's fear, anger, hatred, and suffering.

The fear of loss was the catalyst of Anakin's fall to the Dark Side of the Force. When Anakin was first discovered, he was a young slave of about nine years old living with his mother. He was discovered by two Jedi, one of whom noticed great potential and Force-sensitivity. Young Skywalker was freed from slavery shortly after meeting the two Jedi. However, his mother was not freed, and Anakin was confronted by the fear of leaving his mother. Anakin reluctantly left his mother behind, afraid that he might never see her again. Anakin vowed to return and free her once he was able. His attachment to his mother only fueled his fear of losing her.

The fear of losing his mother was about to transition into anger. After several years, Anakin had grown into a talented and headstrong Jedi apprentice. However, he was being plagued by nightmares about his mother. While on a mission, Anakin sensed that his mother was in great danger. He raced off to his old home planet as quickly as he could. Upon his arrival, he discovered that his mother had been taken prisoner by the Sand People. Anakin tracked down the nomadic tribe of Sand People, sneaked into their camp, and found his mother tied up and near death. He released his weak mother from her bonds and held her close as she looked upon her son for the first time in years; she died in his arms. The anger within Anakin grew so quickly and violently that he slaughtered the entire camp of Sand People. He killed every man, woman, and child. After burying his mother, Anakin vowed to himself that he would become powerful enough to keep those closest to him from dying.

Over the next decade, Anakin's anger began its transition into hate when he began having nightmares again, this time about his secret pregnant wife. He was not going to allow his wife to die, so he sought teachings from a different master: a Master of the Dark Side named Palpatine. Anakin's quest for power began to worry his Jedi Master, Obi-wan Kenobi, and the other members of the Jedi Council, leading Anakin to become distrusted by the other Jedi. He sensed this and came to distrust the other Jedi as well. His new Master, Palpatine, misled Anakin by implying that he was able to teach the ways of stopping death. In this deception, Anakin was no longer fighting his anger and hatred but fueling them. He began to hate everything that he had once stood for because he believed that it had failed him. In an attack on the Jedi Council, Anakin was ordered to destroy his old friends and mentors, including his former Jedi Master, Obi-wan Kenobi. After killing countless young Jedi, Anakin met Obi-wan in combat. Obi-wan tried to reason with Anakin, but Anakin had become blinded by the Dark Side and by his own hatred. The two fought in an epic duel, but Anakin was defeated; his arm and legs were severed, and he was left burning on the bank of a lava river.

Anakin's suffering had only just begun. Palpatine, sensing Anakin's danger, arrived just in time to collect what was left of Anakin's broken, burned body. Anakin was slowly rebuilt with cybernetic limbs but was unable to breath on his own, so he was forced to wear a respirator helmet and a life-support suit. Once his rebuild was complete, Anakin asked Palpatine if his wife was safe. Palpatine informed Anakin that she was dead, sparking the beginning of his true suffering. He had lost everything: his mother, his wife, his hope, and finally himself. That was the day that Anakin Skywalker ceased to be, becoming the evil Darth Vader.

Anakin Skywalker was meant for greatness. He was supposed to be greatest Jedi of all, but his fear became too strong and made him angry. His anger began to blind him and make him hateful. His hate drove him to commit acts that could not be taken back. All of these actions led to immense suffering, not only of the body but of the soul. When Anakin's soul suffered too much, he changed. Thus, Anakin Skywalker became Darth Vader.

STUDENT SAMPLE: EXEMPLIFICATION ESSAY

Alia Machin
Professor Sanders
ENC 1101
04 February 2017

Destiny

Envision a small girl sitting in the corner of a classroom quietly playing all alone. Another toddler approaches this girl and asks sweetly, "Can I play with you?" This timid girl looks down at her toys, back up at this new potential friend, opens her mouth to respond, but words refuse to leave her. This friendly little child backs away scared and confused as to why this seemingly normal girl could not simply say "Yes." That's a small glimpse into what Destiny faced for the first few years of her life. Unfortunately, a speech impediment was not the only obstacle she had faced. At the young age of eleven, both of her parents passed away due to lingering addictions. With no other options, Destiny was forced to move to a distant, unfamiliar state to live with estranged family members. As a result of all this chaos, she developed memory issues that made exceling in academics that much harder. Despite all of these unfavorable odds, this persistent young scholar managed to go from a mute, introverted child to a respected leader at Columbia University.

Regardless of how hard she tried, Destiny was unable to speak simple syllables for the first few years of her life. This shy young girl had to attend years of speech therapy to be able to engage in conversation. This created an introverted lifestyle away from all of her classmates. While all the other children were singing songs, reading aloud, and talking with one another, she was trapped within her own mind. Destiny would not let her disadvantage break her. By the age of five she was able to speak like all of her friends and quickly started to proceed them in school. This was the first, and surely not the last time, that Destiny would have to fight much harder than others to reach success.

After overcoming her speech impediment, Destiny was then faced with a new tragedy. On February 17th 2009, both of her parents passed away and oddly enough, in two separate places at two separate times. Once again Destiny was faced with a drawback completely out of her control. How was she going to deal with this catastrophic turn of events? Now as an orphan, Destiny had to move from her home in New York City to suburbia in Tampa, Florida to begin a new life with distant family members. She soon discovered that these family members were also addicts who struggled with mental health issues. Abuse began to flood this new home but Destiny found solace in her education. She knew that doing well in school was the only way she would make it. Destiny made sure to dedicate every part of her mind to her studies. Despite her circumstances behind closed doors, Destiny started to become one of the top scholars in her high school.

Struggling with the loss of her parents and the abuse at her new home, Destiny started to develop severe memory issues that affected her education. She would come straight home to begin her homework at four in the afternoon and work relentlessly until six in the morning. Education would eventually become her ticket out of this dysfunctional environment, but how could she excel when her memory was now failing her? There were nights full of tears because Destiny knew she would have to fight persistently once again to tackle this new complication. She invested the little money she had into memory aiding vitamins, mental health counseling, and study groups with other struggling scholars. Eventually she learned to work around her memory failure and become Valedictorian at her high school.

All of her hard work finally paid off and Destiny was awarded a full ride scholarship to the college of her dreams: Columbia University. This scholarship provided the means for Destiny to go back to New York City and leave her cruel family behind. However, once she began her studies at Columbia she realized her fight was not over. The courses were much more intense and the other students were much more privileged than herself. Being a low income student, Destiny had to get a part time job to purchase essentials that were not included in her scholarship. The time she invested at her job took away from the time she needed to once again excel in her academics. Destiny knew she would struggle more than her peers but she did not develop an excuse. She pushed herself out of her comfort zone and trained her mind to work with her new crammed schedule. Eventually she became a member of her resident hall, a co-founder to a club for low income students, and attended workshops at other Ivy League schools to motivate other struggling students.

Committing years of her life to hard work, discipline, and academics has transformed Destiny from a timid child to a courageous leader. Despite a speech impediment, the death of her parents, developing memory loss, and managing a part time job with full time school, Destiny still manages to be victorious. She knows her struggles are still present and will be for some time, but she doesn't let these disadvantages stop her. Destiny has never made excuses. She utilizes as many resources as she can to prevail in her studies. Most of all, she remains focused on her overall goal at all times. She is an inspiration to all struggling young adults fighting for total success. Following her example, anyone can succeed despite the shortcomings in their life.

STUDENT SAMPLE: EXEMPLIFICATION ESSAY

Peggy Reyes
Instructor Paquette
ENC 1102
30 May 2017

The Things I Carry

Leaving the place where you felt safe and comfortable is never an easy feat for anyone. For most, doing such a thing leaves them feeling terrified and anxious for a prolonged time. In my previous experiences, leaving home was always a laborious task for me and brought about a sense of dread. In "The Things They Carried," a group of soldiers goes through a very similar experience of having to move away from home and immerse themselves in a world where everything, from the landscape to the language to the culture, is different and overwhelming. If there were another time where I had to do it again and only bring a few objects, I would carry a notebook with a pencil and extra lead and erasers, a phone and its charger and earphones, and a book.

If I were to leave home like the soldiers in the book, one of the things I would bring with me when packing my possessions is my notebook as well as a pencil and extra lead and erasers. Since second grade, writing has always been a passion of mine. The ability to create and destroy worlds with a pen or pencil amazed me, and after trying it out for myself, I fell in love with it. Bringing this notebook with me is necessary to keep my imagination and creativity alive while also staying sane during my travels. In addition, I would also bring a pen or pencil to write down my ideas and stories on the paper. Extra lead and erasers are necessary as well to keep the stories flowing and to fix any mistakes I make.

Another thing I would pack with me is a phone and its charger and earphones. Like most people, my phone is something I must carry with me everywhere at all times. Without it, I would feel lost. Moreover, like most pieces of technology, I would need a charger to keep my phone alive. Having my phone is a necessity; it is my one source of communication with not just my family, but my friends as well, especially if they live hundreds or thousands of miles away. If I ever went away, I know that I would often feel lonely and depressed, and knowing that I can contact my friends for comfort and happiness brings about a great positive aura. Despite the fact that we are miles away, we can still virtually be next to each other, and being on the road to wherever I would go would be less stressful.

Finally, the last thing I would carry with me is a book. As a writer, I am naturally attracted to reading as well. To be able to immerse myself into another world is a reliever for me, and no matter where I would be heading, reading books would always be an escape for me. It has broadened my creative horizons in the past, and it has acted as a security blanket to me. Knowing that there are people, fake or real, that have struggled through something, and being able to relate to those characters would give me hope that I would be okay in my journey.

We all carry something with us. For me, keeping my imagination and my human desire for connection as well as my hope and courage to persevere are things I must bring with me to keep me alive, no matter where I am going. Without these things, I would not be able to endure my journey, and the things I hold so dearly would not last long anymore.

STUDENT SAMPLE: EXEMPLIFICATION ESSAY

James Curry
Dr. Funk
ENC 1101
17 April 2019

Technology Has Doomed Us All

The dependence on modern technology is a sadistic crutch for all of mankind. A crutch can be considered a useful tool to aid in one's life when needed, but the excessive reliance on this tool will cause turmoil when it is suddenly stripped away. The same can be said about our reliance on technology. Most would shrug off the fact that the chance of an apocalyptic event that renders technology useless is surprisingly high. The majority of people today do not have the skill sets to survive in techless world. Every decision people make today is based on technology and the convenience it brings. Convenience from modern technology will be the final nail in the coffin for our so called "advanced" civilization. Do to the advances in technology many have failed to develop skills and attributes required to survive in a wasteland without convenience.

Everyone has fallen victim to the side effects of a bad night's sleep at least once in their life. Unfortunately, prolonged insomnia has become an epidemic in modern society thanks to our easy access to technology. People today would rather lay in their beds and scroll through social media or watch T.V. instead of getting a good night's sleep. They preform this ritual every night just to try and feel some sort of connection to the outside world. The side effects of insomnia that build up over time can be devastating. Negative effects consist of fatigue, poor balance, a weakened immune system, and it can drastically hinder your decision making process. All of these symptoms can be fatal in a wasteland where every decision could be life or death. I can contest to the severity of the negative effects of insomnia though my own personal experiences. While deployed to Afghanistan I suffered from the effects of not getting enough sleep. Which, is unavoidable when deployed to a warzone. The unresolved truth is that the suffering people experience from technology induced insomnia is completely avoidable, and it is making us weak at the core. The long term effects of sleep deprivation can permanently hinder the ability to use any skills that are essential for survival in a technology deprived world.

It is no longer a necessity to be the most physically fit in today's society do to the advances in our technology. This has caused outbreak in obesity worldwide and doesn't show signs of slowing down. In a techless world it is sad to say but the fatties will be the first to go. With just a touch of a button they have their food delivered to the their door, and zero physical effort was put into getting that food. When everything falls apart the absence of developed physical strength and motor skills will be the executioner for most. The lack of physical strength will become the greatest hurtle to those who have no concept of the amount of effort required to "put meat on the table" without clicking a button. The fact of the matter is that these people would starve to death before they could adapt their lifestyle to the drastic changes of a world without technology. The only possible way for individuals fitting in this category to survive would be reliance on others that are more physically capable.

Unfortunately, the art of conversation is now hanging at the gallows because of the isolation technology has inflicted on humanity. A meaningful face-to-face conversation is tragically a thing of the past. Conversation is a skill, and just like all skills it must be honed through practice. The only way to practice conversation affectively is to converse regularly with others. Today's technology has made it possible for people to never come in contact with others that are not on the other side of their screen. The text lingo and the emojis have brought on a new era of broken grammar and the inability to express thought into alluring speech. Charisma could be considered one of the most valuable asset in one's arsenal against the lawless time that the loss of technology would bring upon us. Difficult situations would arise where the only means of survival depends on rhetoric. In a land without technology the social infrastructure would collapse entirely causing an wave of crime without consequence. In this period of lawlessness the ability to sway people's opinion with speech is an essential talent to master in order to thrive amongst the chaos.

In a world ruled by technology's convenience, mankind as a whole has a very gloomy forecast ahead of it. The path of least resistance we have been blindly following will abruptly come to an end in a single global catastrophe. With the likelihood of the end rising every day it feels like it is no longer a matter of if but when. The odds are stacked against us, and the inevitable failure of our precious technology is fast approaching. We can only pray that enough survive with the strength to assist humanity hobble forward into this new world without the weaknesses induced by modern technology.

QUESTIONS FOR CONSIDERATION

What is each essay's thesis?

Explain some of the strengths of the essays.

Identify specific ways these essays could be improved. Consider each essay's focus, organization, development, style, and grammar.

EXERCISES

EXEMPLIFICATION EXERCISE 12.3A
Consider the following writing prompts:

- What could be done to improve your experience at HCC?

- What are your three greatest fears?

- Choose a movie or TV show. What lessons can be learned from watching?

EXEMPLIFICATION EXERCISE 12.3B
The German poet/philosopher Schiller wrote, "Deeper meaning resides in the fairy tales told to me in my childhood than in the truth that is taught by life." What fairy tale from your childhood has helped you find meaning in your life?

EXEMPLIFICATION EXERCISE 12.3C
As you wander along the beach, you stumble upon an old, seaweed-encrusted bottle. As you wipe it off, a genie appears. Thanking you for freeing him from two thousand years of imprisonment, he offers you three wishes. What would they be?

12.4 DEFINITION

Finding a useful definition of a word seems like an easy task. After all, one simply has to consult a respectable dictionary, and the task is completed.

But what about complicated concepts? It may be easy to define the word "chalk," but what about abstract ideas? For example, how does one define "democracy"? Does holding elections automatically make a system of government democratic? Is that enough? (Probably not, as many dictatorships hold elections that are rigged.) What if a large segment of the population is prevented from voting? What if the government relies on representatives? What about the Electoral College in the United States? At what point is a government democratic enough to be accurately called a democracy? And for that matter, how do *you* personally define democracy? (Others will disagree with your definition, and that's okay.) A dictionary will provide a useful starting point, but to capture all the complexities of a concept, a dictionary definition simply isn't enough.

Consider other concepts as well--for example, ideas from the worlds of medicine, law, and ethics. What about the word "alcoholism"? At what point is a drinking problem chronic enough to be called alcoholism? What about "manslaughter"? How does the law definite this term in contrast with murder? (For that matter, how do other states and even other countries define this term, assuming they even make such a distinction?) What about "plagiarism"? At what point has an idea been duplicated blatantly enough to be considered a violation of ethics?

Other words to consider include "friend" (is a social media friend an actual friend?), "wisdom," "culture," and even slang words like "frenemy," "adulting," and "woke."

A definition paper defines a term or concept without simply referring to a dictionary. The idea is to go beyond a simple definition of a concept. After all, if a term can be defined in one sentence, it's probably not worth writing an entire essay about.

The word or concept you choose for a definition essay should probably be an abstract noun, as opposed to a concrete noun. It would be very difficult to write an essay about "chalk" because that simple word can be defined in a few sentences. Instead, choose more complex concepts like "motherhood," "liberty," or "faith," all abstract nouns that require much longer explanations.

When writing a definition essay, it can be easy to fall under the sway of what others say—try to avoid this. This is the time to use personal experiences and ideas to proclaim your truth. Don't regurgitate what others have said; ask yourself, what does this word mean specifically to you?

A. Personal Definition

A definition essay can be a personal one in which you tell what a word means to you—just don't add any first-person references like "to me, a good citizen is someone who . . . . " Instead, just say it as if it were so. After all, everything that you write is your opinion, isn't it? Assume that your readers can distinguish between fact and opinion on their own. Simply write, "A good citizen is someone who . . . . "

B. Stipulated Definition

You may also have a stipulated definition, providing a particular meaning that it might not otherwise have or that might work just for your essay. Stipulated definitions don't attempt to define every aspect of a word. Instead, they limit the definition to a particular area. For example, there are many ways to define democracy, but you might want to write a paper that limits it to the way democracy works in the United States of America.

C. Analytical Definition

You can define by analysis, comparing your word to others in its class and then showing how your word stands out. For example, you might define a muscle car by concentrating on characteristics such as performance, engine size, and body types.

D. Extended Definition

You can define with an extended example, using illustrations, metaphors, similes, or personification. For example, you could describe alcoholism as a "hidden demon," "a scream of terror," or a "home-wrecker."

E. Function Definition

You can define by function, telling how something works or what something does. This type of definition works well for jobs (what is a web designer?) and machinery (what is a CPU processor?).

F. Negative Definition

You can also define by negation, telling what your word is not and then contrasting or comparing it to something someone might confuse it with (e.g., a whale is not a fish). Negation works well as a first developmental paragraph, but keep in mind that ultimately, you must tell your reader what your term actually IS. Therefore, negation won't work for an entire paper.

Some other possible definition topics could be love, trust, communication, honor, bravery, courage, intelligence, power, justice, freedom, success, or responsibility.

Sample Outline: Definition—What is Love?

Thesis: Romantic love is a combination of three main components: communication, respect, and attraction.

Topic Sentence: Romantic love requires communication.

- Couples in love must talk to each other
  - It really doesn't matter what they talk about—just that they talk
- Couples in love have to be willing to share parts of themselves
  - Part of love is sharing intimate parts of the self with the partner

Transition: But none of that matters if the people in love do not respect each other.

Topic Sentence: Romantic love requires respect.

- Couples in love must show respect for each other at all times
  - Even if they disagree, they should do so in a respectful manner
- Couples in love should always show respect when speaking of the partner
  - Love does not allow couples to say disrespectful things about the partner

Transition: While communication and respect are the foundation of romantic love, they could also be the backbone for a great friendship; the difference between romantic love and friendship comes down to attraction.

Topic Sentence: Romantic love requires attraction.

- Couples in love should be attracted to each other mentally
  - Romantic love often begins in the mind

- Couples in love should be attracted to each other physically
  - Romantic love has a physical component

STUDENT SAMPLES

All student samples have been preserved in the form in which they were submitted in class; thus, they contain some errors. After all, papers are never truly done; they are just due.

STUDENT SAMPLE: DEFINITION ESSAY

Amber Imeh
Professor Coursey
English Composition 1101
3 December 2014

Sodium Nitrate in Processed Meat

Grocery stores stock their products from all over the nation. Some products are delivered from right around the corner, but many are shipped for days by train or by plane before reaching their destination on local shelves. How does food stay fresh and safe during all that time? The answer is preservatives. Food preservatives have been used for centuries to maintain freshness and prevent decay caused by "chemical (oxidation), physical (temperature, light), or biological (microorganisms) factors" ("Preservatives"). Food can be preserved by processes including freezing, canning, smoking, drying, and freezing ("Food Preservatives" 40); however, most food is preserved by natural or added chemicals such as salt, sugar, sulfur compounds, sorbic acids, and benzoic acids ("Preservatives"). Over the years, the safety of one chemical compound, sodium nitrate, has been disputed. The concerns over the use of sodium nitrate are unfounded. There is not enough evidence to prove that sodium nitrate is a health risk to consumers, and the benefits and regulation of the chemical make it a safe and effective preservative.

Sodium nitrate is an ionic compound of sodium (Na) and nitrate (NO3). Plants create the compound when they absorb nitrogen from the soil, which is why sodium nitrate is naturally found in vegetables, fruits, and grains (Alfaro). Sodium nitrate is also found in the saliva that helps to break down food as it enters the stomach ("Sodium Nitrate"). Sodium nitrate naturally breaks down into sodium nitrite ("Chemical Cuisine"; Alfaro; Yoquinto). Usually, sodium nitrite is then converted by the body into nitric oxide, a compound that serves many important functions (Yoquinto); unfortunately, under the right conditions, sodium nitrite can also be turned into nitrosamines, a chemical that has been linked with cancer in animals (Yoquinto). The link between nitrates and nitrosamines is the main reason why some people avoid meat preserved with sodium nitrates.

In the past, there were studies that showed a link between eating meat with sodium nitrate and an increased cancer risk ("Chemical Cuisine"). However, recent studies have produced different results. A study by the International Agency for Research on Cancer claims that there is no clear indication that nitrate causes cancer (qtd. in "Sodium Nitrate"). Other organizations, including the

National Academy of Sciences, the American Cancer Society, and the National Research Council, agree that there is no proof that nitrates directly cause cancer in the human body (Alfaro). Even though there have been studies that link coronary heart disease and diabetes with the consumption of processed meat ("Red and Processed Meat"), these studies produced unclear results as to what factor in the meat caused the health risks. Nitrosamines are also a point of concern with consumers. It is a fact that nitrosamines have been linked with cancer in small animals (Yoquinto), but there is no guarantee that the sodium nitrate in processed meat will turn into nitrosamines in the human body. Nitrosamines only form from sodium nitrite under certain conditions in the human body (Yoquinto). Therefore, manufacturers add ascorbic acid (vitamin C) and erythorbic acid to processed meat (Yoquinto). The addition of ascorbic and erythorbic acid in the meat promotes the formation of nitric oxide in the body rather than the formation of nitrosamines (Yoquinto). Even though it is true that sodium nitrate can turn into nitrosamines, there are preventative measures in place to protect consumers.

Sodium nitrate is an excellent preservative for meat. The addition of sodium nitrate in processed meat produces an attractive red coloring, a distinctive flavor, and a shelf life significantly longer than fresh meat alone (Yoquinto; "Sodium Nitrate Q&A").

Sodium nitrate also performs an important duty: it prevents the growth of Clostridium botulinum, bacteria that produce chemicals that cause botulism poisoning (Alfaro). The botulism bacteria grow in anaerobic environments with low acid levels (McGavin). Sodium nitrate is effective in preventing the growth of anaerobic bacteria (McGavin), thus protecting consumers from a paralyzing disease (Alfaro). Despite the clear benefits of sodium nitrates, some food manufacturers attempt to attract customers with labels claiming their food is "nitrate-free" or has "no added nitrates." In fact, these products are more dangerous than meat with added sodium nitrate. Meat with "no added nitrates" is actually preserved with celery juice in an attempt to deny the addition of sodium nitrate; however, as a plant, celery is full of sodium nitrate (Alfaro). In fact, meat cured with celery juice often has more sodium nitrate than regularly processed meat (Alfaro), which can lead to increased health risks because high concentrations of sodium nitrate is toxic (McGavin; "Sodium Nitrate"). Meat without sodium nitrate is even more dangerous; since sodium nitrate inhibits the production of toxins in meat (McGavin), meat without it puts consumers at risk of developing botulism poisoning.

Sodium nitrate is safe for use because of its regulation by the government. Sodium nitrate is approved by the Food and Drug Administration (FDA) for use as a preservative. The FDA has found no indication health risks associated with the preservative at its current level of use ("Sodium Nitrate Q&A"). If it had, the preservative would not be in food for people to eat. Also, to protect consumers from eating too much sodium nitrate, the FDA has released a limit on how much of the preservative can be in meat. People who cure meat at home are safe as well. Pink salt, a mixture of sodium nitrate and table salt, is sold in stores to people who want to cure their own meat (McGavin). The mixture is premeasured with safe amounts of sodium nitrate and has detailed instructions for use to prevent accidental poisonings.

Sodium nitrate is a safe and effective preservative. It keeps meat fresh for weeks and gives it an appealing color and flavor. It prevents botulism, a dangerous disease that grows in uncured meat. No evidence points to nitrates causing cancer in humans. The government has approved its use in commercial food and products. So, why, is there still a controversy over its use in meat? Consumers generally group all food preservatives as harmful. People want nothing to do with preservatives or the recent studies that exonerate the chemicals from wrongdoing. Moderation is the key to understanding sodium nitrate. As with any type of salt, the amount congested should be limited. However, people should not shun sodium nitrate because of its bad reputation; it has positive effects on the body, and produces more benefits than risks.

Works Cited

Alfaro, Danila. "Facts About Sodium Nitrate and Sodium Nitrite." *Culinaryarts.about.com*, About.com, Accessed 26 Nov. 2014.

"Chemical Cuisine Learn about Food Additives." *Cspinet.org*, Center for Science in the Public Interest, Accessed 24 Nov. 2014.

"Food Preservatives Antimicrobials, Antioxidants, and Metal Chelators Keep Food Fresh." *Chemical and Engineering News*, 11 Nov. 2002, p. 40. *ACS Publications*, Accessed 24 Nov. 2014.

McGavin, Jennifer. "Pink Salt - Using Nitrates to Cure Meat." *Germanfood.about.com*, About.com, Accessed 26 Nov. 2014.

"Preservatives to Keep Foods Longer and Safer." *EUFIC*, European Food Information Council, 2004, Accessed 24 Nov. 2014.

"Red and Processed Meat Consumption and Risk of Incident Coronary Heart Disease, Stroke, and Diabetes: A Systematic Review and Meta-analysis." *Ncbi.nlm.nih.gov*, National Center for Biotechnology Information, Accessed 26 Nov. 2014.

"Sodium Nitrate." *Pubchem.ncbi.nlm.nih.gov*, National Center for Biotechnology Information, Accessed 01 Dec. 2014.

"Sodium Nitrite Q&A." *Meatsafety.org*, American Meat Institute, Accessed 1 Dec. 2014.

United States. U.S. Food and Drug Administration. "CFR - Code of Federal Regulations Title 21." *Accessdata.fda.gov*, U.S. Food and Drug Administration, 1 Apr. 2014, Accessed 1 Dec. 2014.

Yoquinto, Luke. "The Truth About Nitrite in Lunch Meat." *Livescience.com*, Purch, 30 Dec. 2011, Accessed 24 Nov. 2014.

QUESTIONS FOR CONSIDERATION

What is each essay's thesis?

Explain some of the strengths of the essays.

Identify specific ways these essays could be improved. Consider each essay's focus, organization, development, style, and grammar.

EXERCISES

DEFINITION EXERCISE 12.4 A

Consider the following writing prompts:

- What is your greatest fear?

- What is love?

- What is a hero?

- What is power?

- What is success?

- What is a successful student?

- What is happiness?

- What is a healthy relationship?

- What is a toxic relationship?

- What is a great job?

- What is a good teacher?

- What is beauty?

- What is art?

- What is truth?

DEFINITION EXERCISE 12.4B

According to Benjamin Franklin, "Those who would give up essential Liberty, to purchase a little temporary Safety, deserve neither Liberty nor Safety." How would you define safety? (You may want to consider what essential liberties you would be willing to give up to acquire it.)

12.5 CLASSIFICATION AND DIVISION

A classification essay groups items according to certain criteria, putting topics into categories based on specific characteristics. Generally speaking, a classification essay takes a larger group of topics and sorts them into categories, whereas a division essay takes one main topic and divides it into several components.

For instance, a classification essay may do the following:

- place daily activities into categories like work, school, and home

- discuss a variety of television shows as they fit in the genres of teen drama, cheesy romance, and police procedural

- evaluate the attributes of fictional characters by considering physical prowess, intellectual capability, and social network

A division essay may do the following:

- consider a movie by looking at the acting, the musical score, and the script

- analyze a song through the lyrics, the vocals, and the musical background

- discuss a painting in terms of colors, textures, and techniques

If you write a paper on different types of something, use classification categories that have some depth or meaning. Classifying different types of anything as expensive, medium-priced, and cheap or small, medium-sized, and large is probably meaningless. Be careful, too, about not using categories that are too broad. Classifying something as good, bad, and okay is not likely to enlighten your readers. Whatever categories that you use, make them parallel.

Classifying different types of Christmas shoppers as impulse shoppers, seasonal shoppers, and shoppers who look for sales is not parallel. The categories overlap. A seasonal shopper might also be an impulse shopper.

Use one single, significant principle for organizing your paper.

Again, one of the keys to writing a good division and classification essay is to choose a topic that is not too broad. This is not usually a problem for a paper about different ways to do something. However, if your topic is different types of something, try to narrow it down.

For example, the topic "different types of movies" is too broad. Even if you choose horror movies, action movies, and comedies as your division (that is, your main categories), you have left out too many other types of movies to make your paper meaningful (westerns, musicals, historical dramas, etc.) To correct this problem, you could narrow the topic down to different types of a specific type (or genre) of movie, such as different types of horror movies.

Classifying different types of movies as comedies, dramas, and horror movies is too broad, but classifying different types of horror movies as comic horror, slashers, and psychological thrillers is more meaningful.

Remember that each classification must also be divided into examples. Rather than merely list some psychological thrillers, differentiate among your examples and then illustrate them.

For example, there are comedic horror movies (the developmental point), but all comedic horror movies aren't the same. There are (Example A) classic horror films that have become comic over time because of their old-fashioned special effects (illustrate with old Japanese films such as *Godzilla*), (Example B) horror films with comedic subplots (illustrate with *Shaun of the Dead*), and (Example C) intentionally funny horror parodies (illustrate with *Scary Movie* series).

This is ONE paragraph of a longer essay. You would then distinguish among the slashers and the psychological thrillers.

Your outline might look something like this:

TYPES OF HORROR MOVIES

I. Comic horror
   A. classic
      1. *Godzilla*
      2. Funny effects, soundtrack synchronized poorly
   B. comic subplot
      1. *Shaun of the Dead*
      2. zombies
   C. parodies
      1. *Scary Movie*
      2. absurd—intentionally fake

II. Slashers
   A. Example
      1. illustration
      2. illustration
   B. Example
      1. illustration
      2. illustration
   C. Example
      1. illustration
      2. illustration

III. Psychological thrillers
   A. Example
      1. illustration
      2. illustration
   B. Example
      1. illustration
      2. illustration
   C. Example
      1. illustration
      2. Illustration

What if you wanted to classify different types of roommates to avoid? You might have an outline that looks like this one:

TYPES OF BAD ROOMMATES

I. **Introduction**
   A. **Topic**: Types of roommates to avoid
   B. **Hook**: One of my friends was unable to sit on his living room couch for six months. Why? His roommate gave a friend permission to "live" on that couch...rent-free.
   C. **Working Thesis Statement**: By learning about the less than admirable types of roommates, those sharing a space with someone can be aware of danger signs and get out of an unfortunate situation before having to renew their lease, and those seeking a roommate can be aware of the possible pitfalls of having a roommate before making the decision to share a living space.

II. Intrusive and Inconsiderate Roommate
  A. Invades your privacy
    1. Barges into your personal space
      a) Goes in your room while you're sleeping, doing homework, or spending time with a significant other
      b) Goes into the shared bathroom when you're using it
    2. Goes through your things
      a) Rifles through your belongings
      b) Opens and reads your mail (or social media accounts)
  B. Expects you to adjust your schedule at their whim
    1. Invites mutual friends over and gets upset if you do not participate in fellowship
    2. Plays loud music at all times of the day
  C. Treats you like a supplier
    1. Use your stuff without asking and neglects to replace it
    2. Doesn't pay bills on time (thinks you can handle all the bills by yourself)
  D. Believes they live alone
    1. Walks around much less than fully dressed
    2. General irritations like going out of town, locking their door, and forgetting to turn off their alarm clock
III. Parent-type Roommate
  A. Desire for information
    1. Eager to know who, what, when, where, why and how of your every move
    2. Gets upset when you don't provide this information
  B. Demands accountability
    1. Hounds you to do your chores
    2. Uses information about deadlines or due dates to constantly harass you to do your work
  C. Overly critical
    1. Picks at every minor detail
    2. States their (unsolicited) opinion on every aspect of your life/Expresses constant disapproval
  D. Tries to be an authoritarian
    1. Thinks you can't make decisions on your own
    2. Thinks they know what is in your best interest
IV. Drama-loving Roommates
  A. The Conniving Roommate
    1. Tries to hit on your significant other
    2. Steals from you
  B. The Angry Roommate
    1. Always in a bad mood
    2. Complains about your every move
  C. The Negative Roommate
    1. Gloomy about everything, including living with you
    2. Tries to draw out negativity in your life
  D. The Self-Absorbed Roommate
    1. Thinks they can do nothing wrong and you are to blame for everything
    2. Only considers their needs and projects their issues onto you
V. **Conclusion:** Get out while you can or make sure your friendship with any potential roommates can withstand the storms that are sure to come when you decide to live together.

Notice how the first two points focus on the behaviors of a specific type of roommate while the third point divides a category even further into different types of drama-loving roommates--and then focuses on the behaviors of those sub-types. You could possibly break this outline into two separate essays--one on the first two types of roommate and another on just drama-loving roommates.

IN-CLASS EXERCISE

Remember that breakfast idea from chapters 5-9? Create an outline based on the ideas you generated. Your outline may look like this:

PATH TO DECODING A PARENT'S ANSWERS: THE RACE TO SUNDAY BREAKFAST

I. **Introduction**
  A. **Hook:** Every Sunday, my mother and one of her close friends met for breakfast. (This "Once Upon a Time" hook lets the reader know that it's story time).
  B. **Background information:** My mother would sometimes buy a small gift for the child who accompanied her to breakfast. Naturally, my brother and I competed for this spot. But my brother and I were often disappointed when our requests were not immediately granted.
  C. **Thesis:** My brother and I had to learn how to understand and deal with the different ways our mom could say no.

II. **Not now**
  A. **Topic sentence:** This alliterative utterance gave us hope.
    1. Grammar
      a) The phrasing pointed toward the possibility of future acquisition
    2. Follow-up
      a) Requests greeted with "not now" needed to be renewed the following week.
        (1) This is the only time my brother and I collaborated. If one of us got a "not now" the previous week, the other would walk away gracefully.

III. **We'll see**
  A. **Topic sentence:** This ambiguous response was puzzling.
    1. Grammar
      a) The use of first-person plural suggested objectivity.
    2. Follow-up
      a) There was no need to follow up. Although my brother and I knew what we wanted, there was no way ALL parties were going to reach an equitable agreement.

IV. **I'll think about it**
  A. **Topic sentence:** This was, paradoxically, the most honest and deceptive response.
    1. Grammar
      a) The first-person singular made it clear our Mother was the sole decision-maker.
    2. Follow-up
      a) Common sense made it clear our single mother, who had to handle the responsibilities of raising five children, had no downtime with which to consider our Sunday requests.

V. **Conclusion**
  A. **Sum up main points:** I'm glad my mother never gave a straight answer.
  B. I learned life lessons and, more importantly, how to appreciate my mother.

SAMPLES

SAMPLE OUTLINE: CLASSIFICATION AND DIVISION—TYPES OF SHOPPERS

I. Year-round shoppers
- A. take advantage of seasonal sales
  1. white sales in January
  2. summer clearance in Sept.
- B. needs may change
  1. children grow, change sizes
  2. change interest—Tickle-Me-Elmo out of favor
- C. forget what they already bought
  1. buy niece a purse in February, hair dryer in June, tickets to a show in October
  2. hide in closet and forget it's there
- D. tie up: get great bargains but may end up wasting money

II. Seasonal shoppers
- A. get in the spirit
  1. carols playing in the store
  2. weather cools
- B. Christmas sales
  1. 50% off before Christmas
  2. slow-moving items
- C. Buy the right items
  1. children same size
  2. know what the hot items are
- D. tie up: busy time but may be worth the effort for the savings

III. Last-minute shoppers
- A. Stress
  1. illustration
  2. illustration
- B. Crowds
  1. illustration
  2. illustration
- C. Best sales
  1. illustration
  2. illustration

SAMPLE OUTLINE: CLASSIFICATION AND DIVISION—DIRTY SOUTH RAP

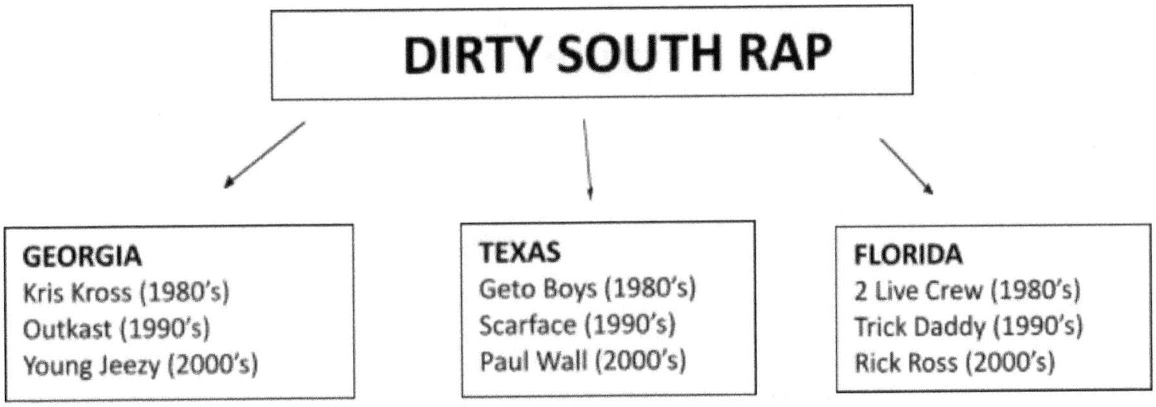

DIRTY SOUTH RAP

GEORGIA	TEXAS	FLORIDA
Kris Kross (1980's)	Geto Boys (1980's)	2 Live Crew (1980's)
Outkast (1990's)	Scarface (1990's)	Trick Daddy (1990's)
Young Jeezy (2000's)	Paul Wall (2000's)	Rick Ross (2000's)

I. **LEAD:** Jermaine Dupri's 2001 hip hop single "Welcome to Atlanta" (feat. Ludacris) declares Atlanta the "new Motown," referencing the city of Detroit, Michigan, which was known for its contributions to popular music, fertile job market, and affordable urban housing in the 1950s to 1980s.

THESIS: The Dirty South style of hip-hop emerged in part from Texas, Georgia, and Florida artists of the 1980s who were able to lay the foundation of what was to come.

II. **GEORGIA**
    A.   1980'S
        1.   KRIS KROSS
    B.   1990'S
        1.   OUTKAST
    C.   2000'S
        1.   YOUNG JEEZY

III. **TEXAS**
    A.   1980'S
        1.   GETO BOYS
    B.   1990'S
        1.   SCARFACE
    C.   2000's
        1.   PAUL WALL

IV. **FLORIDA**
    A.   1980'S
        1.   2 LIVE CREW
    B.   1990'S
        1.   TRICK DADDY
    C.   2000'S
        a)   RICK ROSS

V. CONCLUSION

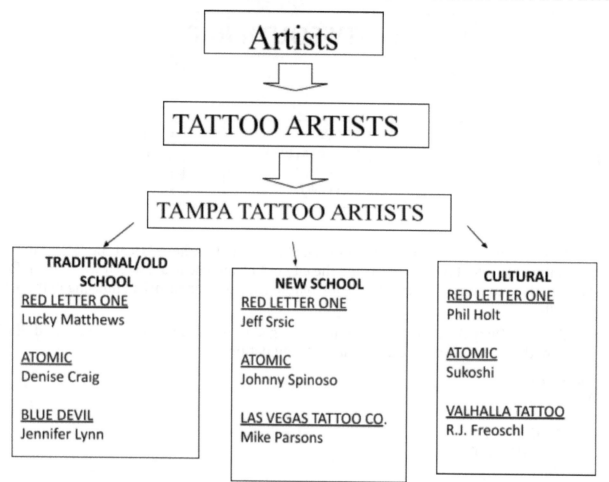

I.   Lead
      3 Points of Development: Three Divisions of Tampa Bay Tattoo Artists Thesis

II. Classification One: Traditional/Old School
    A.   Lucky Matthews
    B.   Denise Craig
    C.   Jennifer Lynn

III. Classification Two: New School
    A.   Jeff Srsic
    B.   Johhny Spinoso
    C.   Mike Parsons

IV. Classification Three: Cultural
    A.   Phil Holt
    B.   Sukoshi
    C.   R.J. Freoschl

V.   Conclusion

SAMPLE OUTLINE: CLASSIFICATION AND DIVISION—LOSING WEIGHT

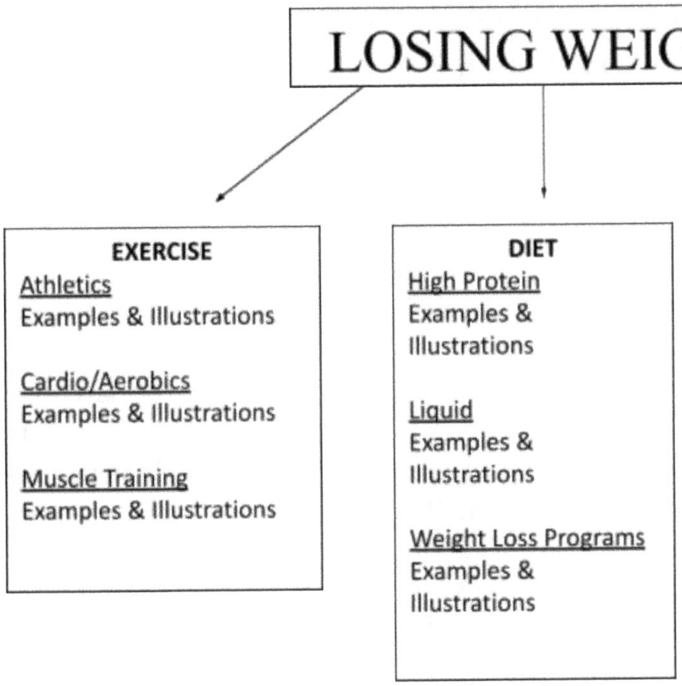

LOSING WEIGHT

EXERCISE
Athletics
Examples & Illustrations

Cardio/Aerobics
Examples & Illustrations

Muscle Training
Examples & Illustrations

DIET
High Protein
Examples &
Illustrations

Liquid
Examples &
Illustrations

Weight Loss Programs
Examples &
Illustrations

MEDICAL
Pharmaceutical
Examples & Illustrations

Surgical
Examples & Illustrations

Therapeutic
Examples & Illustrations

I. Lead
    3 Points of Development: Three Divisions Diets Thesis
II. Classification One: Exercise
    A.   A.   Athletics
    B.   B.   Cardio/Aerobics
    C.   C.   Muscle Training
III. Classification Two: Diet
    A.   High Protein
    B.   Liquid
    C.   Weight Loss Programs
IV. Classification Three: Medical
    A.   Pharmaceutical
    B.   Surgical
    C.   Therapeutic
V. Conclusion

STUDENT SAMPLES

All student samples have been preserved in the form in which they were submitted in class; thus, they contain some errors. After all, papers are never truly done; they are just due.

STUDENT SAMPLE: CLASSIFICATION AND DIVISION ESSAY

Alex Rose
Professor Gaspar
Hawkeye Newspaper
30 March 2015

Florida Man

He's drunk, high, rich, poor, black, and white. He has no respect for the law or himself. His favorite drink is orange juice with meth. He's robbed stores and kidnapped and murdered. He's a citizen, a football player, a lawyer, governor, and a constant pervert. He's your neighbor, your brother, father, uncle and sometimes you. He is Florida Man and there's a little bit of him in all of us.

Florida Man is not one person, but the conglomerate of all Florida residents. No one is safe from him because he is everywhere and everyone, at least in Florida. He has Twitter, Instagram, and Facebook accounts. He even has a new beer made by Cigar City Brewing Company. Combined, he has killed every animal in the state, and eaten most of them, including humans. The only creature to elude Florida Man is the Skunk Ape, and it can't run forever.

The rest of the nation knows that Florida is crazy. Scientists have blamed the fact that we don't have winter. We get to spend more time outside and get in more trouble. But that doesn't account for the sheer insanity and volume of the incidents. It could be because of Florida Man's easy access to guns and unwillingness to learn gun safety. Or maybe his fondness of meth and alcohol drives him to rob. I say it is because Florida Man is in us all, and only in Florida can he exercise his full potential.

Web results for other states bring similar men of this caliber. Georgia Man lives in a similar way, as does Arizona Man, but they do not match Florida Man's track record. Florida gives too many opportunities for insanity to take over. We have swamps, farms, forests, big cities, small towns, and at most three hills. Florida Man is confined by the sea on three sides and has nowhere to go but crazy.

But our state's special brand of insanity has not missed the fairer sex. Florida Woman is also on the prowl, stabbing, shooting, and crashing her car with the same ferocity as her male counterpart. If anything, Florida Woman is more of a threat due to her close proximity to babies. Leaving a child in the care of Florida Woman is inadvisable to anyone but Florida Man.

Taking a look back at some of Florida Man's more famous exploits, we see that he is a talented and determined individual. Florida Man buried his cat, and fought to keep ownership of it when it clawed its way out of the ground five days later. Florida Man shot a teenager, was set free, and continues to assault people. Florida Man ate a guy's face while on bath salts. Florida Man hunts alligators for food and pythons for fun. Florida Woman had an affair with a fourteen year old student and mostly got away with it. Florida Woman killed her baby and walked on lesser charges.

As we reflect on our state's pride and glory, it makes it hard to wonder why anyone would live in Florida in the first place. Maybe we just never left. Or maybe we can't resist the allure of 90 degree, 90% humidity and the constant risk of hurricanes. But really, Florida isn't a state of the nation, it's a state of mind, and no amount of distance will free us from our madness.

Nia Baptiste-Dena
Professor Gaspar
Triad Magazine
27 November 2012

Body Art

Tattoos are a form of body art which can also be considered fashion. Self-expression is taken seriously. It gives us ways so that we can uniquely identify ourselves and others. Tattoos can hold sentimental value to some, whereas for others, it is just another creative way to express who they are.

Ways of expressing ourselves can be through the form of dance, writing, singing, acting, and body art. Body art can sometimes be considered taboo, because to some people it is not of the norm to "decorate "our bodies in such manner. In some societies, they have deemed body art to be a rebellious act and symbolized anti-socialism, versus other societies, where it is for cultural purposes, and body art is embraced and considered unique and is form of self-expression.

Tattoos can be representations of many things. They can be used in remembrance of soldiers who have fallen. Many prisoners who were a part of gangs had certain "symbols" that identified them. Today, any and every group of people one can think of, have some sort of self-expression of body art on them. Moms and dads are even getting tattoos. Naturally tattoos send off a negative influence to society in those who do not believe in and accept "body art".

Some tattoos are too awesome to even be considered covered up. Embrace your body art, and don't let anyone bring you down from it. Embrace its beauty and be happy with your body.

QUESTIONS FOR CONSIDERATION

What is each essay's thesis?

Explain some of the strengths of the essays.

Identify specific ways these essays could be improved. Consider each essay's focus, organization, development, style, and grammar.

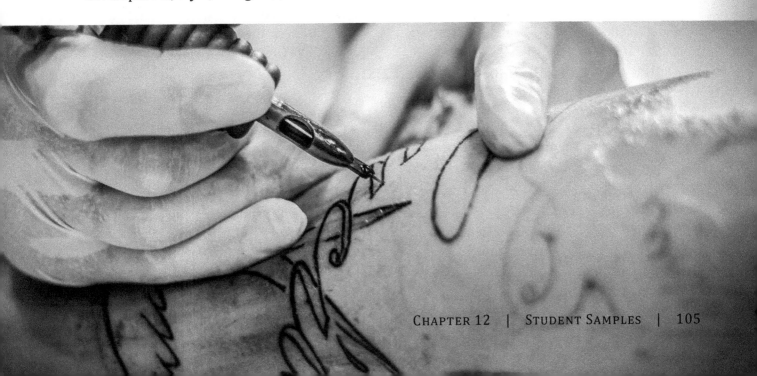

EXERCISES

CLASSIFICATION AND DIVISION EXERCISE 12.5A
Consider the following writing prompts:
- Categorize the things you are willing to die for and the things you are willing to kill for.
- Classify different types of friends.
- Can secrets be dangerous? Categorize different types of secrets.

CLASSIFICATION AND DIVISION EXERCISE 12.5B
After spending all those years listening to our parents (not to mention all those years trying not to listen), is it any wonder that we eventually become them? Discuss the ways you have become your parents.

CLASSIFICATION AND DIVISION EXERCISE 12.5C
Robert M. Adams, in the Preface to Thomas More's *Utopia*, asks the question, "How much repression is a good society justified in exercising in order to retain its goodness?" What do you think? How can you classify the "right" amount of repression? What would these categories be?

CLASSIFICATION AND DIVISION EXERCISE 12.5D
Your cousin asks you for dating advice, specifically on how to recognize the right sort of partner (as opposed to the wrong sort of partner). How can you characterize different types of romantic partners?

CLASSIFICATION AND DIVISION EXERCISE 12.5E
Student stress can be caused by a number of factors, both internal and external. List some stress-inducers in each category.

CLASSIFICATION AND DIVISION EXERCISE 12.5F
People are always telling you what to do. Explain why you shouldn't do something that someone is suggesting you should do (moving in together, taking that job, getting married, getting a tattoo, studying for a test, etc.).

CLASSIFICATION AND DIVISION EXERCISE 12.5G
Classify or divide any of the following topics:

- Country Music
- Rap Music
- Rock Music
- House Music
- Folk Music
- Pop Music
- Reality TV Shows
- Students
- Teachers
- Fathers
- Mothers
- Marriages
- Noise
- Directors
- Actors
- Nurses
- Newscasters
- Bosses
- Wars
- Liars
- Coaches
- Salespeople
- Shoppers
- Drinkers
- Smokers
- Drivers
- Churches
- Dancers
- Lawyers
- Diets
- Ex-Smokers
- Artists

CLASSIFICATION AND DIVISION EXERCISE 12.5H
Classify or divide any of the following topics:

- Studying for a test
- Losing weight
- Disciplining children
- Finding a job
- Training an animal
- Saving money
- Planning a vacation
- Arriving at the truth
- Getting a date
- Turning down a date
- Balancing a budget
- Teaching a class
- Solving a problem
- Making people laugh
- Selling a product
- Getting rich
- Fooling people
- Dealing with an irate customer

12.6 PROCESS

Have you ever found yourself staring at a pile of wood, hammer in one hand and nails in the other, and wondered, "How on earth am I supposed to make a bookshelf out of that?" Or maybe you've thought about making a cake but didn't know where to start. Perhaps you've wanted to learn more about how a caterpillar becomes a butterfly. Chances are you turned to a YouTube tutorial to help you in the hopes that the YouTube tutorial would successfully guide you through the process needed to build the bookshelf, bake a cake, or understand metamorphosis.

A process essay shares characteristics of a YouTube tutorial. It is a detailed, thesis-based approach to explaining how something works or how to do something. A process essay is not simply a list of steps or a series of instructions, though. It goes beyond just explaining what you should do. The essay explains the importance of each step through reflection and analysis. It also includes information about why a specific step is taken over another, and it anticipates potential problems so that your reader learns what to avoid and why.

Going back to YouTube tutorials as an example, there is one particularly popular video of a young woman, Tori Locklear, demonstrating how to use a heating tool on her hair. Tori allows the tool to heat up, sections off a small piece of her hair, wraps her hair around the tool, and within a few seconds opens her mouth in horror as tears well in her eyes: the heating tool had completely burned off a section of her hair. (Link to "Burning My Hair Off" video: https://youtu.be/LdVuSvZOqXM)

A successful remake (revision) of the tutorial could include narrative techniques taken from personal experience, like those in the paragraph above, to share information about how to curl hair, as well as the dangers of not considering hair texture when choosing a heating temperature.

KEY POINTS TO REMEMBER

- You don't want to simply create a list of instructions/steps without presenting an argument and detailed elaboration on how each step supports the argument

- You want to have a point for explaining the process

- You want to be fully knowledgeable of the process you want to explain. If not, conduct some research or choose a different topic.

- If you are detailing a process and want readers to follow along, it is important to explain the steps in the right sequence. The order should allow readers to either recreate a process or understand how a process works from beginning to end. You wouldn't take cooked food out of the oven BEFORE you defrost it (Exception: If you start with a glimpse of the final step in the introduction as a hook. Consider such an approach as a flash forward before you go back to explain the process from the beginning).

- Avoid including terms with which readers are unfamiliar. Make sure you define jargon or less familiar concepts. Reminder: Know your audience.

- Make sure you use signal words to transition from one step to the next.

If you look at the process essay as a journey, you could begin the writing process by asking yourself the following:

- Why should readers embark on this learning journey?

- What have I learned about myself/life/others in my travels down this path?

- Where is the road leading?

- Why is this destination important?

- Why am I choosing this path over others?

- What are the potential roadblocks, and how can I help readers avoid them?

- Are there any shortcuts I can share with readers?

STUDENT SAMPLES

All student samples have been preserved in the form in which they were submitted in class; thus, they contain some errors. After all, papers are never truly done; they are just due.

STUDENT SAMPLE: PROCESS ESSAY

Jasmine Rolph
Professor Sanders
ENC 1101
25 September 2016

How to Serve a Bottle of Wine

Every time a cork is popped on a bottle of wine, the setting turns into an event. People gather to indulge in the celebration of fellowship between friends, family, and coworkers. From red to white, if a big dinner is being served or just a couple of appetizers, the mood is set by the wine, and it is important that it is enjoyed properly. Professional hospitality can be hard to find in today's society, as food and beverage handling becomes a saturated field for college students and adults alike. When a person goes out to eat and experiences bad service, it is often due to lack of education. With the proper training, anything is possible. A guest's experience can always be enhanced with a personable server who knows what product they are selling and can talk about it fluidly and with passion.

When a bottle of wine is ordered, the motive behind ordering should be taken into consideration. Is this a celebration? A special date? Most importantly, different wines go well with different foods. It is almost a sin to enjoy a juicy steak without a robust red, and oh, the complementation of a cool glass of white with a flaky, tender piece of Mahi-Mahi. These are things to consider so the server can provide the appropriate experience for the guest.

Next, there is opening the bottle properly. This is the most crucial point, and it must be mastered before attempting in front of any guest. Professionalism is key. First, take any standard wine key, pull out the knife on the back of the key, and begin cutting the foil around the neck of the bottle in a circular fashion. Carefully peel foil upwards with the thumb. Wipe the neck of the bottle as to clear leftover pieces of foil. Position the corkscrew part of the wine key into the center of the cork. Twist the bottle, not the wine key, until the first lip of the corkscrew reaches the edge of the bottle. Strategically, lever the corkscrew, pulling up on the cork until released. Pull slowly on the cork, and hear the harmonious pop as the cork releases and the bottle unleashes its marvelous aroma and flavor.

Then, there is presenting the bottle of wine in the proper fashion. When people order their immodestly priced bottle of wine, they deserve to be presented with their bottle professionally. The technique of serving in this manner helps people to appreciate what they drink, and enjoy it as it should be enjoyed. Servers should always wine and dine their guest. Make sure to present the label of the bottle of wine to the guest who ordered it. With one hand firmly around the neck of the bottle, and another supporting the back of the bottle, make sure to present the bottle at eye level of guest. The guest will read the label and confirm that this is the bottle they ordered. After taking the steps to properly open the bottle of wine with the wine key, pour out a sample for the guest, twisting the bottle upwards when finished so as to prevent drips down the side. This is the best part. Usually the guest begins swishing around the fermented grapey wonderfulness, taking in the smell, and gulping down the first sip, nodding in approval. Continue to pour out six to nine ounces of wine into the glass. Pay close attention to the guest's consumption and refill the glass accordingly.

To ensure the guest have a good perception, it is important that a bottle of wine be opened at the table every time. Often times, people send the bottle back if the server has the bartender open the bottle at the bar, and then brings it to the guest. It is thought that maybe they have been served an old bottle of wine, or something that has not been freshly prepared. Knowledge on the product being served also helps to execute the utmost professional level of service. If white wine is being served, it must be stored and served in refrigeration, chilling the glass is also important. If red wine is being served, it must be stored and served at room temperature. Distinguishing between a dry wine and a sweet wine will help to suggestively sell bottles for those that lack education in the product they choose to enjoy.

The best kinds of servers are the servers that can enjoy a good wine experience. People often forget to take pride in what they do. Avoid being one of those people. It is better to be completely mad over details, straining for articulation to feed the passion inside, than to leave an already opened bottle of wine at a table to fend for itself amongst the wild creatures who have not yet been properly served their wine.

STUDENT SAMPLE: PROCESS ESSAY

Kristina Piloto
Professor Chamberlin
ENC 1101
March 2017

How to incubate chicken eggs using an incubator

Incubating chicken eggs is a very exciting and easy learning experience for anyone. This development can be utilized as a tool to instill responsibility or it can be a solution to a well-known problem with hens that do not brood. There are many crucial steps that need to be taken to ensure these baby chickens will survive. This twenty one day process is detailed by clarifying the required items necessary, explaining the process of candling the eggs, providing advice on setting up the unit of choice, explaining the importance of a stable environment, and what to expect on the days leading up to the lock down procedure.

Initially, you must gather all the required items. Be prepared to constantly monitor for twenty one days. I would suggest investing in a Hovabator incubator with an automatic turner. This model can hatch up to 40 chicken eggs at a time. For those of you that just want to hatch a few eggs, there are many other incubators sold online that hold less eggs. They are more affordable and achieve the same results as the more expensive units. Once you have the incubator of your choice you can focus on obtaining eggs. If you do not own a rooster and hens for egg production, you can buy all types of eggs off eBay or your local craigslist ads. Now you have the incubator and the eggs all you need is a thermometer that measures the temperature and moisture, a bright flashlight for the candling process that is explained later, and a pencil to mark the collection date on the eggs. Marking the date on the eggs is important to keep track of how long they have been incubating, when they should be showing signs life, and when you should throw them out. You can also have these dates written on a calendar or wherever works best for you.

The candling process is where you use a bright light in a dark room to look into the egg and make sure it is fertile. This process is done on the 7thand 14th day allowing you to watch the growth of the embryos. It is definitely an important step that helps avoid infertile eggs in your incubator. Infertile eggs will literally be cooking and will actually explode when left in the incubator. As you can imagine, it is unpleasant and does not smell very good at all. Make sure you take advantage of the candling experience and avoid an unwanted mess. This step can be very educational and fun. You can watch the embryos grow, stage by stage.

Setting up the incubator is an easy task. First, you must set up the moisture and temperature for your eggs and adjust the incubator accordingly. The temperature in the incubator must stay unchanging between 99.5-100 degrees Fahrenheit. The moisture for chicken eggs must stay below 60%. I find that it is best to keep the moisture at 50%. To produce moisture you must place about 3 teaspoons of water in the tray at the bottom of the incubator. Then, set up thermometer inside the incubator and make sure you can clearly see it from the outside of the incubator when the lid is closed. Turn on the heater and carefully monitor the temperature and the moisture. Set up the auto turner inside the unit and plug it in. Leave the incubator functioning for about a day or two while monitoring the temperature and humidity levels.

Maintaining the environment is priority in this process. The stability of the environment can be altered by nature. Make sure to place the incubator in an area where little to no sun shines in. This is crucial because heat from the sun can alter the temperature inside the unit, causing the incubator to overheat and end up killing the embryos. The area of choice must stay between 70-80 degrees Fahrenheit. It's important to remember that every time the lid is opened the heat and moisture will decrease. This type of alteration must be avoided and is crucial in maintaining the stable environment for the embryos. Once the environment is sustaining a temperature of 99.5 – 100 F and the moisture level is consistent at 50%, you can add your eggs in.

Day one is considered the day the eggs are placed in the incubator. You carefully place the eggs into the proper slots on the auto turner. Some people do not invest in the auto turner and would rather manually move the eggs by hand. The eggs must be manually turned between 3 - 4 times a days. If you choose this method it is easy to alternate by marking each side of the egg with an x and o. If you do not have a lot of spare time on your hands I would highly recommend the automatic turner. When the eggs are added on day 1, you will need to readjust both temperature and moisture. The eggs will be cool, causing the temperature and moisture to change. It is important to check on the incubator every day to add water if necessary or adjust the temperature.

On day seven and fourteen, you must remove the eggs to be candled one by one. You are checking for signs of life. You should see veins and a little moving dot. On day fourteen you must candle the eggs again to get rid of the ones that are not developing. They are not fertile and will not produce chicks. You will know this because they will have no veins and most of them will have a red ring of death. It's a red ring that is clearly visible when candling and can be seen all around the egg. These eggs must be removed and discarded immediately.

The lock down period occurs on day seventeen. This is when the eggs cannot be moved and the lid must stay closed until hatching is complete. The eggs are removed from the turner and placed on the floor of the incubator for the hatching stage. The humidity must be increased and stabilized between 65% - 70%. This makes it easier for the chicks to be able to peck through the egg. This process can take up till the 21st day. Many will say to throw out the ones that have not hatched on the 21st day. It is ultimately your decision to either help them out or get rid of them. From experience it is hard to throw them out, especially when you can hear them inside the egg.

To conclude, I recommend this learning experience to anyone willing to follow these steps to ensure the survival of the chicks. So, next time your hen will not cooperate with nature or you just want to practice this learning development, take it into your own hands and avoid the obstructions involved. Incubate the eggs yourself using this process described. Just think, in twenty one days or less, you will have accomplished your mission, skipped all the hindrance, and have baby chicks to tend to.

STUDENT SAMPLE: PROCESS ESSAY

Rachel Carter
Professor Chamberlin
ENC 1101
March 2017

How to Clip a Show Pig

It was ten in the morning in the wooden pig pen behind my house. I was covered in coarse pig hair and mud, and my back was stiff from leaning down for so long, but it was worth it. For the last two hours I had been completing a process most people probably do not even know exists- clipping a show pig for the Hillsborough County Fair. What is clipping and why would you need to do this you ask? Well clipping is another word for shaving, so you are basically giving your pig a hair cut. Anyone who is exhibiting a pig in a pig show must shave his or her pig in order for the judge to judge them better. Pigs are judged mostly on how muscled their bodies are, but it is not easy for judges to see the pig's muscles when they are covered in long, coarse hair. Just as body builders may shave for a show to better display their muscles, pigs are clipped in order for their muscles to be seen better. Even though clipping a pig may seem like an absurd process to some, it is necessary to those of us who show; after a few hours of washing and clipping, your pig will be show ring ready.

The first thing I do before clipping my pig is wash it. Pigs love to roll around in mud to cool down their bodies, and it is almost impossible to clip them when they are covered in dried mud. My pig pen has two sections- a small section with a wooden floor where my pig eats and drinks its water, and a large section with a dirt floor that is really just a fenced off portion of a pasture. I close my pig into the smaller wooden floor section, this way once my pig is washed, it can not get dirty again by rolling around in the dirt found in the large section of the pen. Next, I make sure that my shampoo- called Sullivan's Brightener, a wash brush- which you can find at your local feed store, conditioner- also found at a local feed store, and a hose with a nozzle made for showering is on hand for the washing process. After gathering all of these supplies up I begin to rinse my pig down with the hose. Once it is all rinsed down, it is time to lather Sullivan's Brightener Shampoo all over my pig's body. It is best to use Sullivan's Brightener because it is made to remove any mud stains found on the pig's white skin. Most show pigs have white skin somewhere on them if they are not all completely white- contrary to the popular belief that pigs are pink. After my pig is lathered down with the shampoo, I use my wash brush to scrub all over its body, making sure not to scrub too hard and leave red marks on my pig. Although your pig will probably not loose points in the show for having red marks, it is still best not to have them because it makes you pig look more cared for and cleaner. Next it is time to rinse all of the shampoo off with the hose. If there are still mud stains on my pig after rinsing, I repeat the shampoo and scrubbing process until my pig is spotless. Once my pig is completely rinsed and cleaned up, I rub conditioner into its skin to leave for a few minutes. Conditioner just assures that your pig's skin stays healthy, especially for clipping. The last step to washing my pig is rinsing out the conditioner with the hose. After finishing that, it is now time to put away my washing supplies and let my pig dry before clipping.

The next step in the show pig clipping process is clipping itself. The first thing I do is prepare my clippers, which are pet clippers that I bought from my local feed store. Next I oil them down and choose what size clipper guard I want to use. A clipper guard goes on the clippers to protect the skin better and also to leave the hair a certain length. I usually use a ½ inch to a ¼ inch guard because this will leave my pigs hair a ½ inch to a ¼ inch long. After that, I turn on the clippers and begin shaving the side of my pig's belly in a straight line, against the grain of the hair. There is no magic place to start clipping a pig, but it is easiest to clip their stomach and back first and work your way to the legs and face. I just continue to clip against the grain of my pig's hair until I have gone over its whole body with the clippers. Once I have clipped my pig's whole body, I am done. I then usually look over my pig and make sure that I have not missed any spots-including their tail, ears, and chest, and that they look trim and tidy. If all the hairs are clipped to perfection and everything is even as it should be, I brush down my pig with a soft bristled brush that I bought at a local feed store.

The last step is to put everything away and clean up. Although it is not essential, I usually sweep the hairs out of the pig pen and make sure my pig has water, food, and is comfortable. Next, I brush all the pig hair out of my clippers with a small brush that came with the clippers. I usually oil the clippers one last time to keep them working at their full potential for the next time they are used. After this, I put all my washing supplies and the clippers into my show box to keep them protected and clean. The end result of clipping always produces one shiny, clipped, blue ribbon pig, but one exhausted filthy clipper. It all makes it worth it once you get to the pig show though, especially when you come home with lots of blue ribbons.

STUDENT SAMPLE: PROCESS ESSAY

Sabrina Arocha
Professor Funk
ENC 1101
27 April 2019

The Process of a Period

Once a month, women go through a painful and uncomfortable ordeal, that prohibits them from acting like sane and rational human beings. On that cursed day, a woman howls in pain, clutching her stomach to somehow ease it, all while her head feels as if it will split into two. And it might as well, considering her personality transforms between: a sweet and polite lady of society, to a vicious untamed beast ready to bite and snarl. Yes, every month women turn into werewolves. Just kidding (unfortunately). Every month women go through their periods. But they might as well be transforming into a fictional creature, because what is taught about periods is non-existent to little. Anything young ladies learn is taught by their mothers or motherly figures. But even then, they do not fully learn the cycle of a period. So, I will be explaining the process of a period through medical research and my own experiences. Disclaimer, like a werewolf transformation, this will contain a lot of gore and blood.

First you have to stock your arsenal. Figure out what you are going to use to stop the flow of blood. Because not only is free-bleeding shunned by society, it is preferable that a lady doesn't appear to have murdered a man with her thighs. Luckily there is a variety of options to choose from; over the last decade, many products have been developed to absorb the blood and chunks of the uterus lining: menstrual cups, period panties and even swimsuits that can be used during your period. But ladies often use either tampons or pads. I use pads and have been using them since I first got my period. For young girls starting their period they are great, because tampons appear to be intimidating and require some practice. I remember I was out of pads, and saw a tampon in an empty box. It was probably a promotional gift, but all I cared about was to stop the blood from oozing out of me. (And it's not like if a man cut himself and started bleeding. Menstrual blood is thicker, and almost has a syrupy consistancey. How do I know? I can feel it pouring out, as do most women). So, I looked up on my phone how to insert a tampon and checked the instructions. After researching, I opened the capsule, took the wad of cotton, and tried to shove it up my woo-ha. It barely entered when I immediately decided against it. It was dry and scratchy, and I was unsure if I inserted it into the right hole. When I took it out, I noticed two things: One, the tampon barely entered me, given the fact only the tip had blood on it, and two it looked like a murdered a man with my bare hands. But from that point on I have never again attempted to use tampons. And although pads are less intimate and more comfortable, it sometimes feels bulky and diaper-ish. But when a woman looks for a period product, they should buy whatever they feel most comfortable with to catch their blood.

But the fun starts before the period does! A couple of days before a lady's period, she experiences pre-menstrual syndrome or PMS. PMS is commonly misused in daily conversation as the symptoms a women experiences during her period; but actually, PMS is the term to describe the symptoms a women experiences *before* her period. A few days prior to the first drop, a lady experiences physical symptoms, such as: tender breasts, bloating, headaches, constipation, and acne. I notice before my period, I get horrible acne and bad headaches. To counteract this, I wear make-up and take some Ibuprofen. But some symptoms aren't as easy to fix. Women also experience mental symptoms: mood swings, anxiety, insomnia, memory problems, sadness, and loss their appetite in food, sex, or both. I try to keep a cheerful disposition, but a few days before my period, I get really agitated and moody. One minute I'm smiling and happy. But the next I'm extremely furious and ranting. For example, I got angry at my younger brother for not doing the dishes. Normally I let him face the consequences and punishments my mother would serve; however, I kept thinking, "Oh how nice it must be to take a nap and do nothing, while your sister does everyone's laundry including yours." And "What is he even so tired from? Staying up late and playing video games? School? I go to school, go to work, and I miracously find time to clean." After stewing in my bitterness, I finally let him have it when he woke up. I compared him to our absent father (who also didn't help in chores) and also spat, "What are you going to do when you have a girlfriend? Make her do everything? I'll tell you right now, when she sees you can't even do dishes, she'll say 'He can't do dishes? He can't do his own fucking laundry? Does he think *I'm* going to pick up after his ass? Never mind. I made a mistake. Peace. I'm gone. See ya later loser." And after that, he began to cry. Wailing how "no girl would like him in the first place" and "who would even notice him." But my brother's pity party didn't stop me from telling him off. My mother had to practically hold me back from ripping his head off. Normally I'm nonconfrontational and would maybe make a snide remark here or there. But after I cooled down, I didn't know why I exploded. Until a day or two later I got my period.

The first drop always creates a mixed emotion. On one hand, it explains why a woman felt crappy and unstable; but it also means she has to suffer for three to five more days. My first few thoughts consist of, "At least I'm not pregnant. Not that I have any reason to be. Unless my body preformed immaculate conception like in that one House episode. Wait do I have pads?" When a woman gets her period, she receives it twenty-one to thirty days after her last; but periods seem to occur when women least suspect it. Typically, I wait a long time for my period to come (around thirty days), so I'm typically caught off-guard. I've gotten my period during the middle of the day, at night, in the morning, during school, during a field trip, and even at my first reptile expo. So it's best to be prepared and I recommend to keep prefered period products on hand.

And once a period starts, it will continue until all of the old utereus lining is out. This will take from two to seven days, and each day will have their own "flow". Flow refers to how much blood and chunks is excreted from a woman's vagina. My periods last for about three to four days; days one and two basically releases an overflowing dam of blood and tissue, while days three and four produces maybe a drop or two. But for my heavy flow days, I often use heavy duty supplies and change my pad often. And my light days, I can sometimes get away with only needing one pad. But if a lady's cycle last for longer, they may have a regular flow or a light flow. Or it could be heavy half the process and spotty the remainder of the week. But each ladies start dates, end dates, and flows are varying (although women who often work or live together can "sync" their cycles. This happened to me and my guard members).

Aside from bleeding from an orfice from their body, women can also experience symptoms: cramps, cravings, back pains or random muscle pains, fatigue, and some symptoms from pre-menstrual syndrome contribute to the pain as well (and the intensity of the effects from PMS become heightened, dulled, or remain the same). But the most common and notable symptom is cramps; the cramps are a side effect of one's body squeezing and pushing out their old lining. I've heard horror stories of women mistaking a ruptured apendixes for period cramps and resuming their day until they fainted from internal bleeding. But this comes from women who suffer extreme pain from their cramps. Cramps can range from uncomfortable to unbearable, depending on the person. In order to ease the pain, women get pain killers and use birth control to ease the pain. And although I keep the acne and occasional headaches from PMS, I lose the mood swings. In place of my mood swings, however, I become increasingly tired and develop cravings. Mostly I want take-out or something fattening; recently I was yearning for a chocolate milkshake and some fries. It's not that bizarre, but I wanted to dip my fries into the milkshake. It created the perfect taste of sweet and savory. As I poured a bit of my shake as a dipping puddle for my fries, my brother gagged, and my mother just shrugged (my mother being an aged veteran herself). But when one's body is punishing them for not producing a child, they may act however one pleases.

This is not how all women experience their period. Some are mildly uncomfortable, while others can be as painful as transforming into a mythical creature. But with some guidance and education, young ladies can prepare for the enevitable effectively.

QUESTIONS FOR CONSIDERATION
What is each essay's thesis?

Explain some of the strengths of the essays.

Identify specific ways these essays could be improved. Consider each essay's focus, organization, development, style, and grammar.

EXERCISES

PROCESS EXERCISE 12.6A

Your sixteen-year-old cousin has come to you for advice. Your cousin is in love and the beloved doesn't even know your cousin exists. Explain to your cousin how a person goes about attracting the attention of someone.

PROCESS EXERCISE 12.6B

'Tis the season to reflect on some of the great myths of this culture: Santa Claus, Rudolph-the-Red-Nosed-Reindeer, the ideal man or woman. We might recognize Santa Claus by his furry red suit, his hardy ho-ho-ho, and the musky reindeer scent which surrounds his bag of toys. We might recognize Rudolph by his sleigh bells and the famous red nose. But the ideal man or woman is much more difficult to recognize—if he or she even exists! How would you recognize this person?

PROCESS EXERCISE 12.6C

When you die, how do you want people to remember you? (Remember, write this as a process essay. Think about how such a topic might present a process.)

PROCESS EXERCISE 12.6D

Describe a process for something unexpected:

- How to fail a test
- How to break-up with someone via text
- How to ruin a fancy dinner party
- How to flunk out of school
- How to get fired
- How to alienate your family
- How to get sunburn
- How to intentionally ruin a first date
- How to fail at boiling water
- How to ruin your laundry
- How to crash your car
- How to drown in five easy steps
- How to lose all of your savings
- How to ruin your social media presence

12.7 Compare and Contrast

Compare and contrast essays do what they say: They compare topics according to similarities and differences. One primary criterion for this rhetorical mode is that you must compare/contrast topics that have enough shared characteristics to withstand such comparison. If you're hungry and trying to choose a dining spot, you would not compare a restaurant to a ballpoint pen.

As you can see with the dining example, you more than likely employ components of the compare/contrast rhetorical mode on a regular basis. If you're shopping, trying to choose between two similar items, you probably make a mental list of what you like and dislike about each item. You then make an informed choice.

Contrary to what you might think, a compare/contrast essay does not need to focus on similarities AND differences (or advantages/disadvantages, likes/dislikes, etc.). In this sense, the better term for this essay is "compare and/or contrast."

You may be wondering how you can focus on just similarities or differences. Imagine your instructor assigns you a prompt to explain the similarities between the leadership approach and speaking style of President John F. Kennedy and President Barack Obama.

A working thesis for such a paper might look like this:

> President Barack Obama's rhetoric and leadership skills are reminiscent of President John F. Kennedy's.

The body of the paper would provide specific and relevant details elaborating on those similarities.

You can also focus on differences:

> With regard to running a country, President Barack Obama and President John F. Kennedy had completely different philosophies.

What if you wanted to focus on similarities AND differences?

> While President Barack Obama and President John F. Kennedy brought great awareness to social issues, they employed different approaches to raising that awareness.

Whether you choose to compare and/or contrast, using a graphic organizer, particularly a Venn Diagram, is useful.

On the far end of each intersecting ring, you would list the characteristics unique to either Kennedy and Obama. Where the rings intersect, you would list the shared characteristics between the two presidents. This visual organizer will help you develop ideas and ensure you are choosing topics that are similar enough to be compared and/or contrasted.

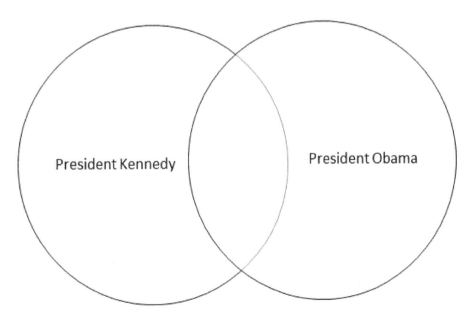

When you prepare to write your compare/contrast essay, you can organize your content using one of two methods: point-by-point or topic-by-topic.

A. Point-by-Point

A point-by-point organizational pattern compares two topics based on the same criteria or point.

- Characteristic of topic A, same characteristic of topic B
- Different characteristic of topic A and topic B
- Another characteristic of topic A and topic B

For example:

- Script in movie A and movie B
- Acting in movie A and movie B
- Visual effects in movie A and B

Many instructors prefer point-by-point organization because it allows readers to see the point you are making about each topic within the same paragraph(s).

Kennedy and Obama

- Rhetoric
  - President Kennedy
  - President Obama

- Leadership Skills
  - President Kennedy
  - President Obama

- Philosophies
  - President Kennedy
  - President Obama

B. Topic-by-Topic

With this method of organization, you detail all the points about one topic. Then, you introduce the same points about the next topic(s).

While topic-by-topic is a perfectly acceptable way to arrange ideas, it is most useful when limited to two topics. There is a possible disadvantage to using this method: If you discuss only one topic for too long, by the time you introduce the second topic, your readers may feel like they are reading two separate essays. If you were to include more than two topics using this method of organization, your readers may be confused as to how the topics connect.

- Topic A
  - Characteristic of topic A
  - Different characteristic of topic A
  - Another characteristic of topic A

- Topic B
  - Characteristic of topic B
  - Different characteristic of topic B
  - Another characteristic of topic B

For Example:

- Script in movie A, acting in movie A, visual effects in movie A
- Script in movie B, acting in movie B, visual effects in movie B

Kennedy and Obama

- President Kennedy
  - Rhetoric
  - Leadership Skills
  - Philosophies

- President Obama

- Rhetoric
- Leadership Skills
- Philosophies

Different topics lend themselves to different organizational patterns, so don't be afraid to explore your options.

Possible Topics:

two related politicians; two internet search engines; two news stations; related sports (softball/baseball, American/ Canadian football, field/arena football—NOT unrelated sports like baseball and football); diet programs; physical therapy/occupational therapy; two sports figures it makes sense to compare or contrast; slander/libel; two types of related dance (like the rumba and the samba, not the rumba and the waltz); two types of related cars or car engines (like the Mini Cooper and the Smart Car, not the Smart Car and the Cadillac)

Weak topics to avoid:

university vs. community college or high school; living at home vs. living in an apartment; public school vs. private school; two places you have lived; two people you have known; very broad topics, like Republicans and Democrats; a contrast of two unrelated or obviously different types of something, like luxury cars vs. economy cars.

These weak topics may seem like simple ones to compare—but that's the problem. They are too simple. What can you say that the reader has not already thought about? It's like writing a paper comparing cats and dogs: would you want to read a paper that reiterates the same old tropes (cats are inside; dogs need to go outside; cats are aloof; dogs are affectionate; etc.)?

This is your chance to say something different. Go for it! Say something new. Say something special. Choose a topic that requires critical thinking, expertise, or creativity.

SAMPLE INTRODUCTION: COMPARE AND CONTRAST

Consider how effective this provocative introduction would be in a Compare/Contrast essay:

Many people believe that the American prison system should not be compared to Pre-Civil War slavery, in that slaves were punished for crimes against humanity. However, if those people looked closely at the thirteenth amendment, they would see that the abolishment of slavery did not truly eliminate the use of slaves. To understand contemporary slavery, and how it is similar to antebellum slavery, one would first need to consider the treatment these people endure. Not only is treatment a point of comparative value, the reasons why slavery and the prison system exist revolve around cost effectiveness and race. These are only compounded by the common living standards that pervade both scenarios of utter injustice. Once examined closely, it is an undeniable truth that the American prison system and the slavery in America's dark past are more similar than different.

SAMPLE OUTLINE: COMPARE AND CONTRAST

SLAVERY: PRE-CIVIL WAR VS CONTEMPORARY SLAVERY IN THE UNITED STATES

POINT BY POINT METHOD

I. Introduction paragraph
- A.   treatment
- B.   Reasons why
- C.   Living standards
   - Thesis:

II. Body 1: treatment
- A.   Pre-Civil War slavery
   - 1.   Authority, abuse, and methods of control
- B.   Contemporary slavery
   - 1.   Authority, abuse, and
   - Methods of control

III. Body 2: reasons why
- A.   Pre-Civil War slavery
   - 1.   Race, cost, and forced labor
- B.   Contemporary slavery
   - 1.   Race, cost, and forced labor

IV. Body 3: living standards
- A.   Pre-Civil War slavery
   - 1.   Education, freedom, and containment
- B.   Contemporary slavery
   - 1.   Education, freedom, and containment

V. Conclusion

Topic by Topic Method

Slavery: Pre-Civil War Vs. Contemporary Slavery In The United States

I. Introduction paragraph
- A. Treatment
- B. Reasons why
- C. Living standards
- Thesis:

Ii. Body 1: slavery Pre-Civil War
- A. Treatment
   - Authority, abuse, and
   - Methods of control
- B. Reasons why
   - Race, cost, and
   - Forced labor
- C. Living standards
   - Education, freedom, and
   - containment

Iii. Body 2: prison contemporary
- A. Treatment
   - Authority, abuse, and
   - Methods of control
- B. Reasons why
   - Race, cost, and
   - Forced labor
- C. Living standards
   - Education, freedom, and
   - containment

Iv. Conclusion

SAMPLE OUTLINE: COMPARE AND CONTRAST

COMPARISON OF THE VIETNAM WAR AND THE WAR IN IRAQ

TOPIC BY TOPIC METHOD

I. Introduction
   Lead:
   Main points:
   Thesis:

II. Vietnam War
   A. Reasons/causes/effects
      Political policies, propaganda, media portrayal, public response…
   B. Tactics
      Weaponry, terrain, equipment, technology…
   C. Treatment
      Civilians, pows, veterans; innocent deaths; physical and psychological damage…

III. War in Iraq
   A. Reasons/causes/effects
      Political policies, propaganda, media portrayal, public response…
   B. Tactics
      Weaponry, terrain equipment, technology…
   C. Treatment
      Civilians, pows, veterans; innocent deaths; physical and psychological damage…

IV. Conclusion

POINT BY POINT METHOD

Comparison Of The Vietnam War And The War in Iraq

I. Introduction
Lead, main points, thesis:

Ii. Reasons/causes/effects
   A. Vietnam War
      Political policies, propaganda, media portrayal, public response…
   B. War in Iraq
      Political policies, etc.

Iii. Tactics
   A. Vietnam War
      Weaponry, terrain, equipment, technology…
   B. War in Iraq
      Weaponry, etc.

Iv. Treatment
   A. Vietnam War
      Civilians, pows, veterans; innocent deaths, physical & psychological damage…
   B. War in Iraq
      Civilians, etc.

V. Conclusion…

STUDENT SAMPLES

All student samples have been preserved in the form in which they were submitted in class; thus, they contain some errors. After all, papers are never truly done; they are just due.

STUDENT SAMPLE: COMPARE AND CONTRAST ESSAY

Wesley Bryan
Sanders
ENC 1101
17 October 2016

Steam or Diesel, Punk?

In the present age of flourishing "nerd culture," many genres of science fiction permeate the landscape. Some of these genres produce unique and intriguing subculture groups, usually referred to as types of "punks": cyberpunk, teslapunk, atompunk, biopunk, etc. Two of the most popular of these groups are known as Steampunk and Dieselpunk. While these groups share numerous attributes, their distinctions provide an in-depth understanding of their own individual appeal.

The most obvious distinction between Steampunk and Dieselpunk is the reference to their time period of influence. Steampunk is essentially a retro-futuristic interpretation of an alternate history that began in the Victorian Era of the late nineteenth century. Steam is viewed as the technology that would power everything from modern computers to space ships. Conversely, Dieselpunk, as the name might suggest, is a retro-futuristic interpretation of an alternate history that focuses on diesel engines becoming the technology that propels humanity forward. Dieselpunk is usually considered to represent a new historical timeline beginning between the interwar period of the 1920s through the 1950s.

For subculture groups with such close timeline proximity, they cerainly exhibit vast differences in fashion style. Steampunk's fashion is most closely associated with two styles: Victorian Era British and American Western. For the Victorian style, most of the outfits for men will include brown or black slacks, suspenders, and a typical working-class button-up shirt. Other accessories usually include bowler hats, circular spectacles, and walking sticks. The women's outfits of the Victorian style will usually include a corset, a loose-sleeved shirt, and a skirt with extra roundness added to the posterior. The American Western outfits are usually the same for men and women. This typical "gunslinger" outfit usually includes dusty-brown slacks, button-up shirts, boots, flattened cowboy hats, and long trench coats. Dieselpunk, however, focuses more on military style uniforms and formal-wear. The military uniforms tend to be of no particular country's military, yet they numerically favor German and American modeled uniforms. These are typically inspired from either World War I or World War II, depending on the wearer's preference. The formal-wear is generally modeled after the pin-stripe suit style for men and flapper dress style for women. This "Gatsby" style is viewed as an elegant remnant of a time long past.

The role of transportation in these communities is mostly part of the artistic representation thereof. Steampunk's main ideal for transportation begins with the steam locomotive. The steam locomotive represents the power and potential of steam as an energy source, not just for land but also for the skies. The rigid airship is another of Steampunk's iconic symbols of power and resourcefulness. In the alternate history created by Steampunk, steam-powered airships become humanity's means of reaching the moon and the stars. In the world of Dieselpunk, transportation is very similar to the real world, minus nuclear power. Planes, trains, and automobiles are all powered by diesel engines; military sea ships run on enormous diesel engines. Diesel engines represent the engineering power and might of warring militaries attempting to develop the most powerful and sophisticated war machines. This ideal carried over into the civilian realm, allowing competing automotive and locomotive companies to produce the fastest and most luxurious forms of transportation.

The architectural styles of these subcultures could not be farther apart. In Steampunk, the Victorian architecture is presented as a very plain and efficient use of space. Aspiring inventors want just enough space to work and tinker yet have easy access to their tools and gadgets. The American West architecture is presented as being less important than making a steam-powered airship into a home or workspace. On the opposite end of the spectrum, Dieselpunk's architectural influence is based on "cubism." This style is best represented in The Chrysler Building. Cubist architecture places an emphasis on geometric symmetry; the people place an emphasis on luxury and elegance.

The overall aesthetic, or main artistic characteristics, for Steampunk and Dieselpunk differs in several ways. Steampunk is characterized artistically by the use of copper as a focal building material. Clockwork is one of the most easily identifiable traits of the Steampunk aesthetic, and it is a testament to the subculture's appreciation with tinkering and inventing. One of the inventions that is very specific to Steampunk is the Rube Goldberg machine: a device that possesses many different moving parts and mechanisms to perform a single, and usually simple, task. The game Mousetrap could be viewed as a very simplistic version of a Rube Goldberg machine. Virtually a world apart, Dieselpunk's aesthetic is best represented in the overarching style of Art Deco. Dieselpunk culture is filled with symmetry, elegance, glamour, and sophistication. Visually, the Art Deco style of Dieselpunk is mostly characterized by the heavy use of chrome, steel, gold, and silver.

Steampunk and Dieselpunk bring about a curiosity and appreciation for times and styles that have long since passed away. Even though these two subcultures appear vastly different on the surface, at their core they both nourish and expand the imaginations of their communities; they allow escape from the shackles of dullness and routine and substitute it with the wonder and excitement for which every person fundamentally yearns.

STUDENT SAMPLE: COMPARE AND CONTRAST ESSAY

Luigi Garcia Otero
Professor Sanders
ENC 1101
4 October 2016

Cristiano Ronaldo vs. Lionel Messi

Cristiano Ronaldo became Real Madrid's all time goal scorer in a match against RCD Espanyol in which he netted five goals. By doing so, Ronaldo reached 231 goals in just 203 games for Real Madrid, overpassing Raul's mark of 228 goals in 550 matches (McMahon par.1). Cristiano Ronaldo who plays for Real Madrid C.F. and Lionel Messi who plays for FC Barcelona, draw the attention of millions of soccer fans every weekend, delighting them with their outstanding and powerful skills. These two prolific goal scorers are the fear of many defenders, goalkeepers, managers, and teams. Not only they are feared by other players, but also they have become inspiration for other forwards to improve their goal scoring skills. Ronaldo and Messi have both achieved exceptional trophies and awards, and broken impressive records. Definitely, neither trophies, awards, nor records seem impossible to attain for these two soccer stars. Although Cristiano Ronaldo and Lionel Messi are the most competitive and gifted soccer forwards at the moment, Ronaldo has a series of skills that make him a more decisive forward than Messi.

Throughout his professional career, Cristiano Ronaldo has become a versatile forward. Not only Ronaldo is able and capable of playing as a Centre forward, but also as a winger on both sides of the field. He has a magnificent notion of where to position himself while his team is attacking, and either create or finalize goal attempts as a winger or striker, respectively. Ronaldo is able to play in multiple positions as he has a tremendous pace to run along the sidelines of the field and a prolific scoring touch to play in the center of the attack. On the other hand, Lionel Messi tends to remain positioned as a Centre forward during matches. Even though Messi is really fast and a tremendous goal scorer too, usually he spends most of the game time walking in the center of the attack, waiting for other teammates to pass him the ball in order to score. Definitely, Messi does not perform the essential role that Ronaldo does for his team. If Messi's teammates fail to accurately pass him the ball, he will simply fail to score, while Ronaldo actively moves around the field creating chances and scoring for his team.

Not only versatility makes Cristiano Ronaldo a more fundamental forward than Lionel Messi, but also his physique. Ronaldo is a really tall and heavy athlete. These physical attributes make him an influential asset for his team. Ronaldo has taken advantage of his stature and has significantly improved his header skills. By being tall and continuously practicing, he is able to finalize goal attempts with his head; therefore, crosses (aerial passes) have become an easy approach for him. Certainly, as he has developed many ways of scoring, he does not waste valuable chances and outscores many other forwards. Also, he benefits from his weight as he uses it to keep ball control, which makes it challenging for other players to displace him from the ball. On the contrary, Lionel Messi is a really short and lightweight athlete. Although Messi has a powerful dribbling, he suffers a lot when he faces strong defenders. Solid and heavy defenders easily displace him from the ball as his weight is not a big deal for them. Moreover, Messi seldom scores using his head as his stature does not help him much to benefit from crosses. Definitely, Ronaldo's physique gives him another alternative to score goals, whereas Messi ends up sometimes struggling by only relying on his dribbling ability to excel.

Besides Cristiano Ronaldo's versatility and header ability, he has another skill that makes him a more prominent player than Messi, which is being two-footed. By being two-footed, Ronaldo is capable of striking the ball with both feet, which increases his chances to score. Regardless of where in the field he receives the ball, he does not hesitate to use either foot to shoot, which makes him more efficient on goal than many other forwards, including Messi. Unlike Ronaldo, Messi's striking ability is just based on his left foot. He is practically unable to shoot the ball with his right foot at all. Frequently, Messi fails to score due to his inability to control his right foot; nevertheless, he compensates this by scoring countless goals with his left foot. Defenders know about the particular issue Messi has with his right foot, so they exclusively focus on not letting him control the ball with his left foot, which makes him uncomfortable during some games. As a matter of fact, Ronaldo's ability to shoot with both feet allows him to score regardless of where he receives the ball, yet Messi limits himself and ends up wasting valuable scoring opportunities due to his poor right foot ability.

In conclusion, even though Cristiano Ronaldo and Lionel Messi are prolific goal scorers, Ronaldo's personal attributes make him a more crucial forward than Messi. Ronaldo has developed and improved outstanding skills that provide him several alternatives to score and assist his team during games, whereas Messi does not help his team much and relies mainly on his dribbling ability to succeed. Indeed, as Ronaldo has more means to score and actively moves along the field, he is a much more valuable asset for his team than Messi. Definitely, Cristiano Ronaldo is a more decisive forward than Lionel Messi as he has the ability to score in diverse ways regardless of the game's circumstances.

Works Cited

McMahon, Bobby. "The Case For Lionel Messi and Cristiano Ronaldo Being Underpaid." *Forbes*, 13 Sept. 2015, http://www.forbes.com/sites/bobbymcmahon/2015/09/13/the-case-for-lionel-messi-and-cristiano-ronaldo-being-underpaid. Accessed 20 Oct. 2016.

STUDENT SAMPLE: COMPARE AND CONTRAST ESSAY

Kelly Gutierrez
Dr. Paquette
ENC-1102-98136
May 25th 2017

Adapting

The fantastic short story, "St. Lucy's Home for Girls Raised by Wolves," by Karen Russel, is related to supernatural beasts adapting to civilized society. The narrator, Claudette, explains in detail how stressful and complicated was for her to become a "naturalized citizen of human society" (Russel 268). Claudette's adaptation process is tightly close to reality, especially to my own reality. When I first arrived at the United States, I struggled from losing most familiar signs of Cuban culture, encountering a different culture, and learning a new language. I, like Claudette, was a victim of cultural shock, and I tried to adapt by undergoing a transformative process that affected me culturally and psychologically.

First, I was brought to the United States when I was a teenager, my parents took the decision of leaving Cuba so I could have a better education. Just like Claudette's parents took the decision for her, mine did for me. In the first two stages of "The Jesuit Handbook on Lycanthropic Cultural Shock," Claudette suppresses her animalistic ways and hides the wild wolf under a properly dressed, well-behaved, bipedal human girl (Russel 267.) I had to suppress a few of my customs such as stop kissing people in the cheek to say hello and bye, apologize for insignificant reasons, and call adults by their last names. Otherwise I would've been considered rude or impolite. The way I used to dress and speak was estrange for American people, they could easily pinpoint that I did not belong to United Sates. The cultural shock made me feel out of place, frustrated, and disoriented.

During this transition period, learning the new language was primordial. Claudette had to suddenly stop talking her mother tongue and move from howling and growling to speaking proper human language. Claudette's "tongue...curl[ed] around [her] false new name" and she felt powerless "in between languages," just like I did and still do on multiple occasions (Russel 273). Learning the English tongue has been challenging, not being able to understand or communicate effectively is extremely frustrating. Even though I was exposed to the language constantly, it was not simple to learn it. This lead to depression and uncertainty about my own person; I even questioned my ability to learn and to adapt. For a long time, I rejected the culture by pointing out every little fault in the system. I wanted to go back home. Not after spending a couple years in the States and improving my language skills, my perspective about American society started changing. I felt more familiarized with the culture, and I slowly embraced my fate: I had to stay and I had to do everything in my power to fit in.

In the story, Claudette exhaustively tries to fit in, especially when she "slunk[s] into the closet and practice[s] the Sausalito two-step in secrete" (274). I did not have to learn how to dance but I had to learn how live the American way: a very agitated self-reliance, extreme hard work, education above everything kind of way. By stage four, Claudette "feel[t] more comfortable in [this] new environment" and strives for successful completion of the program. This is how I felt when I started at taking classes Hillsborough Community College and enrolled in the Honors Program. I wanted to successfully submerge into the culture and take advantage of it. Finally, during the last stage, Claudette shows signs of alienation and rejection after becoming "civilized." Like Claudette's, my mind set has changed and now I act more independent. I do not see myself like part of the family I left behind but more like a lone individual with my own preoccupations and goals. Claudette submerges deeper into the human culture, at the point that "[she] couldn't remember how to find the way back [home] on [her] own". At the end of the story she "[tell[s] [her] first human lie. 'I'm home'", proving that the transition was not completely successful: she could not move "in between the two cultures" (Russel 278). Claudette and I slowly recovered from the stress and anxiety of adapting to a new life. She adapted but partially rejected her lycanthropic culture. However, I am stuck in the middle where I do not feel like I belong to either American or Cuban culture.

Work Cited

Russel, Karen. "St. Lucy's home for girls raised by wolves." *The Norton Introduction to Literature*, edited by Kelly J. Mays, shorter 12th ed., W. W. Norton,2017, pp. 267-273.

STUDENT SAMPLE: COMPARE AND CONTRAST ESSAY

Kelsey Means
Professor Tartaglia
ENC 1102
2 October 2020

Compare and Contrast of "55 Miles" and "The Hit Man"

Murder doesn't have to be such a serious topic. "55 Miles to the Gas Pump" by Annie Proulx and "The Hit Man" by T.C. Boyle are two comedic short stories in which a main character enjoys murdering people. While perusing both works the reader might notice a few similarities and differences between them, with the strongest being the techniques that revolve around style and character.

The styles of the two stories stand out in particular. Both stories rely on diction to accentuate their dark humor and turn the topic of murder into a light-hearted affair. In "The Hit Man," nearly every time the Hit Man makes a kill the author comedically describes him as "wasting" people. Not to mention, Boyle speaks about the Hit Man's killings in a shockingly nonchalant manner. Similarly, in "55 Miles" Proulx makes light fun out of the way that Rancher Croom has killed a bunch of women. When Proulx says, "When you live a long way out you make your own fun" (3), it's obvious that Rancher Croom's murderous habits are simply a hobby to enrich an isolated life. Additionally, the stories also both use a small amount of foreshadowing in their writing styles to force the reader to ask questions before the results hit them. There is a funny little section in "The Hit Man" subtitled "Peas" in which the Hit Man is said to dislike peas. At first, this section seems unimportant until later when the Hit Man "wastes" a waitress for serving him peas. A similar bout of foreshadowing occurs in "55 Miles" when Rancher Croom commits suicide without context. The reader soon learns that Rancher Croom has done some horrible things during his lifetime that led to this suicide. Of course, both authors incorporate these details through dark humor.

The two characters the Hit Man and Rancher Croom both have a few similarities and differences that stick out. There's the obvious way in which both characters are alike in that they're both murderers, but they also both qualify as main characters. The two characters differ in the way that their authors utilized the character technique. Although the Hit Man is the protagonist in

"The Hit Man," Rancher Croom could be considered the antagonist in "55 Miles." This is because his wife, Mrs. Croom, displays more aspects of a protagonist than Rancher Croom does and he acts as her opposing force. In contrast, the wife in "The Hit Man" (Cynthia) is much less of a significant character than Mrs. Croom is in "55 Miles." Another way Rancher Croom and the Hit Man differ is in their motives. For example, the Hit Man strikes people down due to anger and because it's hinted to be his job at one point, but Rancher Croom appears to have killed women for enjoyment. Strangely, Rancher Croom is the character who succumbs to the possibility of guilt and the Hit Man is the one to die from a seemingly natural cause. Regardless, the two characters have similar roles but are written differently.

An exceptionally noticeable way that the two stories compare and contrast is by the levels of information provided by each author in their respective work. Both narratives purposefully leave out background information about the characters, although Boyle describes more about the main character's life than Proulx does. "The Hit Man" provides the reader with information on the main character's family and small portions throughout his entire life span. On the other hand, "55 Miles" only educates the reader on Rancher Croom's suicide and how his wife finds the bodies of his victims. A contradiction of this pattern is how Mrs. Croom is known to have found out about Rancher Croom's "secret" life, whereas it is unknown if Cynthia was aware of the Hit Man's killings.

"55 Miles to the Gas Pump" and "The Hit Man" are two unrelated stories, yet they both have similarities that stand out when reading them. It's important to note that although the two narratives read similarly regarding their writing styles and the hobbies of the main characters, the authors wrote these stories with different character techniques in mind. They also wanted to express different amounts of information in each story. As a result, both works are intriguing texts that will catch the eye of similar audiences without them feeling like they're reading a different version of the same story.

Works Cited

Boyle, T.C. "The Hit Man." Meyer, pp. 33–35. Meyer, Michael and D. Quentin Miller, editors. Literature to Go. 4th ed., Bedford/St. Martin's, 2020.

Proulx, Annie. "55 Miles to the Gas Pump." Meyer, pp. 351. Meyer, Michael and D. Quentin Miller, editors. Literature to Go. 4th ed., Bedford/St. Martin's, 2020.

QUESTIONS FOR CONSIDERATION

What is each essay's thesis?

Explain some of the strengths of the essays.

Identify specific ways these essays could be improved. Consider each essay's focus, organization, development, style, and grammar.

EXERCISES

COMPARE AND CONTRAST EXERCISE 12.7A

Consider the following writing prompts:

- Compare *fact* and *opinion*.

- Compare Hillsborough Community College to another school you attended.

- Compare two different restaurants' pizza.

- Compare two singers (or two athletes).

- Compare the things you are willing to die for to the things you are willing to kill for.

- Having realized that the body is a temple, your younger cousin wants to redecorate and asks your opinion on tattoos and body piercings.

- Discuss the love-hate relationship people have with credit cards.

- Compare one of your relatives to an animal using analogy.

- Consider education in the 1910s, and compare the methods of instruction and material to a modern education.

COMPARE AND CONTRAST EXERCISE 12.7B

"A dog . . . is prose; a cat is a poem," according to American writer Jean Burden. Compare cats and dogs in an essay that you would want to read.

COMPARE AND CONTRAST EXERCISE 12.7C

Consider a place you know well that has changed for the better (or worse). You might focus on a renovated church or school, a rehabilitated neighborhood, or a newly preserved park. Focus on the contrast of before and after.

COMPARE AND CONTRAST EXERCISE 12.7D

Choose two advertisements for the same product or from the same company. Look closely at how the advertisements may differ. Look closely at the varied approaches to reaching a certain demographic. Three elements of a demographic might be the target age, the target class/economy, and the target gender.

COMPARE AND CONTRAST EXERCISE 12.7E

Does slavery still exist in America? Look closely at the prison system and determine the differences or similarities between Pre-Civil War slavery and contemporary slavery found in America.

COMPARE AND CONTRAST EXERCISE 12.7F

Compare the Vietnam War with the War in Iraq, identifying similarities in the causes, development, and outcomes of the wars.

12.8 CAUSE AND EFFECT

A cause and effect essay illustrates a condition or fact and describes what causes it to occur. For instance, a student might analyze recent slumps in the automobile industry and what economic factors are affecting sales.

A cause and effect essay generally begins by establishing the cause, linking it to a specific effect, and then advocating some kind of change in the chain of events. You can focus on causes and work toward the effects, or you can focus on effects and work backward to the causes.

You can focus on a single effect from a single cause:

> Smoking leads to lung cancer.

You may decide to focus on one cause with multiple effects:

> Smoking leads to lung cancer, heart disease, and stroke.

You may prefer to focus on one effect that results from many causes:

> Poor health is a result of bad eating habits and lack of exercise.

Or you may want to tackle what's called a causal chain—one cause and effect that in turn lead to another effect and so on:

> Poor eating habits and little exercise can lead to stage two diabetes, a disease which can cause kidney failure and death if not treated properly.

A. INTRODUCTIONS

The organization of a cause and effect essay determines the effectiveness of your claim. There are several popular methods of introducing your body paragraphs:

1. PROBLEM/SOLUTION

In this pattern, you would open with a statement of a problem and then follow with a possible solution to that problem.

> Ex: Television's contribution to family life has not served to bring families together, but if people would...

2. QUESTION/ANSWER

In this pattern, your first sentence poses a question and is followed by an answer.

> Ex: What has television done to contribute to family life?

3. NARRATION

In this pattern, you would begin with a personal or historical account to develop your ideas.

> Ex: In my family, the television was turned off when it was time to eat dinner.

4. DIALOGUE

In this pattern, you can begin with a quote that relates to your topic and catches the audience's attention.

> Ex: "Dinnertime!" my brother screamed, his little body deliberately blocking my view of the television as he reached for the remote control.

B. BE SURE TO CONNECT YOUR CAUSES WITH YOUR EFFECTS

Cause and effect essays are among the most subjective because information can be "cherry picked" to illustrate a thesis. If you are going to connect a cause with an effect, you must have logical connections between the ideas. Chronological order does not always equal causality. For instance, consider this statement: "Mr. X played a violent video game in the morning and then committed a violent act that evening. Clearly, violent video games cause violent outbursts in players." You are assuming that because one thing happened first (playing the game) and something else happened next (violent outburst) that the two issues are related. You could just as easily use the same logic to say "I wore red socks today, and I got in a car accident. Clearly, my red socks caused my car accident." Chronological order does not automatically imply causality. You have to show the connection with something more than simple time order. In the video game example, you would need to explain the factors that connect the violent game with the violent act—stating it as fact from the start is not acceptable. In fact, it's a logical fallacy (see chapter 12.9 for more details) known as *post hoc ergo propter hoc*.

SAMPLES
SAMPLE OUTLINE: CAUSE AND EFFECT

SLEEP DEPRIVATION
I. INTRODUCTION
    A. Lead: Percentage of people affected by sleep deprivation in this country
    B. Three points of development:
        1. Lifestyle
        2. Medical
        3. Stress
    C. Thesis: The causes of sleep deprivation are numerous and ultimately have the same disastrous effects on one's health and ability to think clearly.
II. Lifestyle (Personal Choice)
    A. Profession
        1. Military (OR)
        2. Two or more jobs
    B. Entertainment
        1. Alcoholic/Drug addict (OR)
        2. Parties
    C. Habits/Habitat
        1. Obesity/College Dorms (OR)
        2. Alaska/Ybor City
III. Medical
    A. Insomnia
        1. ?? (OR)
        2. ??
    B. Medications
        1. ADHD (OR)
        2. Asthma
    C. Depression
        1. ?? (OR)
        2. ??
IV. Stress
    A. Family
        1. Sick relative (OR)
        2. ??
    B. Work
        1. Unemployed (OR)

2. Certain Profession
C. School
   1. ?? (OR)
   2. ??
V. Conclusion
   A. Discuss effects on health and ability to think clearly

STUDENT SAMPLES

All student samples have been preserved in the form in which they were submitted in class; thus, they contain some errors. After all, papers are never truly done; they are just due.

STUDENT SAMPLE ESSAY: CAUSE AND EFFECT

Riley Schmidt
Professor Sanders
ENC 1101
27 September 2016

Homeschooling Creates Less Stressed Students

Some might look back on their high school years and think of fond memories while some might just remember their awkward teenage years. Nowadays, students avoid this entirely by homeschooling, or participating in online school. Homeschooling is not just the stereotypical idea of a mother standing over her child while the child completes an assignment. Online, or virtual school, has become a school in itself, and many high school students receive their diploma from an online program. Homeschooling allows students to complete their school work on their time while also being provided an up to date, certified education. With this flexibility comes both a relief of stress from the teachers who always seem to schedule their most important tests or projects all on the same day, and the mandatory eight hours of schooling that seems to take up most of the day.

A common factor amongst high school students in today's age of AP classes, hundreds of mandatory volunteer hours, jobs, clubs, and other extracurricular activities, is their stress level. This could be caused by these time consuming, equally important activities, which make finding time to complete homework or even finding time to relax or get a good night's sleep, difficult. The reason why all of these activities are equally important is because colleges look for a 'well rounded' student in their applicants. Some students are deciding to make the switch to homeschooling because it allows for the student to have enough time in the day to complete all of the extracurricular activities, and still have enough time for schoolwork. This is because most homeschool programs combine the classwork and homework into one assignment, which cuts the time needed for school in half. Instead of a straightforward eight-hour school day, a student can break the hours up with other activities that they enjoy, and not have to worry about having enough time to complete assignments. Also, the improved online option of homeschooling is more personalized than ever. Many resources are provided for the student, including a schedule for when assignments should be turned in, online textbooks, a group message for the students in the course, and much more. A student may be taking a class that is based off a computer screen, but a real teacher is always available for questions or just to remind a student of their progress on a class. Also, other students are available for support and for every day socializing. A homeschool student is never all alone in a course because someone is always there to help.

Despite the commonly held idea that homeschoolers are unsocial and do not interact with others during the day, many homeschoolers have their own clubs and study groups. Many homeschoolers even play sports for their local public school and this allows them to experience part of the "normal" high school life. Some homeschoolers do not want the normal high school experience, and instead choose to make their own kind of high school experience. In fact, some homeschool programs hold their own school dances and regional graduation ceremonies, so that no student is deprived of any fun activity. One effect of all of these activities are that some colleges actually see homeschoolers as better candidates for their school. This is because these students are seen as more independent and self-sufficient. Also, homeschool students generally have more time to enhance the part of themselves that does not have to do with school. Some students have trouble thinking about who they are outside of school, and when it comes time to think about what career they would like to pursue, it can be confusing and difficult if the student does not know what else they are interested in, or what they are good at. For the homeschool student, they have all the opportunity in the world to explore what they are interested in, whether it be fieldtrips for younger students, or educational internship-type programs for older students. Many younger homeschool students take "fieldtrips," which expose the child to people and places outside of the typical classroom. This helps immerse the child to interact with others, while also learning new things that cannot be learned from a textbook. Some homeschool students have the opportunity to have a part time job during the day in a field of study they are interested in. This helps them decide if this is truly what they would like to pursue as a career. Overall the homeschool student will have more time to experience more of the "real world," and be able to figure themselves out outside of the classroom setting, more than the normal public school student ever will be able to.

There are many negative stereotypes brought with homeschooling about all that a child might miss, but it could actually be better for students who want more time for the activities that are not school related. The new generation of homeschoolers might be the ones that prove the world wrong and show others what it is like to be independent and ready for college, and beyond. Maybe the public school system will take a few pointers from the online programs that seem to allow a more personalized and less stressful form of education.

STUDENT SAMPLE ESSAY: CAUSE AND EFFECT

Jared Kleinkopf
Hawkeye Newspaper
May 2017

Immokalee Protest Continues

"Hey Hey, Ho Ho, Exploitation's got to go!" was chanted by protesters on the sidewalk in front of Publix supermarket on Azeele Street in Tampa, Florida. Over 250 demonstrators showed up to voice their anger toward the two large corporations of Publix and Wendy's on Wednesday, March 29.

The sun was still beaming down at 5 p.m. as activists showed up and began an hour of marching in front of the Publix. The group then walked to the nearest Wendy's on Kennedy Avenue to continue the protest.

Protesters say that the Wendy's claim that it doesn't make financial sense to spend an extra penny per pound of tomatoes on workers is a scam, as the organization still finds the resources to buy multi-million dollar ads during the Super Bowl.

Publix and Wendy's are the last two major companies remaining that haven't signed the fair food pledge to pay more for their produce. The pledge pushes for equality and demands that workers who pick food in fields should be treated with dignity and paid fairly for their sweat and labor. In the past, workers would get paid way below to poverty line for the long hours and labor they put forth to pick produce.

The drums, loudspeakers and voices of the hundreds drew the attention of commuters on their way home from work. Many honked in support and rolled down their windows to express their agreement for the actions being taken. The large, colorful, and visible signs held by most of the protestors showed just how much equality meant to them. Some signs read "Stop farmworker exploitation" while others read, "Fair food now, respect, we want justice and 1 penny more."

"There has always been a place for students to act in solidarity with these farmworkers," explained Alex Schelle, a student of New College in Florida located in Sarasota. She continues, "Students are so important to these causes because they help to apply the pressure to these companies." Besides a multitude of farmworkers and students, there was also a large presence of religious communities that also came to lend a helping hand and support.

Two organizations devoted to the Florida tomato worker's human rights and freedom are the Coalition of Immokalee Worker's and the Fair Food Program. The coalition has been in place for over two decades and has made huge strides in combating human rights abuses in Florida. Local supporter and Tampa native Sydney Eastman joined this cause after already being involved in women's march rallies. She said, "The message really spoke to me and I was happy to show support to a group that liberated 1,200 farmworkers from actual slavery. This movement and women's rights are both looking for the same things," she added.

The gathering of such a diverse group of people showed that equality is still a subject that needs much attention in today's society and also show the power people have when they stand together for a just cause.

Protesters: Photo by Jared Kleinkopf (www.hawkeyenews.net/news/2017/05/17/immokalee-protest-continues/)

Questions for Consideration

What is each essay's thesis?

Explain some of the strengths of the essays.

Identify specific ways these essays could be improved. Consider each essay's focus, organization, development, style, and grammar.

EXERCISES

CAUSE AND EFFECT EXERCISE 12.8 A

Consider the following writing prompts:

- It is the end of the semester, and time to reflect on what we have learned. What did you learn this semester in college? What do you wish you hadn't learned? Or, with the 20/20 vision of hindsight, what would you do differently? Why?

- Where do you see the United States in five years? Why? (You may wish to consider international politics, the economy, global warming, and/or technological advances.)

- If you could change one aspect or action of your parents, what would you change? Why?

- If you could delete one invention of the last two hundred years, what would you delete?

- Entertainers influence viewers. Discuss the effect that one entertainer has had on his/her viewing audience.

- Discuss the effects the Internet has had on students' study habits.

CAUSE AND EFFECT EXERCISE 12.8B

List some causes for and effects of the following topics:

- The failure of a local business, a campus organization, or a recent movie

- Global warming

- Divorce

- Teen obesity

- Rising rate of foreclosures

CAUSE AND EFFECT EXERCISE 12.8C

Student stress can be caused by a number of factors. List some causes. Then, think of some effects of student stress.

CAUSE AND EFFECT EXERCISE 12.8D

Look closely at contemporary culture within the last twenty-five years. What popular trends do you see? Once you have chosen a specific classification of the different popular trends—music, movies/television, clothing, food, etc.—determine what may have caused this particular trend. Who or what is responsible? Or, what are the effects of such a trend? For example, how are people, media, or a culture perceived because of this trend?

12.9 ARGUMENT

Argumentation is not the same as arguing. Brothers and sisters argue over toys and during games. Parents and teens argue about curfews and clothing styles. People can argue about anything from religion and politics to restaurants and shoes. These kinds of arguments, though, are not argumentation. When you engage in argumentation, you are making claims based on facts and logic rather than on intuition.

A. ARGUMENT AS COMMUNICATION

In order to understand argumentation, you should consider what it really means to communicate. Communication generally involves three elements: transmitter, channel, and receiver. The transmitter is the person generating the idea (writer, presenter, speaker, etc.). The channel is the mode of communication (essay, movie, commercial, etc.). The receiver is the audience for the message (reader, viewer, listener, etc.).

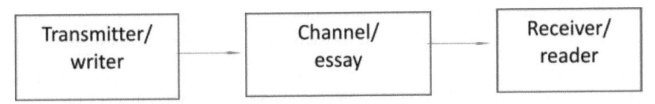

The one-way communication model, or information model, is generally attributed to Claude E. Shannon back in 1948 and the modified Shannon-Weaver Model in the early 1950s. This model still applies to the writing of argumentation today.

To convince your reader that your position is the "correct" one, you need to clearly transmit the idea to the receiver, but before you can be an effective transmitter, you need to be a competent receiver (basing your argument on facts and logic). Doing research is vital to developing a successful argument.

For example, if you wanted to make the argument that election day should be a national holiday, you would need to do some research on the history of elections and the people impacted by the current practice. As a researcher, you are acting as a receiver evaluating new information. At this point, you should ask yourself the following questions:

- How can I prove my claim?

- What factual, verifiable, logical "evidence" is available to support my position?

- How can I incorporate this evidence into my argument?

Then, as a writer, you become the transmitter, using that information to build an effective argument for your claim. As you cite sources, you use evidence to support your claim about election day becoming a national holiday. You not only state your opinion, but you also support it logically. You write the essay, and the reader reads the essay. The one-way communication has been completed.

B. PURPOSE OF ARGUMENT

Arguments can have many purposes. In *A Handbook of Public Speaking*, Richard Letteri explains several reasons for presenting an argument.

The general intent of argumentative writing is to convince the audience to do at least one of the following:

- to accept the idea

- to adopt the value

- to engage in the action advocated in the essay

Other intentions of argumentation might include asking the audience to do the following:

- to question its previous beliefs

- to change its attitudes about the topic

- to view the topic from an alternative perspective

You will notice that each of these six specific intentions requires your readers to change their thoughts or actions in some way.

Letteri uses "argumentation" and "persuasion" interchangeably. However, not every writer does the same. Many writers distinguish between argumentation and persuasion. In future composition courses, you may encounter different schools of thought.

Barbara Clouse, author of *Patterns for a Purpose: A Rhetorical Reader*, a book often used in college composition courses, distinguishes the two terms:

- **argumentation** relies on reasoning, evidence, and logic to move an audience to action.

- **persuasion** appeals to emotions, values, and beliefs, qualities often embraced in interpretations.

In *The Longman Reader*, Judith Nadell goes a bit further:

- **argumentation** also includes "clear thinking" and "a particular opinion on a controversial issue," suggesting that you are expected to defend one side of the argument.

- **persuasion** uses "emotional language and dramatic appeals" to achieve its purpose through word choice.

Andrea Lunsford and John Ruszkiewicz in *Everything's an Argument* add that:

- **argumentation** uses evidence and reason to "discover some version of the truth" to convince an audience "that a claim is true or reasonable or that the course of action is desirable."

- **persuasion** may "aggressively" change opinions, moving readers from conviction to action.

The most important point for Lunsford and Ruszkiewicz is the emphasis on "truth" as the end result, whether through argumentation or persuasion, and the claim being made is just another way of talking about the purpose.

Thus, **argumentation** refers to how you lead your audience to the truth about your claim. Another way to consider argumentation is to think of it as an appeal to reason and thoughtful consideration. **Persuasion** is the search for the same truths, but it further engages the readers not only to recognize the logical and reasonable elements of the argumentation but also to have an emotional response that changes beliefs or even inspires action.

C. ELEMENTS OF ARGUMENTATION

1. THESIS

An effective thesis statement clearly communicates your essay's main idea, as discussed in Chapter 7. It tells the reader not only what your essay is about but also how you are going to approach the topic. It reflects your purpose and should be more than a general truth.

When planning an argumentative essay, you need to have a logical and clear thesis (the major claim or dominant position taken in your essay). You will begin with a working thesis, and during the writing process, you will continue to refine your ideas.

Letteri suggests that a working thesis:

- should reflect your topic, position, and purpose
- should be a simple sentence (often the answer to the question you asked yourself when considering the topic)
  - For example, if asked whether election day should be a national holiday, your answer/ thesis may be "Election day should be a national holiday because..."
- should use words that reflect your intent in a clear, concise manner

Words have meaning, even in a thesis statement. Letteri recommends a restatement or reinforcement of the thesis throughout the essay— not necessarily the exact same words but in intent and focus.

Sarah and David Skwire in Writing with a Thesis provide further details about thesis statements. A thesis statement:

- establishes the basic stand you take in the essay
- expresses your opinion
- details the points you make about your specific subject
- presents a valid perspective
- should be restricted, specific, and unified
- is not a title, an announcement, or a statement of fact

These are important elements to keep in mind while you refine your thesis statement through the drafting process. Remember that the first iteration of your thesis statement is not necessarily the final version of that thesis. The thesis can evolve as you develop the argument, especially as you learn more about your topic.

2. CLAIMS

Your argumentative essay will consist of claims that support your thesis statement. Claims can be divided into three general categories: claims of fact, claims of value, and claims of policy.

a. Claims of Fact

This claim focuses on empirically verifiable evidence. A claim of fact may attempt to answer the following questions: what is or is not true, what does or does not exist, or what did or did not happen?

A claim of fact can be argued in a court of law, as in the 2021 case in Minneapolis, Minnesota. A former Minneapolis police officer was charged with committing the crime of killing George Floyd. The jury had to determine whether the killing on May 25, 2020 was second-degree unintentional murder, third-degree murder, or second-degree manslaughter.

American law states that a person charged with a crime is innocent until proven guilty, so the prosecutors in this case had to prove that the former police officer was guilty of the charges. If they could not prove the claim of fact, the charge would be dismissed, establishing the official court record of what happened.

Claims of fact can only be argued when there are at least two opposing points of view. For instance, you cannot argue that West Virginia is west of Virginia—no one can logically disagree with this fact. Remember that your thesis statement needs to be both logical and arguable such as questions of innocence and guilt.

b. Claims of Value

This claim focuses on opinions, attitudes, beliefs, or other subjective evaluations. A claim of value considers what is good/bad, moral/immoral, just/ unjust, etc.

Sometimes referred to as a matter of taste or preference, a claim of value can never be satisfactorily argued. Have you ever had a discussion with friends about why you like or dislike DC's *Justice League* but have been unable to change their mind? You probably value different qualities in movies, so you might as well be trying to convince them to like chocolate over vanilla ice cream.

Claims of value are subjective and, therefore, almost impossible to argue effectively. While you can argue your points, decided readers rarely change their preference (though you may have more success convincing undecided readers).

c. Claims of Policy

This claim focuses on current laws or procedures that need to be changed in order to achieve a goal, solve a problem, or effectively administer services. Most frequently, a claim of policy seeks to reject a statute or procedure in favor of an alternative.

For example, many colleges require general education courses: English, math, science, and history. Some students feel that this is an unnecessary repeat of the high school curriculum and argue that this requirement should be removed. (Other students may see the value in learning advanced skills in these subjects.) Such an argument would be a claim of policy.

A claim of policy may utilize cause and effect to help build a case for change. Often, claims of policy call for a specific action.

These three claims are not mutually exclusive. Your argument may use a combination of claims of fact, claims of value, and claims of policy.

3. REASONING

Your argument will be organized around specific reasons that support your claim. There are several ways to arrange your points, but inductive and deductive reasoning are two of the most popular.

a. Inductive

Inductive reasoning moves from the specific to general, so you may collect a range of evidence to support your position and use that information to focus your argument. When using inductive reasoning, be sure that your evidence supports the conclusion you reach in your argument. Consider any exceptions that are important enough to negate your conclusion.

For example, consider the following pieces of evidence:

- Ben Zobrist was a leader on the Chicago Cubs for the 2016 season.
- Ben Zobrist played primarily at second base but also spent time in left and right field.
- Ben Zobrist was respected as a clubhouse professional by his younger teammates.
- Ben Zobrist offered a stellar performance during the 2016 World Series:
  - He had a batting average of 357 (10 hits in 28 at-bats, with two doubles and one triple).

- He had an on-base percentage of 419.
- He had a hit in six of the seven games.
- He had an OPS of 919 (On-base plus slugging [OPS] is a baseball statistic calculating a player's ability to get on base and to hit for power, two important offensive skills).
- He had the sixth highest leverage hit in the history of the World Series.

- "Ben is a winning baseball player," Cubs President of Baseball Operations Theo Epstein said. "He's been one of the more valuable players in the game for a long time."

CONCLUSION: Ben Zobrist deserved to be selected as the Most Valuable Player in the 2016 World Series!

Note the specific evidence used to argue this point: statistical data, summarized assessments, and a direct quotation from an expert authority. All are used to prove why Ben Zobrist was the MVP in the 2016 World Series. Inductive reasoning starts with specific examples and details and uses them to prove a broader thesis.

b. Deductive

Deductive reasoning moves from the general to the specific (or from the generalization you want to prove to the specific conclusion that your argument reaches).

The basic form for deductive reasoning is the syllogism, a type of argument that includes three elements:

- a major premise (the generalization used as the basis for the argument—often a statement of fact generally agreed upon)
- a minor premise (a specific instance used to support the generalization)
- the conclusion (the point reached when the specific example is applied to the generalization)

For example, consider the syllogism used by Susan B. Anthony when she argued on behalf of a woman's right to vote. In the 1800s, women in the United States had few legal rights and did not have the right to vote.

Anthony delivered the speech "On Women's Right to Vote" after her arrest for casting an illegal vote in the presidential election of 1872, arguing that:

- Webster, Worcester, and Bouvier all define a citizen to be a person in the United States, entitled to vote and hold office.
- Women are persons.
- Therefore, women are citizens. (14th Amendment)
- No state has a right to make any law, or to enforce any old law, that shall abridge a citizen's privileges or immunities. (15th Amendment)
- Therefore, women cannot be denied the right to vote.

Reminder: The 14th Amendment granted citizenship to anyone born or naturalized in the US and the 15th Amendment states that the right of citizens to vote shall not be denied or abridged.

Anthony's argument is a perfect syllogism. It would read as follows:

- Citizens cannot be denied their right to vote. (self-evident fact)
- Women are citizens. (specific example)
- Therefore, women cannot be denied the right to vote. (irrefutable conclusion)

In a syllogism, you need to convince the reader that because your major and minor premises are true; therefore, your conclusion must also be true. Syllogisms use deductive reasoning to accomplish this goal—starting with general statements and narrowing down to your specific conclusion.

4. RHETORICAL APPEALS

In addition to inductive or deductive reasoning, your argument will also involve a combination of ethos, pathos, and logos. These concepts originate with Aristotle, an ancient Greek philosopher, who (along with Plato and Socrates) laid much of the basis for western world philosophy. Whether readers are familiar with Aristotle or not, they will still expect an argument to establish the writer's credibility, the intended emotional response from the reader, and the logical reasons that support the claims.

a. Ethos

Ethos refers to the credibility of the writer. Readers need to understand why they should trust the writer. Questions that the readers could ask about you as the author might include:

- What is the author's background?
- What expertise or personal experience does the author have?
- Why should I trust the author?
- How credible is the evidence being used?
- How up-to-date is the research that supports the claims?

The readers' perceptions of the author's character influence how believable or convincing the readers find the argument. Readers are more likely to be persuaded by a writer who has personal warmth, consideration of others, a good mind, and solid learning. The argument conveys an impression of the author's character through clear word choice. The words you choose will determine both your ethos and whether you effectively communicate your idea.

The basic sentence structure is important to enhancing your ethos or credibility. Following proper grammar and mechanics while avoiding colloquialisms, text language (such as emojis and abbreviations), and bias can help build your ethos.

Ethos goes beyond simply writing essays. Whether written or spoken, you should always establish your credibility.

Ronald Adler and George Rodman in *Understanding Human Communication* (Oxford University Press) explain how to establish ethos in the following three ways:

- Competence: Cite relevant research and stress the credibility of your sources.
- Character: Show a genuine concern for the audience, be fair to your subject matter, and respect values.
- Charisma: Demonstrate a positive outlook with enthusiasm and empathy, and connect to your audience.

The ethical writer is perceived as moral, trustworthy, and of good intentions, making it easier for readers to trust you.

b. Pathos

Pathos refers to emotional appeals, that is, how you want your audience to feel after reading your argument (though not necessarily how you feel). It is often argued that the use of pathos is inappropriate because it is not entirely based on logic. However, readers will nevertheless have an emotional response to your argument. Considering pathos allows you to develop the emotional side of what you are advocating.

Remember that some people will use the word argument to refer to lines of reasoning that rely solely on logic, while others use persuasion to refer to claims that intertwine emotions with logic. The difference in terminology often depends on the specific background of the speaker. For example, speech experts may use one term while English instructors use another. Observe how your discipline uses the terminology and follow that example.

Pathos is largely based on word choice. Think about the denotation (dictionary definition) and the connotation (associated concepts) of a word when crafting your argument (see Chapter 18.3 Diction). When using emotional appeals, you should respect the sensitivities of your readers. The use of emotion should never become offensive, which is a lesson from Aristotle, who emphasized using language carefully when advocating a position.

But this is not to say that you cannot use words that vividly describe a situation or event. Sometimes, strong words or images can be an effective strategy to convince your readers.

The website of World Vision posted an article titled "Syria Refugee Crisis: Facts You Need to Know" (April 13, 2017), which illustrates pathos through effective word choice:

Six years of war has torn Syria apart. Violent reactions to peaceful protests throughout the country descended Syria into chaos in early 2011. Syrian children and families have borne the brunt of the conflict's disastrous consequences. Hundreds of thousands have been killed and more than half of the population 11 million people has been displaced from their homes.

March 15 marks the sixth anniversary of the war's outbreak. Since then, 5 million Syrians have fled to other countries as refugees and more than 6 million have been displaced within the country. In many cases, children caught up in this crisis have fared the worst, losing family members or friends to the violence, suffering physical and psychological trauma, or falling behind in school.

As you read these paragraphs, you cannot help but feel something for these displaced Syrians, especially the children. The word choice and the brief examples of what has happened to the children and families are powerful emotional appeals. The reaction to these examples will vary based on the reader's personal needs, so keep that in mind and adjust your argument accordingly.

Appealing to the emotional needs of the audience can be appropriate. However, if those appeals are likely to incite fear, anxiety, or distrust among your readers, you should re-evaluate your approach to the topic.

c. Logos

Logos refers to the sound reasoning and evidence in your argument, arranged logically and expressed in a clear writing style. Your argument will likely be organized using inductive reasoning or deductive reasoning, while your claims will be supported by evidence.

One way to look at evidence is to distinguish between fact and opinion. Facts are those items that everyone will agree have been empirically established. Facts don't change: a yard equals 36 inches and the sun rises in the east.

The following are examples of facts that can support your claims:

- statistical data
- known historical events
- reports of direct observations
- expert testimony
- case studies

Opinions, on the other hand, are subjective and vary from person to person (like claims of value).

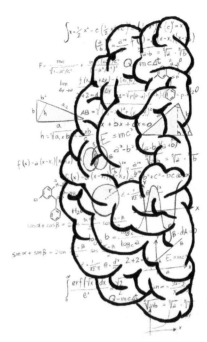

Although an opinion may be widely accepted, popularity alone does not make that opinion a fact.

The following are examples of opinions that cannot be adequately supported:

- Ed Sheeran is the best guitarist of all time.
- The *Harry Potter* audiobooks are the best way to experience the story.
- Comedians who joke about dating are the funniest performers ever.
- Dogs with floppy ears are cuter than any other type of animal.

While you may agree with these statements, they are difficult to effectively argue because they are based on taste, value, and personal preference; these are not based on logic. This is not to say that you cannot use opinions. Opinions can be a valid part of your argument if they are combined with evidence and reason.

The following are examples of well-reasoned opinions that can be adequately supported:

- The MINI Cooper is safer than the FIAT. (crash statistics, safety tests)
- Using refillable water bottles reduces shoreline pollution. (eco statistics, water tests)
- Online classes help students achieve success. (former student testimonials, graduation rates)

The facts (the evidence) support the opinions being expressed, but your paper will likely involve ethos, pathos, and logos. The insights provided by Aristotle thousands of years ago still hold true today.

5. FALLACIES

Fallacies are arguments that appear logically sound but are actually flawed. Recognizing logical fallacies is important because they are based on faulty reasoning and will weaken your argument. In addition to improving your reading and writing skills, identifying logical fallacies makes it easier to spot them in academic arguments, political rhetoric, and social commentary.

In fact, once you recognize logical fallacies, you will be surprised at how often people rely on them and how easy they are to counter. An argument that relies on fallacies is not convincing—and readers tend to distrust those who use such faulty reasoning.

Here are some of the more common fallacies.

A. IT DOES NOT FOLLOW (NON SEQUITUR)

This formal fallacy reaches a conclusion that does not follow the premise, occurring when a line of reasoning jumps from one idea to the next without any connection.

> Example: I had a crazy science teacher in elementary school. Science creates maniacs.

These two ideas may be completely coincidental.

B. EITHER/OR (FALSE DILEMMA)

This fallacy oversimplifies a complicated situation so that only two sides are presented when there may be more.

> Example: Either we bomb North Korea, or we face nuclear Armageddon.

This argument ignores any other diplomatic solution to this issue.

C. SLIPPERY SLOPE

This fallacy always ends with a presumed catastrophe, claiming that a chain reaction will take place, but there's really not enough evidence for that assumption.

> Example: If you borrow the car, you might crash into someone, that person might sue us, and we will lose the house!

Borrowing the car does not automatically lead to homelessness.

D. FALSE CAUSE AND EFFECT (POST HOC ERGO PROPTER HOC)

Latin for "after this, therefore, because of this," this fallacy, usually called simply post hoc, assumes that because one thing happened first and something else happened next, there must be a causal relationship between them. This doesn't mean that cause and effect can be ignored—the connection just needs to be proven by more than chronological order.

> Example: If we do not restrict pesticide use, the bee will disappear forever.

Granted, science shows that bees are in trouble, but other than pesticide use, there may be other reasons why they are in jeopardy. There is a correlation in time, but correlation isn't the same as causation.

E. BEGGING THE QUESTION (PETITIO PRINCIPII)

This fallacy states a debatable premise as if it were true. This type of circular fallacy contains an obvious question that is not answered but presumed answered.

> Example: A civil society would not permit the death penalty.

This assertion begs the obvious question, "How do we know society is civil?" (Please note that the phrase "begs the question" is often used incorrectly in common discourse to mean "raises the question.")

F. CIRCULAR REASONING (CIRCULUS IN DEMONSTRANDO)

This fallacy makes an argument that circles back on itself (like begging the question).

> Example:
> Enlisting in the military is patriotic and the right thing to do for our country.
> Why is it the right thing to do for our country?
> Because it's patriotic.
> Why is it patriotic?
> Because it's the right thing to do for our country.

This argument just goes around in circles and never makes any valid points.

G. RED HERRING

This fallacy is all about distraction. It diverts attention from the key issue, bringing up an unrelated argument to distract from a current argument (which may be going badly).

> Example:
> You are late. You should have called to let me know, but you never think of my needs.
> But what about last week when you promised to put the laundry away but didn't for two entire days? You don't think of my needs!

The first speaker addresses being late, but the second speaker ignores the main point and brings up an unrelated topic (laundry).

H. APPEAL TO AUTHORITY (ARGUMENTUM AD VERECUNDIAM)

This fallacy assumes that something is a fact because someone in a position of authority said it. In your argument, your evidence may include authority figures/experts, but you must be sure that the authority is an expert in the area under discussion.

> Example: Professor Dante Trebon is the world's leading expert on medieval history; clearly, we can adopt his thoughts on fidelity.

This professor is an expert in a specific area, and he shouldn't be used as an authority in an area beyond the scope of his expertise.

I. AT THE PERSON (AD HOMINEM)

This logical fallacy attacks the character of the speaker rather than the idea itself.

> Example: People who think a border wall will solve our immigration problems are stupid.

Calling a group of people stupid accomplishes nothing for your argument. Instead of attacking the person with the idea, critique the idea itself.

J. YOU TOO (TU QUOQUE)

This logical fallacy is another form of the "at the person" fallacy that suggests that the speaker's opinion isn't valid because the speaker is guilty of the same behavior.

> Example: The CEO shouldn't drug test employees because she parties on the weekend.

In this example, the author focuses on the CEO's drug-using behavior to discredit her rather than the drug testing policy.

K. APPEAL TO TRADITION (AD ANTIQUITATEM)

This logical fallacy argues that something has value because it is traditional (it's the way things have always been done so it shouldn't be changed).

> Example: There is no reason to get rid of the Electoral College. It's been working in the U.S. since 1804.

Simply saying "that's the way it's been done before" isn't a valid way to make your point.

L. BANDWAGON APPEAL/TO THE PEOPLE (AD POPULUM)

This fallacy appeals to the prejudices of the people, suggesting that because many people believe something, it must be true.

> Example: Everyone knows that teenagers can't be trusted.

Not everyone agrees with this, and even if most people did, their belief would not necessarily make it true.

M. STRAW MAN

This fallacy focuses on a fake argument that has been created, as if out of straw, rather than the one being discussed, setting up an oversimplified or misrepresented version of an argument that is easier to refute.

Example:
Person 1: "We should think about adding more vegetables to our diet."
Person 2: "Why do you hate protein?"

This argument derailed quickly, shifting away from Person 1's claim. Person 2 focuses on the easier "protein argument," which is not present in the original claim, instead of addressing the topic of needing more vegetables.

N. CHERRY PICKING/CARD STACKING

This fallacy uses only supporting data while deliberately rejecting any dissenting evidence, slanting the argument with selective information.

> Example: The student success course enjoyed unprecedented student demand last semester (all sections filled); clearly, students value the content.

This argument ignores any other reasons for the class's popularity (maybe it was a requirement) and focuses only on the high level of registration. What about passing rates or student reviews?

O. GENETIC FALLACY

This fallacy assumes certain qualities of a person based on inherited characteristics.

> Example: Mr. Santini must love wine; he's Italian.

Belonging to a certain nationality does not mean a person behaves a certain way.

P. HASTY GENERALIZATION (SECUNDUM QUID)

This fallacy assumes a general statement based on one or two examples, often making a broad assumption that may not be true.

> Example: That's the second woman I saw putting on makeup in the car while driving this   morning; clearly, women don't pay attention when they are behind the wheel.

Two examples are not enough information to make a broad statement like this.

6. COUNTERARGUMENT

When planning an argument, you will need to consider at least one other position that differs from your own. If everyone agrees with your position, then you won't have an argument. If you choose to develop the opposition's position within your own paper, you are including what is called a counterargument. Some instructors appreciate seeing a strong counterargument as a way to show that you have done research on both sides of the argument and that you do not hold any bias for your own position. However, arguments can be successful without a counter included. Your argument should be built with claims that have support through evidence and well-reasoned opinions.

Still, even though a counterargument doesn't need to be included, considering opposing points of view can build a stronger argument. You will know how to approach your own claims after considering how your opposition may critique your ideas. Remember your audience. Your audience will include people who do not agree with you. What objections will those readers have to your position?

When examining your counterargument, you need to fairly review those points, taking into consideration both the opposition's strengths and weaknesses (as you should with your own). Then, if you develop it in your writing, you will have the opportunity to respond by either providing a rebuttal, concession, or alternative.

With a rebuttal, you analyze the opponents' arguments by evaluating and questioning their claims. When you concede to their point, you are admitting their point is strong and you cannot argue it. An alternative to their point simply means providing a different perspective that they haven't considered.

As an example, consider the language for the following rebuttal, concession, and alternative.

Also, observe how they differ in responding to the same idea. Keep in mind that the position is not a thesis statement and that the examples do not include supporting research.

- **Your position:** Social media should have more restrictions.
- **Opposition's position:** Social media should not have more restrictions.
  - **Opposition's claim:** Having restrictions on social media would limit a person's ability to connect with others around the world to engage in social media activism.
    - **Rebuttal:** Social media activism is an important element of using social media; however, because of targeted algorithms that provide one-sided information (creating echo chambers and bubbles), those with mental health issues are especially vulnerable to misinformation about current events. Restrictions in the form of stricter guidelines could improve the quality of information that users receive.
- **Concession:** Admittedly, the opposition's claim that social media allows the global community to facilitate positive change is accurate.
  - Note: At the conclusion of your argument, while you may concede to one point, the other claims made by the opposition need to be rebutted. If you concede to every claim the opposition makes, you need to reconsider your argument.
- **Alternative:** The opposition hasn't considered that even with social media restrictions, activism can be done locally to facilitate community change; grassroots efforts can grow into larger movements, especially with the support of healthy users who are not targeted by misinformation.

Counterarguments can strengthen an argument by anticipating readers' objections, but they can also remind readers of the reasons to disagree. Remember your purpose and audience when considering a counterargument.

IN-CLASS EXERCISE

Choose one of the sample essays in this chapter and analyze the counterarguments it contains. If you can't find any, suggest some.

D. MODELS OF ARGUMENT

1. ARISTOTELIAN MODEL: RHETORICAL APPROACH

This classic method of argument uses a blend of the three appeals to convince readers:

- Ethos: establishes the writer's credibility
- Pathos: evokes a specific emotional response to the topic
- Logos: uses logical claims to support the argument

2. TOULMIN MODEL: COURTROOM APPROACH

The Toulmin Model, devised by philosopher Stephen Toulmin, is similar to the stages of deductive reasoning, except that terminology differs. Toulmin's three components include claim, grounds, and warrants.

- Claim: argument being made
- Grounds: evidence that supports the claim
- Warrant: underlying assumption about the claim

Example:

- Claim
  - The Tampa Bay Buccaneers deserve the support of the Tampa Bay communities.
- Grounds
  - The Tampa Bay Buccaneers organization is active in many positive ways in the greater Tampa Bay area.
  - The Tampa Bay Buccaneers have invested in building a football team of quality players that won the 2021 Super Bowl.
- Warrant
  - An organization that is active and invested in the Tampa Bay community has earned the support of the Tampa Bay area.

3. ROGERIAN MODEL: COMMON GROUND APPROACH

Psychologist Carl Rogers' approach to argument contends that argumentation does not have to be adversarial. When thinking about argument, writers often assume they are required to take a side to prove a point. The Rogerian approach looks for ways to avoid controversy and seeks compromise and a cooperative approach.

- Acknowledge Opposition: present counterarguments accurately and fairly
- Find Common Ground: think of it as a prism through which all sides can see the issue
- Present Evidence: establish your position as most reasonable

E. OVERVIEW: COMPONENTS OF ARGUMENT

Subject/Issue: What are you arguing for/against? What stance have you taken on your topic?

Note: This is not the time to equally examine both sides and leave the interpretation up to the reader—that's what an informative essay does. This is the time to take a stand on a topic and convince the reader that your perspective is the right one.

- Claims/Thesis
  - What are you advocating?

- Logos
  - grounds, evidence, examples, facts, opinions
  - the logical arguments you make

- Pathos
  - the emotional appeals in your argument
  - How do you want your readers to feel?

- Ethos
  - your credibility as a writer
  - Why should readers trust you?
  - There are two ways to establish credibility: personal experience and research.

- Counterarguments/Opposing Viewpoints
  - What do those who disagree with you say?
  - How can you respond to their arguments?

SAMPLE OUTLINE: ARGUMENTATIVE ESSAY—2008 RECESSION

Topic: An essay or research paper about the recession in 2008.

Thesis Statement/Major Claim: The Great Recession of 2008 resulted in companies from Fortune 500 companies to small businesses failing, causing unemployment and leaving many Americans facing an uncertain future.

1. Claim 1: Under the resulting economic conditions in 2008, many corporations either downsized or shut down operations altogether, leaving a growing class of unemployed Americans uncertain about where they would find themselves at retirement age.
   a. Companies downsized operations and laid off employees with little or no advance warning.
   b. Ultimately, Fortune 500 companies filed bankruptcy and totally shut down operations.
      i. "The biggest loser of them all: Insurance giant AIG. The company posted a $99.3 billion loss."
      ii. "Thirty-eight companies disappeared from the Fortune 500 list altogether. Bear Stearns and Lehman Brothers may be no surprise, but it was also the "last call" for brewer Anheuser Busch" ("2008 'Worst Year'").
      iii. Records were broken: Eleven of the top 25 largest corporate losses in list history took place last year.
      iv. "No fewer than 25 federally insured U.S. banks failed in 2008" ("The Year in Bankruptcy").
2. Claim 2: Rising unemployment rates and a dismal job market contributed to the increasing uncertainty that many newly unemployed and displaced Americans faced.
   a. "The hemorrhaging of American jobs accelerated at a record pace at the end of 2008, bringing the year's total job losses to 2.6 million or the highest level in more than six decades" (Goldman).
   b. Nearly four in five businesses have no employees at all, and they make an average of $45,000 per year, according to the U.S. Census Bureau (Kavoussi).
   c. More than 170,000 small businesses in the U.S. closed between 2008 and 2010, according to an analysis by the Business Journals of U.S. Census Bureau (Thomas).
3. Claim 3: With the loss of employment and ballooning mortgage rates, foreclosures escalated, leaving many Americans uncertain about the future of their homes.
   a. Americans had to deal with subprime rates, declining home values, and unsympathetic lenders while attempting to retain their homestead: the one remaining vestige of the American Dream.
   b. More than 1 million U.S. homes were lost to foreclosure since the housing crisis began in August 2007, according to RealtyTrac, an online marketer of foreclosure properties (Christie).

Works Cited

"2008 'Worst Year' in Fortune 500 History." *CBS News*, CBS Interactive, 19 Apr. 2009, www.cbsnews.com/news/2008-worst-year-in-fortune-500-history/.

Christie, Les. "Foreclosures up a Record 81% in 2008." *CNNMoney*, Cable News Network, 15 Jan. 2009, money.cnn.com/2009/01/15/real_estate/millions_in_foreclosure/.

Fiorillo, Steve. "What Was the Subprime Mortgage Crisis and How Did It Happen?" *TheStreet*, 7 Sept. 2018, www.thestreet.com/personal-finance/mortgages/subprime-mortgage-crisis-14704400.

Goldman, David. "Worst Year for Jobs since '45." *CNNMoney*, Cable News Network, 9 Jan. 2009, money.cnn.com/2009/01/09/news/economy/jobs_december/#:~:text=Annual%20loss%20biggest%20since%20end,Unemployment%20rate%20rises%20to%207.2%25.&text=NEW%20YORK%20(CNNMoney.com),in%20more%20than%20six%20decades.

Kavoussi, Bonnie. "Instagram Isn't The Only Company Making Big Bucks With Few Workers." *HuffPost*, 7 Dec. 2017, www.huffpost.com/entry/instragram-economy-_n_1417277.

Thomas, G. Scott. "Recession Claimed 170,000 Small Businesses in Two Years." *The Business Journals*, American City Business Journals, 2012, www.bizjournals.com/bizjournals/on-numbers/scott-thomas/2012/07/recession-claimed-170000-small.html.

"The Year in Bankruptcy: 2008: Insights." *Jones Day*, Jan. 2009, www.jonesday.com/en/insights/2009/02/the-year-in-bankruptcy-2008#:~:text=No%20fewer%20than%2025%20federally,extensive%20holdings%20in%20subprime%20assets.

You can find an early version of this outline in Ch. 10.

SAMPLE OUTLINE: ARGUMENTATIVE ESSAY

Below is an example of a possible outline for an argumentative essay. You can find the final version of this essay on the next page. (Note: This outline was not created by the student.)

Immunization

I. Introduction
   A. Hook: Inconsistencies in immunization policies
   B. Background information: How communities are affected by immunization rates
   C. Thesis: To prevent the spread of infectious diseases, it is vital to strengthen and make equal for each state immunization policies in order to elevate immunization rates and protect the health of each individual, especially those whose immune systems are weak.
II. Inconsistency in immunization policies at the state level
   A. CDC recommendations
   B. Hepatitis A immunization requirements
   C. Hepatitis B immunization requirements
   D. Difficulty of keeping the national immunization rate balanced
III. Exemptions
   A. Medical
      1. All states have medical exemptions
      2. Immunizing children protects not just themselves but those who can't due to medical reasons
   B. Religious
      1. First Amendment considerations
      2. Jacobsen vs. Massachusetts decision
      3. Beliefs must be sincere, and religious exemptions often require evidence
   C. Philosophical
      1. 17 states allow philosophical exemptions
      2. Often the result of poor education about immunization
IV. College and university requirements
   A. Not all states require immunization for college students
      1. Some states require immunization only for students living on campus
      2. Some states require immunization for all college students
V. Herd immunity
   A. Successes and problems globally in controlling measles
   B. Vulnerability of children who cannot be immunized due to medical reasons
VI. Conclusion
   A. Success of vaccines generally
   B. Legal implication: The importance of having consistent immunization laws

STUDENT SAMPLES

All student samples have been preserved in the form in which they were submitted in class; thus, they contain some errors. After all, papers are never truly done; they are just due.

STUDENT SAMPLE: ARGUMENTATIVE ESSAY

Laura Vazquez
E. Coursey
ENC 1101
6 June 2015

Immunization

Immunization is required by law for children attending public school in all states of the U.S. On the other hand, private schools and universities do not always require immunization records. Students can be exempted from immunization for medical, religious, and philosophical reasons. These exemptions lead to a lack of immunization during childhood and youth having an impact on the immunization rates of each state. When immunization rates go down in a specific community, that community becomes a perfect environment for vaccine-preventable diseases (VPD's), which affects not only the young population but also the elderly population. Even though VPD's have been controlled in the U.S, the continuing migration of people to the states keeps bringing diseases into the country. These diseases, later, are transmitted among the population causing outbreaks. To prevent the spread of infectious diseases, it is vital to strengthen and make equal for each state immunization policies in order to elevate immunization rates and protect the health of each individual, especially of those whose immune systems are weak.

In the United States, each state decides which immunization plan is required for the enrollment and attendance at child care facilities, schools, and universities located in the pertinent state. Because of this, each state has its own immunization requirements which can be updated or changed regularly. Immunization requirements per state cover a series of vaccines for childcare, kindergarten, middle school, high school, and university/college.

The vaccines recommended by the Centers for Disease Control and Prevention (CDC) for children are Hepatitis A and B, DTaP (to fight Diphtheria, Tetanus, and Pertussis), Influenza,Chickenpox, MMR (to fight Measles, Mumps, and Rubella), MCV (Meningococcal), IPV (Polio),

PCV (Pneumococcal), RV (Rotavirus), and the Whooping Cough vaccine. ("VFC"). Besides the recommendations, regulations for these vaccines are not the same for every state. Some states may require some of these vaccines for children entering kindergarten but not middle school. Others require just the first dose of the vaccine, and in some cases there might be no requirements at all. For example, the Hepatitis A vaccine is not required for childcare and kindergarten in 44 states while in 11 states and/or territories of the U.S., including Oregon, Texas, and Wyoming, it is mandatory, with the exceptions of Nevada, West Virginia, Tennessee, North Dakota, New Mexico, and Georgia where the vaccine is just mandatory for child care and not for kindergarten ("School"). By contrast, the Hepatitis B vaccine is mandatory for every state and territory for childcare and/or kindergarten with the exception of Alabama ("School"). In the case of the TDP vaccine, 37 states do not require the vaccine at all ("School"). Due to the disparities in the regulation of immunization on each state, it is hard to keep the national immunization rate balanced.

The immunization records established by each state are mandatory for all children or students wanting to attend a public institution located in that state. However, exceptions are allowed by the law. These exceptions are given due to medical conditions, religious beliefs, and/or philosophical reasons. Just as regulations vary in every state, exceptions vary as well, with the exception of the medical condition exemption which is a granted by every state. Also, some states allow vaccination exemptions for certain diseases if medical documentation shows proof of immunity. Immunity can be proven if the child had the natural disease.

For medical exemptions, a written statement by a physician indicating that the child cannot receive the vaccine because the components can compromise his or her health is required. This permit can be temporary or permanent, and the definition in each state varies. All states have medical exemptions, either temporary, permanent, or both ("Medical"). Children that cannot be immunized due to medical conditions are usually the victims of VPD's because they do not have the same protection that immunized children have. The protection of unimmunized children is one of the reasons why other children (whose health is not compromised by getting vaccines) should get immunized. When children get immunized, they not only protect themselves from getting VPD's but protect other children that were not immunized as well.

Religious exemption is the one that exempts children from receiving vaccines because of religious beliefs. The religious exemption is granted based on the U.S. Constitution's First Amendment which gives the right to freely hold and exercise religious beliefs. "A state must have a 'compelling State interest' before this right can be taken away" ("Religious"). In the Supreme Court decision Jacobsen v. Massachusetts (the right of the states to mandate smallpox vaccine was affirmed), the Court decided that limiting the spread of communicable diseases was a "compelling State interest." All states allow religious beliefs exemptions with the exception of Mississippi and West Virginia. Religious beliefs must be sincere, and some states might require proof of religious membership and others a signed affidavit from the spiritual advisor of the parent who wants the religious exemption ("Religious").

In the case of philosophical exemptions, the child is exempted from immunization due to personal beliefs. The use of philosophical exemption to avoid immunization tends to cluster geographically, making some communities at greater risk for outbreaks. There are currently 17 states with philosophical exemptions. "In some states parents or children old enough to give consent (usually age 12 or older) must object to all vaccines and not just one vaccine."

("Philosophical"). States like California, Washington, and Oregon require that the parent obtains a signature from a medical doctor or another health care provider in order to obtain a philosophical exemption. Also, in Oregon, parents are required to complete a state vaccine education program. ("Philosophical"). Philosophical exemptions are the result of poor education about immunization. When parents do not know how vaccines work and their importance, the parents are more likely to reject vaccines and avoid getting their children immunized.

Some states also have immunization laws for colleges and universities. College and university students, according to the CDC, should receive the Influenza vaccine and the HPV vaccine which protects against the human papillomavirus that causes most cervical cancers, anal cancers, and genital warts ("Vaccine"). Not all states require immunization for colleges and universities. Some states might require vaccines like Hepatitis B just for public universities, such

as in Ohio, others just for entering students that plan on living on-campus, and others for students with more than 12 credits, like in New Jersey. And others states, like Florida, mandate immunization for all educational institutions. ("Hepatitis B"). In general, not many states require immunization for college and university students which expose these students to VPD's that can be easily transmitted among the students especially the ones who live on-campus.

Vaccinating people also contributes to the immunity of the community. Herd immunity or community immunity occurs when most members of a certain community have been immunized against an infectious disease. Because of the immunization, the disease is contained, offering protection to the people that cannot be immunized at the time but live in the same area, people such as pregnant women, newborns, the elderly, and people that could not receive the vaccine

due to medical conditions.

Importation of measles into the U.S. emphasizes the importance of sustaining and increasing vaccination coverage rates to prevent outbreaks of VPD's. Complications are more common in children younger than age five and in adults. Measles cases and outbreaks still occur in countries around the world. In fact, according to the CDC, about 20 million people get measles each year; about 146,000 die. Each year, unvaccinated people get infected while in other countries and bring the disease into the United States and spread it to others ("Measles"). Measles was declared eliminated from the U.S. in 2002. Since that year, the annual number of people reported to have measles ranged from a low of 37 people in 2004 to a high of 668 people in 2014. Most of these originated outside the country or were linked to a case that originated outside the country. Measles can be prevented with the MMR vaccine with almost 100 percent of effectiveness ("Measles").

VPD's are constantly affecting people who did not received vaccinations. With the possibility of being exempt from immunization laws, some parents do not vaccinate their children without thinking that their decisions will compromise the health of their child in the future, and perhaps, their child's life. Also, when these children do not get immunized and contract an infectious disease, they transmit the disease to other children that might have not been immunized due to medical conditions. These children later might encounter serious health complications. VPD's also have a costly impact, resulting in visits to the doctor, hospitalization, and other medical expenses. Looking from any perspective, lack of immunization has no favorable results. It affects the health of the person who contracts the infectious disease, the economy of that person or parents if the affected is a minor, and compromises the health of the people who live around the infected person.

In contrast of religious and philosophical beliefs, vaccines are the only proven way to protect people from getting infectious diseases. In some cases vaccines are the only option available to people to protect themselves from diseases that do not have a cure yet, like the HPV vaccine which fights human papillomavirus. For these reasons, states should reinforce immunization laws and reduce exemptions. It is important for the country and the health of its citizens to have equal immunization laws. People are in constant migration, traveling from one state to the other. If immunization laws are strong in one state, but not in the other; people won't be protected against VPD's because they might contract them when moving to one state or from another person who traveled from that state to the other.

Works Cited

"Hepatitis B prevention mandates for college and universities." *Immunization Action Coalition*, Centers for Disease Control and Prevention, Accessed 24 June 2015.

"Measles Vaccination." *Centers for Disease Control and Prevention*, Department of Health and Human Services, 15 Feb. 2015, Accessed 24 June 2015.

"Medical Exemptions." *National Vaccine Information Center*, National Vaccine Information Center, Accessed 24 June 2015.

"Philosophical Exemptions." *National Vaccine Information Center*, National Vaccine Information Center, Accessed 24 June 2015.

"Religious Exemptions." *National Vaccine Information Center*, National Vaccine Information Center, Accessed 24 June 2015.

"School and Childcare Vaccination Surveys." *Centers for Disease Control and Prevention*, Department of Health and Human Services, 21 July 2011, Accessed 24 June 2015.

"Vaccine Information for Adults." *Centers for Disease Control and Prevention*, Department of Health and Human Services, 18 Sep. 2014, Accessed 24 June 2015.

"VFC Program." *Centers for Disease Control and Prevention*, Department of Health and Human Services, 15 Feb. 2015, Accessed 24 June 2015.

STUDENT SAMPLE: ARGUMENTATIVE ESSAY

Jo Neuman
Professor Coursey
ENC 1102
2 May 2011

Human Nature at its Worst

When Shirley Jackson's "The Lottery" was first published in *The New Yorker* in 1948, it struck a nerve with readers. "The story was incendiary; readers acted as if a bomb had blown up in their faces . . . Shirley struck a nerve in mid-twentieth-century America . . . She had told people a painful truth about themselves" (Oppenheimer 129). Interestingly, the story strikes that same nerve with readers today. When my English class recently viewed a video production of the story, those students who had not previously read the story reacted quite strongly to the ending. I recall this same reaction when I was in high school. Our English teacher chose to show the video before any student had read the story. Almost every student in the class reacted with horror at the ending. Why do people react so strongly when they read the story or see the video? What is it about "The Lottery" that is so disturbing? To understand, one must examine the very nature of humankind.

Man's propensity for violence has been around since Cain killed Abel. In the Old Testament, the Bible speaks frequently of wars and killing. "And it came to pass . . . that all Israel returned unto Ai, and smote it with the edge of the sword. And all that fell that day, both of men and women, were twelve thousand" (Josh. 8. 24-25). The ancient Romans were known for their bloodlust. "The ancient Romans loved gladiators. They loved the men, the weapons, the fighting and the bloodshed. They also loved the death" (Baker 2). While most people today would be horrified by "what the historian Michael Grant has called 'the nastiest blood-sport ever invented' [it] was much loved in ancient Rome" (Baker 3). It is also well known that over the years, various cultures have practiced human sacrifice. "The Aztecs probably offered up more sacrificial victims than any other people in recorded history. In this, they were enacting a Mesoamerican tradition that originated far back in the region's past" (Allan 19). Throughout more modern history, wars have been fought resulting in the deaths of millions. Murders and other violent crimes are inescapable. Throughout mankind's history, it can be shown that man's capacity for evil has no limits. But is this what troubled readers of Jackson's story?

"We cannot, in all honesty, make any serious claim that our own culture really abhors violence. . . . Modern society still feels the need to watch violent events, whether it be at a boxing match or spattered across the cinema screen" (Baker 5). Society today is bombarded with violence. There is graphic, and often gratuitous, violence in movies and video games. Most people do not give this type of violence a second thought. This may be because they know that the violence in the movies or games is not real, but "The Lottery" was just a story; it, too, was not real. So what is it about Jackson's story that hits readers so deeply? What makes "The Lottery" so disturbing?

For years, critics have been trying to answer these questions. Some have focused on the story's symbolism, while others have focused on its relationship to the horrors of World War II. Jay Yarmove writes, "Coming after the revelation of the depths of depravity to which the Nazis sank in their eagerness to destroy other, 'lesser' peoples, 'The Lottery' upsets the reader's sense of complacency" (242). He goes on to say that

there were many Americans who, after the end of World War II . . . smugly asserted that such atrocities could happen in Nazi Germany but not in the United States. . . . Jackson's story help[s] to create the specter of a holocaust in the United States. (Yarmove 245)

James Evans believes that

since the story was written in the immediate aftermath of World War II and the holocaust, it raised (and can still raise) important questions concerning 'the power of mass psychology, the possibility that blind adherence to tradition will forestall

judgment, and the ease with which responsibility can be denied.'" (J. Stark qtd. in Evans 119)

Other critics simply focus on man's inhumanity to man. Helen Nebeker notes:

Numerous critics have carefully discussed Shirley Jackson's "The Lottery" . . . pointing out its obvious comment on the innate savagery of man lurking beneath his civilized trappings. Most acknowledge the power of the story, admitting that the psychological shock of the ritual murder in an atmosphere of modern, smalltown normality cannot be easily forgotten. (100)

Jackson herself once said,

Explaining just what I had hoped the story to say is very difficult. I suppose, I hoped, by setting a particularly brutal ancient rite in the present and in my own village to shock the story's readers with a graphic dramatization of the pointless

violence and general inhumanity in their own lives. (Friedman 33–34)

While a case can be made for each of these interpretations, I believe there is more to the story.

Very subtly throughout the story, Jackson shows that the townspeople feel no individual responsibility in committing what can only be termed murder. The lottery was treated as just another social event. "The lottery was conducted–as were the square dances, the teenage club, the Halloween program–by Mr. Summers" (248). As people assembled on that day, the women "greeted one another and exchanged bits of gossip" while the men spoke "of planting and rain, tractors and taxes" (247). As they begin the process, the people "only half listened to the directions" as they "had done it so many times" (250). Old Man Warner, the oldest man in the town, makes it clear "there's always been a lottery" and that this is his "seventy-seventh time"

(250). It is apparent that at one time, long before the characters in the story were alive, the lottery held a deep significance to the people. According to Old Man Warner, there "used to be a saying that 'Lottery in June, corn be heavy soon'" (250), intimating that the ritual was born out of a desire to ensure prosperity for the town. Over the years, however, "much of the ritual had been forgotten or discarded" (248), indicating that the current townspeople really had no idea why they continued to conduct the lottery.

It is obvious at times that some of the villagers are uncomfortable with the whole process, but no one ever overtly criticizes or speaks out against the lottery. Mr. Adams tells Old Man

Warner "that over in the north village they're talking of giving up the lottery," and Mrs. Adams adds that "some places have already quit lotteries" (250). Yet, neither of these two individuals had the courage to stand up and say, "Why are we still doing this? Perhaps we should stop, too." Many of the townspeople were obviously nervous during the process, fully comprehending what the end would bring. As Mr. Delacroix went to get his slip, Mrs. Delacroix "held her breath" and the men who had already selected their slips stood in the "crowd . . . holding the small folded papers in their large hands, turning them over and over nervously" (250). Yet again, no one dared to question, or better still, condemn the process. Even Tessie Hutchinson, after her husband drew the deadly slip of paper, did not condemn the lottery itself. She simply stated, "It wasn't fair. . . . I think we should start over" (251). She apparently had no issue with the lottery, just that her family was selected. This conjures up images of the German people during World War II or the 38 people who did nothing as they watched their neighbor, Kitty Genovese, brutally murdered (Darley 417). Readers are troubled by the fact that no one in the village had the courage to take a stand against the lottery. Readers believe that had they been in the village, they would have been willing to speak up. This begs the question as to whether or not readers today would have behaved any differently than the villages of the story.

Many psychologists have studied the effects of crowds, or mobs, on individuals. The fact that the entire town participates in the ritualistic murder allows individuals to abdicate their own responsibility. "Diffusion of responsibility . . . explain[s] that being in a group leads one to feel as if one is less responsible" (Garcia et al. 845). Graham Tyson, a South African psychologist,

described the phenomenon of deindividuation (sic) and concluded . . . on the basis of [his] assessment of the psychological literature, that it is highly probable that an individual in a mob situation will experience deindividuation and that this . . . will lead to diminished responsibility. . . . The dense crowding . . . appeared to have caused some . . . to become deindividuated and therefore less aware than they normally were of their individual identity and accountability. (Colman 1072-3).

In other words, people do not feel responsible for their actions when they are in a group. Because everyone in the town, from young children to Old Man Warner, participated, the individual citizens felt no personal responsibility. Psychologist Jerry M. Burger notes the "absence of responsibility has often been cited by psychologists as a contributing factor to aggressive and abhorrent behavior" (3-4). When an individual perceives that someone or something else is responsible for a particular action, he is capable of doing things that he otherwise would not.

Part of what disturbs readers is that fact that no one wants to believe that an otherwise normal human being could commit a reprehensible and violent act like that depicted in "The Lottery." Burger, in talking about Stanley Milgram's obedience studies of the 1960s, states "most social psychologists appear to agree . . . [Milgram's] studies are a dramatic demonstration on how individuals typically underestimate the power of situational forces when explaining another person's behavior." Burger goes on to say that "our culture socializes individuals to obey certain authority figures" (3). It is likely that the townspeople in "The Lottery" viewed Mr. Summers as an authority figure. As the man who "ran the coal business" (248), Mr. Summers was probably the richest, most powerful man in the town. As such, individual townspeople would have been hesitant to speak out against the lottery as Mr. Summers, a man of authority, was in charge of it. Readers may dismiss this thought believing they would never succumb to this kind of pressure. In fact, Burger points out that there has been "a persistent question about Milgram's research" and whether his findings could be repeated today as people are "more aware of the dangers of blindly following authority" (4). But are people today really any different? Burger recently conducted a "partial replication of Milgram's procedure" and found that average Americans react to this laboratory situation today much the way they did 45 years ago. Although changes in societal attitudes can affect behavior, [Burger's] findings indicate that the same situational factors that affected obedience in Milgram's participants still operate today. (9)

The villagers in "The Lottery" not only had Mr. Summers as an authority figure, but they had the group dynamics of having the entire town involved, effectively absolving them of their personal responsibilities.

A phenomenon known as "bystander apathy" may also help to explain the townspeople (Garcia et al. 843). There are numerous contemporary news accounts of people witnessing a brutal act yet failing to help the victim. Most people are genuinely horrified to hear such accounts. But what is it that would make someone stand idly by and watch someone get murdered? It seems the more bystanders there are, the less likely any of them will be to act. "Even if a person defines an event as an emergency, the presence of other bystanders may still make him less likely to intervene. He feels that his responsibility is diffused and diluted" (Darley 420). This could explain why the townspeople in "The Lottery" were reluctant to speak out against the practice. Because the entire town was participating, they no longer felt any individual

responsibility for what was to occur.

The responsibility-diluting effect of other people was so strong that single individuals were more than twice as likely to report the emergency as those who thought other people also knew about it . . . [an individual's] reactions are shaped by the reactions of others." (Darley 421)

When Mrs. Adams commented on the villages that have stopped the lottery, the only person to respond was Old Man Warner who exclaimed that those who had given up the lottery were a "pack of young fools" (250). No one else spoke in support of ending the lottery. While they did not speak up, it is quite possible that some of the townspeople, while present, did not actually participate in the stoning. This can be inferred from Mrs. Dunbar telling Mrs. Delacroix, "You'll have to go ahead and I'll catch up to you" (252). Readers can choose to believe that Mrs. Dunbar had no intention of catching up. "Marked by the loss of her son [to the lottery, Mrs. Dunbar] may still be a victim but she will not be a perpetrator" (Nebeker 105). Readers can also wonder where Mrs. Adams was at the time of the stoning. Jackson makes it very clear as the stoning begins, "Steve Adams was in the front of the crowd of villagers, with Mrs. Graves beside him" (252). Where was his wife? It is logical to conclude that because Mrs. Adams had commented earlier that "some places have already quit lotteries" (250), Jackson's exclusion of her at this point in the story is intentional. It is likely that while Mrs. Adams was certainly present, she did not actually participate. This may be the only glimmer of hope in an otherwise dark and troubling tale.

What perplexes readers is, unlike most modern movies, there are no discernible good guys or bad guys in the story. The characters are regular people, just like those reading the story. Until the end, readers can picture themselves as one of the townspeople. Yet when these seemingly regular people commit a horrifying, heinous act, readers struggle to comprehend their actions. Readers are forced to ponder whether they would have acted any differently than the townspeople. Would they have gone against Mr. Summers' authority? Would they have had the courage to tell the group what they were doing was wrong? While most readers will tell themselves that they would have intervened, sadly, as we have seen, most would not.

As long as humans exist, Jackson's story will remain relevant.

Man, [Jackson] says, is a victim of his unexamined and hence unchanged traditions . . . Until enough men are touched strongly enough by the horror of their ritualistic, irrational actions . . . man will never free himself from his primitive nature and is ultimately doomed. (Nebeker 107)

If the disturbing nature of "The Lottery" causes readers to look more closely at themselves, perhaps there will be a time when individuals will do what they know is right, regardless of who is in charge or how many people are around.

Works Cited

Allan, Tony, et al. *Gods of Sun and Sacrifice*. Duncan Baird, 1997.

Baker, Alan. *The Gladiator: The Secret History of Rome's Warrior Slaves*. St. Martin Press, 2000.

Burger, Jerry M. "Replicating Milgram: Would People Still Obey Today?" *American Psychologist*, 64, 1, 2009, pp.1-11. *PsycArticles EBSCO*, Accessed 26 Apr. 2011.

Colman, Andrew M. "Crowd Psychology in South African Murder Trials." *American Psychologist*, 46, 10, 1991, pp.1071-79. *PsycArticles EBSCO*, Accessed 26 Apr. 2011.

Darley, John M. and Bibb Latane. "Why People Don't Help in a Crisis." *The Longman Reader*, edited by Judith Nadell, John Langan, and Eliza A. Comodromos, 8th ed, Pearson Education, 2007, pp.417-21.

Evans, Robert C. "Short Fiction: A Critical Companion." 1997, pp.112-9. *Library Reference Center Plus*. Accessed 25 Apr. 2011.

Friedman, Lenemaja. "Shirley Jackson." *Bloom's Major Short Story Writers: Shirley Jackson*, edited by Harold Bloom, Chelsea House Publishers, 2001, pp.32-4.

Garcia, Stephen M., et al. "Crowded Minds: The Implicit Bystander Effect." *Journal of Personality and Social Psychology*, 83, 4, 2002, pp.843-53. *PsycArticles EBSCO*. Accessed 25 Apr. 2011.

Jackson, Shirley. "The Lottery." *Literature: An Introduction to Fiction, Poetry, and Drama*, edited by X.J. Kennedy and Dana Gioia, 10th ed, Longman, 2007, pp.247-52.

Nebeker, Helen E. "The Lottery: Symbolic Tour de Force." *American Literature* 46, 1, 1974, pp.100-7. *EBSCO, Accessed* 23 Apr. 2011.

Oppenheimer, Judy. *Private Demons: The Life of Shirley Jackson*. G. P. Putnam's Sons, 1988.

The Holy Scriptures According to the Masoretic Text. Jewish Publications Society of America, 1917.

Yarmove, Jay A. "Jackson's The Lottery." *Explicator*, 52, 4, 1994, pp.242-45. *EBSCO, Accessed* 26 Apr. 2011.

STUDENT SAMPLE: ARGUMENTATIVE ESSAY

Laura Dilts
Professor Coursey
ENC 1102
3 December 2014

The Yellow Wallpaper

As early as 1900 BC, all the way up until the 19th century, it was widely stated by medical professionals that simply having a womb would drive a person to illness and insanity (Tasca). Physicians stated that the uterus would wander about inside the female body, causing trouble wherever it went. The clinical term for it was "wandering womb" or "hysteria" ("Hysteria"). Does this sound ridiculous? To us it may, but at the time Charlotte Perkins Gilman wrote "The Yellow Wallpaper," it was still a common notion that women were somehow innately mentally ill for simply being female. They were encouraged to not exert themselves, were isolated whenever they showed signs of rebellion, and told they were mad for wanting to be less dainty and breakable (Tasca). This socially accepted notion gave a seemingly valid excuse to control, manipulate, and discredit all women, which led many to a breaking point, to fulfil that prophecy of madness bestowed upon them.

In "The Yellow Wallpaper," Gilman tells a tale of this kind of fall to madness caused by the mistreatment of women. We can infer that it is the story of a woman named Jane who lived in the late 1800s and suffered from severe postpartum depression. The woman's husband, John, takes her to a large rental house away from her home and essentially imprisons her in her quarters until she behaves again. Her husband is a doctor, and though modern medicine was transitioning to a better understanding of mental illness (Tasca), he seems to be of the opinion that Jane should be subdued to cure herself (Gilman).

One could argue that his actions seem less than "doctoral." We see what is being done to her through off-handed comments, like when she mentions that her husband sometimes strikes her. She is forbidden from seeing who she wants to see and only allowed certain interactions that he approves of. He is controlling and abusive, yet she still insists that she is being treated rather than mistreated and abused. He gives her infantilizing nicknames, calling her a "little girl" and "silly little goose." He demeans everything she says and asks her to behave for his sake and their child's sake (Gilman). These are classic signs of a manipulative abuser ("Abuser Tricks").

It is interesting to see the first person perspective in Gilman's story. It puts us inside of a mind that has been punished and oppressed. We can see her protagonist's attempts to defend her persecutors, to justify what is happening. Like many abused women who try to rationalize a controlling spouse's behavior as protective, she calls her husband "careful and loving" because he gives her "a schedule prescription for each hour in the day" (Gilman). Most would call that kind of micromanaging very domineering, and it is also a common sign of abuse ("Abuser Tricks").

And truly, one could argue that the whole idea of the diagnosis of female hysteria is really a controlling device. In medical literature, it has been described as

a manifestation of everything from divine poetic inspiration and satanic possession to female unreason, radical degeneration and unconscious psychosexual conflict...a physical disease, a mental disorder, a spiritual malady, a behavioural [sic] maladjustment, a sociological communication, and as no illness at all. (Fairclough)

So basically, ... everything? Everything a woman could do to displease society, or simply to be, is cast in a sickly light. Nothing she can do is truly right. In abusive relationships, we see abusers often convince the abused that there is something wrong with them; it makes them easier to manipulate at the whim of the abuser ("Abuser Tricks").

We can see Jane's descent into madness. The longer she is imprisoned, the more she is cowed, the more her frustration emerges as insanity (Gilman). Sadly, the author has divulged that this story is based on personal experience. A well-respected psychiatrist said it was the best portrayal of that kind of illness that he'd ever read, and she admitted that it was because she had been there herself ("Why I Wrote Yellow Wallpaper," Gilman). And judging by the fact that a medical professional was so vividly reminded of the symptoms, many other women had been too.

Through other literature, we can see this theme of control causing distress, even to the point of death. In a short story by Kate Chopin, the protagonist, Mrs. Mallard, is ill in some way and her husband is implied to be overbearing and controlling. Yet the speaker still feels obligated to defend him. She does not betray that her silence and reclusion is borne of joy rather than mourning at his supposed death. Her dismay at her husband being alive, that the hope for freedom she'd kindled in that short time she thought him dead suddenly being snuffed, was enough to kill her. There seems to be no explicit indication of physical abuse in this story, but Mrs. Mallard still felt she was not allowed to live her own life or to feel free in the presence of her husband. Chopin says it well in a moment of clarity before Mrs. Mallard finds her husband to be alive:

There would be no one to live for during those coming years; she would live for herself. There would be no powerful will bending hers in that blind persistence with which men and women believe they have a right to impose a private will upon a fellow-creature. A kind intention or a cruel intention made the act seem no less a crime as she looked upon it in that brief moment of illumination (Chopin).

Her husband was not as bad as John from "The Yellow Wallpaper," but still, that pressure was there. We can postulate that it is within the relationship dynamics between men and women of the time where the true problem lies.

It is a subtle thing, to be oppressed, one hard to grasp in a meaningful and articulable way. As Betty Friedan said in *The Feminine Mystique*, what keeps a woman from feeling truly fulfilled was a "problem that has no name." Many women feel it, but few can concisely say what it is (Friedan 63). It creeps up, creeping like the woman in Jane's hallucinations (Gilman). To explain it, once it has festered for centuries and boiled over, well, it does make us look quite mad, no? It is difficult to say there is something wrong between men and women without seeming to shout blame at every man in existence, whether he is an abusive John, or a simply present Mr. Mallard. It is like trying to catch shadows to show proof that something is standing between you and the light. But that shadow is there, twisting and crying out from behind the yellow wallpaper in every woman's mind.

Works Cited

"Abuser Tricks." *New Hope for Women,* 2012, Accessed 22 November 2014.

Chopin, Kate. "The Story of an Hour." *Literature: An Introduction to Reading and Writing,* edited by Edgar Roberts and Robert Zweig, 10th ed, Pearson, 2010, p. 337.

Fairclough, Victoria. "The History of Hysteria." *Bronte Heroine,* 16 August 2011, Accessed 22 November 2014.

Friedan, Betty. *The Feminine Mystique.* W.W. Norton and Company, 1963.

Gilman, Charlotte Perkins. "The Yellow Wallpaper." *Literature: An Introduction to Reading and Writing,* edited by Edgar Roberts and Robert Zweig, 10th ed, Pearson, 2010.

Gilman, Charlotte Perkins. "Why I Wrote 'The Yellow Wallpaper.'" *Literature: An Introduction to Fiction, Poetry, Drama, and Writing,* edited by X.J. Kennedy and Dana Gioia, 11th ed, Pearson, 2010, p. 447.

"Hysteria." *Wikipedia,* Wikimedia, Accessed 22 November 2014.

Tasca, Cecilia, Rapetti, Mariangela, and Fadda, Bianca. "Women and Hysteria in the History of Mental Health." *National Center for Biotechnology,* 19 Oct. 2012, Accessed 22 Nov. 2014.

STUDENT SAMPLE: ARGUMENTATIVE ESSAY

Jo Neuman
Professor Coursey
ENC 1102
9 March 2011

Satire Squared

Upon first reading Kurt Vonnegut's "Harrison Bergeron," readers often interpret it solely as a satire on the evils of egalitarianism. Set in the future, the story begins by declaring that everyone was finally equal. "They were equal every which way. Nobody was any smarter than anybody else. Nobody was better looking than anybody else. Nobody was stronger or quicker than anybody else. All this equality was due to . . . the unceasing vigilance of agents of the

United States Handicapper General" (216). The tone of the narration is immediately negative, leading readers to the natural conclusion that the author believes equalization is bad. But is that really what Vonnegut intends? Even a cursory review of his political leanings indicates that Kurt Vonnegut was a proponent of socialism. How can the seemingly anti-egalitarian message of "Harrison Bergeron" be reconciled with Vonnegut's personal feelings and beliefs?

On the surface, the story blatantly satirizes a time when everyone is physically and mentally made to be exactly the same as everyone else. This interpretation has been used countless times as an argument against egalitarianism. Murray Rothbard, in *Egalitarianism as a Revolt Against Nature,* refers to "Harrison Bergeron" as "a pithy and . . . bitterly satirical short story depicting a comprehensively egalitarian society" (289) which he describes as "a world of

faceless and identical creatures, devoid of all individuality, variety, or special creativity" (6). This certainly describes the world of Harrison Bergeron, where the purpose of the Handicapper

General is to ensure that no one is "better than anybody else" (216). Rothbard uses "Harrison Bergeron" to further his ideals that humans are "uniquely characterized by a high degree of variety, diversity, differentiation; in short, inequality" and that "the egalitarian goal

is . . . evil" (8). Others use the story to combat the idea of one-size-fits-all education. Tracy Cross, in an article for *Gifted Child Today*, writes:

In 1961 Kurt Vonnegut wrote the short story "Harrison Bergeron" about America's quest for equality that had gone so far as to create a position of Handicapper General. This person's role was to create ways in which society could equalize the natural human variations so that everyone would be the same. . . . Vonnegut's story can be instructive to those of us in gifted education. (14)

She uses the story to support her contention that "Our current conceptions of fairness and equity have led us to . . . harm many of our most able students" (Cross 15). Clare Fugate uses the story to denigrate the No Child Left Behind law. After referencing the opening paragraph of the story describing how everyone was finally equal, she asks:

Any of this science fiction sound familiar? Currently, No Child Left Behind . . . decrees that . . . all students must be proficient for their grade level in reading and math. Who among us thinks that this is a reasonable, logical expectation? Who among us believes that each student has the same intellectual capabilities? Who among us believes that a one-size-fits all, cookie-cutter test actually measures an individual student's academic achievement? (71)

Both Cross and Fugate use Vonnegut's words to bolster the absurdness of trying to equalize students. Most Americans would agree, but would Vonnegut?

Some critics theorize that Vonnegut wrote the story simply to appeal to a particular audience. "Vonnegut wrote this piece in the era of 'the Communist threat.' Magazines publish what people will read, and at that time, readers wanted to . . . feel superior and correct in their defense of democracy" (Stuckey 89). Darryl Hattenhauer, in "The Politics of Kurt Vonnegut's 'Harrison Bergeron,'" echoes this sentiment:

As a struggling writer, Vonnegut had to put a surface on this story that would appeal to his audience. And it did. More specifically, it did so because it appeared to rehearse central tenets of the dominant culture's ideology. It appealed to the

literal-minded with such accuracy that William F. Buckley's National Review reprinted it as a morality tale about the dangers of forsaking private enterprise. (2)

Having written the story in 1961 when the Cold War was in full swing, it may be that Vonnegut was simply capitalizing on the fears the American people had of communism and socialism. It is

also quite probable, as Hattenhauer concluded, that the depiction of the forced equality in the story was written as a means of exposing America's misunderstanding of what equality really means (2). In other words, embedded in the blatant satire of an unrealistic egalitarian society is the hidden satire of what Vonnegut perceived Americans erroneously believed about socialism. What Vonnegut created was a satire within a satire; one written for the masses and another for

those willing to look a little deeper. Vonnegut himself said, "As I get older . . . I say what I really think. I don't hide ideas like Easter eggs for people to find" (*Playboy*). Since "Harrison Bergeron" was written early in his career, it is logical to conclude that the secondary satire hidden in the story was intentional. The blatant satire of what equality means is so over-the-top, it is reasonable to conclude, as Hattenhauer did, that Vonnegut is intentionally poking fun at the American people through the story.

This is clearly shown through his depiction of Hazel, who "had a perfectly average intelligence" (216). Hazel may have been average in the made-up world of Harrison Bergeron, but she would not be average today, nor would she have been average back in 1961 when the story was written. An average person is capable of remembering things from one moment to the next; an average person is capable of understanding death and mourning the loss of a loved one. Hazel "couldn't think about anything except in short bursts" (216). When she sees her son,

Harrison, killed, she cries, but just moments later, is unable to recall why. Consider the dialog between Hazel and her husband right after their son was killed:

"You've been crying," he said to Hazel.

"Yup," she said.

"What about?" he said.

"I forget," she said. "Something real sad on television."

"What was it?" he said.

"It's kind of mixed up in my mind," said Hazel. (219)

This is not representative of the average person. By equalizing everyone to Hazel's level, a below-average level, Vonnegut was clearly showing the absurdness of the story, as well as what he considered were the erroneous beliefs of the American people.

While readers tend to choose one interpretation over the other, I believe both are valid and do not contradict Vonnegut's beliefs. Vonnegut's idea of socialism was very different from what he perceived the majority of Americans believed. He did not believe that everyone should be the same but that those who are more capable should take care of those who are not. He confirmed this when he said "thousands of people in our society found out they were too stupid or too unattractive or too ignorant to rise. They realized they couldn't get a nice car or a nice house or a nice job. Not everybody can do that, you know" (*Playboy*). He went on to say, "I just know that there are plenty of people who are in terrible trouble and can't get out. And so I'm impatient with those who think that it's easy for people to get out of trouble. I think there are some people who really need a lot of help. I worry about stupid people, dumb people. Somebody has to take care of them because they can't hack it" (*Playboy*). He worried about people with less ability and felt those with greater ability should help them. He did not believe that those with ability should be

brought down to the same level as those without. As a writer, an artist, I believe he appreciated individuality and respected talent. In talking about the "big money and . . . heavy praise some of

[his] contemporaries were getting for their books," Vonnegut stated, "I'm going to have to study writing harder, because I think what I'm doing is pretty good, too" (*Playboy*). He did not think those other writers should be handicapped to equal him; he was going to have to work harder to improve himself.

Vonnegut's idea of a perfect society would not be what he portrays in "Harrison Bergeron." I contend it would include people with varying abilities and talents, but those with more ability would assist those with less ability simply for the purpose of making the society as a whole better. He confirmed this in an article he wrote later in life where he stated, "Many years ago, I was so innocent I still considered it possible that we could become the humane and reasonable America so many members of my generation used to dream of" (Cold Turkey). His perfect society was not one in which there was no variation, as in "Harrison Bergeron," but one where people cared for one another.

Through "Harrison Bergeron," Vonnegut very cleverly disguised his satire of what he believed was most Americans' misguided perception of socialism by wrapping it in the blatant satire of totally unrealistic egalitarianism. Both messages are consistent with Vonnegut's core philosophy. While he felt most Americans misunderstand socialism, he also valued individuality. Those who only see one side of this coin will never be able to appreciate the mixed satire Vonnegut skillfully hid among his words like "Easter eggs" for people to find (*Playboy*).

Works Cited

Cross, Tracy L. "Disrupting Social Contracts that Affect Gifted Students: An Homage to Harrison Bergeron." *Gifted Child Today*, Fall 2009, pp.14-15. *Academic OneFile.* Accessed 1 Mar. 2011.

Fugate, Clare. "Vonnegut Warned Us." *Phi Delta Kappan*, Sep. 2007, pp.71-2. *OmniFile Full Text Mega,* Accessed 1 Mar. 2011.

Hattenhauer, Darryl. "The Politics of Kurt Vonnegut's 'Harrison Bergeron.'" *Studies in Short Fiction*, Fall 1998, pp.387-92.

OmniFile Full Text Mega, Accessed 1 Mar. 2011.

Stuckey, Lexi. "Teaching Conformity in Kurt Vonnegut's 'Harrison Bergeron.'" *Eureka Studies in Teaching Short Fiction*, 2006, pp.85-90. *Literary Reference Center Plus, Accessed 1* Mar. 2011.

Vonnegut, Kurt. "Cold Turkey." *In These Times*, 10 May 2004, Accessed 2 Mar. 2011.

---. "Harrison Bergeron." *Literature: An Introduction to Fiction, Poetry, Drama, and Writing,* edited by X. J. Kennedy and Dana Gioia, 11th ed, Longman, 2010, pp.216-219.

---. Playboy Interview: Kurt Vonnegut, Jr. *Playboy,* Playboy Enterprises, Inc., July 1973, Accessed 2 Mar. 2011.

STUDENT SAMPLE: ARGUMENTATIVE ESSAY

Xye Borg
Prof. Mangione
ENC 1101
30 Oct. 2019

Hjonk: Dadaism's Reflection in Millennials and Gen Z's

A teenage girl at a park can be seen looking down at her phone, as most young people are commonly seen doing. An elderly couple gazes at her with discontent, disparaging thoughts flooding their minds while they whisper of disapproval to one another. Unbeknownst to the couple, the girl is busy planning a peaceful sit-in with her associates to protest the Trump Administration's stance on the Green New Deal. Negative generalizations like this are continuously pinned on younger generations by their older counterparts, despite the reality that contradicts the immediate assumptions. Weighty stressors unfamiliar to many older individuals are imposed upon newer generations, but almost never taken into consideration because of a trend of immediate dismissal. Millennials and Gen Z's are often seen as shallow and apathetic by older generations, but their striking resemblance to the politically and socially charged Dadaist art movement shows that younger people have a culture of compassionate awareness that inspires activism and change.

Political and social environments of early twentieth-century Europe are similar to political and social environments of contemporary times, placing levels of stress on the Millennials and Gen Z's that are comparable to those that were placed on the Dadaists. Witnessed by the Dadaists of Europe during the infancy of the 1900's, a blight of nationalism and militarism plagued the continent's front. According to William Eckhardt and Alan G. Newcombe, militarism is defined as "the belief in military deterrence, or the reliance on military strength to defend one's nation and its values, or aggressive foreign policy in general" (210). After the Franco-Prussian War in 1870, militarism become prominent throughout Europe. "Causes of World War I" explains how "Militarism in particular helped to transform Europe into a tense, hostile environment, with millions of troops and newly industrialized warfare ready to be mobilized in the event of war" (7). Toxic nationalist mindsets present at the time were the motivation behind the assassination of Archduke Franz Ferdinand of Austria, which sparked the beginning of World War I (Shen 8). What followed was a horrendous war fueled by the vast militaristic powers within Europe. Today, a resurgence of nationalist ideals is being observed. Pazzanese, a Harvard Staff Writer, identifies the growth of nationalist-based politics in Europe: "Trump's surprise election has proved a political windfall and an inspirational template to far-right candidates in Europe... These rightist groups predate Trump politically and tie themselves more tightly to nationalism, but they are also happy to ride on the coattails of his victory." As seen many times in the past, most notably with WWI and the Cold War, the culmination of nationalistic and militaristic aspects within a country can, and usually does, have severe consequences on the mental wellbeing of the country's populous. At the front lines of this mental assault in today's times are the youngest generations, adding just one more added stressor to their already disadvantaged lives. The subjugation of Millennials and Gen Z's to modern nationalist and militaristic political environments mirrors the experiences of the Dadaists in early twentieth-century Europe.

The manner in which Millennials and Gen Z's views have been molded in response to the plights in their environments exemplifies the generations' connection to the nature of Dada. The practitioners of Dada in the early 1900's were notably liberal and often supported socialistic ideals. As described by "Police, Politics, and Anti-Art," political and social beliefs of the Dadaists were embedded into the aspects of Dada culture, making Dada into a politically fueled, avant-garde movement: "...The First International Dada Fair of 1920 opposed military and capitalistic institutions that inflicted violence upon minorities" (Alonso 106). Today, Millennials and Gen Z's in the U.S. and Europe are following the same path of opinions on the same subjects. Studies on political stances of different generations in the U.S. say, "...majorities in Gen Z and the Millennial generation say government should do more to solve problems, rather than that government is doing too many things better left to businesses and individuals..." (Parker). Even separated by decades, younger modern generations and the Dadaists hold concurring opinions.

Absurdist themes are present in Dadaism in the same way that Absurdist themes are present in Millennial and Gen Z humor: as a method to cope with the distressing state of society, which usually generates awareness about the issue being addressed in the art piece or joke. Confronted with a bloody, violent war, Dadaists sought to call out the poor justifications for such death and destruction created by the established powers at the time. According to Hans Arp, "Dada wanted to destroy the deceptions of reason and discover an irrational order" (Elger 9). The Dadaists wanted to display the horrors promoted and carried out by institutions in Europe as unbelievably nonsensical and monstrous; a savagery that would only be allowed to thrive under a system just as nonsensical and monstrous as the acts within the war itself. Millennials and Gen Z's seek to find an outlet for their stress under their current societal pressures as well, but they do so through their humor. TheDalekHater, a user of the website *Reddit*, created a meme based off struggles with mental illness – an adversity tragically familiar to Millennials and Gen Z's (Hoffower and Akhtar; Wasserman):

Fig. 1. An edited screenshot of a notification screen. TheDalekHater. "Hjonk hjonk." Reddit, r/memes, 13 Feb. 2019, https://www.reddit.com/r/memes/comments/aqcdh7/hj%C3%B6nk-hj%C3%B6nk/

In the meme, the two messages from "Anxiety" and "Depression" represent the doubts an individual with the two illnesses frequently experience. The "Scandinavian Clown" message is the joke of the meme. A disheartening atmosphere is built up by the first two messages and then subsequently interrupted by the meaningless nature of "Hjonk." While the nonsensical, lazy essence of a Scandinavian Clown saying "Hjonk" as a joke is an example of absurdist humor on its own, combining the joke with a preexisting theme of authentic despair is signature to Millennials and Gen Z's. Through grouping major tribulations with meaningless statements or visuals in a humorous format, they reduce the mental impacts inflicted on them caused by living under harrowing circumstances. All the unnecessary pain resulting from broken or corrupt systems is painted as outrageous for any human to undergo, thus subtly encouraging the reformation of systems that enable human anguish. Young people's access to the internet nowadays has made them painfully aware of the devastation and suffering that fills the world. They are constantly reminded of a bleak present with even bleaker prospects for the future. Absurd humor is their way of coping with the despair they experience from an unrelenting awareness of illogical, but seemingly unstoppable doom (Mercado).

Older generations, however, connect the Millennial and Gen Z culture surrounding electronics and unconventional humor to superficial values and apathy. They claim that the perceived decline of face-to-face human communication reduces younger people's ability to empathize with others. Participation in social media creates a self-centered generation of youth that are driven by a shallow desire for attention in the eyes of many older individuals. Being exposed to all the barbarity of the world is affirmed to cause desensitization in the youth, adding to their seemingly inherent quality of selfishness. Contrary to these beliefs, younger generations are exhibited as more politically active. Their exposure to the world's atrocities instead breeds a determination to fight injustice. Millennials and Gen Z's recognize that it's their future and the future of humans yet to be born that's at stake. They are fully capable of comprehending the reality of the world, and desensitization worries them more than it prevents them from empathizing. They are educated about what is happening in the word, too; "Gen Zers' views about climate change are virtually identical to those of Millennials and not markedly different from Gen Xers. About half in all three generations say the earth is getting warmer due to human activity" (Parker et al.). Activism is prominent among younger people; they are driven to change the future for the better since it will directly impact their quality of life.

Millennials and Gen Z's nature and response to their circumstances are comparative to the Dadaists of early twentieth-century Europe. Political aspects of modern day that Millennials and Gen Z's live under mirror the political state of early twentieth-century Europe. Dadaists share the need to cope with the ridiculously depressing condition of society, only this reveals itself within the Dada art itself. Younger generations are a bit different in this department, employing dark and absurdist humor to deal with the despondent future they see ahead of them. They share general ideals with the Dadaists, corresponding opinions on the role of government and economic handling relate the groups together. Regardless of the negative assumptions held by older generations, Millennials and Gen Z's are working towards fixing a world they discern as being broken by those before them and by established powers. Their awareness stretches past many of the generations before them, and they chose to use that awareness for the greater good.

Works Cited

Alonso, Leticia Perez. "Police, Politics, and Anti-Art: The Case of Berlin Dada." *South Atlantic Review*, vol. 83, no. 3, 22 Sep. 2018, https://link.gale.com/apps/doc/A554787592/AONE?u=lincclin-hcc&sid=AONE&xid=c62d886b.

Cornwell, Neil. "Chapter 3: The Twentieth Century: Towards the Absurd." *Absurd in Literature*, Manchester University Press, 2006, pp. 66–98. http://search.ebscohost.com/login.aspx?direct=true&db=lkh&AN=44766121&site=lrc-plus.

Eckhardt, William, and Alan G. Newcombe. "Militarism, Personality, and Other Social Attitudes." Journal of Conflict Resolution, vol. 13, no. 2, June 1969, pp. 210-219, https://journals.sagepub.com/doi/abs/10.1177/002200276901300204.

Hoffower, Hillary and Allana Akhtar, "Lonely, burned out, and depressed: The state of millennials' mental health in 2019." *Business Insider*, Business Insider, 10 Oct. 2019, https://www.businessinsider.com/millennials-mental-health-burnout-lonely-depressed-money-stress.

"How Gen Z led a climate change youthquake." *London Evening Standard*, Evening Standard Limited, 15 Feb. 2019, p. 25. Gale In Context: Opposing Viewpoints, https://link.gale.com/apps/doc/A574224264/OVIC?u=lincclin-hcc&sid=OVIC&xid=038d6ee6.

Mercado, William, "The Shocking and Absurdist Humor of Gen Z." *Medium*, Medium, 17 June, https://medium.com/@williamfmercado/the-shocking-and-absurdist-humor-of-gen-z-f3d6e363d42b.

Parker, Kim, et al., "Generation Z Looks a Lot Like Millennials on Key Social and Political Issues." *Social and Demographic Trends*, Pew Research Center, 17 Jan. 2019, https://www.pewsocialtrends.org/2019/01/17/generation-z-looks-a-lot-like-millennials-on-key-social-and-political-issues/.

Pazzanese, Christina. "In Europe, nationalism rising." *The Harvard Gazette*, Harvard University, 27 Feb. 2017, https://news.harvard.edu/gazette/story/2017/02/in-europe-nationalisms-rising/.

Quinn, Jimmy. "The Lost Generations?" *National Review*, vol. 71, no. 9, National Review, Inc., 20 May 2019, p. 32. https://search.ebscohost.com/login.aspx?direct=true&db=edsgao&AN=edsgcl.584329086&site=eds-live.

Shen, Elana. "Causes if World War I." *The Menlo Roundtable*, Menlo School, Spring 2013, https://roundtable.menloschool.org/issue15/2-Shen-MS-Roundtable15-Summer-20132.pdf.

TheDalekHater. "Hjonk hjonk." *Reddit*, r/memes, 13 Feb. 2019, https://www.reddit.com/r/memes/comments/aqcdh7/hj%C3%B6nk-hj%C3%B6nk/.

Wasserman, Todd. "Half of millennials and 75% of Gen Zers have left their job for mental health reasons." *CNBC*, CNBC, 11 Oct. 2019, https://www.cnbc.com/2019/10/11/mental-health-issues-cause-record-numbers-of-gen-x-z-to-leave-jobs.html.

QUESTIONS FOR CONSIDERATION

What is the thesis statement of each essay?

Explain some of the strengths of these essays.

Identify specific ways these essays could be improved. Consider each essay's focus, organization, development, style, and grammar.

EXERCISES

LOGICAL FALLACIES EXERCISE 12.9A

Identify the following logical fallacies by type/name.

1. Of course he's gay; he's a hairdresser.

2. That engineering major cheated on his exam. Everyone in that department is corrupt!

3. Everyone else is going green to save the environment. You should, too.

4. Sure Remi knows how to cook well—he's French!

5. As a professional racecar driver, I can assure you that string theory is the future of physics.

6. If you let your kids play rough with the dog, it won't be long before your kids are torturing small animals to death.

7. If the milk in the fridge is bad, then the meat must be bad, too.

8. Mrs. Jones may not be qualified for this position, but she certainly looks great in her uniform.

9. That woman was putting on makeup while she was driving. Women just don't pay attention when they are behind the wheel!

10. Jane thinks that Clayton behaved inappropriately with Tarzan on the island, but she is engaged to a man who was raised by apes.

11. Her outfit doesn't match. She must be colorblind.

12. He's an Olympic athlete, so he must be in great shape.

13. If that man is elected to office, we are guaranteed a nuclear war that will destroy all life on earth.

14. Obviously, Joe is a tough guy; he has tattoos all over his arms!

15. That guy has to be married or gay.

16. The unfair calls cost the team the championship because the referees were biased.

17. Tom Cruise says that psychiatry is a pseudoscience; therefore, I don't need my medication.

18. Mr. Dewey may have embezzled millions from the company, but he is such a devoted husband to his terminally ill wife.

19. You don't think Tony is in the Mob? He's Italian!

20. What does Alcee know about managing his money? He owes me $100!

21. All the cool kids are doing it! You should do it, too!

22. You're either with me, or you're against me.

LOGICAL FALLACIES EXERCISE 12.9B

Review the following statements for logical fallacies, identifying and explaining the fallacy in each.

1. All people from the north look down on southerners as inbred, illiterate folks who say "you'll" or "y'all." Never say "you'll" with a southern drawl and you will not be looked down upon by a northerner.
2. Many students should not use certain useless websites for their sources, such as Wikipedia.
3. Many students, by the time they reach college, know how to read and write. Therefore, there is no need to have classes designed for teaching literature and composition.
4. He should not have to go to jail because he broke his back and leg jumping from the second story of a building while trying to flee the scene of the crime.
5. Poverty causes young women to become strippers and prostitutes.
6. Four out of five doctors claim that Trident gum will help whiten teeth.
7. Over the past few years, a number of Catholic priests have been accused of pedophilia. The Catholic Church has seen steady decline in their membership. The pedophile priests have caused this decline.
8. Binge eating and binge drinking are both addictive habits that cause harm, so they should both be illegal.
9. Eithers prisons need to release criminals who have been convicted of drug charges, or we will continue to see a rise in overcrowded prisons.
10. She uses a cane, so she must have foot problems.
11. Tom Paulin, a well-known poet, has been invited to speak to the poetry department at Harvard. I oppose this symposium because his anti-Semitic views have caused great controversy in the past.
12. Many listeners of rap music use the n-word as do many of the rappers who make the music. This music instigates racial slurs and, therefore, should be banned.

ARGUMENT EXERCISE 12.9C

Consider the following writing prompts:

- According to Heraclitus, "You cannot step into the same river twice." If people could, should they?
- My 75-year-old mother-in-law recently quit driving. The reason? Her 86-year-old boyfriend drives her everywhere she has to go. Should there be a mandatory stop-driving age?
- If you had to lose one of your five senses (taste, touch, smell, vision, or hearing), which would you choose to live without?
- Should professional athletes be paid millions of dollars?
- Should college athletes be paid?
- Does the state of the economy dictate the music that we listen to?
- To what extent does television/film/music/etc. contribute to the dehumanization of minorities?
- What are the three best forms of investment right now? Real estate, traditional IRAs, Roth IRAs, stocks, bond, mutual funds, index funds...?
- Given the wild popularity of violent films, write an argument about why the dark hero, or even the villain, is idolized.
- Examine the different factors that affect, disrupt, or deny upward social mobility.

ARGUMENT EXERCISE 12.9D

The Statue of Liberty, holding the torch of freedom, stands before the "golden door."

"Keep ancient lands, your storied pomp!" cries she
with silent lips. "Give me your tired, your poor,
Your huddled masses yearning to breathe free,
The wretched refuse of your teeming shore.
Send these, the homeless, tempest-tost to me,
I lift my lamp beside the golden door!"

With immigration laws coming under scrutiny, are those doors still golden?

ARGUMENT EXERCISE 12.9E

Examine the decline in male college student enrollment. Provide an argument, backed by support, as to why this phenomenon has occurred in the last ten, twenty, or even forty years.

ARGUMENT EXERCISE 12.9F

Earth is about to be attacked by an aggressive race of intergalactic pirates. The President has heard about the supraluxthoric city shield that you invented and has asked for your assistance. Since you have manufactured only three shields, you are able to shield only three cities in the world. You get to decide which cities to save. Which cities you will save? Why?

ARGUMENT EXERCISE 12.9G

In an attempt to capture the desirable adolescent demographic, television and movies have increasingly focused on the experiences of adolescents. Choose a television show or movie and argue whether or not it does a particularly good or bad job of portraying the experiences of adolescents. How do the portrayals of the characters coincide or differ from the research on adolescence/early adulthood? How adept are movies at handling issues of diversity, in terms of socioeconomic status, race, gender, sexuality, or geographical location?

ARGUMENT EXERCISE 12.9H

What is your position on the issue of whether convicted sex offenders should be required to register with local authorities? Should registration be required even though they have already served their sentences in prison? Should people have the right to know the identity of any sex offenders living in their neighborhoods, or is this an invasion of privacy? Research sex offender registration, and write an essay arguing for or against such measures.

ARGUMENT EXERCISE 12.9I

You decide to go out for breakfast before your final exam. Driving to class, you spy a phone booth-shaped object by the side of the road. Shades of Bill and Ted, it is...a...a...tesseract! (Or a tardive?) Now that you hold the key to time travel, you decide to have breakfast with a very important person. Whom did you visit for breakfast?

Chapter 13

TYPES OF WRITING

In addition to the previous modes, there are some other types of writing that you may encounter in your college classes.

- Academic Writing

- Essay Exams

- Visual Analysis

- Emails

- Public Writing

- Journals

13.1 ACADEMIC WRITING

Academic writing is the type of writing you will be expected to compose in college. This kind of writing is usually serious in content, formal in tone, and organized around a thesis. Plus, you have to follow the rules of grammar and style.

When writing college papers, consider your audience. Use language that your reader will appreciate and understand. Discuss your topic in a manner befitting the situation.

Some general guidelines for academic writing:

- Follow the thesis statement you establish. Avoid tangents.
- Use 3rd person point of view (he/she/it/they) unless there is a compelling reason not to.
- Use jargon sparingly if necessary. Remember your audience.
- Avoid contractions. Spell out all words if possible, but again, consider your audience.
- Use a logical organizational method that follows the logic of your argument or commentary.
- Use active voice when possible. Use passive voice when necessary.

ACADEMIC WRITING EXERCISE 13.1A

Review one of your essays for a college class. Revise your language to reflect the academic writing guidelines presented here.

13.2 ESSAY EXAMS

Taking an exam is stressful. Writing an essay is also taxing. Put these two tasks—taking an exam and writing an essay—together, and you have the daunting job of writing an essay exam. However, preparing and planning for an essay exam can help you succeed in the task.

A. PREPARING FOR AN ESSAY EXAM

What's the difference between preparing and planning for an essay exam? Preparing is a long-term task. However, preparing for an essay exam will help you understand the task, study for it, and practice relevant skills.

Begin by understanding the task. Ask yourself—and your professor—the following questions:

- *Who* is the audience for this essay exam? Ordinarily, your teacher serves as your audience. However, ensure that your instructor does not want you to write for a particular audience, especially if you are taking an essay exam in a writing course.

- *What* is the purpose of the essay exam? For example, does your instructor want you to inform, displaying your knowledge in a particular area? Alternatively, does your instructor want you to argue on the topic, advocating one particular view?

- *What* materials can you use during the exam? Some instructors do not allow the use of any materials. In contrast, other instructors allow the use of a book, particularly so that you can quote or paraphrase from it.

- *Where* will your essay exam take place? Will it take place in a computer lab? If your exam will take place in your regular classroom, will you need to handwrite your exam (rather than type it)?

- *When* will the exam take place? Some exams take place during your regular class session. However, many colleges create a specific schedule for mid-term and final exams.

- *How* will the essay exam be evaluated? Not all instructors provide specific grading information, but they may tell students what to study and review. For example, aside from content knowledge, do you need to use correct grammar and punctuation?

- *How* much time will your instructor give you to take your essay exam? Will you have part or all of the class session to complete the exam?

Note: Some, but not all, instructors provide detailed information about an essay exam. Do not badger your professor for information, but do ask these important questions.

After you understand the task to the best of your ability, you need to study for it. What should you study? First, study the necessary content. For example, if you know your essay exam will cover everything you have learned during the first half of the semester, review all the relevant notes, quizzes, and tests. In contrast, if your essay exam will cover a list of special topics, study those topics carefully. Review any related notes, quizzes, and tests as well.

Last, but certainly not least, practice writing an essay exam. When you practice, simulate as many conditions of the upcoming exam process as possible. If your instructor tells you that you will have one hour to write a persuasive essay on a topic, study for the essay exam, and then practice writing a persuasive essay in one hour. If your instructor plans to let you use a book during the exam, use your book during your practice exam, and quote from it. If you will not be allowed to use your book during the actual essay exam, do not use it during your practice exam.

Ideally, you should spend at least two weeks preparing for an essay exam. If, however, your exam is scheduled for next week—or even tomorrow—do as much long-term preparing as you can and read about planning for your essay exam.

B. Planning for an Essay Exam

Planning for an essay exam is a short-term task—one that you can accomplish in approximately five to six minutes—but you should never skip this step. Planning for your essay exam moments before writing it will enable you to stay calm, manage your time, and do well.

- Begin your planning by reading the prompt carefully. Underline any details that you may forget during the exam, such as a required word count.

- Next, create a thesis statement. The thesis statement is the main idea of your essay. Ensure that your thesis statement matches the purpose of the essay exam.

- After you have written a thesis statement, it is time to create an outline. You can compose either an informal or formal outline. If you do not create an outline, you may accidentally forget a main point or run out of time.

- Next, start writing. Devote no more than 10 percent of your allotted time to planning, such as reading the prompt and composing an outline. Additionally, spend no less than five percent of your total time on proofreading. For example, if you need to take a 60-minute essay exam, you should spend at least three minutes on planning and one to one-half minutes on proofreading.

Many students view taking an essay exam as a menacing task. However, preparing and planning can turn this menacing task into a manageable one.

Essay Exams Exercise 13.2A
Have you taken an essay exam? Relate your experience in a short essay. What did you do well? What could you have done better? If you haven't taken an essay exam, consider what you will do when faced with one in the future.

13.3 Visual Analysis

Images are visual texts. They speak through visual signs and are representations of the human world in which we live. As you begin to explore how a specific image communicates, you might want to think about where the dominance is located in the text and how it speaks. What is the relationship of the dominance to the other objects in the image? Think about the elements in the text and identify how the narrative is displayed. Is it a narrative of phenomenon (a monumental occurrence) or is it a narrative of pathos? Is the narrative told through the setting, the action, or a relationship? Maybe it is a combination of all the above.

Once you establish the organizational scheme of the text, then you want to begin to employ your critical thinking to explain what and how the image communicates. You might begin with two simple questions:

1. What do I see?
2. What do I wonder?

As you begin to wonder about the image, ask yourself what leads you to this questioning:

1. Where is your eye drawn?
2. What stands out for you?
3. What details seem interesting and why?
4. How does the image make you feel?
5. What is in the foreground and the background?
6. How do the elements of the image complement or critique each other?
7. To what issue does the image seem to speak?
8. What does the image say, and how does the image say it?

IN-CLASS EXERCISE: VISUAL ANALYSIS

Sometimes, writing may involve analyzing an image. Writers may not know how they feel about a visual until they start writing about it, questioning themselves as they note new details. Writing as exploration can be useful in this situation. Consider the following photograph of a man and dog (both wearing shoes!) in a snowy setting:

When you are faced with a visual image, begin with some basic questions:

- What is my dominant impression of the image?
- Where is my eye drawn and why?
- What details stand out to me?
- What other significant elements do I notice?

As your analysis develops, exploring the significance of your answers leads to further questions:

- What does each element of the image mean to me?
- What does the image as a whole mean to me?
- What concrete ideas does this image capture—how and why?

These considerations can be essential to a deeper understanding of the image. Now is the time to consider how your ideas connect with one another:

- What is a reasonable conclusion to make about this text?
- What does this image say, and how does the image say it?

Let's say, for the sake of argument, you draw the conclusion that the image speaks to the old adage that dogs are man's best friend. You should then ask the following questions:

- Why is this idea significant?
- Where do I go from here?
- How do I move this conclusion forward?
- What else might this image be saying?

Consider this example of a visual analysis:

> The first thing I notice is the dog standing next to the man. I immediately see all the snow, the coldness of which seems to contrast with the seemingly warm relationship between the man and the dog. They both are bundled up against the weather as expected for a man, but when I look closely, I notice that even the dog's feet are protected from the harsh elements. All this warmth and protection is balanced against the cold, un-shoveled right side of the image. Although this image could be about that old adage of "dog as man's best friend," I can also see an interplay between the attempts to battle the weather on the left with the desire to simply give up and get through it (as evidenced by the paths of frozen footfall in the piles of snow) on the right. The man may want to fight the elements by putting shoes on the dog, but it's a small thing, almost insignificant, in the grand scheme of things—but given the attitude of the dog (seemingly content with his master), perhaps this small gesture is enough.

Here are some other issues to consider in your analysis:

- Are there words in the image? How does the written text look and function?
- How does the placement of items help inform communication? Look at layout, organization, spacing, etc.
- How does color contribute to the image?
- How does this image fit into a broader context?

VISUAL ANALYSIS EXERCISE 13.3A

Select one of the following images and write a well-organized paragraph discussing what idea is presented in the image and how this idea is presented. As you make your conclusions, please ask yourself the following: Why did I say that? How can I qualify that? As you do so, you will begin to clarify your thoughts and present them with concrete reasoning. Be sure to begin with a clear topic sentence, followed by specific details to explain that introductory sentence.

VISUAL ANALYSIS EXERCISE 13.3B

Choose an advertisement and analyze the argument it makes. Study the composition of the advertisement and explain how it works.

Write an analysis that explains the message of the advertisement as well as how that message is created. Be sure to create a valid argument about what the ad communicates by speaking specifically about the image. Use the details of the image to make your point.

13.4 EMAIL

You may find yourself sending an email to your professor. Remember that emails should use proper English—not shorthand or texting shortcuts.

Here is a short checklist of things to keep in mind when writing emails:

1. Is this something that should be conveyed over email? Would it be more effective to use another medium (phone call, text message, etc.) for this information?

2. Is your message direct and specific? Will the receiver of the email understand the message you are sending? Include relevant details so that the receiver knows what you are talking about. This means, if you are emailing your professor, you should include your name, the class you are in, and if possible, details about the specific assignment you are asking about.

Don't:

hey prof what's the homework for tomorrow?

Do:

Hello Professor X,

I am in your ENC 1101 class (Monday/ Wednesday at 9:30), and I see that we have "Paper Three" on the course schedule for tomorrow. Where can I find the explanation for that assignment?

Thanks,

Sally Student

Remember that your professor probably teaches many different classes with different assignments. Help out with the details so you can get the response you want. Of course, please make sure you already reviewed possible places where the assignment can be found before sending an email such as this. If the assignment is on the homepage, the professor will think you have not even taken the time to look for it.

3. Did you ask the receiver for some specific action? What is your goal in sending this email? Did you ask the receiver to do something to help you achieve this goal?

4. Did you proofread for grammar? Yes, it's an email. No, it's not an essay. But that doesn't mean it shouldn't use English the way it is intended to be used. The receiver may judge you for your writing style. Check your message for errors.

5. Have you used the proper tone? Would you say it like this to the person's face? Choose the appropriate words for the occasion. Consider your audience. Is this message to a person in a position of authority? If so, you should probably use proper grammar without slang or unneeded abbreviations.

What NOT to do:

hey prof i didnt finish my paper can i get extension

What TO do:

Hello Professor Smith, may I have an extension on the paper due tomorrow? I'm in your Tuesday/ Thursday ENC 1102 class at 9:30.

6. Did you sign it? Yes, emails have an easy-to-use "reply" button, but it's always nice to include your name at the bottom anyway. If you are emailing a teacher, remember that your teachers may have more than a hundred students each semester.

While we're talking about signing emails, consider the email address that you are sending this message from. Is your email kittybooboo@mail.com? Maybe it's time to get a new address that just uses your name.

7. Are you sending it to the right person? Double-check that email address. Make sure you are sending this message to the proper receiver.

Beware of the "Reply All" button on emails. There are few occasions that warrant the use of this option—use it wisely. Avoid clogging up everyone's inbox with unnecessary information.

Professional emails should follow the following guidelines:

- Emails should be short and get to the point immediately.

- You should understand your audience. Is this someone familiar or someone you don't know? Is this a superior or a colleague? These things will determine the tone of your email.

- State your purpose concisely and if background is needed, please give it.

- Do not assume that your readers have you at the top of their mind (unless, of course, you have been having an ongoing and very recent conversation). Provide all information needed to understand your point before you get to your point.

- No chattiness such as "how are you?" or other emptiness. Get to your point. Your ideas should be substantial and specific, so please provide all the information that your reader needs to know in order to follow your thought.

- If your email is simply to provide information, then make sure your reader understands why this information is relevant.

- Be polite and sincere.

EMAIL EXERCISE 13.4A

Send an appropriate email to your instructor.

13.5 Public Writing

A. Social Media

Writing, reading, and responding to social media are activities most students engage in every day. In fact, Michelle Klein, Head of Marketing for North America at Facebook, shared at a social media conference that the average millennial will check his or her phone 150+ times per day. Writing for social media encompasses most of the same rules as most public writing. Here are three key concepts to follow when writing for social media:

1. Accuracy

Be accurate when writing, posting, or sharing social media. Be skeptical about what you read and how you respond online. If the post reads "Golden Eagle Snatches Kid," be sure to check the sources or accuracy before sharing or responding.

2. Transparency

Be transparent when writing, posting, or sharing social media. Identify your sources. Provide your readers with attribution for sources.

> Don't simply write:
> Check this out. . . a Golden Eagle snatched a kid.
> Instead, provide attribution:
> According to a YouTube video uploaded by MrNuclearCat, a Golden Eagle tried to snatch a baby in Montreal.

3. Honesty

Be honest online. Remember, there is no privacy on the web. Don't believe it? Type your name in to WaybackMachine (web.archive.org) and see how many pages you find. What you post, share, and respond to on the web represents your social media credibility. Be careful to protect your online reputation.

So, it might take you a few seconds longer to be accurate, transparent, and honest with your social media posts, but in the end, it will improve your credibility and writing. If you apply these to the "Check this out. . . a Golden Eagle snatched a kid" post, you will be much more credible:

> According to a YouTube video uploaded by MrNuclearCat, a Golden Eagle tried to snatch a baby in Montreal. However, NPR revealed the video was a hoax by three college students in a 3D animation and design class.

B. Blogs

Blogs encompass all genres of writing. Who wrote the first blog is up for debate, but weblogs started populating the internet in the 1990s. In the 2000s, blogs exploded in popularity. According to Technorati's State of the Blogosphere report (2010), by the end of the decade, there were 8 million blogs online. Today, Technorati estimates there are nearly 4 million blogs published each day. Ready to add to that number? If so, here are some key concepts to keep in mind:

1. Organization

Keep your blog organized. Most blogs are organized by pages and posts. Both pages and posts can be categorized by topics. Some blogging platforms provide themes to help keep your writing structured. WordPress is the largest blogging platform in the world and is free to set up and use. You can also pick a WordPress theme to keep your pages and posts organized.

2. Focus

Find a niche you like. Most blogs focus on a specific genre or topic. For example, Mugglenet is widely known as the "World's #1 Harry Potter Site." Mugglenet has expanded to include podcasts, videos, and an annual conference, MuggleNet Live!

3. Relevancy

Blog pages and posts should have a relationship. Readers expect to read *Harry Potter*-related posts on Mugglenet. Blog titles, content, and links should have a consistent focus, content, and message. For example, on the Mugglenet *Fantastic Beasts* pages, readers can find posts on the films, books, and music.

Public Writing Exercise 13.5A

Make a post on social media or a blog that follows these guidelines. The website 100words.com is free and easy to use. Try it!

Public Writing Exercise 13.5B

Find a post on social media or a blog and analyze how well it follows these guidelines.

13.6 JOURNALS

Journals can range from the classic "Dear Diary" outpourings to structured observations of life. The goal of any journal, public or private, organized or random, is to record your thoughts. Focus on getting the words down on paper (or on the screen) instead of worrying about grammar and formatting. Those things can come later. The goal of a journal is to capture the thoughts and ideas as they come to you. Think of your journal as a judgment-free zone, a place where you can write down your innermost thoughts and save them for later.

Note: If you have a journal assignment for a class, do keep in mind that your instructor will likely read your journal. Don't write down ideas that you do not want your instructor to know!

JOURNAL EXERCISE 13.6A

Keep a private journal for one week, writing every day about something—anything. The goal is to keep the words flowing.

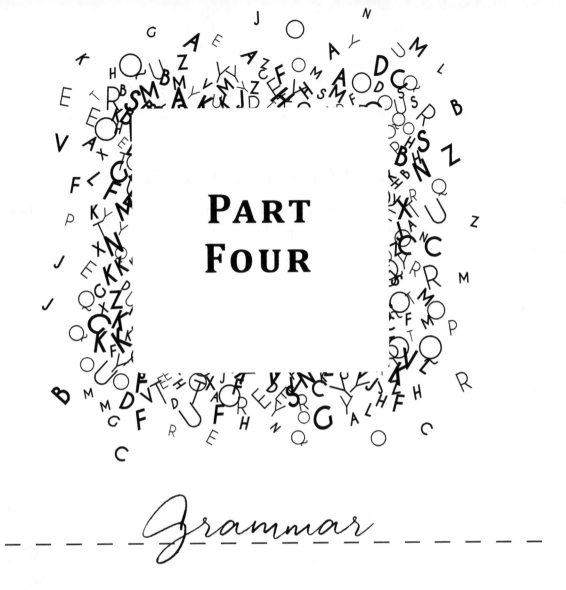

PART FOUR

Grammar

- -

OVERVIEW

A few things to know before beginning:

- Grammar isn't always set in stone. People still argue about the details.

- That said, there are some rules that everyone agrees on. In fact, the definition of the word grammar is the usage of a language as agreed upon by the educated users of that language.

A note on the structure of this section:

- Part Four begins with an overview of the parts of speech.

- This part continues with a look at sentence structure.

- The next part contains all of the punctuation rules.

- After that, this section covers the common errors.

- Finally, this section ends with a discussion of style and reference.

Chapter 14

PARTS OF SPEECH

Words can be grouped into categories that are useful when discussing language. These categories are called parts of speech, and they include the following:

- Nouns
- Verbs
- Adjectives
- Adverbs
- Pronouns
- Prepositions
- Conjunctions
- Interjections

14.1 Nouns

Nouns can be a person, place, thing, or idea. They can be broken down into the following categories:

COMMON NOUNS

- Common nouns are usually things that are not capitalized: foot, chair, tree, mug, box; they can be singular or plural.

PROPER NOUNS

- Proper nouns identify a specific person, place, or thing that begin with a capital letter: Mr. Jones, Composition I, Spring Break, Hillsborough Community College; each proper noun is singular.

COUNT NOUNS

- Count nouns are words that can be counted: glasses, shirts, steps; they can be singular or plural, depending on the context.

NON-COUNT NOUNS

- Non-count nouns are words that identify something that cannot be counted: love, milk, anger, sugar; non-count nouns are usually singular.

COLLECTIVE NOUNS

- Collective nouns are words used to represent a group of people, animals, or things: army, family, team; they can be either singular or plural, depending on the context.

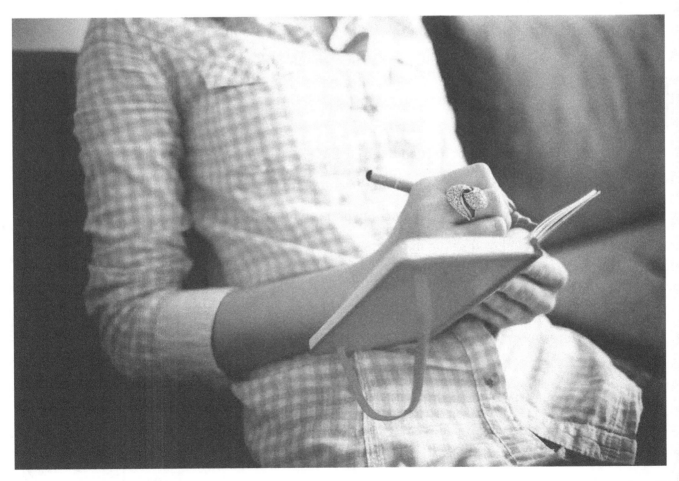

EXERCISES

NOUNS EXERCISE 14.1A

Find the nouns in the following sentences. Identify what type of noun it is: common, proper, count, or non-count.

1. Florence Nightingale tended many sick people.

2. Ibu greeted his guests with a bow.

3. The bulletin warned that heavy rains would follow.

4. They called her Magnanimous Tillie, or "Mag" for short.

5. When in doubt, stamp and shout.

6. The kindly old mayor helped the candidate to his seat.

7. Frantic Jacob hurtled sideways into the crowded elevator.

8. Having been left in the sun too long, the milk turned sour.

9. Racing frantically down the aisle, the tardy groom upset more than chairs.

10. Creepy crawlers commonly dominate Jane's troublesome dreams.

NOUNS EXERCISE 14.1B

Find the nouns in the following sentences. Identify what type of noun it is: common, proper, count, or non-count.

1. The house was a mess and needed to be cleaned.

2. Richard retrieved the newspaper from the end of his driveway each morning.

3. Mr. Thomas enjoyed reading the morning paper while drinking a cup of coffee.

4. Samson the cat enjoyed laying in the sun.

5. The water in the pool was gloriously warm.

6. The hot sun beat down on the beachgoers as they swam in the waves.

7. The surfers were riding the waves as they crashed into the shore.

8. There was not a shark in sight when the beach was filled with people.

9. Sarah thought she saw a fin out in the waves, but it was just another surfer sitting on his board.

10. Alligators infest the Everglades.

14.2 VERBS

Verbs show action. They come in many shapes and size, but they can be divided into type and then identified by tense and mood.

A. VERB TYPES

Verbs come in four types:

- Linking Verbs (LV)
- Transitive Verbs (TV)
- Intransitive Verbs (ITV)
- Modal Verbs (MV)

1. LINKING VERBS

Linking verbs literally link the subject to the subject complement, a word or words that usually describe or rename the subject. Subject complements can be an adjective or a noun. The most popular linking verb is **to be (is, am, are, were, was),** but there are other linking verbs as well, such as **seems, tastes,** and **smells.**

> The picture **was** lovely.

"Was" is a linking verb. "Lovely" is a subject complement, an adjective which tells the reader more about the subject, "picture."

> Sara **is** the leader.

"Is" is a linking verb. "Leader" is a subject complement, a noun that renames the subject, "Sara."

2. TRANSITIVE VERBS

Transitive verbs allow the subject to "go across" the sentence and affect the object or object complement. Direct objects directly receive the action of the verb. Object complements describe the direct object. (Trans means across.)

> Sally **held** the book.

"Held" is a transitive verb. What is being held? The book. The book is the direct object.

> Becky **called** her friend.

"Called" is a transitive verb. Who or what is being called? Her friend. Her friend is the direct object.

Now, let's add some fun to it:

> Kathy **considered** the sale successful.

"Considered" is a transitive verb. Considered what? The sale. The sale is the direct object. But it doesn't end there! What was the sale considered? Successful. Successful is the object complement, telling the reader more information about the direct object (it's complementing the object!).

Note: Sentences with transitive verbs may also have indirect objects. Indirect objects indirectly receive the action of the verb.

> Anna **gave** me the book.

"Gave" is the transitive verb. What was given? The book. The book is the direct object. But what is "me"? "Me" is indirectly receiving the action here—since ultimately that's where the book ends up. "Me" is the indirect object.

3. INTRANSITIVE VERBS

Intransitive verbs take no objects or complements. The verb alone conveys the intended meaning.

> The girl <u>laughed</u>.

"Laughed" is the intransitive verb. The girl isn't laughing anything (compared to her saying something or seeing something or singing something), so there is nothing to cross over to. The sentence is over. There is no need for anything else.

> The couple <u>smiled</u>.

"Smiled" is the intransitive verb. The couple doesn't smile anything (compared to them saying something or holding something or touching something).

VERBS IN ACTION

1. The sunset **is** beautiful.

> Is =linking verb.
> Beautiful = subj. complement (adj).

2. The reorganization of Exxon **may be** a disaster.

> May be= linking verb.
> Disaster = subj. complement (noun).

3. The cat *ate* the chicken stew.

> Ate = transitive verb.
> Stew = direct object (DO)

4. Grandma *will knit* you a warm scarf.

> Will knit = transitive verb.
> You = (Indirect Object) IO.
> Scarf = DO.

5. At Christmas, uncle *bought* me a model train.

> Bought = TV.
> Me = IO.
> Train = DO.

6. The painter *made* Joan's painting beautiful.

> Painting = DO.
> Beautiful = Object Complement (OC).

7. Capt. Jim Smith *named* his boat Queen of Joy.

> Boat = DO.
> Queen of Joy = OC.

8. The bird <u>flew</u>.

> Flew = intransitive verb. Nothing receives the action.

9. Stuff <u>happens</u>. The universe <u>exists</u>.

> Happens and exists are both intransitive.
> No object.
> Note: some verbs can be either transitive or intransitive, such as to fly or to eat.

10. Uncle Ben *flew* his plane to Chicago.

> Flew = transitive verb.
> Plane = DO.
> Chicago = OP (object of preposition).

11. Are you hungry? I have <u>eaten</u> already.

> Eat = intransitive verb.
> In example 3 above, eat (past tense ate) is transitive.

4. MODAL VERBS

The ten (10) modal Verbs are can, could, may, might, must, shall, should, will, would, and ought to.

- Modals show the mode of an action
- Modals show certainty, necessity, contingency, or possibility
- Modals do not change form to indicate tense.

Modals are also called Modal Auxiliary Verbs (OED) or Modal Helping Verbs.

Note: **Shall** is becoming less used in British and American English, being replaced by the more common **will**. **Ought to** is not always regarded as a modal verb. Unlike the other modals, the verb following **ought to** does take the infinitive with to, not the "bare infinitive" (base form without to) of the other modals.

> So, we must go / we might go / we will go, but we ought to go.

Modals and the following verbs do not change form to indicate tense.

> The art museum **will** launch its fundraising campaign next month.

Modal *will* followed by base form of launch—not launches (present tense).

> The translator **could** speak many languages...

Modal *could* followed by base form of speak—not spoke (past tense).

> The base form of the verb (launch or speak) is the infinitive without the "to."

a. Can
Possibility

> Anyone can make a mistake.

General ability (present tense)

> Jim can play soccer.

Informal requests/permission

> Can you tell me where I can find Maria?

More on Can from the *OED*

- To know how (to do anything); to have learned, to be intellectually able. (***OED*** II.3)
- To be able; to have the power, ability or capacity. (Said of physical as well as mental, and of natural as well as acquired ability; = Latin ***posse***, French ***pouvoir***.) (***OED*** 3.a.)

Can was originally (1000 AD) an independent verb meaning *to know.* Compare the Scottish *to ken* (to know) or the noun *cunning* (ability, skill, cleverness, knowledge).

b. Could (past tense of can)
Possibility

> His mood could change at any time.

General ability (past tense)

> When he was three, he could read.

Polite requests/permission

> Could I borrow your pen?

c. May
Formal requests/permission

> May I see the report?

Possibility

> I may try to finish tonight.

Expressing a wish

> May he find peace at the end.

d. Might (past tense of may)
Possibility

> We might arrive by 7:00 pm.

e. Must (past tense of mote, an obsolete verb)
Necessity (present or future)

> You must go to the Final Exam.

Strong probability

> Amy must be nervous (= she probably is).

Near certainty (present or past)

> I must have left my wallet at home
> (= it seems almost certain…)

f. Shall
Simple future tense (in 1st person).

> I shall go back to England in 2018, I hope.

Determination (in 2nd and 3rd person)

> They shall pay for this insult, I promise you.

Expressing the speaker's determination to bring about

> "You shall not pass," proclaimed Gandalf.

(or, with negative, to prevent) some action, event, or state of things in the future" (***OED***).

> Congress shall make no law…

Also legal uses

> The owner shall be responsible for the roof.

g. Should (past tense of Shall)
Suggestions or advice

> While here, you should see the Dali Museum.

Obligations or duties

> Students should pay tuition fees by the 1st.

Expectations

> The textbooks should arrive by next Monday.

More on Shall

The original meanings of **shall** in Old English were:

- To owe money (975 AD).
- To owe allegiance (1325 AD).

But there are many other meanings and uses for this ancient and complex verb **shall**.
Note that the ***OED*** has forty-nine (49) pages on **shall**.

h. Will
Certainty

> If we don't leave now, we will be late.

Simple Future (2nd and 3rd)

> By now, she will be in France

Fut + Determination (1st)

> Whatever happens, I will make it to the summit.

Requests

> Will you help me study for the psychology exam?

Promises and offers

> Jonah will arrange the carpool for us.

Habitual actions (OED)

> "Men, by their nature, are prone to fight;
> they will fight for any cause, or none" (Ruskin, 1865).

Shall / Will
The original usage, see the *OED*. But getting rarer now, both in American and British English.

SIMPLE FUTURE TENSE	FUTURE + DETERMINATION, OBLIGATION, OR PURPOSE
Shall in 1st , but **Will** in 2nd and 3rd	**Will** in 1st person, but **Shall** in 2nd and 3rd person
I shall go	I will go
You will go	You shall go
She/he/it will go	She/he/it shall go
We shall go	We will go
You (pl.) will go	You (pl.) shall go
They will go	They shall go

i. Would (past tense of will)
Polite Requests

> I would appreciate a cup of coffee.

Habitual or repeated actions (past tense)

> Whenever I needed some good advice on financial matters, I would call Michael, my banker brother.

In Conditionals

> "That which we call a Rose, By any other name would smell as sweet" [Shakespeare, *Romeo and Juliet*].

j. Ought to (originally, the past tense of owe)
Obligation /duty (present)

> You ought to ask her forgiveness.

Obligation /duty (past) [with have + participle]

> "We have left undone those things which we ought to have done" (*Book of Common Prayer*).

Possibility or probability

> You ought to be able to see the sea from the summit.

Suggestions or advice

> Friends advised me that I ought to see a doctor. Note: Unlike other modals, **ought to** takes the infinitive with **to** with following verb.

MODALS—A DEEP STRATA OF OUR LANGUAGE
The earliest use of each modal (according to the *OED*)

1. *Can*	1000 AD		6. *Shall*	831 AD
2. *Could*	893 AD		7. *Should*	888 AD
3. *May*	1200 AD		8. *Will*	825 AD
4. *Might*	1200 AD		9. *Would*	825 AD
5. *Must*	800 AD		10. *Ought to*	800 AD

Sources and Further Reading on Modals

Hacker, Diana and Nancy Sommers. *Rules for Writers.* 7th Ed, Bedford/St. Martin's, 2012.

MEU Burchfield, R. W. *The New Fowlers Modern English Usage.* Rev. Ed, Clarendon, 1998.

OED Oxford English Dictionary. Online ed, Oxford, 2014, 7 Sept 2014.

Verb Types Exercise 14.2A

Find the verbs in the following sentences. Identify the type of verb: linking, transitive, intransitive, or modal.

1. Harry handed his hat to the lady at the checkout register.

2. The child on the swing in the playground laughed out loud with delight.

3. The children were in the sandbox.

4. I should go to the party tonight, but I don't want to go.

5. I love the food at Guadalajara Restaurant.

6. Sara wanted to visit Disneyland in California.

7. George answered the riddle correctly and won a prize.

8. Gollum could not answer the riddle correctly and lost the contest.

9. Bilbo went home with a magic ring.

10. He should have left the magic ring in the cave.

Verb Types Exercise 14.2B

Find the verbs in the following sentences. Identify the type of verb: linking, transitive, intransitive, or modal.

1. The students studied hard for the test.

2. The teacher planned a difficult midterm.

3. Final exams can be stressful for teachers and students.

4. John shared his class notes with Brenda.

5. You should spend more time on your math homework this semester.

6. The driver cruised the highway in his convertible with the top down.

7. Samson definitely missed his hair after the haircut.

8. You are my best friend.

9. We could be heroes just for one day.

10. Why are you here today?

B. VERB TENSE

The English verb brings <u>action</u> or <u>state of being</u> to the sentence. The verb also brings energy and passion, but also:

- A sense of **time or tense** (*present, past or future tense*) to the sentence, and also

- The **kind of action** being described (*simple, perfect,* or *progressive*).

So, tense and time are crucial to our narrative writing and storytelling, indeed to all of our use of language. We need, therefore, to understand with confidence the complexity and variety of the English verb system.

There are three main verb tenses:

- Past: It already happened

- Present: It is happening now

- Future: It will happen later

These tenses have three modes:

- Simple

- Perfect

- Progressive

A NOTE ON VERB FORMS

Verb forms are NOT tenses. They are different forms (spellings) of verbs that can be combined with various helping verbs to create the twelve verb tenses in English. Following are the four verb forms:

- **The infinitive** (PRESENT tense plus "to," a.k.a. the "plain form") – to walk, to swim, to go, to run

- **The past tense** – walked, swam, went, ran

- **The present participle** (the "-ing" form) – (to be/am/is/are/was/ were) walking, (am...) swimming, (am...) going, (am...) running

- **The past participle** – (have/has/had) walked, (have/has/had) swum, (have/has/had) gone, (have/has/had) run

Things can happen at any one time – **past, present,** or **future** – so we have a tense for each of those. These are called the simple tenses, and you are probably familiar with those. However, things can also begin at one time and continue to a certain point or forever. This means that we need more tenses, and that is where HELPING VERBS and VERB FORMS come into play. By using helping verbs in different tenses along with various verb forms, we can create nine tenses in addition to the three simple tenses.

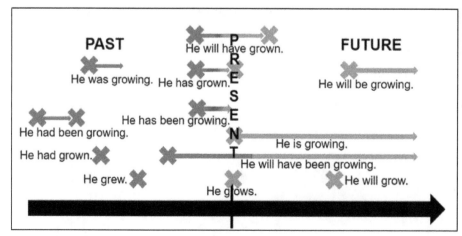

1. Simple Tenses

Simple tenses are used for actions that happen at only one time. They use no helping verb other than "will" or "shall" in simple future. They add "s" for simple present tense when the subject is third-person singular ("he," "she," "it," or any word that could be referred to with "he," "she," or "it," like "Jerry," "Dr. Smith," or "the dog").

- **Simple past:**
  - Nick walked while they swam.
  - Ana went more quickly because she ran.

- **Simple present:**
  - Nick walks while they swim.
  - Ana goes more quickly because she runs.

- **Simple future:**
  - Nick will walk while they will swim.
  - Ana will go more quickly because she will run.

SIMPLE TENSES CHART

For general facts, states of being, and habitual actions

SIMPLE PRESENT	BASE FORM OR S-FORM
General facts	Students often **study**.
States of being	Water **becomes** steam at 100 Celsius.
Habitual actions	We **donate** to a different charity each year.
Scheduled future events	The train **arrives** tomorrow at 6:30 pm.
SIMPLE PAST	**BASE FORM + -ED OR –D OR IRREGULAR FORMS**
Completed actions at a specific time in the past	She **drove** to Montana three years ago.
Facts or states of being in the past	When I **was** young, I **walked** to school.
SIMPLE FUTURE	**WILL + BASE**
Future actions, promises, predictions	I **will exercise**.
	It **will begin** around at midnight.
SPECIAL FUTURE USES	**WILL AND SHALL + BASE**
Simple future (1st person) may use	I **shall go** to the movies this Friday. [more Brit-English]
Future + determination (**shall** in 2nd and 3rd)	"You **shall** not **pass**," cried Gandalf (Tolkien, *LOTR*).
Future + determination (**will** in 1st person)	No matter what, I **will complete** my mission.
Shall in legal uses and prohibitions (2nd and 3rd)	"Congress **shall make** no law abridging ..."

2. Perfect Tenses

Perfect tenses are used for actions that are completed or that started in the past before something else that happened in the past. They use the past participle form of the main verb (which sometimes ends in "d," "n," or "t") and a form of "to have" as a helping verb ("had," "have," "has," "will have," or "shall have").

- **Past perfect:**
  - Nick had walked while they had swum.
  - Ana had gone more quickly because she had run.
- **Present perfect:**
  - Nick has walked while they have swum.
  - Ana has gone more quickly because she has run.
- **Future perfect:**
  - Nick will have walked while they will have swum.
  - Ana will have gone more quickly because she will have run.

Perfect Tenses Chart

For actions that happened or will happen **before** another time

Present Perfect	Has, Have + Past Participle
Repetitive or constant actions that began in the past and continue to the present	I **have loved** cats since I was a child.
	Alicia **has worked** there for ten years.
Actions that happened at an unknown or an unspecified past time	Steven **has visited** Wales three times.
Past Perfect	**Had + Past Participle**
Actions that began or occurred before another time in the past	She **had** just **crossed** the street when the runaway car crashed into the building.
Future Perfect	**Will + Have + Past Participle**
Actions that began or occurred before another time in the future	By July 2018, I **will have lived** in the USA another time in the future for thirty-five years.

3. PROGRESSIVE TENSES

Progressive tenses are used for actions that happen over a period of time. They use the present participle form of the main verb (the "ing" form) and a form of "to be" as a helping verb ("was," "were," "am," "is," "are," "will be," or "shall be").

- **Past progressive:**
  - ◦ Nick was walking while they were swimming.
  - ◦ Ana was going more quickly because she was running.

- **Present progressive:**
  - ◦ Nick is walking while they are swimming.
  - ◦ Ana is going more quickly because she is running.

- **Future progressive:**
  - ◦ Nick will be walking while they will be swimming.
  - ◦ Ana will be going more quickly because she will be running.

PROGRESSIVE TENSES CHART

For continuing actions happening now, or that happened in the past, or that happened in the past **before** another time

PRESENT PROGRESSIVE	AM, IS, ARE + PRESENT PARTICIPLE
Actions in progress at the present time, continuing indefinitely	The students **are taking** an exam in room 105.
	The valet **is parking** the car.
Future actions (with **leave, go, come**)	I **am leaving** tomorrow morning.
PAST PROGRESSIVE	**WAS, WERE + PRESENT PARTICIPLE**
Actions in progress at a specific past time	They **were swimming** when the storm hit.
Plans that did not happen (**were going**…)	We **were going** to drive, but the car broke down.
PRESENT PERFECT PROGRESSIVE	**HAS, HAVE + BEEN + PRESENT PARTICIPLE**
Continuous actions that began in the past and continue to the present	Yolanda **has been trying** to get a job in Boston for five years.
PAST PERFECT PROGRESSIVE	**HAD + BEEN + PRESENT PARTICIPLE**
Actions that began and continued in the past until another past action	By the time I moved to Georgia in 2003, I **had been supporting** myself for five years.

4. PERFECT PROGRESSIVE TENSES

Perfect progressive tenses are used for continuing actions that happen before another action happens. They use the present participle form of the main verb (the "ing" form) and a form of "to have" <u>and</u> a form of "to be" as helping verbs ("had been," "have been," "has been," "will have been," or "shall have been").

- **Past progressive:**
  - ◦ Nick had been walking while they had been swimming.
  - ◦ Ana had been going more quickly because she had been running.

- **Present progressive:**
  - ◦ Nick has been walking while they have been swimming.
  - ◦ Ana has been going more quickly because she has been running.

- **Future progressive:**
  - ◦ Nick will have been walking while they will have been swimming.
  - ◦ Ana will have been going more quickly because she will have been running.

The Five (5) Basic Verb Forms

VERB FORM	REGULAR VERB	IRREGULAR VERB	IRREGULAR VERB
	To Help	**To Give**	**To Be**
Base form	Help	Give	Be
Simple Past Tense	Helped	Gave	was, were
Past Participle	Helped	Given	Been
Present Participle	Helping	Giving	Being
s-form she/he/it	Helps	Gives	Is

For information about Verb Tense Shifts, see Ch 17.1 Verb Errors.

VERB TENSE EXERCISE 14.2C

Identify the verb tense of the following verbs.

1. Has been walking
2. Will have visited
3. Helps
4. Helped
5. Has helped

VERB FORM EXERCISE 14.2D

Identify the verb form of the irregular verbs below.

1. Was
2. Been
3. Being
4. Is
5. Am

C. Verb Mood

Hang in there—we're almost finished with verbs!

Verbs also come in three different moods. Verb mood tells you what information and in what manner the verb is conveying the action.

1. Indicative Mood

The indicative or declarative mood is a clear statement. It can appear in any tense.

Past: I disliked vinegar.

Past Perfect: I had disliked vinegar.

Present: I dislike vinegar.

Present Perfect: I have disliked vinegar.

Future: I will dislike vinegar.

Future Perfect: By the time I reach thirty, I will have disliked vinegar for twenty-eight years.

2. Imperative Mood

The imperative mood gives a command or order. It usually appears in the present tense.

Take out the garbage, please.

Do your homework now.

3. Subjunctive Mood

The subjunctive mood expresses information that is a wish, a doubt, or an idea contrary to fact.

If I were a rich man, I would have many cars.

If you were my dream partner, I would marry you this moment.

Verb Mood Exercise 14.2E

Identify the verb mood in the following sentences.

1. John likes to talk walks in the evening.

2. Lucy, take out the garbage!

3. If you were in charge, this place would be much better.

4. Listen to me!

5. The movie begins promptly at noon.

14.3 ADJECTIVES

Adjectives are words that describe nouns or pronouns. They tell which one, what kind, or how many.

> The thick, heavy, boring textbook

> An oversized, multicolored, plastic, golf umbrella

Adjectives in English generally follow a specific order:

Opinion	lovely, wonderful, overbearing, unwelcome
Size	big, small, tiny
Physical quality	rough, smooth, rugged, thin
Shape	round, triangular, square, cylindrical
Age	young, old, elderly, childlike
Color	blue, orange, green
Origin	British, Chinese, Italian
Material	metal, plastic, aluminum
Type	four-sided, refillable, disposable
Purpose	golfing, cleaning, walking

So, for example, you might describe a tiny, green Chinese metal candle holder (but not a Chinese, metal, tiny, green candle holder).

> My grandmother makes wonderful Italian meals.

> Joey drank from a cylindrical, blue, refillable water bottle.

> A rocker all his life, he enjoyed listening to rough British metal bands at full volume.

> The teacher brought round plastic plates to the class picnic.

You may have noticed that some of the examples above use commas between adjectives, and some don't. The coordinate adjective comma rule explains why. Adjectives are coordinate if they are equally important in the sentence, and coordinate adjectives get commas between them.

Here are two tests:

- Can you flip the words and have the sentence mean the same thing? If so, they're probably coordinate, so use a comma.

- Can you insert the word "and" between the two words and still mean the same thing? They're coordinate and need a comma.

For instance, think of a red brick house. This is a specific material. If you flip those words to describe a brick red house, that's a color. So these words aren't coordinate and do not need a comma.

Now, consider the example above about Joey's water bottle. It's **blue** and **refillable**, so those are coordinate, but it's not a **water refillable** bottle (that sounds weird, right?), so those aren't coordinate.

EXERCISES

ADJECTIVES EXERCISE 14.3A
Identify the adjectives.

1. The soda can had a red logo on the side.

2. The red-haired student was always late to English class.

3. Sam laid down on the brown leather sofa for a nap.

4. The new keyboard on the laptop computer was giving her some difficulty while typing her essay.

5. The gorgeous models paraded down the runway wearing the best of Italian fashion design.

ADJECTIVES EXERCISE 14.3B
Check the order of the adjectives in the following sentences. Revise any that do not follow the guidelines.

1. I am staring at a U-shaped, metal, blue-painted, ancient, rough screwdriver.

2. I was supposed to use the rough, ancient screwdriver to screw in these unusual, tiny, round, plastic fasteners.

3. I peered at the confusing, frustrating, vague instructions on the IKEA pamphlet.

4. Deciding that I am a strong, independent, modern woman of the times, I forge ahead, tightening round, plastic, rough fasteners into mismatched, four-sided holes.

5. After five more minutes, I decided to call on the burly, old, Italian painter next door for some help.

14.4 ADVERBS

Adverbs are words that describe verbs. They can also describe adjectives, other adverbs, or entire groups of words. They will tell you:

- How?
  - Josh skipped **happily** down the hallway.
  - Henry trotted **languidly** into the field.

- Where?
  - The cereal is right **there** in the closet.
  - The form is **here** on your desk.

- When?
  - I had a midterm in class **today**.
  - The paper was due **yesterday**.

- In what manner?
  - Billy **hurriedly** washed the dishes.

When identifying adverbs that modify verbs, you can use the simple questions above as a guide. Also, consider the many other functions of adverbs:

- Adverbs can describe adjectives.

- That movie was **really** scary. Scary is an adjective. How scary? Really scary. Really is an adverb modifying an adjective.

- Adverbs can describe other adverbs.

- The Olympic athlete ran **very fast**. Fast is an adverb. How fast? Very fast. Very is an adverb modifying an adverb.

- Adverbs can describe other groups of words or entire sentences.

- **Generally**, Bob is a great employee. Generally is an adverb. How is Bob a great employee? Generally.

Both adjectives and adverbs have three levels of comparison that affects their usage:

- Base form
  - I am tall.
  - The old man walks slowly.

- Comparative form—used when two things are being compared.
  - I am taller (than she is).
  - The old man walks more slowly (than she does).

- Superlative form—used when three or more things are being compared.
  - I am the tallest (member of my three-person family).
  - The old man walks the slowest (out of three walkers).

A. Conjunctive Adverbs

These are a special class of adverbs often used in transitions to connect ideas. If they appear in the middle of two independent clauses, they get a semicolon before and a comma after:

> My neighbor John and I shared the fence along the property line; **hence**, when the time came to replace it, we shared the cost of the installation.

accordingly	consequently	hence	instead	otherwise	undoubtedly
additionally	contrarily	henceforth	likewise	rather	yet
also	conversely	however	meanwhile	similarly	
anyway	elsewhere	in addition	moreover	still	
again	equally	in comparison	namely	subsequently	
almost	eventually	in contrast	nevertheless	that is	
as a result	finally	incidentally	next	then	
besides	for example	in fact	nonetheless	thereafter	
certainly	further	in particular	now	therefore	
comparatively	furthermore	indeed	of course	thus	

B. Adjectives and Adverbs

Let's look at the following sentence as an example of how *adjectives* and **adverbs** can lend more description to a sentence.

> I **usually** understand *Dr. Romano's* lectures **well**, but his case of laryngitis made his presentation **barely** *audible* **today**.

The adverbs usually and well give more information about how the writer understands the lectures. The presentation is already described with an adjective -- audible -- but the adverb barely is important here because it shows in what manner the lecture was performed. The sentence also uses the adverb today to show when the action takes place.

EXERCISES

ADVERBS EXERCISE 14.4A
Identify the adverbs in the following sentences.

1. John stalked angrily to his car last night.

2. He was very unhappy that Dana had decided to end their relationship.

3. Only yesterday, he had been thinking about marriage proposals.

4. Clearly, he was more invested in the relationship than she was.

5. Eventually, John will get over Dana, but not any time soon.

ADVERBS EXERCISE 14.4B
Revise the following sentences for errors in usage.

1. My sister is taller than her.

2. I am the tallest between my sister and me.

3. Davison is the fastest runner in the entire class of students.

4. Marta wonders who the happier person at HCC is.

5. John thought he was in the better relationship in the world.

ADJECTIVES AND ADVERBS EXERCISE 14.4C
Circle the adjectives and underline the adverbs in the following sentences.

1. Though he is usually considered the calmer of the two executives, it was Jared -- not Ralph -- who brazenly began the meeting today with a stinging criticism of the original contract.

2. Raizel defiantly broke her agreement with the greedy company who published her most recent memoir.

3. An unparalleled controversy arose when her devoted readership learned the book was actually written by her recluse sister, Ari.

4. I truly appreciate Professor Rivera's expertise in the often complex but always rewarding field of Botany.

5. Of all the science instruction I've had, Professor Rivera's concise explanations are the simplest and yet most insightful.

14.5 Prepositions

Prepositions bring space-time into our sentences. They give context and position.

- Prepositions indicate the context or position of nouns or pronouns in a sentence. More importantly, maybe, they tell us where and when the main action of the verb occurs.

- Prepositions indicate that context in terms of space, time, or relationship.

- The preposition comes before *nouns* or *pronouns* – which are called the objects of the prepositions. There may be determiners like the/an/a or adjectives in between.

Consider these examples:

1. **In** the *morning*, **before** *breakfast*, Mary Jane ran.

     time   time

2. She stood **on** the <u>rock</u>, **in** the <u>shadow</u> **of** the <u>cliff</u>.

           space   space   relationship

3. **During** <u>lunch</u>, **in** the <u>lunchroom</u>, we met.

     time   space

4. **Before** <u>graduation</u>, **in** <u>August</u>, I shall do it.

     time   time

5. James was a member **of** <u>several groups</u> **in** <u>college</u>.

             relationship   relationship

The whole phrase—beginning with the preposition and ending with the noun (or pronoun)—is called a prepositional phrase. These phrases function either as adjectives or as adverbs. Understanding them will add greatly to your writing style and precision.

Remember that nothing in a prepositional phrase can ever be the subject of the sentence. So, identify the prepositional phrases, but then look for the subject elsewhere. In the following sentences, the subject is easier to see because the prepositional phrases have been struck out.

1. Each of the children (relationship) from various schools (space) around the country (space) gathered to march to City Hall (space) today.

2. After Conor's testimony (time) in the courtroom (space), Blake decided to confess.

3. A team member of the Aeronautics Club (relationship) on the East campus (space) of the university (relationship) will interview new candidates.

The noun or pronoun is the object of the preposition; therefore, it is in the objective case.

1. **Under** the <u>elm trees</u> **beyond** the <u>tall reeds</u>, **on** the <u>north side</u>, you should find a great fishing spot.

2. **At** the <u>edge</u> **of** the <u>old swamp</u>, **near** the <u>oil derrick</u>, **beyond** the <u>abandoned barge</u>, we found his body.

3. The tabby cat sat **on** <u>him</u> [not he] in preference to sitting **on** the <u>hard floor</u>.

4. We walked very slowly **toward** <u>her</u> [not she], but she nervously backed away **from** <u>us</u> [not we].

COMMON PREPOSITIONS

about	before	except	instead of	on behalf of	throughout
above	behind	for	into	on top of	toward(s)
according to	below	from	like	out of	under
across	beneath	in	near	outside	underneath
after	beside	in addition to	next	outside of	until
against	between	in case of	next to	over	up
along	by	in front of	of	past	upon
among	by way of	in place of	off	since	with
around	down	in regard to	on	than	within
at	down to	in spite of	onto	to	without
because of	during	inside	on account of	through	

EXERCISES

PREPOSITIONS EXERCISE 14.5A
Identify the prepositions in the following sentences.

1. I put the lotion on my skin.

2. The basket is lowered into the pit.

3. On the table, next to the napkin holder, is my purse.

4. Can you open the second door on the left when you go inside?

5. I was standing next to the lead singer down by the backstage entrance.

PREPOSITIONS EXERCISE 14.5B
Identify the prepositional phrases in the following sentences.

1. Can you grab the stack of books on the table in the front room for me?

2. Jane handed Benjamin a pile of papers along with several large textbooks.

3. The phone on the desk was ringing for hours.

4. Her email inbox was filled with frantic messages from desperate students.

5. The soda can in the refrigerator belonged to her roommate.

PREPOSITIONS EXERCISE 14.5C

Strike through the prepositional phrases and identify the subjects in the following sentences.

1. An investigator from the Grammar Police Department at the local university will attend today's presentation at lunch time.

2. After the twins' departure in the morning, Manny secretly played their video games.

3. One of the athletes on the team fell and sprained her ankle.

4. The accident occurred at about 6 p.m. on the off ramp of I4.

5. To avoid overwatering his begonias, the gardener uses an app for tracking the days he tends his flower beds.

14.6 PRONOUN

A pronoun is a word that takes the place of a noun or another pronoun. Pronouns come in many varieties:

- Personal Pronouns
- Possessive Pronouns
- Demonstrative Pronouns
- Relative Pronouns

- Reflexive Pronouns
- Interrogative Pronouns
- Indefinite Pronouns

A. PERSONAL PRONOUNS

Personal pronouns represent people or things. They take different forms depending on whether they are the subject of the sentence (the word doing the action) or the object of the sentence (the word receiving the action in the sentence).

USED AS SUBJECTS			USED AS OBJECTS	
Singular	Plural		Singular	Plural
I	we		me	us
you	you		you	you
he, she, it	they		him, her, it	them

Example: Kathy loves running at the park, and **she** wished **she** could stay longer.

> *She* refers to Kathy. *She* is the pronoun.

B. POSSESSIVE PRONOUNS

Possessive pronouns show ownership.

Singular	**Plural**
mine	our _____ /ours
your	your _____ /yours
his, her, its	their _____ / theirs

Example: After going to the pet store, Sam bought a cat for **his** daughter.

> *His* in this sentence is explaining that the daughter is the daughter belonging to Sam.

C. DEMONSTRATIVE PRONOUNS

Demonstrative pronouns are used to replace specific people or things that have been previously mentioned (or are understood from context).

this   that   these   those

Example: Jim pointed to the pen and asked "Can I please have **that**?"

> *That* refers to the pen.

Example: I love **these**. Do you love **those**?

> The use of *these* provides us with the knowledge that the speaker pointing to something nearby, possibly in the speaker's hands. *Those* refers to what the speaker is pointing to that is probably farther away—maybe in the hands of the other person.

D. Relative Pronouns

Relative pronouns are used after a noun to make it clear which person or thing you are talking about and to tell more about a person or thing. Relative pronouns are used to mark a relative clause.

who   whom   which   that   whose

Example: Annabelle, **who** is tall, is my best friend.

Who refers to Annabelle. The relative clause is between commas because the clause is unnecessary for the purpose of the sentence. The fact that Annabelle "is tall" does not matter to the fact that she "is my best friend."

Example: The dog that won the competition belongs to my neighbor.

Which dog belongs to my neighbor? *That* competition-winning dog. There is no comma here to offset the clause because without that information, I don't know which dog belongs to my neighbor.

E. Reflexive Pronouns

Reflexive pronouns are used when referring back to the subject of the sentence or clause. Reflexive pronouns end in - self or -selves.

myself	ourselves
yourself	yourselves
himself, herself, itself	themselves

Example: Brian cooks **himself** dinner only once a week.

,Himself refers to Brian.

Example: You two should go shopping for **yourselves**.

Yourselves refers to you two (the people who should go shopping).

F. Interrogative Pronouns

Interrogative pronouns are used when asking questions. Interrogative pronouns represent unknown things or answer questions.

who   whom   which   whose   what

Example: **What** do you want? I want cookies.

What refers to cookies.

Example: Which dress did you buy?

Which refers to the dress.

Interrogative pronouns can be distinguished from relative pronouns because they introduce a question, while relative pronouns (often the same words) are introducing a relative phrase or clause.

G. Indefinite Pronouns

Indefinite pronouns refer to people or things without saying exactly who or what they are.

anything	anybody	anyone	each
everything	everybody	everyone	either
something	somebody	someone	neither
nothing	nobody	no one	one

Example: **Nothing** at this restaurant tastes good.

Nothing refers to "all of the items" at the restaurant in a negative way.

Example: **Something** smells great in the house.

Something refers to an unknown item that is presumably a "thing" and not a "person."

EXERCISES

PRONOUNS EXERCISE 14.6A

Identify the pronouns in the following sentences.

1. When you have a cold, you should drink plenty of fluids.
2. I enjoy having a Coke with my lunch each day because it really quenches my thirst.
3. No one should work in a noisy atmosphere without earplugs.
4. The winner was congratulated every day until she retired from the sport.
5. He dialed her number, which only rang again and again.
6. If I were you, I would be more careful with those.
7. Another example of a marsupial would be a kangaroo.
8. This recipe makes the best chocolate cake ever.
9. Justin asked if I had any questions.
10. Since he already has a date, he can't go out with you.
11. Who is in charge of this debacle?

PRONOUNS EXERCISE 14.6B

Choose the correct pronoun for the blank.

1. ____ going to judge me if I want to be an Elvis impersonator? (Who, Who's, Whose, Whom)
2. ____ will join me at the SGA meeting this week? (Who, Who's, Whose, Whom)s
3. To ___ should I address my concerns? (Who, Who's, Whose, Whom)
4. This is the student ____ essay won the contest. (Who, Who's, Whose, Whom)
5. The debate team members got ___ into trouble with the university. (themselves, themselves, theirself, theirselves)
6. "The trophy is ___!" claimed the opposing team. (ours', our's, ours)
7. The Psychology club changed the time for ___meeting. (its, it's, its')
8. If you forget to attend meetings, the loss is ___. (your's, yours, yours')
9. When I attended the party, I didn't know _____ in the room. (any body, anybody, any-body)

14.7 Conjunctions

Conjunctions come in three types: coordinating, subordinating, and correlative.

A. Coordinating Conjunctions

These conjunctions can be memorized with the convenient mnemonic device:

F	For
A	And
N	Nor
B	But
O	Or
Y	Yet
S	So

These FANBOYS are used to connect ideas together, showing that each idea is equally important to the sentence. They are coordinating because they are on equal footing.

You should be prepared, **for** winter is coming.

I want peanut butter **and** jelly.

Sarah wasn't the savior, **nor** was she the one mentioned in the prophecy.

I love the outfit, **but** that hat is awful.

You're either with me **or** against me!

I know the romance is over, **yet** whenever I look at her, I see my future.

I woke up late this morning, **so** I was late to class.

Note: When you use a FANBOYS to connect two independent clauses (two complete sentences), place a comma before the FANBOYS.

I was waiting for the bus, **and** it began to rain.

B. Subordinating Conjunctions

These conjunctions cannot be memorized with a mnemonic device—there are just too many. Here are some examples:

after	even if	rather than	when
although	even though	since	whenever
as	if	so that	where
as if	if only	than	whereas
as long as	in order that	that	wherever
as though	now that	though	whether
because	once	unless	while
before	provided that	until	why

Subordinating conjunctions have two jobs in the sentence. First, they give the relationship between the two ideas (cause/effect, chronological, etc.). Second, they give importance to one idea over the other, subordinating one to the other.

> I woke up late **because** my alarm didn't go off this morning.
> **If only** I hadn't said that, we would still be together.
> **Even if** I hadn't said that, we would have broken up anyway.
> **Wherever** you are, I will be with you.

Note: If the dependent clause is before the independent clause, put a comma before the start of the independent clause: Because I overslept, I was late for school this morning.

If the independent clause is before the dependent clause, do not use a comma at all: I was late for school this morning because I overslept.

C. Correlative Conjunctions

Correlative conjunctions, like coordinating conjunctions, connect or link two grammatically equal items in a sentence. (Subordinating conjunctions, which connect a dependent or subordinate clause with an independent clause; to paraphrase Orwell, all conjunctions connect things, but things that coordinate or correlate are more equal than those that subordinate.) Correlative conjunctions establish a mutual or reciprocal relation or correspondence between two things, concepts, ideas—fixed or variable—that move in the same or a positive direction and offer a choice.

For example, in this sentence—I want either the cheesecake or the frozen hot chocolate—the grammatical subject, "I" is presented with two choices, cheesecake or hot chocolate, and correlated by the conjunction "either/or."

Correlative Conjunctions Work in Pairs

Correlative conjunctions come in pairs of words, and both terms in the correlative conjunction must be used, though they are used in different places in a sentence. They get their name from the fact that they work together (co-) and relate one sentence element to another.

Example: I didn't know *whether* you'd want to go to Disney *or* Universal, so I got tickets to both.

Example: *Both* Pete Weber and his father, Dick, were major celebrity stars in the Professional Bowling Association, and *both* have their roots in St. Louis.

Example: In ENC 1102, *not only* did I learn to enjoy prose fiction, *but* I *also* came to appreciate poetry, much to my surprise.

Example: Bowling is *as* much fun *as* playing tennis or golf and more challenging.

Example: We think Tim Tebow would *rather* be playing football *than* baseball.

This box lists all the most commonly recognized correlative conjunctions.

as/as	just as/so	if/then	no sooner/than
both/and	either/or	not only/but also	scarcely/when
from (this)/to (that)	hardly/when	neither/nor	not (this)/but (that)
rather/than	what with/and	whether (this)/or (that)	

D. Conjunctive Adverbs

accordingly	furthermore	meanwhile	similarly
also	hence	moreover	still
besides	however	nevertheless	subsequently
consequently	indeed	next	then
conversely	instead	nonetheless	therefore
finally	likewise	otherwise	thus

For more information on conjunction usage, see Ch 15.3 Coordination and Subordination.

EXERCISES

CONJUNCTIONS EXERCISE 14.7A
Connect the following sentences with a coordinating conjunction.

1. Superman is from Krypton. His nemesis is Lex Luthor from earth.
2. Thor is a member of the Avengers. Loki is not a member of the team.
3. Batman uses clever devices to fight crime. He has no special physical superpowers.
4. The Flash runs really fast. People can't even see him run by them.
5. Wonder Woman comes from another planet. She fights evil and injustice everywhere.

CONJUNCTIONS EXERCISE 14.7B
Connect the following sentences using subordinating conjunctions.

1. Megan was frantically writing her paper before class. Her laptop died just as she hit submit.
2. She was so angry. She had just lost all of her work from the last hour.
3. She promised to do it sooner next time. She wouldn't wait until the last minute.
4. She walked dejectedly into class. She didn't have her homework.
5. This was the very last time she would do her work before class. She promised herself.

CONJUNCTIONS EXERCISE 14.7C
Connect the following sentences using correlative conjunctions.

1. John is a surfer. John is also a poet and painter.
2. You can have pizza for dinner tonight. You can have tacos for dinner tonight.
3. The beach wedding had just started. Rain began to pour on the unhappy guests.
4. The elephants were trying to stay cool in the oppressive heat. The lions were hiding in the shady canyons.
5. Sheila preferred to stay in her current position. She did not want to find another job.

CONJUNCTIONS AND PREPOSITIONS EXERCISE 14.7D
Circle the conjunctions in the following sentences; underline the prepositions.

1. The newest installment in the Star Wars movie series was not only entertaining on the surface, but also brimming with mythological resonance.
2. The movie didn't make as much money as predicted on the first weekend, so some fans thought the lack of performance was due to a shoddy film.
3. In fact, the movie underperformed that first weekend because it was competing against several other blockbusters in the same genre.
4. Over time, the movie made way more money than the projected income, yet some fans still refuse to see it because they think it must not be any good or worth their time.
5. Eventually, the naysayers will see that the newest installment in the series is worth their time and money.

14.8 Interjections

Interjections are extra words that do not perform any grammatical function when they are added to a sentence. They are words like *boom, woot, hooray, wow, uh huh, hey*, etc.

Because interjections are considered to be informal, you should limit your interjections in academic writing to those that are **absolutely necessary**.

Interjections do have legitimate uses in less formal types of writing, however. Always consider your audience. Imagine if the following sentences were found in an email at work:

Hey, do you mind if I stop by your office today? I have a few questions for you.

In the above sentence, the interjection "hey" does nothing grammatically. Try removing the word and see what changes. In terms of the sentence's basic meaning, nothing gets lost.

So what does the word "hey" actually do in the above example? Is it pointless? Not exactly. The word indicates that the message is intended to be informal. The writer's intentions are not hostile. The message is, perhaps, not urgent. It assumes that a friendly relationship has already been established between the two individuals. However, be careful with these sorts of assumptions--it is rude to treat a work relationship as being more casual than it actually is.

Consider this other work message:

I heard the bad news about the failed sales campaign. Ugh. What's our next step?

What is the nonsensical word "Ugh" doing there? Is it pointless? Grammatically, yes, but emotionally, no. It shows that the writer is upset about the failure and is, perhaps, motivated to find a solution. It also, as above, assumes that a friendly relationship has already been established between writer and reader--again, be careful not to be presumptuous or rude in any other way.

Consider, also, other forms of writing. What if you were to write a fictional short story? You would most likely strive to create realistic dialogue--that is, your characters would speak the way real people speak. Because people use interjections all the time to help convey emotion, your characters probably would as well:

"Did you hear about the proposal?"
"Huh?"
"Scott and Zelda. They're getting married!"
"Oh really? Wow!"
"I know, right?"
"Yay!"
"So now we'll probably have to buy nice dresses."
"Expensive ones, too. Damn."
"Uh-huh. I know."
"Ah, well. I'm happy for them."
"Me, too!"

In the above exchange, see if you can count the number of interjections, and consider what role each one plays. What emotions are being conveyed? How does each interjection push the conversation forward?

One final example:

Yay! We have finished the Parts of Speech chapter.

REVIEW EXERCISE

Identify the part of speech of the word in bold in each sentence.

A. Noun   B. Verb   C. Pronoun   D. Adjective

E. Adverb   F. Conjunction   G. Preposition   H. Interjection

_____ 1. The clown chased a dog around the **ring** and then fell flat on her face.

_____ 2. The geese **indolently** waddled across the intersection.

_____ 3. **Yikes**! I'm late for class.

_____ 4. Bruno's **shabby** thesaurus tumbled out of the bag when the bus suddenly pulled out into traffic.

_____ 5. Mr. Frederick angrily **stamped** out the fire that the local hooligans had started on his verandah.

_____ 6. Later that summer, she asked herself, "What was **I** thinking of?"

_____ 7. She thought that the twenty zucchini plants **would** not **be** enough, so she planted another ten.

_____ 8. **Although** she gave hundreds of zucchini away, the enormous mound left over frightened her.

_____ 9. Everywhere she went, **she** talked about the prolific veggies.

_____ 10. The manager **confidently** made his presentation to the board of directors.

_____ 11. Frankenstein **is** the name of the scientist, not the monster.

_____ 12. Her greatest fear is that the world will end before she finds a comfortable pair **of** pantyhose.

_____ 13. That suitcase is **hers**.

_____ 14. **Everyone** in the room cheered when the announcement was made.

_____ 15. The sun was shining as we **set** out for our first winter camping trip.

_____ 16. **Small** children often insist that they can do it by themselves.

_____ 17. **Dust** covered every surface in the locked bedroom.

_____ 18. The census taker knocked **loudly** on all the doors, but nobody was home.

_____ 19. They wondered if there truly was honor **among** thieves.

_____ 20. Exciting new products **and** effective marketing strategies will guarantee the company's success.

Chapter 15

SENTENCE STRUCTURE

Now that parts of speech, or what categories words fit into, have been covered, it's time to talk about putting those words into sentences.

This section covers the basic structure of a sentence, beginning with the parts of sentences, moving into how to categorize sentences, and ending with some tips on how to create effective sentences.

- Parts of a sentence

- Sentence types, patterns, and structure

- Coordination and subordination

- Modifiers

- Parallelism

15.1 PARTS OF A SENTENCE

A. SUBJECT AND PREDICATE

These are the most basic parts of a sentence.

The subject – who or what the sentence is all about. The **subject** performs the action of the verb. He or she (or it) is the actor, the protagonist.

The predicate – says something significant (complete idea) about the subject. It must include a main verb.

1. She *runs*. **[Runs]** is the predicate, a single verb.

2. We *want* the <u>prime rib.</u> **[Want the prime rib]** is the predicate.

3. American troops *need* more <u>armor.</u> **[Need more armor]** is the predicate.

Sentences need a subject. Sentences must have a predicate. This topic of subject and predicate is the most basic characteristic and structure of a sentence. Therefore, the two crucial questions to ask of any sentence are:

*   Who or what is the subject? Who or what is this particular sentence about?

*   What is the predicate? What is happening to the subject – and maybe why and where?

The predicate may be simply a verb (1: runs), or it can include a verb and a direct object (2: want prime rib and 3: need armor). Direct objects are underlined in (2) and (3) above. The predicate may also include indirect objects and other words and phrases.

B. SUBJECT, VERB, AND OBJECTS (SVO)

A complete sentence must include a subject and a verb. Someone or something (subject) must do something (verb). Sometimes, the subject does something to something else—that other thing is called the object. Objects receive the action of the verb. Objects can be direct and/or indirect.

John carried the bag.

*   John is the **subject**. He is the doer, the actor, in the sentence.

*   Carried is the **verb**. It is the action in the sentence.

*   Bag is the **object**. The bag is the thing being carried, so it is affected by the verb.

Once you recognize the subject and the verb, you need to ask if there are any direct objects and/or indirect objects, and you need to distinguish between them. What is a direct object (DO)? What is an indirect object (IO)?

*   A <u>direct object</u> (DO) receives the action of the verb (Bill threw the <u>ball</u>). It will be a noun or pronoun.

*   An **indirect object** (IO) tells us to whom or for whom the action was done: Bill threw the <u>ball</u> to **Jim**.

If we put **to** or **for** in front of an indirect object, it becomes clearer. With **to** or **for**, the IO then usually goes after the direct object: He threw **me** the <u>ball</u> = He threw the <u>ball</u> to **me**.

Some SVO sentences will include both <u>direct</u> and **indirect** objects:

At Christmas, when I was eight, my uncle bought **me** a model <u>train</u>. He gave my **sister** <u>perfume</u>.

What did your uncle buy? A train. Train is the direct object. Who received the train? Me. Me is the indirect object. What else did your uncle buy? Perfume. That's the direct object of the second sentence. Who received the perfume? Sister. She is the indirect object.

Has the mailman given **Mary** the <u>package</u>? No, he left **me** the <u>package</u> since she was out.

What did the mailman give? To whom did he give it? What did the mailman leave? To whom did he leave it?

The catcher caught the <u>ball</u>. He threw <u>it</u> to First Base. First Base threw **me** the <u>ball</u>. I tagged the <u>player</u> at second base.

What did the catcher do? Who received the action?

C. CLAUSES AND PHRASES

Writers often refer to clauses and phrases when discussing the building blocks of English. This is one way of categorizing language so that we can all talk about it.

1. CLAUSES

A clause is a group of words that includes a subject and a verb. Clauses are divided into independent and dependent.

I walked. The dog barked. I stood up after sitting all afternoon.

Independent clauses are complete sentences that can stand on their own:

I stood up. I walked. The dog barked. The girl on the swing laughed loudly.

Dependent clauses are sentences with a subject and a verb, but they are still dependent on more words to form a complete sentence. Often, this is because they have an extra word or phrase attached to them:

Because I stood up.

In this example, I need the rest of the thought here. I do have a subject "I" and a verb "stood up" but I also have a "because," implying that there is more to the thought—so it is a dependent clause.

When I walked.
As the dog barked.
While the girl on the swing laughed loudly.

All of these sentences leave the reader hanging, waiting for more information. They are incomplete ideas, also called Sentence Fragments (see ch. 17.5 for more information).

2. PHRASES

A phrase is a group of words that does not have a subject and a verb.

On the edge, before class, the open door, that awesome hand lotion on the shelf

Each of these phrases is more than one word, but they are not clauses because they do not contain subjects and verbs. They are building blocks of sentences, but they are not enough on their own—they need more in order to form a complete sentence.

EXERCISES

PARTS OF A SENTENCE EXERCISE 15.1A
Find the subject. Find the predicate.

1. The burden of proof lies on the plaintiff.
2. In the eyes of a lover, pockmarks are dimples.
3. In golden pots are hidden the most deadly poisons.
4. Never go to bed mad. Stay up and fight.
5. The structure of every sentence is a lesson in logic.
6. Keep your mouth shut and your eyes open.
7. Three women and a goose make a market.
8. The greatest right in the world is the right to be wrong.
9. In war, all delays are dangerous.
10. Most of the disputes in the world arise from words.

PARTS OF A SENTENCE EXERCISE 15.1B
Identify the subject, verb, and indirect/direct objects in the following sentences.

1. The man riding the scooter carried his grocery bags.
2. Lucy handed her backpack to her mother when they walked into the house.
3. The man in the elevator delivered pizza to the hotel room.
4. Salvatore gave Iris the notes from class today.
5. John watched the blockbuster movie the day it came out in theatres.

PARTS OF A SENTENCE EXERCISE 15.1C
Identify the following as a phrase or a clause.

1. standing on your head
2. you should wear a helmet
3. the best sunscreen I've ever used
4. the hot summer sun beats down
5. the children laugh

15.2 Types, Patterns, and Structure

English divides sentences into types, patterns, and overall structure.

- Sentence types: What is the sentence doing?

  - Declarative
  - Imperative
  - Interrogative
  - Exclamatory

- **Patterns:** How is the sentence put together?

  - S-LV-SC
  - S-TV-DO
  - S-TV-IO-DO
  - S-TV-DO-OC
  - S-ITV

- Structure: What clauses make up the sentence?

  - Simple
  - Compound
  - Complex
  - Compound-Complex

A. Types

The easiest way to describe sentences is by what they are doing. In this sense, there are four options: **declarative, imperative, interrogative, and exclamatory.**

1. Declarative

Declarative sentences literally declare something.

> **Ex**: Today is Tuesday.
> My name is Jean.
> The weather is lovely today.
> I read books to my children.
> Javier collects unusual postcards from around the world.
> My company laid off over one hundred employees.

2. Imperative

Imperative sentences give orders or make requests.

> **Ex**: Take out the garbage.
> Come here!
> Help me.
> Have a nice day.
> Get well soon.
> Let me get that door for you.
> Please let me know if you have any questions.
> Stop that!
> Watch out for that pothole!
> Don't forget my birthday!

(Note that imperatives can use either periods or exclamation points.)

In sentences giving orders or instructions, the subject, usually you (2nd person singular) or you (2nd person plural) can be omitted. The subject is understood from the context. Imperative sentences (orders or requests) are the one exception to the rule that all sentences must have an explicit subject.

> "You" (singular or plural) is assumed.
> Fire! Shoulder arms! [An order or command]
> "You guys" (plural) is assumed.
> Help unload the car! [Still in tone a command]
> "You" does not have to be omitted.
> Please would you help unload the car? [More polite, a request]

3. Interrogative

Interrogatives ask something and generally end with a question mark.

> **Ex**: Who are you?
> Where are we going?
> Why are we going this way?
> Do you like to cook?
> Does anybody here know CPR?
> How do I open a retirement account?

4. Exclamatory

Exclamatory sentences are excited about the information and usually end with an exclamation point.

> **Ex**: This is crazy!
> I can't believe it!
> I'm utterly shocked!
> The ordeal was over!

Sentence Types Exercise 15.2A

Identify the sentence type for the following sentences.

1. Take out the garbage!

2. Where are you going?

3. I am going out to dinner!

4. Where do you want to have dinner?

5. I'm not sure where we are going for dinner.

B. Sentence Patterns

Sentence structure in English can be complicated, but often, it follows this simple pattern: Subject + Predicate. The subject is the actor in the sentence. It is whatever is doing what the verb describes. The predicate includes the rest of the sentence—the verb or the action in the sentence—and anything else that the verb is affecting.

Most simple English sentences conform to these five (5) patterns:

1. Subject—Linking Verb—Subject Complement (S LV SC)

> Ex: Good researchers are curious.
>   S   LV   SC

What is the sentence about? The subject is "researchers."
What are the researchers doing? They "are" being something.
What are they being? Curious. "Curious" is complementing the subject here, giving more information about it—the subject complement.

> Ex: The weather is lovely.
>   S   LV SC

What is the sentence about? The subject is "weather."
What is the weather doing? The weather "is" being something.
What is the weather being? Lovely. "Lovely" is complementing the subject, telling readers more about the weather, so it is the subject complement.

> Ex: Thessaly is still a puppy.
>   S   LV   SC

What is the sentence about? The subject is "Thessaly."
What is Thessaly doing? Thessaly "is" being something.
What is Thessaly being? A puppy. So, "puppy" is complementing the subject, telling readers more about Thessaly, so it is the subject complement.

2. Subject—Transitive Verb—Direct Object (S TV DO)

> Ex: An antihistamine may prevent an allergic reaction.
>   S   TV   DO

What is the sentence about? The subject is "antihistamine."
What is the antihistamine doing? It "may prevent" something.
What is being prevented? The allergic reaction. The reaction is directly receiving the action of the verb, so it is the direct object.

> Ex: The dog chewed the bone.
>   S   TV   DO

What is the sentence about? The subject is "dog."
What is the dog doing? It is "chewing." "Chewing" is the verb.
What is being chewed? The bone. Therefore, "the bone" is the direct object.

> Ex: The volcano destroyed many homes.
>   S   TV   DO

What is the sentence about? The subject is "volcano."
What is the volcano doing? It is "destroying."
What is being destroyed? Homes. Therefore, "homes" is the direct object.

3. Subject—Transitive Verb—Indirect Object—Direct Object (S TV IO DO)

> Ex: The curry gave Jane severe indigestion.
>   S   TV   IO   DO

What is the sentence about? The subject is "curry."
What is the curry doing? It already "gave." "Gave" is the verb.
What is being given? Indigestion. The verb "gave" applies to the indigestion, making this the direct object.
Who is also indirectly receiving the action? Jane. "Jane" is being given indigestion, so she is the indirect object here.

> Ex: I gave John my   notes.
>   S TV   IO   DO

What is the sentence about? Me, or in this case, I. The subject is "I."
What did I do? I "gave" something to someone.
What did I give? My notes. "Notes" is the direct object; it is what is given.
Who indirectly received my notes? John, so "John" is the indirect object.

> Ex: Ron gave Hermione a dozen roses.
>   S   TV   IO   DO

What is the sentence about? Ron.
What did Ron do? He gave something to someone.
What did Ron give? Roses. "Roses" is the direct object.
Who received those roses? Hermione. "Hermione" is the indirect object.

4. Subject—Transitive Verb—Direct Object—Object Complement (S TV DO OC)

Ex: The reviewer called the film a masterpiece.
      S   TV   DO   OC

What is the sentence about? The reviewer. The subject is "reviewer."

What is the reviewer doing? The reviewer "called," so "called" is the verb

What is being called? The film. "The film" is directly receiving the action of the verb called, so it is the direct object.

But what is the film being called? A masterpiece. So masterpiece is giving more information about the direct object, complementing it—so it's the object complement.

Ex: The Senate elected Senator Palpatine Supreme Leader.
       S   TV   DO   O

What is the sentence about? The Senate (subject).
What did the Senate do? Elected someone (verb).
Who was elected? Senator Palpatine (direct object).
What else do we know about the direct object here? Supreme Leader (object complement).

Ex: We painted the room blue.
      S TV   DO OC

Who is the sentence about? We (subject).
What did we do? Painted (verb).
What did we paint? The room. "Room" is the direct object.

What else describes the room in this sentence? Blue. "Blue" complements the direct object "room," so it's the object complement.

5. Subject—Intransitive Verb (S ITV)

Ex: The kettle whistles.
      S   ITV

What is the sentence about? The kettle. "Kettle" is the subject.

What is the kettle doing? Whistling. This is the verb. It's called intransitive because this verb doesn't "go across" the sentence to affect any other words. The kettle isn't whistling anything—it's just whistling. Intransitive verbs do not take objects.

Ex: The child on the swing laughed.
      S   ITV

What is the sentence about? The child (subject)
What did the child do? Laughed (verb). That's it for this sentence. The prepositional phrase "on the swing" tells which child (the one on the swing) is doing the laughing.

Ex: The monkey to the left of the lion grinned at the people at the zoo.
      S   ITV

What is the sentence about? The monkey (subject).
What did the monkey do? Grinned (verb).
That's it for the sentence. Everything else is a prepositional phrase--and though prepositional phrases are great and give a lot of information, they perform no grammatical function in the sentence (they cannot be subjects, verbs, objects, or complements).

Review of Terminology

LV = Linking Verbs take a subject complement, **not** an object (pattern 1).

TV = Transitive Verbs take an object, either a direct object alone (pattern 2) or direct and indirect object (pattern 3) or a direct object and object complement (pattern 4).

ITV = Intransitive Verbs take no object (pattern 5).

DO= Direct Objects directly receive the action of the verb (patterns 2, 3, and 4).

IO= Indirect Objects indirectly receive the action of the verb (pattern 3).

SC= Subject Complements are nouns, pronouns, or adjectives that rename the subject (usually connected by a linking verb) (pattern 1).

OC= Object Complements are nouns, pronouns, or adjectives that rename the direct object at the end of the sentence (pattern 4).

Meaning **flows** from subject > verb > objects, etc. Hence, these are **SVO** sentence patterns.

Note: Prepositional phrases do not have a grammatical function in sentences. They add flavor and detail but cannot do any of the "heavy lifting" in the sentence. They cannot be subjects, verbs, objects, or complements.

For more information about types of verbs, see Ch 14.2 Verbs.

SENTENCE PATTERNS EXERCISE 15.2B

Identify the pattern of the following sentences by labeling the function of each word.

    Example: I   handed   Tom   the   soda.
               S   TV   IO   DO

1. The child on the swing laughed.
2. The book was heavy.
3. We waited in line for hours!
4. He handed Maria a vase of a dozen roses.
5. My car is a Mini Cooper.
6. I found the meal delicious.
7. Good students work hard in school.
8. The plan is to finish her novel.
9. Alanna attends the meeting every other Wednesday night.
10. Erika has many plans for her future.

SENTENCE PATTERNS EXERCISE 15.2C

Identify the pattern of the following sentences by labeling the function of each word.

    Example: Joe drives a big truck.
              S   TV   DO

1. The weekly meeting was always held on Wednesday evening.
2. The kids in the park played in the sandbox.
3. Jane loaned Jesse the first season of *Game of Thrones*.
4. The new car sped along the highway.
5. Mr. Johnson teaches math class.
6. Her boss thought her behavior inappropriate.
7. I was sad at the end of the season.
8. Publishing a book is a big job.
9. Jason washed the car in the driveway.
10. The teacher gave Norman his graded essay.

C. SENTENCE STRUCTURE

Another way to look at sentences is seeing them as a mixture of four (4) different types or structures: **simple, compound, complex, and compound-complex.**

This is based on their structure in terms of the different kinds of clauses (**independent and dependent)** that they contain instead of the individual word functions.

An independent clause has a subject and a predicate and can stand on its own as a complete sentence.

> Ex: I arrived late.
> Ex: The bus ride was long.

A dependent clause has a subject and a verb, but it has some other words that make it dependent on the rest of the sentence to be complete.

> Ex: When I arrived late . . .
> Ex: Because the bus ride was long...

Note: This is a fragment; it needs the rest of the thought to be complete. What happened when the speaker arrived late? Ex: When I arrived late, I missed the birthday song. Because the bus ride was long, I read a good chunk of my book.

Now this is a combination of a dependent clause ("When I arrived late" and "Because the bus ride was long") and an independent clause ("I missed the birthday song" and "I read a good chunk of my book").

Using a mixture of these four (4) different sentence types will give variety to writing, making it more interesting and thoughtful and matching the structure (grammatical and style) to the writer's thoughts and intentions.

1. SIMPLE

A simple sentence contains one independent clause (IC).

> Ex: I   drove   the   car.
>   S   V
> Ex: I   walked   to   school   in   the   driving   rain.
>   S   V
> Ex: My grandmother and grandfather met in New York years ago.
>   S   S   V
> Note: All of the patterns 1-5 in section B are simple sentences.

2. COMPOUND

A compound sentence contains two independent clause (IC IC) connected by a coordinating conjunction.

> Ex: I   drove the car, and   I   listened to the radio.
>   S   TV   DO   S   ITV
>   IC   IC
> Ex: I wanted to mow the grass, but it was raining outside.
>   S   TV   DO   S LV   SC
>   IC   IC
> Ex: I   was tired, so   I   went home early.
>   S   LV   SC   S   ITV
>   IC   IC

3. COMPLEX

A complex sentence contains one independent clause and one or more dependent clauses (IC DC) or (IC DC DC).

> Ex: I drove the car   while I listened to the radio.
>   IC   DC
> Ex: I drove the car   while I listened to the radio   because my favorite song was on.
>   IC   DC   DC

Note: The order of the clauses doesn't matter when identifying sentence types—only that the sentence has them at all.

Ex: While I listened to the radio,   I drove the car.
      DC   IC

Ex: Because my favorite song was on   while I listened to the radio,   I drove the car.
      DC   DC   IC

(Though this last sentence has subtly shifted the sentence's meaning, it's still a complex sentence.)

4. COMPOUND-COMPLEX

A compound-complex sentence contains two independent clauses and one or more dependent clauses (IC IC DC) or (IC DC IC) or (DC IC IC) etc.

Ex: I drove the car,   and my brother told me where to turn   while I listened to the radio.
    IC   IC   DC

Ex: My brother told me where to turn   while I listened to the radio,   and I drove the car.
    IC   DC   IC

Ex: While I listened to the radio,   I drove the car,   and my brother told me where to turn.
    DC   IC   IC

SENTENCE STRUCTURE EXERCISE 15.2D

Identify the following sentences as simple, compound, complex, or compound-complex.

1. I walked on the beach.

2. After a long day in the sun, I had sunburn on my shoulders.

3. I had a delightful time at the beach with my family.

4. I met my friend in Orlando when she flew down from New York.

5. It was so late, but she couldn't go to sleep yet.

6. While she was working on the last part of the essay, Sara swore that she would never wait until the last minute again.

7. She was angry when he left her, but she knew he would regret his decision.

8. They got married on the beach, and their family celebrated afterward with a reception.

9. Planning the wedding was hard work.

10. Seeing the couple so happy on the beach, she knew all of her hard work was worth it.

15.3 Coordination and Subordination

English allows writers to combine ideas in many different ways. Two ways to combine sentences are coordination and subordination.

Coordination means that you are combining two independent clauses so that they are equal in terms of emphasis and importance in the sentence.

Subordination means that you are combining clauses so that one of them is independent and the other is dependent, usually showing that part of the sentence is more important than the other, or one part depends on the other for meaning.

A. Coordination

There are three ways to connect sentences using coordination:

1. Use a FANBOYS word (coordinating conjunctions= for, and, nor, but, or, yet, so) between two Independent Clauses (IC, FANBOYS, IC.)

Ex: She came early, and she opened the store.

2. Use a semicolon if the two sentences are closely related.

Ex: I entered the library; she was already there.

3. Use a semicolon and a conjunctive adverb (however, furthermore, consequently, etc.)

Ex: The shop opened again in June; however, it had closed for good by September.

Note: Using coordination allows you to create Compound Sentences.

B. Subordination

Connecting independent and dependent clauses using subordination means that the IC has more emphasis than the DC.

DC: When his class was finished IC: He came over

Ex: When his class was finished, he came over.

Ex: He came over when his class was finished.

DC: Before the others arrived IC: We had agreed on a plan

Ex: Before the others arrived, we had agreed on a plan.

Ex: We had agreed on a plan before the others arrived.

DC: Until the end of the day arrived IC: We didn't know if it would work

Ex: Until the end of the day arrived, we didn't know if it would work.

Ex: We didn't know if it would work until the end of the day arrived.

Note: Using subordination creates complex sentences.
Another note: Notice the comma use with these sentences! Here's the rule:

IC DC.= When the independent clause comes first, do **not** use a comma in the middle of the sentence.

DC, IC.= When the dependent clause comes first, **do** place a comma before the start of the independent clause.

(For more information, see Conjunctive Adverbs in Chapter 14.7)

C. USING BOTH COORDINATION AND SUBORDINATION

Sometimes, it's fun to have a party with all different sentence types. Go for it! Just keep in mind the average attention span of the reader and have sympathy. A series of long sentences can boggle the mind. But used sparingly, coordination and subordination can make writing sing with detail and purpose.

IC= he went to college

DC= when he left the army

IC=he kept his uniform

Ex: He went to college when he left the army, but he kept his uniform. (IC DC IC)
Ex: He kept his uniform when he left the army, but he went to college. (IC DC IC)
Ex: When he left the army, he kept his uniform, but he went to college. (DC IC IC)
Ex: When he left the army, he went to college, but he kept his uniform. (DC IC IC)

Each sentence emphasizes something slightly different.
Or you can really have some fun:

DC= before she entered his life

IC=he seemed somewhat lost

IC= nobody was very surprised

DC= when they married in the fall

DC= although his former beloved didn't approve at first

IC= she eventually saw how happy he was and gave the happy couple her blessing

Ex: Before she entered his life, he seemed somewhat lost, so nobody was very surprised when they married in the fall; although his former beloved didn't approve at first, she eventually saw how happy he was and gave the happy couple her blessing.
(DC IC IC DC DC IC).

Note: When a sentence has two verbs, but only one subject, it is still considered a simple sentence with one independent clause--it simply has a compound verb. For instance, "she saw how happy he was and gave her blessing" may seem like two independent clauses, but there is only one subject (she) and two verbs (saw and gave).

What a mouthful! But occasionally, a long sentence like this is a welcome challenge for readers to tackle.

COORDINATION EXERCISE 15.3A

Revise each of the following sentence pairs by combining each of the two ideas to form one sentence. Use a coordinating conjunction, and be sure to express the idea in brackets.

Example:

ORIGINAL: I keep a detailed schedule on my phone. I still can't manage to get everything done on time. [Show that one idea contrasts with or contradicts the other.]

REVISED: I keep a detailed schedule on my phone, but I still can't manage to get everything done on time.

1. I intend to stay focused on my long-term goals. I am determined to succeed. [Show that one idea adds to the other.]

2. Jerry said he might take his dog to the park tonight. He might go to the movies. [Show that one idea is an alternative to another.]

3. Brianna is worried that she'll be bored this summer. She has applied to several jobs and intends to do some volunteer work as well. [Show that one idea is the reason for the other.]

4. I'm looking forward to buying a new car. I'm not looking forward to the car payments. [Show that one idea contrasts with or contradicts the other.]

5. I have not seen that notoriously violent horror movie. I am not planning on it. [Show that one idea is a negative alternative to the other.]

6. Tampa and Atlanta are two very different cities. They have a few surprisingly similar features. [Show that one idea contrasts with or contradicts the other in an unexpected way.]

7. I am grateful for technology like word processing and texting. Sometimes I miss the personal touch of a handwritten letter. [Show that one idea contrasts with or contradicts the other.]

8. Colleen intends to graduate from college by the end of the next year. She hopes to become a social worker right away. [Show that one idea adds to the other.]

9. Colleen wants to become a social worker. She wants to make a difference in her community. [Show that one idea is the reason for the other.]

10. Colleen wants to make a difference in her community. She knows she's going to need to work hard. [Show that one idea contrasts with or contradicts the other.]

SUBORDINATION EXERCISE 15.3B

Revise each of the following sentence pairs by combining each of the two ideas to form one sentence. Use a subordinating conjunction, and be sure to express the idea in brackets.

ORIGINAL: The work meeting is finally over. We will go out to dinner. [Show that dinner will follow the meeting.]

REVISED: After the work meeting is finally over, we will go out to dinner.

1. I refuse to go up in my dark, dusty attic. I am terrified of spiders. [Show that one idea is the reason for the other.]

2. I get my paycheck. I won't be able to afford a new suit. [Show that one idea sets a time frame based on a condition.]

3. We are going to reduce air pollution. We need to rethink the way we design cities. [Show that one idea is the condition for the other.]

4. The air conditioner was malfunctioning. Everybody was sweating. [Show that one idea is the reason for the other.]

5. Tyler is in San Diego. He has several family members. [Show that one idea is related to another in terms of a physical or geographical location.]

6. I'll be happy to pick up your prescription from the pharmacy. I finish grocery shopping. [Show that one event will happen following another.]

7. Tonya enjoyed the movie. She wished it hadn't been so vulgar. [Show that one idea is a concession to another.]

8. Kerri installed a new fan in her bedroom. She hoped it could keep the room cooler at night. [Show that one idea is the reason for the other.]

9. Richard will not quit his job. He finds a new one. [Show that one event is the condition for the other.]

10. I've been on this stringent diet for so long. I'm starting to miss my favorite foods. [Show that one idea is the reason for the other.]

15.4 MODIFIERS

A modifier is a word or a phrase that describes another word in your sentence.

If you think about modifiers as being similar to adjectives, it may help you to understand their function in a sentence. For example, you may remember that an adjective describes something about a noun. In this example, this real estate advertisement uses several adjectives in bold to describe the noun (house):

This **quaint** and **cozy little 1940s** house is located in a prime location in the Seminole Heights community.

Since marketers know that potential home buyers are reading many house listings, they want to keep their readers' attention on the important details in the most concise way possible. Both adjectives and modifiers can be persuasive to readers by directing their attention to specific features of your topic.

Used correctly, modifiers can help you to create more sentence variety and details in your essay. Consider the following sentence, which was written as part of a scholarship application:

While visiting Puerto Rico as part of my school's service learning program, I learned about a non-profit organization that educates people about overfishing.

In the example given, the writer uses one sentence instead of several to explain relevant information about both her academic career and her particular interest in environmental issues. Notice that the modifier in bold describes the nearby subject, which is the pronoun I.

A. Misplaced Modifiers

The reader expects that a modifier will relate to the word closest to it in the sentence, as in the above example. A common error, the misplaced modifier, occurs when the writer does not follow the modifier with its intended subject. As you can see from this example, misplaced modifiers can be both confusing and funny:

I gave the old coins to my nephew **I keep in a safe.**

Although the sentence sounds like cause for alarm, its error can be fixed by moving the modifier, which is in bold, closer to the word it should be modifying. We can assume that the writer does not keep any family members in a safe, so we can just rearrange the sentence for clarity:

CORRECT: I gave the old coins **I keep in a safe** to my nephew.

Walking across the hardwood floor, the porcelain statue slipped from my hand.

Was the statue walking? Probably not, but the sentence implies that it was. Here's what the writer actually meant:

CORRECT: **Walking across the hardwood floor,** I dropped the porcelain statue.

As a nominee for the award, your name will be prominently displayed in the hall.

This sentence implies that "your name" will be the nominee. Well, no. The actual *person* (and not merely the *name* of the person) will earn the nomination.

CORRECT: **As a nominee for the award**, you will be honored by having your name displayed prominently in the hall.

CORRECT: **Because you were nominated for the award**, your name will be displayed prominently in the hall. (Notice that the word "you" has been included in the bold part of the sentence.)

Stranded outside in the rain, Sara's door refused to budge.

This sentence implies that "Sara's door" was stranded outside in the rain.

CORRECT: **Stranded outside in the rain**, Sara could not budge her door.

As a new hire, I would like to welcome you to the company.

This sentence implies that the person speaking as "I" is the new hire. However, why would a new hire be welcoming somebody new? This scenario seems backward. More likely, the speaker ("I") is already established with the company and is welcoming somebody ("you") who is new.

CORRECT: I would like to welcome you to the company.

CORRECT: I would like to welcome you, **a new hire**, to the company.

CORRECT: **As a new hire**, you are welcome at the company.

B. Dangling Modifiers

Another kind of modifier error, the dangling modifier, occurs when the writer does not include the word that it was intended to modify:

At seven years old, my father taught me how to play guitar.

Because the modifier is immediately followed by "my father," which is the subject, the sentence actually says that the writer's father was seven years old when he gave her guitar lessons. Clearly, this is not what the writer intended. However, moving the modifier around in the sentence, as you can to correct misplaced modifiers, will not fix this error. Instead, an effective way to correct the problem is to change the modifier to a dependent clause:

CORRECT: **When I was seven years old,** my father taught me how to play guitar.

To apply for graduation, the form must be filled out in its entirety.

The *form* will not be applying. The *person* will be applying.

> CORRECT: **To apply for graduation**, please fill out this form in its entirety. [Note that this imperative sentence, also called a command, has the implied subject "you."]

The modifier errors seem obvious to us when we are isolating them from the rest of a paragraph. However, remember that these errors frequently occur in all types of writing. After all, when you are typing your rough draft, you are correct to focus more of your attention on your ideas rather than on grammar and mechanics. Just be sure to proofread your rough draft for errors in modifiers.

C. Limiting Modifiers

Limiting modifiers get their name because they specify conditions that restrict the word they are modifying. This error often occurs with words like "only," "just," and "almost." Here is an example:

> It's **just** not the best phone available right now.

In this sentence, the speaker doesn't like the phone and believes there are better options available.

> It's not **just** the best phone available right now.

In this sentence, the speaker likes the phone—and also feels that it has more benefits than just being the "best," like maybe it's also the cheapest or newest.

> My sister **only** eats the green candies.

As the sentence stands, it is stating that the writer's sister does nothing but eat green candies—she doesn't sleep or work or do anything but eat candy. You could also assume the modifier "only" applies to the rest of the sentence (eats the green candies), in which case, she doesn't sell the candy or deliver the candy—she only eats it. Similar to misplaced modifiers, this error can often be amended by moving the modifier closer to the word it should be modifying, but sometimes you need to add words for clarification:

> CORRECT: **Only** my sister eats the green candies.

> CORRECT: My **only** sister eats the green candies.

> CORRECT: When she has a bag of jelly beans, my sister eats **only** the green candies.

Moving the word changes the meaning of each sentence.

Also, consider the shifts in meaning in the following sentences.

The word "only" modifies the next word or phrase in the sentence:

> **Only** John said he loved Susan.
> John was the only one who said it.
> John **only** said he loved Susan.
> Perhaps he didn't mean it?
> John said **only** he loved Susan.
> John is telling people that he is the only one who loves Susan.
> John said he **only** loved Susan.
> Does he even like her? No. Just love.
> John said he loved **only** Susan. John said he loved Susan **only**.

Apparently, Susan is the only one for John.

> Note: If "only" is the final word in the sentence, it refers to the previous word or phrase.

A Note on YOLO

The phrase YOLO has been used as a short version of "You only live once." The users of this phrase think that this sequence of words suggests that they are living in the moment--because you only have one to live, live in the moment, seize the day (*carpe diem*), etc. This sentiment, however, is not what YOLO tells the listener. Think of how the word "only" works--it modifies the word after it in the sentence.

You **only** <u>live</u> once.

This sentence says that the only thing you will do once in your life is live. Everything else in life, you must do twice. Skydiving? Do it again. Awful breakup? Twice. YOLO tattoo? Get two of them.

Joe **almost** won $100. (He came close to winning the contest, but he lost.)
Joe won **almost** $100. (Perhaps he won $99 or so.)
This new device **just** costs $50. (This placement is awkward and unclear.)
This new device costs **just** $50. (This sentence implies that the price is surprisingly low.)
I was **just** driving slightly over the speed limit, but I got a ticket, anyway. (The placement is awkward and unclear. When did this happen? Recently? Or, does this mean that the speaker was only driving—not texting, not on the phone, etc.?)
I was driving **just** slightly over the speed limit, but I got a ticket anyway. (Perhaps the driver was clocked at 58 mph in a 55 mph zone.)
I was **just** calling you, and I didn't expect you to be offended. (The call isn't a big deal.)
I was **just** calling you, and then you walked into my office. (The call happened recently. Or, it could also mean that the call isn't a big deal.)
I was **just** now calling you, and then you walked into my office. (The call happened recently.)

D. Squinting Modifiers

Another kind of error, the squinting modifier, occurs when the writer places a modifier between two words or grammatical structures without clearly modifying either of them.

The celebrity the audience expected enthusiastically entered the room.

In the sentence above, it is unclear whether: 1) the audience was enthusiastically expecting the celebrity, or 2) the celebrity enthusiastically entered the room. This sentence can be corrected by having the modifier clearly describe the correct word or phrase.

CORRECT: The celebrity the audience **enthusiastically** <u>expected</u> entered the room.

CORRECT: The celebrity the audience expected <u>entered</u> the room **enthusiastically**.

The girl I dated recently was in a Broadway show.
Was the dating recent? Or was she in a show recently?

CORRECT: The girl I **recently** <u>dated</u> was in a Broadway show.

CORRECT: The girl I dated <u>was</u> **recently** in a Broadway show.

EXERCISES

MODIFIERS EXERCISE 15.4A

Correct modifier errors in the 10 sentences below, or write "No Revision."

1. As a hungry Labrador, I knew the stray dog would need food soon.
2. I discovered a love for Spanish guitar while I was taking a music course.
3. Driving my motorcycle near the Everglades, an alligator chased me.
4. By the age of six, Latrice spoke three languages.
5. After breaking my leg, the rescue team responded to my phone call and arrived very quickly.
6. By driving to the nearest pharmacy, my child was able to get her last dose of antibiotics on time.
7. This semester, my financial aid did not arrive on time.
8. Professor Busari only eats at Starbucks on Monday.
9. Before reading the article, Jae shared it on Facebook to see if it was credible.
10. While taking my exam, Dr. Torres accused me of cheating.

MODIFIERS EXERCISE 15.4B

Read the ten sentences below, identify the type of modifier error in them, and rewrite any sentences with errors.

1. Swinging in the hammock, we silently envied my Uncle Fred.
2. My sister only goes to a yoga class on Tuesday.
3. Before printing the article, Alicia ensured that it was from a credible journal.
4. Doing your homework quickly will improve your grade.
5. While I was waiting for my friend, I called my mom to wish her happy birthday.
6. Having arrived late for his appointment, the appointment needed to be rescheduled.
7. The book you finished recently went missing.
8. Drinking a glass of ice water, envious looks were shot Stephanie's way as the other volleyball players wished they could quench their thirst.
9. The bus I usually take to work did not arrive on time today.
10. With a gasp of pleasure, applause for the musical commenced.

15.5 PARALLELISM

Effective writers make their sentences "flow." Their sentences are easy to follow and easy to understand because they don't jump around between different styles. Instead, parallel sentences are structured in a way that makes them almost poetic.

Parallelism refers to using elements in sentences that are grammatically similar or identical in structure, sound, meaning, or meter. This technique adds symmetry, effectiveness, and balance to the written piece.

Here is an example of a sentence with incorrect parallel structure:

I like to study, sleeping, and to go to the beach.

In this example, which mentions three activities, the list does not use parallel structure. The terms are not parallel. There are two infinitives (to study, to go to the beach) and one gerund (sleeping). To put it another way, the three items in this list don't match. This sentence is grammatically incorrect.

Here is an example of a sentence with correct parallel structure:

I like studying, sleeping, and going to the beach.

In this example, all three items in the list are gerunds (studying, sleeping, going). They match. The list is parallel, and the sentence is grammatically correct.

A. THE FUNCTION OF PARALLELISM

What is the purpose of parallelism? Without parallel structure, writing is awkward. Parallel structure improves coherence, consistency, and readability. Allow the following examples to illustrate:

To change her diet, my mom purchased some supplements, lots of leafy green vegetables, and gym clothes.

To change her diet, my mom purchased supplements, leafy green vegetables, and gym clothes.

Analyze both sentences and pay close attention to the extra words in the first. Is the first sentence able to be understood? Yes.

Does the second sentence have better coherence and consistency? Yes, and it is more concise and professional as well.

B. PARALLELISM IN GRAMMATICAL STRUCTURES

As noted above, parallelism is essential for clear, concise writing. This rule applies across a number of different grammatical units like lists, phrases, and clauses.

1. PARALLEL STRUCTURE IN LISTS

When creating lists, the items in the list should be parallel. For example, in your list, you might have three nouns separated by commas, or you might have three adjectives separated by commas.

Please note the use of the Oxford comma (or "serial comma") when creating lists. The use and misuse of this comma can change the meaning of your sentences. Consider these examples:

My heroes are my two uncles, George Washington, and Martin Luther King, Jr.

This sentence implies you have four heroes: One uncle, another uncle, Washington, and King.

My heroes are my two uncles, George Washington and Martin Luther King, Jr.

This sentence implies that you have two uncles who are both major figures of American history.

a. Parallel Examples with "a" or "to"

Incorrect: I couldn't decide if I wanted to wear a formal dress, fun skirt, or jeans and a t-shirt.

This one is tricky, but notice the use of the word "a."

Correct: I couldn't decide if I wanted to wear *a formal dress, a fun skirt,* or *jeans and a t-shirt.*

Incorrect: At this new job, expect to work with emerging technology, to develop innovative solutions, and collaborate with talented professionals. (Hint: Watch the word "to.")

Correct: At this new job, expect *to work* with emerging technology, *to develop* innovative solutions, and *to collaborate* with talented professionals.

Correct: At this new job, expect to *work* with emerging technology, *develop* innovative solutions, and *collaborate* with talented professionals.

2. Parallel Structure in Certain Constructions

a. Parallel examples with correlative conjunctions (not only … but also, either …. or, neither … nor, both … and)

The use of a correlative conjunction requires parallel structure of both clauses or both phrases in the sentence. If a verb follows the first correlative conjunction, then a verb should follow the second conjunction in the set. Consider the alternative ways you can construct sentences around each pair of words to maintain parallel structure:

Using verbs: *Whether* you write *or* edit for the school paper, you have a very important free press responsibility to tell the truth.

Using nouns: Amber is *as* friendly a person *as* she is an informed and aware scholar.

Using prepositional phrases: Search Engine Optimization (SEO) is useful *not only* for businesses *but also* for consumers.

Using adjective phrases: There are many aspects to SEO, *from* the words on your page *to* the way other sites link to you on the web.

Incorrect: When deciding whether to travel by car or plane, travelers must consider not only the cost but also know how far the destination is.

"Cost" is a noun; "know how far" is a phrase.

Correct: When deciding whether to travel by car or plane, travelers must consider not only the *cost* but also the *distance*.

Incorrect: Many college students must balance not only part-time jobs but also taking full-time course loads.

"Part-time jobs" is a noun; "Taking full-time course loads" is a phrase.

Correct: Many college students must balance not only *part-time jobs* but also *full-time course loads*.

(For more information, review Chapter 14.7 Correlative Conjunctions.)

b. Parallel examples with comparisons

Incorrect: To make new friends, Jessie thought running on the track team was better than membership in the chess club.

"Running" is a gerund; "membership" is a noun.

Correct: To make new friends, Jessie thought *running on the track team* was better than *joining the chess club*.

3. Parallel Structure in Voice

Incorrect: You can either pay the service fee now, or the bill can be paid later.

You should have a consistent subject (you) doing both things.

Correct: You can either pay the service fee now, or you can pay the bill later.

Correct: The service fee *can be paid now*, or the bill *can be paid later*.

(For more information, review Chapter 18.2 Voice.)

4. PARALLEL STRUCTURE IN PHRASES AND CLAUSES

a. Parallel examples with phrases

Incorrect: Please place the football on the counter or you can put it in the shed.
Correct: Please place the football *on the counter* or *in the shed*.

b. Parallel examples with clauses

Incorrect: My parents did not approve of my actions or what I said.
Correct: My parents did not approve of *what I did* nor *what I said*.

c. Parallelism in Action

Incorrect: According to my taxes, I donated money to a women's center, children's hospitals, and a public school last year.
Correct: According to my taxes, I donated money to <u>a</u> women's center, <u>two</u> children's hospitals, and <u>a</u> public school last year.

Incorrect: I taught my sister to speak properly, eating correctly, and saying "thank you."
Correct: I taught my sister <u>to speak</u> properly, <u>to eat</u> correctly, and <u>to say</u> "thank you."
Correct: I taught my sister to <u>speak</u> properly, <u>eat</u> correctly, and <u>say</u> "thank you."

Incorrect: Arts and crafts projects encourage kids to be creative, to be patient, and allows them to feel a sense of accomplishment.
Correct: Arts and crafts projects encourage kids to be creative, to be patient, and to appreciate a job well done.
Correct: Arts and crafts projects encourage kids to be creative, to be patient, and to accomplish tasks that can boost their self-esteem.
Correct: Arts and crafts projects encourage kids to be creative, to be patient, and to take pride in their work.

Incorrect: Wikipedia is an ambitious project that lacks sufficient credibility for college work but as an example of "crowdsourcing" it is intriguing.
Correct: Wikipedia is an ambitious project that lacks sufficient credibility for college work but provides an intriguing example of "crowdsourcing."

Incorrect: To complete this ceiling fan installation, you will need a screwdriver, wrench, a pair of pliers, two standard light bulbs, electrical tape, and patience.
Correct: To complete this ceiling fan installation, you will need a screwdriver, a wrench, a pair of pliers, two standard light bulbs, electrical tape, and patience.

Incorrect: In some parts of the country, a carbonated beverage is called "soda," whereas "pop" is used in other parts of the country.
Correct: In some parts of the country, a carbonated beverage is called "soda," whereas in other parts of the country, it is called "pop."

Incorrect: The best American western movies look as though they were filmed on location in the American west, but Europe was the shooting location for many of them.
Correct: The best American western movies look as though they were filmed on location in the American west, but many were actually filmed far away in Europe.

Incorrect: Many controversial works of literature have been banned from school libraries. Examples include "Howl," a poem by Allen Ginsberg; the great Mark Twain novel *The Adventures of Huckleberry Finn*; and J.D. Salinger's young adult favorite *The Catcher in the Rye*; and even the Bible has found itself banned at times as well.
Correct: Many controversial works of literature have been banned from school libraries. Examples include "Howl," a poem by Allen Ginsberg; *The Adventures of Huckleberry Finn*, the great novel by Mark Twain; *The Catcher in the Rye*, the young adult favorite by J.D. Salinger; and even the Bible.

Incorrect: "The vessel also has a 1,380-seat theater that will show the Broadway musical Grease, comedy club, jazz club, casino, aquatheater and karaoke bar."
Sloan, Gene. "Largest cruise ship ever sets sail on inaugural voyage." *USA Today, 23 May 2016.*
Correct: The vessel also has a 1,380-seat theater that will show the Broadway musical Grease. The theater also acts as a comedy club, jazz club, casino, aquatheater, and karaoke bar.

EXERCISES

PARALLELISM EXERCISE 15.5A

Identify each sentence as correct or incorrect. Revise the sentences that are incorrect.

1. Circling above, the hawks scanned the ground for tiny field mice, for baby raccoons near streams, and some chipmunks were running in the wheat field.

2. Red-tailed hawks perch on fence posts along the back road and on electric poles near the city.

3. Doctors are encouraging patients to consume more water and exercising three times a week.

4. The hotel clerk told Geoffrey to cancel his reservation or he should pay for the room in cash.

5. Her father said he would take the family either to the Grand Canyon or they could see the Painted Desert.

6. A news story on the cable networks today is not so much a news story as it is a questionable manipulation of the truth.

7. Have watching television, using computers, and cell phones negatively impacted our culture?

8. Is cable news today reliable, unbiased, and accurate?

9. Employees must not only wear protective covering but also ID badges should be carried at all times.

10. It is better to show up for work on time than running behind schedule.

PARALLELISM EXERCISE 15.5B

Mark correct or incorrect for parallel structure. Revise the sentences that are incorrect.

1. During Isabella's trip to Florence, she visited the Uffizi Museum, toured St. Peter's Cathedral, and went shopping in Florence.

2. To her relief, many Italians spoke English to visitors and were translating Italian for American tourists.

3. She was most impressed by the sculptures of Michelangelo, including *David*, the *Pieta,* and the one of Moses.

4. If you travel to Florence, be sure to visit the small shops along the narrow alleys where hand-made leather suitcases, briefcases, and purses are sold.

5. Also, be sure to pack lightly, to purchase train tickets ahead of time, and to carry two credit cards.

6. In her travel article, Olive Ventini claims that tourists can visit the Duomo di Firenze as long as they arrive early and taking pictures is avoided.

7. The English-Italian dictionary is helpful not only to those who speak Italian but also many people trying to learn.

8. Finding a cheap hotel room is difficult during winter months, but hostels are a great alternative if you do not mind sharing a room and sleeping on a hard mattress.

9. Michelangelo, a true Renaissance man, was a great painter and he made many sculptures.

10. Either plan to stay in Rome for several weeks or making a quick visit is a possibility.

11. Some argue that getting enrolled into college classes is harder than to take the actual courses.

12. According to those who practice mindfulness, it is easier to begin meditating for a few minutes than to sit for fifteen minutes.

13. George and Martha learned it is better to trust their intuition when traveling than listening to advice from strangers.

14. Taking notes requires summarizing key points, highlighting details, and be sure to use a consistent method.

15. Running the 100 meter hurdles is easier than when you run the 300 meter hurdles.

PARALLELISM EXERCISE 15.5C
Mark correct or incorrect for parallel structure. Revise the sentences that are incorrect.

1. At the park Jimmy enjoys climbing on the monkey bars, swinging on the tire swing, and to play in the sandbox.
2. Gas prices are near record highs; drivers must carpool, to check their tire pressure, and driving no faster than the speed limit.
3. Jessica made an "A" on her science project, a "B" on her math quiz, and her English quiz was 100 percent.
4. College is difficult; students must read all the assignments, complete all the homework, and attend all the classes.
5. In order to succeed in college, one must study hard, manage one's time, and take advantage of opportunities for assistance.
6. To make a good grade, reading the book, to turn in the homework assignments, and attendance must be priorities.
7. The grade was based on the score on the final exam, the number of labs completed, and if we missed too many classes.
8. Your assignment may be done in pencil, pen, or type it on a computer.
9. The library has three sections: the circulation desk, the reference area, and the study rooms.
10. Even when he works out and will eat healthy, Jonathan has a hard time keeping slim.

PARALLELISM EXERCISE 15.5D
Mark correct or incorrect for parallel structure. Revise the sentences that are incorrect.

1. Because Sue neither eats well nor is exercising, she has no hope of losing weight before her wedding.
2. Yoshi loves music, conversation, and to go dancing in clubs.
3. Steven enjoys playing video games, listening to heavy metal, and skateboarding.
4. Leslie prefers watching television, reading a good book, or a romantic movie.
5. Jim is always on his iPhone talking, texting, or when he checks his e-mail.
6. The country's biggest problems are economic, social, and the conflicts in the Middle East.
7. In his speech, the candidate addressed the financial meltdown, the war in Afghanistan, and the health care system.
8. Luis likes not only spaghetti and salad but also to grill burgers on the barbecue.
9. The babysitter forgot to give the baby a bath, to wash the dishes, and to take out the trash.
10. The job application asked for my address, my educational level, and what my work experience is.

Chapter 16

PUNCTUATION

Punctuation includes the following:

- End Punctuation
- Commas
- Semicolons
- Colons
- Apostrophes
- Hyphens
- Dashes
- Parentheses
- Ellipsis
- Brackets
- Quotation marks
- Italics

16.1 END PUNCTUATION

A. PERIODS

Periods are used at the end of a declarative sentence.

The movie was over.

John stared out the window at the stars.

I was late to class because I overslept.

B. QUESTION MARKS

Question marks are used at the end of an interrogative sentence, a sentence that asks a question.

Did you see that movie yet?

What is John staring at?

Why were you late to class?

C. EXCLAMATION POINTS

Exclamation points are used at the end of exclamatory sentences. They show excitement or strong emotion. Generally speaking, you should avoid exclamation points in academic writing. Rely on your words to show emphasis instead of punctuation marks.

That movie was awesome!

John, look at me!

I can't believe I overslept again!

EXERCISE

END PUNCTUATION EXERCISE 16.1A

Revise the following sentences for end punctuation problems. Sometimes, using a period or exclamation point is debatable, so be prepared to discuss your answer.

1. How am I supposed to live without you.

2. I will never give you up or let you down?

3. If you liked it, then you should have put a ring on it?

4. I'll love you with all of the madness in my soul.

5. You've got to fight for your right to party.

16.2 COMMAS

Commas can do a number of wonderful things! See the list below for all of their abilities.

A. COORDINATING CONJUNCTIONS
Commas separate two independent clauses joined by a coordinating conjunction (FANBOYS).

> Ex: Harvey was a great man, and Leslie was an amazing woman.
> Ex: The party ended late, so I spent the night at my friend's house.

B. ITEMS IN A SERIES
Commas separate items in a series.

> Ex: You need nuts, bolts, and screws.
> Ex: I drove with Jessica, Suzy, and Lisa to the hockey game.

Note: The comma before the "and" in a series of three is referred to as the Oxford comma. In certain fields, this comma is regarded as extraneous. Nonetheless, this comma performs an important function.

When you have a comma and then two items, you are telling the reader that both of those things are examples of the previous item.

> Ex: My heroes are my parents, Bill Clinton and Oprah Winfrey.

In this example, you are the child of Bill Clinton and Oprah Winfrey (and they both happen to be your heroes). If that's what you mean, leave it as is!

But, if you meant to say that you have several heroes—parents, Clinton, and Winfrey—you need that comma there to show the difference.

> Ex: My heroes are my parents, Bill Clinton, and Oprah Winfrey.

C. INTRODUCTORY PHRASES
Commas are used after introductory phrases of more than two words.

> Ex: By four in the afternoon, traffic is scary on I-275.
> Ex: In the morning, I require a large cup of coffee.
> Ex: At my computer, I answer a lot of emails.

D. DEPENDENT CLAUSES
Commas separate dependent clauses at the start of the sentence from the independent clause.

> Ex: Because her alarm clock was broken, she overslept and missed the bus.
> Ex: When I stay up late, I make sure that my alarm is set to a loud setting.

Note: If the clauses are reversed so that the independent clause starts the sentence, you do not need a comma.

> Ex: She overslept and missed the bus because her alarm clock was broken.
> Ex: I make sure that my alarm is set to a loud setting when I stay up late.

E. TRANSITIONAL EXPRESSIONS
Commas are used to set off transitional expressions.

> Ex: Ferns, for example, need less light than other plants.
> Ex: John, for instance, would make a great driver.

F. PARENTHETICAL ELEMENTS
Commas also set off parenthetical elements.

> Ex: By the way, did you see Jim today?
> Ex: In the meantime, can you hold this for me?

G. APPOSITIVES
Commas set off appositives (phrases which rename nouns or pronouns).

> Ex: Judy, our new pitcher, was late to the playoff game.
> Ex: Sasha, the new clerk in the office, was still learning how to login to his computer.
> Ex: Darth Vader, Lord of the Sith, conquered many star systems.

One word appositives are not set off when they are essential to the meaning of the sentence.

Ex: The poet Shelly wrote "Ode to the West Wind."
Ex: The poet's wife, Mary, wrote *Frankenstein*.

H. Nonrestrictive relative clauses

Commas are used with nonrestrictive relative clauses (clauses that start with "who," "which," or "that" that are not necessary to the meaning of the sentence). These phrases can be crossed out or removed without changing the essential meaning of the sentence.

Ex: Tom, who is a part-time aviator, loves to tinker with machines of all kinds.
Ex: My cat, who never missed a meal in his life, was nowhere to be seen at dinnertime.

Commas are not used with restrictive relative clauses (clauses that begin with who, which, or that that are necessary to the meaning of the sentence).

Ex: People who complete their work on time make good students.
Ex: The dog that won the contest was sure to win again this year.

I. Correlative conjunctions

Commas are used in a special way with correlative conjunctions (see Ch 14.7 for more information). The general rule is not to use a comma to separate the two key terms of any correlative conjunction.

No Comma Between: From off-site blogs to strategic recommended keyword placement, Greg knows everything about Search Engine Optimization.

Too many writers just throw in a comma between a set of correlative conjunctions without knowing why the comma is there and cannot justify the comma when asked about it. However, exceptions occur when the sentence structure is grammatically incorrect without the comma or the comma serves required grammatical function in the sentence.

Yes, Comma Between: **Not only** did Jeff need a textbook, **but** he **also** needed a laptop for his college classes.

When there is a non-restrictive or non-essential clause in the sentence, then the comma—and most frequently a pair of commas—should be used even if it separates the two terms of the correlative conjunction.

Yes, Comma Between: **Both** the article about roofing, which I know little about, **and** the article about plumbing interested me.

The pair of commas enclosing the interrupting non-essential clause are required to indicate the non-restrictive or non-essential insertion in the sentence. The sentence without the interrupting clause reads: Both the article about roofing and the article about plumbing interested me.

J. Addresses

Commas are also used between the elements of an address.

Ex: Send payment to 300 West Road, Stanford, CT 06860.
Ex: He lives in Seattle, Washington.

K. Dates

Commas also separate the elements of a date.

Ex: The wedding is December 12, 2004.
Ex: Her 10th birthday party is September 6, 2016.

Note: If you use the superscript after the number, you do not also need a comma.

Ex: The wedding is December 12th 2004.
Ex: Her 10th birthday party is September 6th 2016.

Do not use a comma with a single-word address or date preceded by a preposition.

Ex: He arrived from Baltimore in January and stayed awhile.
Ex: She lived in New York for the month of February.

L. REPLIES/DIRECT ADDRESS
Commas are used after answering a question with *yes* or *no*.

Ex: No, I do not like this.
Ex: Yes, I will marry you!

Commas are used when addressing someone specific.

Ex: Annie, where did you get your gun?
Ex: Are you going to class today, Mark?

Note: This comma can save lives.

Ex: Let's eat, Adam! (We have invited Adam to eat with us.)
Ex: Let's eat Adam! (We have invited everyone to eat Adam. Creepy.)

Commas are needed after interjections like ah, oh, etc.

Ex: Ah, this water is refreshing.
Ex: Oh, you are the best!
Ex: Woohoo, we won the big game!

M. CONTRAST
Commas are also used to contrast.

Ex: Harold, not Roy, is my favorite player.
Ex: *Return of the Jedi*, not *The Empire Strikes Back*, is my favorite Star Wars movie.

Note: The contrast comma is often a matter of stylistic choice. It may not be wrong to leave it out, but it typically makes the sentence easier to comprehend for the reader.

N. CONFUSION
Commas are used to avoid confusion. Consider this sentence:

Ex: To George Harrison is a great drummer.

Are you confused? It starts one way but then goes somewhere else. Let a comma help.

Ex: To George, Harrison is a great drummer.

Commas can add clarity to a confusing situation.

O. COMMA ABUSE: WHEN NOT TO USE A COMMA
Commas are great, even powerful, but they can only do so much. Don't overwork them!
1. Do not use a comma to separate a subject and a verb.

NOT: John's cat, wanted to go outside.
BUT: John's cat wanted to go outside.

2. Do not use commas when you need something more permanent like a semicolon or period. Connecting two independent clauses with a comma creates a comma splice (see chapter 17.4).

NOT: I was working hard, I forgot to eat lunch.
BUT: I was working hard; I forgot to eat lunch.
OR: I was working hard. I forgot to eat lunch.
OR: I was working so hard that I forgot to eat lunch.

3. Do not use commas when you have a compound subject or object.

NOT: The music teacher, and the art teacher went on a date, and saw a movie.
BUT: The music teacher and the art teacher went on a date and saw a movie.

4. Do not use a comma when your sentence begins with an independent clause.

NOT: I was exhausted, until I had my morning coffee.
BUT: I was exhausted until I had my morning coffee.

EXERCISES

COMMAS EXERCISE 16.2A

Check the following sentences for comma use in a series, coordinating conjunctions that separate independent clauses, and introductory elements. If a sentence is already correct, label it "Correct."

1. Before the fisherman throws the seine net he spots a large school of minnows off the beach.
2. Throwing a net requires practice and patience.
3. A variety of bait fish can be caught and used to catch yellow tail, whiting and trout.
4. Juan and his father prefer freshwater fishing because they catch more fish in the lake near their home.
5. However, Maggie and Diana like to fish off the beach, and their friends join them later in the day around sunset.
6. Putting a live shrimp on the hook, can result in pricking yourself, so it is best first to push the hook into the shrimp's thorax.
7. After the hook punctures the shell of the thorax push the hook through the shrimp's body toward the head.
8. Many prefer to cut up squid and use a piece on the end of the hook as bait.
9. The rostrum is the spike-like extension of the shrimp's head, and it is very sharp.
10. While some are picky eaters most Florida fish will eat cut up pieces of squid, pin fish, and sardines.
11. Before casting the fishing rod, it helps to chum the water with small pieces of bait fish.
12. Off St. Petersburg beach, locals catch sting ray, catfish and needle fish, none of which are kept and eaten.
13. Because Florida requires that people purchase a fishing license fewer people fish today than they did in the past.
14. Jose, Ray, and Dommi challenge Mikel, Mark, and Marie to a fishing contest each July.
15. Marie always wins, and she is a good sport about it.

COMMAS EXERCISE 16.2B

If the sentence needs a comma, add one, and then write the relevant comma rule next to the sentence. If the sentence does not need a comma, write "C" next to the sentence. You do not need to write a rule if the sentence does not need a comma.

1. She gave him her opinion but he did not want to listen.
2. Give me liberty or give me death.
3. He appreciates her efforts but doesn't want to pay her for her time.
4. Whenever I hear music I want to dance.
5. In the middle of the third act he dropped his popcorn on the floor.
6. I gave you my heart my soul and my money.
7. She held him in her arms kissed him on the forehead and told him goodbye.
8. He is a stubborn egotistical fool.
9. She gave him three new Dell computers.
10. Children who misbehave will not be permitted to stay up late.
11. My sister who rarely remembers my birthday sent me a beautiful bouquet.
12. Cats that scratch the furniture should remain outdoors.
13. Chloe my calico cat thinks she is a dog.
14. The play *Death of a Salesman* was written by Arthur Miller.
15. Therefore you must always remember to proofread your work.
16. My father-in-law however is the chairman of the board.
17. The stock market according to most analysts will reach 12,000 next year.
18. Her temper flaring she drove away without saying goodbye.
19. I want two small pizzas not one large one.
20. Those who can pay for the tickets in advance are allowed to go to the concert.
21. Although we were wearing our raincoats we were soaked after the storm.
22. I like baked potatoes yet always order french fries with my meal.

Commas Exercise 16.2C
Check the following sentences for comma use for dependent and independent clauses, use in a series, coordinating conjunctions, and introductory elements.

1. A winter day in Oklahoma is often freezing in the morning and warm in the afternoon.
2. Oats, hay and wheat are common cash crops in the central and eastern part of the state.
3. Although snow falls in the winter, most streams dry out before the end of January.
4. Concerned that Stella had not come home Ryan called her friends, boss, and sister.
5. When Stella met Ryan a meteor shot across the sky.
6. Stella was sure it was a sign, but Ryan laughed it off as a coincidence.
7. Under the canopy of elm many white-tailed deer scratch the snow on the ground for berries and bark.
8. A harvest moon appears to rest on the horizon for hours before finally floating into the night sky.
9. In rural areas of Oklahoma Native Americans build sweat lodges designed for purification rituals.
10. Porous rocks are burned for five hours, lifted with antlers into the sweat lodge and doused with water.

Commas Exercise 16.2D
Remove all unnecessary commas. If a sentence does not contain any incorrect commas, write "Correct."

1. Leah was confident she would someday become a therapist, or a social worker.
2. Although Luke had never been on a road trip, he was excited to travel across the country, and visit many national landmarks.
3. By the time Andrew finally reached his favorite restaurant, the kitchen was closed.
4. The first animated movie Nathan could remember seeing, was *The Little Mermaid*.
5. After reading the recipe carefully, Anna knew she would need to buy butter, sugar, and sea salt.
6. Jack listened carefully, and could hear a wolf howling in the distance.
7. Connor didn't mind driving to work in Washington, D.C., but he preferred the convenience of the subway.
8. Charlotte was excited about starting her new job, but did not know exactly what to expect from her new supervisor, who had a reputation for being harsh, yet fair.
9. Minors, who are not permitted to drink, are welcome to join the event, if they arrive with a parent, or legal guardian.
10. I decided to go to my favorite restaurant, because I wanted to celebrate my promotion.

COMMAS EXERCISE 16.2E

Choose the correct answer.

1. Which is correct?
   a. My iPad, which is vital to today's class lesson, was stolen.
   b. My iPad which is vital to today's class lesson was stolen.
2. Which is correct?
   a. John, who loves his expensive toys, parks his RV in my yard.
   b. John who loves his expensive toys parks his RV in my yard.
3. Which is correct?
   a. I knew he was bad news, when he walked in the door.
   b. I knew he was bad news when he walked in the door.
4. Which is correct?
   a. Although he was homeless during his internship, Chris Garner would succeed.
   b. Although he was homeless during his internship Chris Garner would succeed.
5. Which is correct?
   a. The rain poured down, and soaked Austin to the skin on his way to work.
   b. The rain poured down and soaked Austin to the skin on his way to work.

16.3 SEMICOLONS

Semicolons separate related ideas of equal importance. They have four major uses:

A. CLOSELY RELATED IDEAS

Use a semicolon to connect two complete sentences that contain closely related ideas.

> Ex: The concert was brilliant; the crowd gave the band a standing ovation.
> Ex: I said I'd do it; I didn't say when I'd do it.

B. SERIES OF ITEMS

Use a semicolon to separate a series of items if the items are long or if they contain commas.

> Ex: The *Millenium Falcon* blasted out of Mos Eisley with Obi-Wan Kenobi, the Jedi Master; Luke Skywalker, the untried farm boy; Han Solo, the scoundrel; and Chewbacca, the hairy co-pilot.
> Ex: I have lived in Chicago, Illinois; Miami, Florida; Cleveland, Ohio; and Tampa, Florida.

C. TRANSITIONAL PHRASES

Use a semicolon to separate two complete sentences joined with transitional phrases (on the other hand, in fact, for example).

> Ex: The Force only works on the weak minded; for example, the stormtroopers whom Obi-Wan tricks into thinking their droids weren't the ones they were looking for are easily fooled.
> Ex: *Star Wars: A New Hope* ends on a celebratory note; on the other hand, *The Empire Strikes Back* is much more somber.

D. CONJUNCTIVE ADVERBS

Use a semicolon to separate two complete sentences joined with conjunctive adverbs such as also, anyway, finally, hence, however, instead, next, therefore, and thus.

> Ex: The cantina was filled with alien life forms; however, the two droids were not allowed inside.
> Ex: Luke's attempt to keep his head down are unsuccessful; instead, he is threatened by two angry aliens when he walks in the bar.

E. WHEN NOT TO USE A SEMICOLON

1. Do not use a semicolon to introduce a list or a quote.

NOT: Dr. Johnson observed; "This is a wonderful idea!"
BUT: Dr. Johnson observed, "This is a wonderful idea!"
OR: Dr. Johnson observed: "This is a wonderful idea!"

2. Do not use a semicolon to introduce a series or explanation.

NOT: I have traveled to; China, Japan, and West Africa.
BUT: I have traveled to China, Japan, and West Africa.

3. Do not use a semicolon between a dependent and independent clause.

NOT: The city is in danger; because of rising water levels.
BUT: The city is in danger because of rising water levels.
NOT: The mountain in impressive; nearly 30,000 feet tall.
BUT: The mountain is impressive, nearly 30,000 feet tall.
OR: The mountain is impressive at nearly 30,000 feet tall.

EXERCISE

SEMICOLONS EXERCISE 16.3A

In the following sentences, add semicolons where they are needed, and remove them where they are not.

> Hint: In some cases, removing a semicolon will require the addition of a comma. If a sentence is already correct, label that sentence "correct":

1. Some people don't like the outdoors, others spend as much time as they can outside.

2. Although I didn't grow up in a town with many things to do, places to visit, or things to see; I always found a way to have fun with friends, with family, and even with complete strangers.

3. On our next vacation, we could go to Disney World, which is fun but expensive, St. Augustine, which could be more affordable, depending on our budgeting, or Busch Gardens, which may turn out to be the most convenient option.

4. I will probably get a dog; because the house feels somewhat empty without a pet, and I would like a loyal companion.

5. On stormy days, I like to sit on my porch with a cup of coffee, and I watch the rain fall.

6. My sister enjoys playing baseball, however, she confesses that she's not as passionate about the sport as she used to be.

7. My neighbor's backyard has a small, rusty shed filled with forgotten tools; a pool filled with the greenest, murkiest water I've ever seen; and an upside-down wheelbarrow.

8. The dog cowered in the corner he hated baths and was trying to hide.

9. Some writers use semicolons frequently; others, such as Kurt Vonnegut, deliberately construct their sentences so that semicolons are not necessary.

10. Some small businesses are successful, others fail quickly, even after their owners have down as much research, preparation, and analysis as possible, and others ride a roller coaster of success and setback before finally stabilizing.

16.4 COLONS

The colon has specific grammatical functions which are very useful. Generally, colons are used to separate items of unequal importance: what follows the colon in a sentence is less important than what precedes the colon, but what follows often provides a detail or an example or explanation of that content of the first part of the sentence. Note also that a colon always follows an independent clause (complete sentence), but the relationship and the grammatical structure is different from the relationship between an independent clause and a following subordinate clause.

A. EMPHASIS

The colon can be used to emphasize a phrase or single word at the end of a sentence, often providing an explanatory phrase or an appositive.

> After weeks of deliberation following a months-long trial, the O. J. Simpson jury finally reached a verdict: not guilty.
> His travels throughout his military career were extraordinary: five continents, three dozen countries, and over a hundred cities.

B. INTRODUCE A LIST

The colon is used to introduce a list.

> I have lived in the following cities: New York, Chicago, Miami, and Tampa.
> The bookstore specializes in three subjects: art, architecture, and graphics.

C. BETWEEN INDEPENDENT CLAUSES (SENTENCES)

The colon is used between independent clauses when the second explains or details the first. In such usage, the colon functions in much the same way as the semicolon. As with the semicolon, do not capitalize the first word after the colon unless the word is ordinarily capitalized.

> I have very little time to learn the language: my new job in France starts in five weeks.
> A college degree is still worth something: a recent survey revealed that college graduates earned roughly 60% more than workers with only a high school diploma.

However, when two or more sentences follow a colon, capitalize the first word following the colon.

> He made three points: First, the company was losing over a million dollars each month. Second, the stock price was lower than it had ever been. Third, no banks were willing to loan the company any more money.

D. INTRODUCE A QUOTATION

Colons are used to introduce a formal quotation or when the quotation is introduced by a complete sentence.

> Upon the occasion of his death, Nathan Hale supposedly declared, "My only regret is that I have but one life to give for my country."
> Upon the occasion of his death, Nathan Hale supposedly declared: "My only regret is that I have but one life to give for my country."
> The spectators only had one thing to say: "He was a true patriot."

E. Non-grammatical uses of the colon

Colons are used to display time and ratios.

> At 11:35 a.m., the odds were set at 3:2 for the favorite horse to win the race.

Colons are used for chapter and verse in classic plays and religious texts.

> John 3:16 is a popular verse from the Bible.

The colon is used to separate the volume from page numbers of a cited work, with no space before or after the colon, or to separate the city of publication from the publisher.

> Higgenbotham, Evelyn Brooks. "African American Women's History and the Metalanguage of Race." *Signs 17* (Winter 1992): 251-274.
>
> Gomez, Michael. *Reversing Sail: A History of the African Diaspora* (New York: Cambridge University Press, 2005).

The colon is frequently used in business and personal correspondence.

> Dear Ms. Smith:
> cc: Tom Smith
> Attention: Accounts Payable
> PS: Don't forget your swimsuit.

F. When NOT to use a Colon

Do *not* use a colon when the listed items are incorporated into the flow of the sentence. For example, do not use a colon before a list if it follows a verb or preposition or "such as" or "including" that would not otherwise require any punctuation in that sentence.

> NOT: The most well-known actor is: Brad Pitt.
> BUT: The most well-known actor is Brad Pitt.
>
> NOT: I was going to: the store later on.
> BUT: I was going to the store later on.
>
> NOT: The bookstore specializes in: art, architecture, and graphic design.
> BUT: The bookstore specializes in art, architecture, and graphic design.
>
> NOT: I wanted to purchase the finest items, such as: caviar, lobster, and truffles.
> BUT: I wanted to purchase the finest items, such as caviar, lobster, and truffles.
>
> NOT: I have lived in the following cities, including: New York, Chicago, Miami, and Tampa.
> BUT: I have lived in the following cities, including New York, Chicago, Miami, and Tampa.

EXERCISES

COLON EXERCISE 16.4A

Correct the punctuation errors in the following sentences. In particular, look for missing or incorrectly included colons. If a sentence is already correct, simply label it "Correct." HINT: It may be helpful to review the rules regarding both colons and semicolons.

1. My best friend has three phobias, spiders, snakes, and bridges.
2. On the wall in Abel's office, one can find a plaque on which his favorite saying is engraved; "Good things come to those who wait."
3. Although I would love to go on a cruise, there is one thing I fear about such a vacation; motion sickness.
4. I don't usually enjoy camping: however, I had a wonderful time during my last trip.
5. A sign in my aunt's nursing home declares that the facility has three priorities; safety, safety, and safety.
6. I have never minded doing laundry; most other household chores are far more unpleasant to me.
7. At 915 a.m., our minister opened his sermon by reading Corinthians 13,4: "Love is patient; love is kind. It does not envy; it does not boast; it is not proud."
8. My husband enjoys shopping for furniture: I would rather stay at home.
9. I intend save money for: a new phone, a new jacket, and a new pair of shoes.
10. Filiberto would forever cherish the memories from his bachelor party; he knew he had the best friends ever.

COLON EXERCISE 16.4B

Correct the punctuation errors in the following sentences. In particular, look for missing or incorrectly included colons. If a sentence is already correct, simply label it "Correct." HINT: It may be helpful to review the rules regarding both colons and semicolons.

1. My favorite shows of the 1990s are: *The Simpsons*, *Friends*, and *MTV Unplugged*.
2. Although much of the Bible is debated by religious scholars; most agree that Matthew 21:17 is uncontroversial.
3. My day was quite productive I went to the bank, I washed the car, and I bought a new hat.
4. Many people in my family have had a career in medicine, my father, my sister, and my cousin Brett.
5. After he crashed his bike into the fence, a single word echoed throughout the neighborhood: "Help!"
6. I usually enjoy watching classic movies; this one was disappointing, however.
7. My grandmother didn't learn to drive until she was 55: living in New York City, she didn't feel it was necessary.
8. According to the police report; the arrest happened at 3:13 a.m.
9. Her best friend had some bad habits: not putting laundry away, neglecting to clean the shower, and letting the car get far too cluttered.
10. Many movies depict crimes, such as: burglary, fraud, and blackmail.

REVIEW EXERCISE

PUNCTUATION REVIEW EXERCISE 16A: END PUNCTUATION, COMMAS, SEMICOLONS, AND COLONS

Please correct all punctuation errors in the following sentences. Look for missing or incorrectly placed commas, semicolons, and colons. If a sentence is already correct, label it as "Correct."

1. Carolina had never enjoyed: swimming, camping, or anything else outdoors.

2. Although I had never done well with math in high school; I found my college algebra instructor to be inspiring and helpful.

3. All writing contest entries must contain the following: a cover page, an on-topic essay, and a list of references.

4. He wasn't planning on buying a new phone, an intriguing ad convinced him that he should save money for one.

5. By his second year of middle school, Jacob's room was filled with Harry Potter memorabilia; posters, shirts, and countless figurines.

6. Of all the household chores on Alberto's "to do" list, there was one he dreaded most of all: laundry.

7. Daniella was excited about starting the new fitness plan, it had been recommended to her by all her friends.

8. The dinner was formal and elegant, but the food was disappointing.

9. Joanna researched the graduate programs at many colleges, USF, UCF, NYU, and several other schools around the country.

10. Because I stayed up late last night; I pressed the snooze button several times this morning.

16.5 APOSTROPHES

Apostrophes are used for three main reasons:

- To show possession or ownership

- To show omitted letters in contractions

- To show when letters or words are used in special ways

A. POSSESSION OR OWNERSHIP

To show ownership using apostrophes, there are a few rules to remember:

1. When the possessive noun is singular, use an apostrophe and s to show ownership.

The girl's toy	the store's window	the car's door
An umbrella's handle	a fox's tail	a book's cover

2. When the possessive noun is plural, use an apostrophe to show ownership.

The girls' toys	the stores' windows	the cars' doors
The umbrellas' handles	the foxes' tails	the books' covers

3. When the possessive noun is single and ends in s, use an apostrophe.

Ulysses' crewmates	Chris' bedroom	Thomas' car

4. When the possessive noun is plural and doesn't end in s, use an apostrophe and an s.

The children's clothing	the women's section	the men's room

5. When more than one person owns the object, put the 's on the second word.

Jane and Chris' house	Bill and Joe's boat	Sam and Ted's restaurant

6. In a compound word, put the 's on the final word.

My mother-in-law's coat	The Bailey-Smith's house

Note: Do NOT use an apostrophe when the word is simply plural but not possessive. If there is more than one thing, just add *s* or *es* as spelling rules dictate. Apostrophes only show ownership, not plurality.

B. CONTRACTIONS

To show omitted letters in a contraction, use an apostrophe in the place of the missing letters.

Cannot = can't	did not = didn't	was not = wasn't	I am = I'm
2017 = '17	It is = It's	were no t= weren't	I would = I'd

Note: Contractions are considered informal, so in academic writing, you should spell out your words instead.

C. SPECIAL USE

To show when letters are being used in a special way, or to avoid confusion, you might use an apostrophe for clarification.

1. If you have lowercase letters, use 's to pluralize them.

> Your b's are improving!

Note: For uppercase letters, you do not have to use an apostrophe unless it is A or I.

> Those two assignments were the first Cs he ever received.
> He finally received all A's.

2. You do not need an apostrophe to pluralize abbreviations.

> There were four PhDs at the wedding yesterday.

3. You do not need an apostrophe when you pluralize a word, unless it's in quotes.

> I'm tired of your *Yeses* and *Sures*.
> I'm tired of your "yes's" and "sure's."

EXERCISE

APOSTROPHES EXERCISE 16.5A

Correct all apostrophe errors in the following sentences. Some apostrophes are unnecessary, and some need to be added. If a sentence is already correct, write "Correct."

1. After Jayden signed up for a streaming service, he sold all of his DVD's and other video's.

2. My computer wont start Window's, and it's going to be difficult to find a solution.

3. To find recalls for your car, do an online search for it's make and model.

4. "It's starting to rain," David observed, "but didn't the news forecast a sunny day?"

5. Jackson borrowed his wifes iPad to complete his online homework.

6. After Paul put in his two week's notice at work, he was overcome with mixed feeling's.

7. Dana scanned the row of plain white car's in the lot and couldn't tell which one was his'.

8. "We could have the party at Dan's house," Jeb said, "or we could have it at Tim's."

9. James was hoping to spend the holiday's at his parents' house and was glad that his mother and father were both still healthy and happily married.

10. Logan had a bad habit of using apostrophe's to form plural's.

16.6 HYPHENS

Hyphens (-) are used for four reasons:

A. Combine words

Hyphens are used to combine words.

>Ex: Samantha Smith-Jones was my mother-in-law.

B. Two adjectives

They are also used to join two adjectives together when they appear before a noun.

>Ex: Will Smith is a well-known actor.

Note: Hyphens are not used with adjectives when they appear after a noun.

>Ex: The actor Will Smith is well known.

C. Fractions/compound numbers

Hyphens are also used for fractions or compound numbers.

>Ex: I was three-fourths through my textbook by chapter twenty-seven.

D. Awkward words/spellings

Hyphens are also used to clarify awkward words or spellings.

>Ex: The t-shirt I wanted was out of stock, so I had to show some self-control.

>Ex: When she asked me to resend the email, I told her I re-sent it.

EXERCISE

HYPHENS EXERCISE 16.6 A

Add and remove hyphens as needed. If a sentence is already correct, write "Correct."

1. Felipe knew he would be grounded if he didn't complete every item on his todo list on-time.

2. Although Madison had graduated from high-school twenty-five years ago, he still had fond memories of his favorite teacher, Ms. Smith-Stevenson.

3. The television program was attempting to reach the 18 - 35 demographic.

4. Joshua loves his brand-new, state-of-the-art phone.

5. Maya thinks her husband is a good-looking man, but she loves his sense of humor most-of-all.

6. Although Samantha prefers to shop at small, family-owned stores, she sometimes shops at Walmart as well.

7. According to your most recent email, our building passed its most recent safety-inspection.

8. My thirty-year-old son is the proud father of a cute two-year-old.

9. Over one-third of this community's residents will likely retire within ten years, but many others are on a twenty-year plan.

10. I couldn't help but roll my eyes at Mr. Look-How-Great-I-Am.

11. My sister didn't have a long-term relationship until after she had graduated college.

16.7 Dashes and Parentheses

A. Dashes

Dashes are used as interrupters to add more information. They often indicate a shift in thought or can even set off nonessential elements.

Ex: I was planning on going to class—but we'll get to that part.

Ex: I wanted to tell you—I really did—but I just couldn't do it.

Dashes in formal writing stand out—they make a powerful statement—forcing the reader to stop and take in the extra information. They are the written equivalent of a hand banging on the desk, a stop sign, a demand for attention at this very moment—don't overuse them.

B. Parentheses

Parentheses are used to insert extra information, but in a more subtle way than dashes. Where the dash demands the reader's attention, the humble parenthesis is more of a whisper, a polite request to look at the extra information without the extra push.

Ex: Herpetology (the study of snakes) was not something Indiana Jones wanted to investigate further.

Ex: I wanted to let Sam (my brother-in-law) know about the change right away.

Parentheses are also use for in-text citations. For more on citation, see Part Five.

EXERCISES

DASHES AND HYPHENS EXERCISE 16.7A

Add hyphens and dashes where they are necessary. If you are writing your revisions by hand, be sure to use a very short line to indicate a dash, and a much longer line to indicate a hyphen.

1. I have never held a dangerous job my worst ever work injury was a paper cut but I respect those who face the risk of severe injury every day.
2. The period of 2012 2015 included four of the most exciting years of my life.
3. Although off campus living seems exciting, I prefer the convenience of living on campus.
4. My co worker is quite good looking I can't deny that but a romantic relationship could cause problems.
5. My two year old child behaves as if she is already four years old.
6. Because I am twenty four years old, it may be difficult or expensive for me to rent a car from even a discount rent a car service.
7. Although I may disagree with my uncle we've certainly had our share of heated debates I can respect his ultra conservative politics and he can respect my more liberal point of view.
8. My ex boyfriend seems so self aware now that he realizes what he truly wants in life.
9. Some people believe in an all knowing deity, but one can find many different belief systems in the world.
10. This cage looks escape proof the bars are strong and the locks are authentic but Mark can escape it Houdini style.

DASHES AND PARENTHESES EXERCISE 16.7B

Add parentheses and dashes where appropriate. Remove commas as necessary. If a sentence is already correct, label it as correct. Be prepared to explain your choices.

1. I've never used a typewriter, I've never had the chance, but I want to see what it's like.
2. My mother-in-law doesn't like me, there's no way you can deny that depressing fact.
3. He thanked me again, although I was happy to do it, for giving him a ride home.
4. I look forward to our meeting in my office, room 145 in the old building, tomorrow.
5. I've been trying to lose weight for a long time, well, who hasn't?
6. There is only way I could describe my experience of tripping over a cactus, painful.
7. My friend got in trouble for "borrowing" items from a store, if you know what I mean.
8. For dessert, Dad served us key lime pie, my favorite.
9. There's no real reason to register for classes early, unless, of course, you'd prefer to take the classes that truly interest you.

16.8 ELLIPSIS AND BRACKETS
A. ELLIPSIS

Ellipsis are the three dots that are used to show either a pause in the speech or that you've left something out of the quote.

Example: "And then," Prince Lir said, "she looked at me..." Here he paused while remembering the lovely face of his beloved.

Example: "And then," Prince Lir said, "she looked at me...and I was sorry I had killed the thing--sorry for killing a dragon!"

Most often, you will not just drop an entire quoted passage into your discussion. Instead you will want to take portions out or adapt the syntax to fit your own more effectively. When you want to leave out a part of the quotation to make the passage more direct, you will use ellipses to account for the missing material:

One critic has commented that "'revenge tragedy' customarily...portrays the ghosts of the murdered urging revenge, a hesitation on the part of the avenger, a delay in proceeding to his vengeance, and his feigned or actual madness. The antagonist's counter-intrigue against the revenger may occupy a prominent position in the plot" (Bowers 63-64). With these criteria in mind, one can immediately see that Hamlet is not by any means a unique play, but that it does work within the conventions of the genre.

When quoting, you should not put ellipsis before or after the quote. Readers assume more came before and after what you've quoted.

Incorrect: Colonel Sanders explains why "...the chicken is finger lickin' good!" (Jones 22).

Incorrect: Colonel Sanders explains why "the chicken is finger lickin' good..." (Jones 22).

Incorrect: Sanders explains why "...the chicken is finger lickin' good..." (Jones 22).

Correct: Colonel Sanders explains how "the chicken is finger lickin' good!" (Jones 22).

B. BRACKETS

Brackets [ ] are used to show that you have changed something in the quoted material. Sometimes you have to "adapt" the wording of the quoted material so that it blends with the syntax of your own sentence. In this case, you will use brackets **[ ]** to indicate that you have added or changed material:

Bowers explains how "this revenge constitutes the main action of the play . . . [and it] must be the cause of the catastrophe" (63).

EXERCISE

ELLIPSIS AND BRACKETS EXERCISE 16.8A

The original quote from Jane Goodshaw on p. 28: "Cats can be quite challenging pets for young children because they don't always respond immediately, refuse to be cuddled on command, and display their discontent with sharp claws."

1. Which sentence uses ellipsis properly?
   a. Goodshaw explains that "...cats can be quite challenging pets for young children..." (28).
   b. Goodshaw explains that "cats can be quite challenging pets...because they don't always respond immediately" (28).
2. Write a sentence using the above quote that uses ellipsis.
3. Which sentence uses brackets properly?
   a. The author [Jane Goodshaw] explains how cats "refuse to be cuddled on command" (Goodshaw 28).
   b. The author explains how cats can "refuse to be cuddled on command, and [they] display their discontent with sharp claws" (Goodshaw 28).
4. Write a sentence using the above quote that uses brackets.

16.9 QUOTATION MARKS AND ITALICS
A. QUOTATION MARKS
Quotation marks have many uses.

1. DIRECT SPEECH
Quotation marks show what someone has directly said.

> Ex: "But I wanted to feed the fish tonight!" the tired child exclaimed.

Note: If you have a quotation within a quotation, as in you are quoting someone who is also quoting someone, you would use a single quotation mark inside the double quotation marks.

> Ex: "So then I heard her yell, 'But I wanted to feed the fish tonight!' so I knew she was really exhausted," I explained to my friend over the phone.

2. DIALOGUE
There are some rules for writing down a conversation. Each time a new person speaks, you should indent so that readers can follow who is speaking.

> "Why are you following me?" Samantha whirled on her pursuer, anger creasing her features into hard lines.
> "I'm not following you," the man behind her exclaimed. "I'm walking to the library." He was bundled up against the weather, so she couldn't see anything except his lips moving.
> "Why should I believe you?" she demanded. "You've been back there for three blocks already."
> He pointed at the well-lighted building halfway up the block. "I'm going to the library, lady. I have some studying to do." He adjusted the shoulder straps of his backpack and continued walking down the street in front of her.

3. QUOTATIONS FROM SOURCES
The information set off in quotation marks may not be what someone *said* but what someone *wrote* (as in a book or journal article). In this case, the quotation may be followed by an in-text citation in the form of a parenthetical reference giving credit to the source of the information.

> Ex: "I'm a curious person. Like all journalists, I'm a voyeur. I write about what I find fascinating" (Roach 14).

> Ex: According to science journalist Nancy Roach, "I'm a curious person. Like all journalists, I'm a voyeur. I write about what I find fascinating" (14).

Note: An indirect quotation is when you say what someone else said but *in your own words*. Do not use quotation marks in an indirect quotation.

> Ex: The tired child said she wanted to feed the fish tonight.

> Ex: Mary Roach said that she writes about what she finds fascinating.

Indirect quotations can be distinguished from a direct quotation by the shift in pronoun use (from first person to third) and may include the use of the word *that*. These changes indicate that the words are not the exact words of the speaker.

> **Rule of Thumb to test direct from indirect quotations:** Pretend you are the speaker and try to say the sentence. Does it sound like something you would say about yourself? If you were the child, would you say that *she* wanted to feed the fish or "I want to feed the fish"?

4. Longer Quotations

If you are quoting a statement that is four typed lines or less, follow the rules as stated above.

a. Block Quotations

If you have five typed lines or more, you must use a block indent format. This requires NO quotation marks but beginning the quoted material on a new line and indenting the quoted material 1 inch from regular left margins only. The block indent format informs readers that the material is a quotation. If a citation is needed to reference the material, place a period at the end of the quotation and then add source citation following the period and start new line to return to the regular paragraph.

> Many psychologists have studied the effects of crowds, or mobs, on individuals. The fact that the entire town participates in the ritualistic murder allows individuals to abdicate their own responsibility. "Diffusion of responsibility . . . explain[s] that being in a group leads one to feel as if one is less responsible" (Garcia et al. 845). Graham Tyson, a South African psychologist,
>
> > described the phenomenon of deindividuation (sic) and concluded . . . on the basis of [his] assessment of the psychological literature, that it is highly probable that an individual in a mob situation will experience deindividuation and that this . . . will lead to diminished responsibility. . . . The dense crowding . . . appeared to have caused some . . . to become deindividuated and therefore less aware than they normally were of their individual identity and accountability. (Colman 1072-3)
>
> In other words, people do not feel responsible for their actions when they are in a group. Because everyone in the town, from young children to Old Man Warner, participated, the individual citizens felt no personal responsibility. Psychologist Jerry M. Burger notes the "absence of responsibility has often been cited by psychologists as a contributing factor to aggressive and abhorrent behavior" (3-4). When an individual perceives that someone or something else is responsible for a particular action, he is capable of doing things that he otherwise would not.

(See Student Sample Argumentative Essay--"Human Nature at its Worst" in Chapter 12.9 for more of this essay)

b. Quoting Poetry

If you are quoting poetry of one or two lines, continue in paragraph using quotation marks to open and close the quotation. Use a slash (/) to indicate end of original lines of poetry (this is also known as a line break).

> Most students will recognize the opening lines from this famous poem: "Once upon a midnight dreary, while I pondered, weak and weary,/over many a quaint and curious volume or forgotten lore--" (Poe, lines 1-2).

If more than three lines are quoted, use block indent format, maintaining the original sight lines of the poem (hit Enter at each line break), but do not add slashes.

> Most students will recognize the opening lines from this famous poem:
> Once upon a midnight dreary, while I pondered, weak and weary,
> Over many a quaint and curious volume or forgotten lore--
> While I nodded, nearly napping, suddenly, there came a tapping,
> As of someone gently rapping, rapping at my chamber door.
> (Poe, lines 1-4)

c. Long Speeches

If you have someone speaking for more than one paragraph (as sometimes happens in fiction when someone is telling a story), indent and open quotation marks for the person speaking and then open each additional paragraph with an indent and quotation marks for the same speaker but don't close quotation marks until the last paragraph of this speaker's dialogue--this instance is the only time that quotation marks don't come in pairs.

> "I belong to that classification of people known as wives. I am A Wife. And, not altogether incidentally, I am a mother.
>
> "Not too long ago a male friend of mine appeared on the scene fresh from a recent divorce. He had one child, who is, of course, with his ex-wife. He is looking for another wife. As I thought about him while I was ironing one evening, it suddenly occurred to me that 1, too, would like to have a wife. Why do I want a wife?
>
> "I would like to go back to school so that I can become economically independent, support myself, and, if need be, support those dependent upon me. I want a wife who will work and send me to school. And while I am going to school, I want a wife to take care of my children. I want a wife to keep track of the children's doctor and dentist appointments. And to keep track of mine, too. I want a wife to make sure my children eat properly and are kept clean. I want a wife who will wash the children's clothes and keep them mended. I want a wife who is a good nurturant attendant to my children, who arranges for their schooling, makes sure that they have an adequate social life with their peers, takes them to the park, the zoo, etc. I want a wife who takes care of the children when they are sick, a wife who arranges to be around when the children need special care, because, of course, I cannot miss classes at school. My wife must arrange to lose time at work and not lose the job. It may mean a small cut in my wife's income from time to time, but I guess I can tolerate that. Needless to say, my wife will arrange and pay for the care of the children while my wife is working."
>
> (from "I Want a Wife" by Judy Brady)

5. Special Sense

Quotation marks can be used to set off words that are being used in a special sense.

Ex: I always worry when the sign in the bathroom says "Employees must 'wash' hands."

What does it mean to "wash" hands?

Ex: I wasn't stealing this—I was just "permanently borrowing" it.

6. TYPES OF SOURCES

Quotation marks are also used to distinguish certain types of sources. See the following chart for guidelines of when to use quotation marks or italics around titles (in MLA format—for APA guidelines, see Ch. 25). For use of quotation marks for citing sources, see Part Five.

"Short Works" and "Sections of Longer Works"	Long Works and Collection of Short Works
1. "Title of a Short Poem" Ex: Edgar Allan Poe wrote "The Raven."	Title of an Epic Poem, Book-Length Poem, or Collection of Poems Ex: *The Odyssey* is about a long journey. Ex: The book *Ariel* collects some of Sylvia Plath's most famous poems.
2. "Title of a Short Story" Ex: "Young Goodman Brown" was composed by Nathaniel Hawthorne.	Title of a Novel or Book Ex: *The Scarlet Letter* was also composed by Nathaniel Hawthorne.
3. "Title of an Essay" Ex: Our textbook included "Letter from Birmingham Jail" by Martin Luther King.	Title of a Collection or Anthology of Essays Ex: *The Norton Anthology of Literature* is a heavy book.
4. "Title of a Short Song" Ex: "Zombie" is a popular song by the Cranberries.	Title of a CD, Cassette, or Album Ex: *Rubber Soul* by the Beatles is celebrated as a classic rock album.
5. "Title of an Article in a Newspaper" Ex: I enjoyed "My Thoughts on that Thing."	Title of a Newspaper Ex: *The New York Times* is my favorite newspaper.
6. Title of "Individual Episode" in a Television Series Ex: My favorite *Star Trek* episode is called "The Trouble with Tribbles."	Title of a Television Series as a Whole Ex: *The Simpsons* has been on for many years.
7. "Page on a Website" Ex: "How to take care of your new betta fish" was incredibly helpful.	Website Title Ex: I spend a lot of time on *Wikipedia* when I want to learn something new.
8. "Title of a Chapter in a Book" Ex: My favorite chapter in the novel has been "Many Meetings."	Ballet or Opera Ex: *The Nutcracker Suite* and *Aida* are famous performances.
9. [Most movie titles are italicized. Depending on your style guide, however, very short films are sometimes placed in quotation marks, sometimes italicized. Consult your style guide to be sure.]	Title of a Play or Film Ex: *The Importance of Being Earnest* is one of Oscar Wilde's best plays. Ex: I did not enjoy *Star Wars Episode II: Attack of the Clones*.

WHERE DO I PUT THE QUOTATION MARKS?

Generally speaking, your punctuation, whether a comma or a period, goes after the quotation and inside the ending quotation mark according to standard practice. Exceptions include the following:

1. If you document the source of the quotation with an in-text citation, then the end punctuation, whether a comma or a period, goes after the in-text citation identifying the source of the quotation.

Example: "The U.S. Department of Agriculture states that, 'about half of the hired workers employed in U.S. crop agriculture were unauthorized'" (Goodman).

2. If the use of the quotation marks requires a colon or a semicolon, the colon or the semicolon follow the end quotation mark.

Example: "I'll huff and I'll puff and I'll blow your house down": this was the threat from the big bad wolf.

3. If the quotation ends with a question mark, an exclamation point, or a dash, **that** punctuation remains inside the end quotation mark; if you document the quotation with an in-text citation, the terminal punctuation goes after the in-text citation and is usually a period.

Example: "The day of her graduation, she announced that she is part of the 11 million illegal immigrants!" (Richmond).

4. If the quotation is included in a question or an exclamation or requires the use of the dash, then the end punctuation follows the quotation marks.

Example: Was it in The Declaration of Independence that was written, "We hold these truths to be self-evident, that all men are created equal, that they are endowed by their Creator with certain unalienable Rights, that among these are Life, Liberty and the pursuit of Happiness. We hold these truths to be self-evident, that all men are created equal"?
Example: His behavior of constantly lying is the "worst"!
Example: One of the most quoted lines from a love poem—"How do I love thee? Let me count the ways"—was penned by Elizabeth Barrett Browning.

B. ITALICS

In addition to the uses in the chart above, italics have a few more uses.

1. Planes, trains, and ships

Italics are used to distinguish names of planes, trains, and ships.

Example: The president flew on *Air Force One* while I sailed on the *Queen Mary* and Jane rode on the *Polar Express.*

2. Works of Art

Italics are used for works of visual art.

Example: I went to see the *Mona Lisa* at the Louvre in Paris.

3. Foreign words/emphasis

Italics are also used for foreign words or for emphasized letters.

Example: The Old English word *gefronen* is pronounced with a *ye* sound at the start.

EXERCISES

QUOTATION MARKS EXERCISE 16.9A

Most of the following sentences use quotation marks incorrectly. Revise as needed. Be aware that this process may involve changing capitalization and commas. If the sentence is already correct, label it "Correct."

1. The widely-respected repair company advertised that they provided "friendly" service.
2. My mother used to tell me, "that she would ground me for life if she ever caught me smoking."
3. The corrupt lawmaker claimed that the bribes he took were "only" a few thousand dollars, but we knew better.
4. My dad thought his old car was a "bucket of bolts," as he described it, but I loved its vintage appeal.
5. "What now"? He asked, getting up to answer the door, "who could be ringing the bell at this hour?"
6. My grandfather taught me that I would need to work hard to succeed in life.
7. Although my grandmother was born in the age of rock and roll, she refused to listen to anything but "classical" music and referred to popular music as "garbage music."
8. My husband used to tell me that "he loved me" every single day, but even so, he became more and more distant until our marriage fell apart.
9. "The Raven", "Annabel Lee", and "The Bells", are three great poems by Edgar Allan Poe.
10. Jed used to shrug his shoulders and say it is what it is every time something bad happened.

QUOTATION MARKS AND ITALICS EXERCISE 16.9B

Underline words that should be italicized and put quotation marks around words that require them.

1. When the poet addressed the audience, he explained the meaning of the word alliteration and provided an example from one of his poems.
2. St. Lucy's Home for Girls Raised by Wolves is one of the students' favorite short stories in their textbook The Norton Introduction to Literature.
3. Before you leave for the beach, please be sure to pack the sunscreen, said Keira.
4. An article in a local newspaper noted that Sorry Not Sorry by Demi Lovato stayed on the Billboard Hot 100 list for weeks.
5. Many people are confused about the difference between the words lay and lie.
6. One of my favorite films is Il Postino, a story about a postman who delivers mail to the exiled poet Pablo Neruda and learns about poetry and love.
7. One of Jaspar's favorite paintings by Georgia O'Keefe, Ladder to the Moon, is on display at the museum downtown.
8. Ain't No Mountain High Enough, written by Ashford and Simpson, was made a hit by both Marvin Gaye and Diana Ross.
9. Like other musicians of his time, Marvin Gaye used his lyrics to bring attention to controversial issues in the 1960's . His lyrics, Father, father / we don't need to escalate / You see, war is not the answer / For only love can conquer hate are still relevant today.
10. When Baxter visited Georgia O'Keefe's home in Abiquiu and looked out of the windows at the New Mexican landscape, her painting Red Hills and Pedernal immediately came to mind.

11. The Tampa Bay Times reported that about 13,000 attended the March for Our Lives rally organized by local high school students.
12. In the Masterpiece Cakeshop v. Colorado Civil Rights Commission, the Supreme Court ruled in favor of Masterpiece Cake.
13. Another coup d'etat for the Republicans Senator Wassup mused.
14. Speak truth to power has become quite a popular phrase, but it's origin dates back decades.
15. For there is nothing either good or bad, but thinking makes it so, said Hamlet to Rosencrantz.

QUOTATION MARKS AND ITALICS EXERCISE 16.9C
Paragraphing and Punctuating Dialogue: Rewrite the dialogue below in correct paragraphs.

Faye asked her friend Anisha, "How could you lie to me about Rick? You know we've been dating since January." Anisha said, "I – I -- I know, but I thought Rick worked at Greenwise. This guy works at Starbucks." Faye hesitated. She pulled her cell phone out of her back pocket and started scrolling through her pictures.

Anisha said, "Please, Faye, you have to believe me. I wouldn't have told him if I...." "Does this look like him?" Faye asked. "No. That's not the guy I'm talking about. This guy Rick is a bass player. He's got blonde hair." "Blonde hair? Not black hair and a beard?"

"Listen, Faye, I think we are talking about two different guys." "I think so, too, Anisha." "What a relief!"

QUOTATION MARKS AND ITALICS EXERCISE 16.9D
Punctuate and paragraph the following dialogue:

Juan asked Sarah Did you see the game Friday night? We killed 'em. I scored two touchdowns and Josh kicked the winning field goal

I found out from Stephan. He said you guys made the Wildcats look like an amateur team Sarah responded.

No joke. Their quarterback couldn't get a pass off and he fumbled three times Juan laughed. We didn't fumble once.

So now the team goes to Regionals, right Sarah wondered.

REVIEW EXERCISES

PUNCTUATION REVIEW EXERCISE 16B: END PUNCTUATION, COMMAS, SEMICOLONS, COLONS, APOSTROPHES, HYPHENS, DASHES, PARENTHESES, QUOTATION MARKS

Insert the necessary punctuation. Write "C" next to any sentence that does not require any additional punctuation.

1. He gave away the storys ending.
2. The four dancers tap shoes were placed on the shelves.
3. She sees the error of her ways.
4. He said I drink my coffee without cream
5. She asked Do you take cream in your coffee
6. Did he say I never skip a meal
7. Did she ask What would you like for dinner
8. Toni Cade Bambara wrote the short story "The Lesson
9. He gave the following responses yes, no, maybe, and of course not.
10. He needs several supplies, such as hiking boots, a lantern, and a tent.
11. He likes many classical composers Mozart, Beethoven, Chopin, and Brahms.
12. Some of my favorite movies are Star Wars, Field of Dreams, and One True Thing.
13. I enjoy the song "America in fact, it is one of my favorites. (Add a ; and ")
14. He is a well adjusted individual.
15. That proverb is well known.
16. A carefully crafted poem packs a lot of meaning into a few words.
17. One eighth of this pie has been eaten.
18. My ex husband called me the other day.
19. Its a shame that you can't join us.
20. The kitten licked its paws and scampered away.
21. The childrens toys are scattered all over the place.

END PUNCTUATION EXERCISE 16C: END PUNCTUATION, COMMAS, SEMICOLONS, COLONS, APOSTROPHES, HYPHENS, DASHES, PARENTHESES, AND QUOTATION MARKS

Most of these sentences contain errors involving end punctuation. Revise as needed using the skills covered in all of this chapter. If a sentence is already correct, label it "correct."

1. When I propose to my girlfriend, should I say the traditional, "Will you marry me," or should I ask, "May I have your hand in marriage?"

2. After years of hard work and dedication, the gymnast was finally able to complete an elaborate, near-flawless routine that seemed to inspire everyone?

3. "Ouch," he shrieked as the car door slammed on his finger!

4. The young writer gazed into the distance and asked, "Didn't Edward Albee, the writer of *Who's Afraid of Virginia Woolf?*, pass away in 2016"?

5. "What did you say?," she asked as she looked up. "Sorry, I wasn't paying attention".

6. I couldn't believe he actually got up and left the restaurant, leaving me with the expensive bill! How rude!

7. [*In an email at work*] Good morning! I hope you're doing well. When you have a moment, could you send me that progress report? I was hoping we could present our findings to the team today? If you have any questions, please let me know? Thanks!

8. Although it looks a bit like a Dr. Seuss book, wasn't it actually somebody else who wrote *Are You My Mother?*?

9. Wasn't it Shakespeare who wrote the line, "If you prick us, do we not bleed?"?

10. "Could you repeat the question." he asked from the podium. "Also, would you mind speaking a little louder."

Chapter 17

COMMON ERRORS

 New writers often make the following mistakes when composing sentences:

- Verb Errors
- Pronoun Problems
- Run-on/Fused Sentences
- Commas Splices
- Sentence Fragments
- Mixed Sentences
- Writers may also misuse Commonly Confused Words.

17.1 VERB ERRORS

Verbs can be tricky! The two most common errors writers run into with verbs are subject/verb agreement and verb tense shifts.

A. SUBJECT/VERB AGREEMENT

Have you ever left the house with mismatched socks or shoes and failed to realize it until it's too late? It can be awkward. In the same way, your writing can sound awkward if your subjects and verbs are not matched in number. You need the subjects and verbs in your sentences to agree the same way you want your socks or shoes to match. The general rule is this: singular subjects need singular verbs, and plural subjects need plural verbs. However, determining if the subject is singular or plural can be challenging at times. Use these rules below to help you remember how to have your subjects and verbs agree.

1. SINGULAR AND PLURAL

Basic Rule: A singular subject takes a singular verb; a plural subject takes a plural verb.

Singular: **Professor Smith** enjoys discussing short stories.
Plural: **Her students** enjoy discussing short stories.

Find the actual subject. The object (noun) of a preposition can NOT be the subject. Common prepositions to watch for are *of, in, on, with*, and *to.*

Incorrect: The instructor of literature **studies** enjoy discussing short stories.
Correct: The **instructor** of literature studies enjoys discussing short stories.

Usually two nouns connected by the conjunction **and** take a plural verb.

Professor Smith *and* her students enjoy discussing short stories.

If a phrase beginning with *along with, as well as, besides, together with* or something similar follows the subject, then ignore the phrase and use the base subject to determine whether it will take a singular or plural verb.

Incorrect: **Professor Smith**, along with her **students**, enjoy discussing short stories.
Correct: **Professor Smith**, along with her students, enjoys discussing short stories.

When *or, either/or, neither/nor, not only/but also* connect the subjects, only use the subject closest to the verb to determine if the verb will be singular or plural. In other words, make sure the verb agrees with whichever subject comes last.

Correct: Whenever I sit down to write, *either* the bickering **kids** *or* the ringing **phone** interrupts my train of thought.
Correct: Whenever I sit down to write, *either* the ringing **phone** *or* the bickering **kids** interrupt my train of thought.

Correct: Every single evening *either* the horned **owl** *or* the squabbling **cats** wake Samantha with their racket.
Correct: Every single evening *either* the squabbling **cats** *or* the horned **owl** wakes Samantha with its racket.

Correct: *Neither* **Professor Smith** *nor* the **student**s enjoy discussing short stories.
Correct: *Neither* the **students** *nor* **Professor Smith** enjoys discussing short stories.

Note: Since the second example can sound awkward to the ear, many people will make sure that if one subject is singular and the other one is plural that the plural subject is placed closer to the verb to avoid the awkward sound.

2. Indefinite Pronouns

Singular	Can be singular or plural	Plural
either, neither	all	few
one, each, every	most	many
anyone, anything, anybody	any	several
someone, something, some-body	some	both
everyone, everything,	none	
everybody		
no one, nothing, nobody		

Most indefinite pronouns (see chart above) are always considered singular, and thus always take a singular verb.

> **Everyone** enjoys discussing short stories.
> **Neither** of the students enjoys discussing short stories.

A couple of indefinite pronouns (*few, many, several, both*) always take a plural verb.

> **Several** enjoy discussing short stories. **Both** enjoy discussing short stories.

Indefinite pronouns that indicate portions (such as *all, most, any, some, and none, a number, a part, a majority, percent, fraction, etc.*) can be singular or plural, depending on the subject in the "of" phrase.

> **All of the** *students* enjoy discussing short stories.
> **Most of the** *class* enjoys discussing short stories.

3. Here and There
Here and there are never considered subjects; therefore, with *There is/There are* and *Here is/Here are* sentences, the subject comes after the verb.

> Here is a **discussion** on the short story.
> There are **short stories** to discuss.

4. Collective Subjects
If a distance, a period of time, a sum of money, etc. is considered as a unit, then use a singular verb.

> **Two hours** is the normal length of our class discussion.
> **Eight dollars** was the price of my textbook.

A collective noun (*class, faculty, crowd, senate, herd,* etc.) is also considered as a unit when all parts of the noun are working together, so it typically requires a singular verb. However, if it is clear that the people within the unit are functioning as individuals, then the unit takes on the plural.

> The **class** enjoys discussing short stories. ("It" enjoys it all together).
> The **faculty** grade their students work each weekend. ("They" grade individually, not as a group.)

Some plural nouns (*glasses, pants, scissors, pliers, tongs,* etc.) are the only form of the noun; consequently, they require a plural verb unless they are preceded by a phrase like "A pair of."

> Her **glasses** help her read the short story.
> A **pair** of scissors is the murder weapon in the story.

Some nouns (*mathematics, physics, statistics, billiards,* etc.) appear to be plural at first glance because they end with the letter "s," but really these nouns are one item. Therefore, these nouns require a singular verb.

> **Statistics** is a subject many English majors avoid.

B. VERB TENSE SHIFTS

For many college courses, essays should be written in present tense because it creates a sense of immediacy and activity. They should use other tenses only when events happen at different times. However, check with the instructor to find out what tense(s) should be used in a particular course or a specific assignment. For example, a science teacher may instruct students to use past tense to record the results of an experiment that was conducted. A history essay may use past tense to relate events that actually happened in the past. A résumé may use past tense for previous job experience that actually happened in the past.

1. CONSISTENT TENSES

Verb tenses indicate when things happen, so they should not change unless events are occurring at different times. For example,

> Alicia mowed the grass yesterday when the weather was nice.
> Alicia mows the grass daily when the weather is nice.
> Alicia will mow the grass tomorrow because the weather will be nice.

When things are happening at the same time but different tenses are used, this error is called a **verb tense shift**.

> **Incorrect:** Alicia mowed the grass yesterday when the weather is nice.
> **Incorrect:** Alicia mows the grass daily when the weather will be nice.
> **Incorrect:** Alicia will mow the grass tomorrow when the weather was nice.

If events are taking place at the same time, <u>do not change tense</u>! This is called a "faulty tense shift."
To avoid faulty tense shifts, take a second look at the verbs throughout your sentences and essays. Do they have <u>helping verbs</u>? As a general rule, if your essay is set in present tense, the verbs should NOT have helping verbs unless they tell of something that is happening at a <u>different time</u>.

2. WRITING ABOUT LITERATURE

One instance where tense-shift errors are especially problematic is when writing about literature. Sometimes, a work of literature (like a short story, novel, poem, or play) may be written in the past tense, but your instructor wants your essay to be in present tense. Use PRESENT TENSE when writing about anything that happens in a work of literature:

> **Correct:** Louise **puts** her arm around her sister's waist as they **descend** the stairs in Kate Chopin's "The Story of an Hour."
> **Correct:** In "The Star," Arthur C. Clarke's narrator **travels** to a distant galaxy and **begins** to question his faith.

However, when referring to something that happened <u>before the story begins</u> or in the past in real life, a PAST TENSE is correct:

> **Correct:** Louise **acknowledges** that her husband **treated** her kindly. (A tense shift is correct because she acknowledges in the story that her husband treated her that way before the story begins.)
> **Correct:** In "The Star," a priest **finds** the remnants of a supernova that **destroyed** a civilization. (A tense shift is correct because the supernova destroyed the civilization long before the priest arrives.)
> **Incorrect:** Kate Chopin often **writes** stories about women's issues. (Present tense is wrong because Chopin is not still writing stories. She died in 1904.)
> **Correct:** Kate Chopin often **wrote** stories about women's issues. (Past tense is correct because Chopin is not still writing stories. She died in 1904.)

3. USING QUOTATIONS

Tense shifts can be especially problematic when an essay includes **quotations** from a work of literature. If a quotation in your sentence is a <u>complete</u> sentence (capitalized and separated from the rest of the sentence with a colon or a comma and source phrase), a tense change is probably OK:

> **Correct:** Kate Chopin **describes** Louise's initial reaction dramatically: "She **wept** at once, with sudden, wild abandonment" (40).

If you use a quotation that is <u>not</u> a complete sentence, the tense of the quote must be consistent with the rest of the essay. Whenever you change something in a quote, put the change in square brackets [ ].

> **Incorrect:** Because Josephine and Richards **worry** about Louise, "great care **was** taken to break to her as gently as possible the news of her husband's death" (Chopin 40).
> **Correct:** Because Josephine and Richards **worry** about Louise, "great care **[is]** taken to break to her as gently as possible the news of her husband's death" (Chopin 40).

EXERCISES

SUBJECT/VERB AGREEMENT EXERCISE 17.1A

Choose the correct word in the parentheses.

1. The chances of your being promoted (is, are) excellent.
2. Four years of research (has, have) gone into making our software suitable for the Japanese market.
3. Each of the twenty-five actors (was, were) given a five-minute tryout.
4. The most significant lifesaving device in automobiles (is, are) air bags.
5. The dangers of smoking (is, are) well documented.
6. Shelters for teenage runaways (offers, offer) a wide variety of services.
7. Every year, during the festival, the smoke of village bonfires (fills, fill) the sky.
8. When food supplies (was, were) scarce, the group had to make do with the less desirable parts of the animals.
9. There (is, are) several pots of herbs on the balcony.
10. Hidden under the floorboards (was, were) a bag of coins and a rusty sword.

SUBJECT/VERB AGREEMENT EXERCISE 17.1B

Choose the correct word in the parentheses.

1. There is no proof that life (exists/exist) beyond this planet.
2. The choice of these flowers (was/were) correct.
3. This suitcase, as well as my three duffle bags, (is/are) too heavy to lift.
4. Jogging and weight lifting (is/are) both great exercise.
5. Neither my orange tree nor my gardenia bush (needs/need) watering.
6. Either your child or her children (is/are) making too much noise.
7. A feather or a sequin (makes/make) a good addition to this hat.
8. Everyone in these three rows (is/are) assigned the odd numbered questions.
9. Neither of the puppies (was/were) sold.
10. The audience (nods/nod) in approval.
11. There (is/are) fourteen people in this class.
12. Each parakeet and canary (was/were) chirping.
13. The parakeet and the canary each (was/were) chirping.
14. (Was/Were) there any reasons given for the explosion?
15. The most frustrating part of the delays (is/are) the costs.
16. The most important reason to study (is/are) your grades.
17. She is one of the girls who (repairs/repair) the computers.
18. He is the only one of the men who (needs/need) a ride tonight.
19. Physics (is/are) a fun class when Dr. Jenkins teaches it.
20. *The Lost Boys* (is/are) a movie about vampires.
21. Finding lost loves (is/are) an exciting pastime.
22. Thirty dollars (is/are) a lot to pay for these tickets.
23. A number of questions (is/are) missing from the exam.
24. The number of dropouts (has/have) increased.

Verb Tense Shifts Exercise 17.1C

Identify the complete verb(s) and tense(s) in the following sentences.

1. In 1941, Dr. William Moulton Marston created Wonder Woman as a contemporary crime fighter, but the setting of the 2017 movie is World War I.

    A.   created (past tense), is (present tense)
    B.   created (past tense)
    C.   created (past tense), setting (present tense), is (present tense)

2. Professor X has been teaching at HCC since he left the X-Men in 2004.

    A.   has (present tense), left (past tense)
    B.   .has been teaching (present perfect progressive tense), left (past tense)
    C.   teaching (present tense), left (past tense)

3. I will be finishing my research soon; later, I will begin writing the essay.

    A.   will (future tense), will begin (future tense)
    B.   will be finishing (future tense), begin (present tense)
    C.   will be finishing (future progressive tense), will begin (future tense)

4. Louis had submitted his research paper before the assignment closed on Canvas.

    A.   had submitted (past perfect tense), closed (past tense)
    B.   had (past tense), closed (past tense)
    C.   had submitted (past tense)

5. When the timer buzzes, the children will enjoy Grandma's cookies.

    A.   buzzes (present tense), will enjoy (future tense)
    B.   buzzes (present tense), enjoy (present tense)
    C.   timer (present tense), enjoy (present tense)

6. Wanting a game room, Jessica has begun to remodel her garage.

    A.   wanting (present tense), has (present tense)
    B.   wanting (present tense), has begun (present tense)
    C.   has begun (present perfect tense)

7. Students are looking forward to a day without classes when the next holiday happens.

    A.   are (present tense), happens (present tense)
    B.   are looking (present progressive tense), happens (present tense)
    C.   are looking (present tense), happens (present tense)

8. Since the Industrial Revolution began in 1760, air pollution has been increasing exponentially.

    A.   began (past tense), has been increasing (past tense)
    B.   began (past tense), has been increasing (present perfect progressive tense)
    C.   began (past tense), has been increasing (past progressive tense)

9. California farmers had hoped for rain last week; however, they have gotten none.

    A.   hoped (past tense), rain (present tense), have gotten (past perfect tense)
    B.   had hoped (past tense), have gotten (present tense)
    C.   had hoped (past perfect tense), have gotten (present perfect tense)

10. To prevent napping in class, one instructor demands jumping jacks from sleepy students.

    A.   to prevent (present perfect tense), demands (present tense)
    B.   prevent (present tense), napping (present tense), demands (present tense), jumping (present tense)
    C.   demands (present tense)

Verb Tense Shifts Exercise 17.1 D

Identify the complete verb(s) and tense(s) in the following sentences.

1. Dr. Martin Luther King Jr. led the American civil rights movement in the twentieth century.

    A. A. led (past tense)
    B. B. rights (present tense)
    C. C. movement (present tense)

2. King's birthday is celebrated on the third Monday of January.

    A. A. is (present tense)
    B. B. is celebrated (present perfect tense)
    C. C. celebrated (past tense)

3. King was serving as pastor of the Dexter Avenue Baptist Church in Montgomery, Alabama, when he led a bus boycott there in 1955.

    A. A. was (past tense), serving (present progressive tense)
    B. B. was (past tense), led (past tense)
    C. C. was serving (past progressive tense), led (past tense)

4. Since the U.S. Supreme Court declared bus-segregation laws unconstitutional in 1956, people of all races have ridden the bus as equals.

    A. A. declared (past tense), have ridden (present perfect tense)
    B. B. declared (past tense), have (present tense)
    C. C. declared (past tense), have ridden (past perfect tense)

5. King modeled his techniques on the nonviolent protests that Mahatma Gandhi had led in India a few decades earlier.

    A. A. modeled (past tense), had led (past perfect tense)
    B. B. modeled (past tense), protests (present tense)
    C. C. modeled (past tense), protests (present tense), led (past tense)

6. King is best known for his work in 1963, which includes his "Letter from Birmingham Jail" and the March on Washington.

    A. A. is (present tense), includes (present tense)
    B. B. is known (present perfect tense), includes (present tense)
    C. C. is best known (past perfect tense), includes (present tense)

7. The 2014 film *Selma* has reignited interest in the voting-rights marches King and others organized in 1965.

    A. A. reignited (past tense), organized (past tense)
    B. B. has reignited (present perfect tense), organized (past tense)
    C. C. has reignited (past perfect progressive tense)

8. By the time that King died in 1968, he had traveled millions of miles and had given thousands of speeches.

    A. A. died (past tense)
    B. B. died (past tense), had traveled (past perfect tense), had given (past perfect tense)
    C. C. died (past tense), traveled (past tense), given (past tense)

9. Convicted criminal James Earl Ray assassinated King in 1968 while the civil-rights leader was standing on the balcony of a motel in Memphis, Tennessee.

    A. A. convicted (past tense), assassinated (past tense), was (past tense)
    B. B. assassinated (past tense), was (past tense)
    C. C. assassinated (past tense), was standing (past progressive tense)

10. Since 1991, the Lorraine Motel has been serving as a civil-rights museum.

    A. A. has been serving (past progressive tense)
    B. B. serving (present progressive tense)
    C. C. has been serving (present perfect progressive tense)

17.2 Pronoun Problems

A. Pronoun-Antecedent Agreement

Pronouns and antecedents need to agree in person, number, and gender.

Person refers to 1ˢᵗ, 2ⁿᵈ, or 3ʳᵈ, categories that are used to describe pronouns. Number refers to how many things the pronoun refers to—singular means one; plural means more than one. Gender refers to male or female. English does have a gender neutral pronoun—one—but this may alter the tone of your paper.

So, what does it mean to agree with the antecedent? Antecedents are the word(s) that the pronoun replaces or refers to. The pronoun and antecedent have to match.

> Example: **Laura** goes swimming because **she** enjoys it.
> *Laura* is an antecedent because Laura is replaced by the pronoun *she*.
> *Swimming* is also an antecedent because swimming is replaced by the pronoun *it*.

1. Number

The pronoun has to agree with the antecedent in number.

> **Incorrect**: The little *girl* could not wait to hold *their* stuffed animal.
> singular antecedent - plural pronoun

There is only one girl, so the pronoun cannot be the plural their.

> **Correct**: The little *girl* could not wait to hold *her* stuffed animal.
> singular antecedent - singular pronoun

Note: When you are connecting two antecedents with a correlative conjunction, the following pronoun should agree with the second antecedent, so the antecedent mentioned last should agree with the pronoun that follows. This is similar to the pronoun choice when using the coordinating conjunction "or."

> **Correct**: *Neither* Melinda [singular] *nor* the writers [plural] expressed *their* [plural] relief when the deadline was extended.
> **Correct**: *Neither* the writers [plural] *nor* Melinda [singular] expressed *her* [singular] relief when the deadline was extended.

Sometimes, however, the context emphasizes the subject of the sentence, in which case the pronoun following the correlative conjunction relates back to the subject as the antecedent; then the pronoun matches the antecedent.

> **Correct**: Mary [singular subject] realized that her teammates *not only* could run as fast *but also* could jump as high as she [antecedent is the subject].
> **Correct**: Mary's teammates [plural subject] realized that *not only* could Mary run faster than they *but also* could jump as high as they [antecedent is the subject].

Note: When writers do not want to assign gender to singular subjects, they may use the singular they. Consider your audience and purpose when making this choice.

2. GENDER
The pronoun and antecedent need to agree in gender.

> **Incorrect**: The young *man* went to *her* bedroom to study.
>   masculine antecedent - female pronoun
> **Correct**: The young *man* went to *his* bedroom to study.
>   masculine antecedent - male pronoun
> **Incorrect**: The author went on his book tour.
> **Correct**: The author went on his/her book tour.
> **Correct**: The author went on a book tour.

Note: If you want to avoid giving the antecedent a gender, reword the sentence to avoid pronoun use, as above, or if it won't change the meaning of the sentence, make the antecedent plural.

3. AMBIGUITY
Avoid being ambiguous when using pronouns.

> **Incorrect**: When he went shopping, he thought the milk was too expensive.

Who is *he*? Unless it is clear from the previous sentence, make sure you have an antecedent.

> **Correct**: When Dylan went shopping, he thought the milk was too expensive.

Here it is clear that *he* refers to Dylan.

> **Incorrect**: The mom and her daughter shopped for a dress for her.

Who is *her*? Is it for the mother or the daughter?

> **Correct**: The mom and her daughter shopped for a dress for the daughter.

This example may seem a bit wordy, but now it is clear who needs the dress.

4. REPETITION
Avoid repetition when using pronouns.

> **Incorrect**: In "Let Teen-Agers Try Adulthood," by Leon Botstein, he argues in favor of education reform.
>   It is wordy and unnecessary to include the author's name followed by the pronoun.
> **Correct**: In "Let Teen-Agers Try Adulthood," Leon Botstein argues in favor of education reform.

This example avoids needing both the author's name and the pronoun. To avoid ambiguity, you need to provide the antecedent if you have not done so in a previous sentence.

B. PRONOUN CASE
English pronouns are divided by person and case. Person refers to 1st, 2nd, or 3rd.

> 1st person: I, we, me, us, my, mine, our, ours
> 2nd person: you, your, yours
> 3rd person: he, she, it, they, him, her, them, his, her, hers, their, theirs

Pronouns are also divided into cases. Case describes what the pronoun is doing in the sentence.

1. Subjective
The subjective case means that the word is acting as the subject of the sentence:

> I, you, he, she, it, we, they

2. Objective
The objective case means that the word is receiving the action of the verb (remember direct and indirect objects?):

> Me, you, him, her, it, us, them

3. Possessive
The possessive case means that the word shows ownership:

> My, mine, your, yours, his, her, hers, our, ours, their, theirs

4. Reflexive
The reflexive case shows intensity:

> Myself, yourself, himself, herself, itself, ourselves, yourselves, themselves

	USED AS SUBJECTS	**USED AS OBJECTS**	**USED AS POSSESSIVES**	**USED AS REFLEXIVE**
Singular	I	me	my, mine	myself
	you	you	you, yours	yourself
	he	him	his	himself
	she	her	hers	herself
	it	it	its	itself
Plural	we	us	our, ours	ourselves
	you	you	your, yours	yourselves
	they	them	their, theirs	themselves
Singular or plural	who	whom	whose	

Note: Pronouns acting as the subject of the sentence should be in the subjective case. Pronouns that receive the action of the verb should be in the objective case.

> Example: I went to the store.
> NOT: **Me** went to the store.

> Example: She was standing in line with him.
> NOT: She was standing in line with **he**.

Note: If you have a compound subject, sometimes it may be difficult to discern which pronoun you need. In that case, remove the other word and read the sentence with just the pronoun. Decide whether you need the subjective, objective, or possessive case to make the sentence make sense.

> Example: Sheila and she waited for the movie to begin.
> **She** waited for the movie to begin, not **her** waited for the movie to begin.

> Example: The teacher handed the books to Seth and me.
> The books were handed to **me**, not to **I**.

C. INDEFINITE PRONOUNS

Indefinite pronouns take a singular or plural verb depending on what they are.

Take the singular verb	everyone	someone	anyone	no one
	everybody	somebody	anybody	nobody
	everything	something	anything	nothing
	each	another	either (of)	neither (of)
	one (of)	much	such (a)	
Take the plural verb	both	few	many	several
Take singular or plural	all	any	more	most
	none	some		

EXERCISES

PRONOUN PROBLEMS EXERCISE 17.2 A

Revise problems with pronoun-antecedent agreement in each sentence.

1. Each swimmer must submit their application to the athletic department before they are assigned a number for the 400-meter heat.
2. Everyone must bring their student identification to the swim meet to gain free entry.
3. Before the girl left town for the winter, she wanted to make sure her friends knew how to reach them.
4. A news report on cable networks is not so much a news story as they are a political rant.
5. In her travel article, Olive Ventini claims that anyone can visit the museum as long as they arrive early.
6. Every traveler who walks across the Pont des Arts bridge in Paris places their padlock on the rail and throws the key in the river.
7. Spoken word performances entertain students on college campuses, and he enjoys the live impromptu gatherings.
8. An employee must not only wear protective covering, but they must also carry their ID badges at all times.
9. Ricki said anyone who wanted to attend the opening performance could as long as they arrived on time.
10. A shopper today must be careful to check their receipt because many items do not make it into the grocery bags.

PRONOUN PROBLEMS EXERCISE 17.2B

Choose the correct pronoun for the following sentences.

1. Earl and (she, her) were both late for class.
2. Linda sent her parents and (us, we) postcards.
3. If you need a ride, tell Susan or (I, me).
4. The taxi passed Dad and (I, me) at the intersection.
5. Uncle Sam named (we, us) boys in his will.
6. (Us, We) members of the family have to stick together.
7. To Bob and (she, her), he left the summer home.
8. Larry is a better skater than (he, him).
9. No one on the team is faster than (I, me).
10. No one can blame (us, ourselves) for the mistake.

PRONOUN PROBLEMS EXERCISE 17.2 C

Revise shifts in person in each sentence.

1. College students must prepare for class by reading the chapters in the psychology textbook, or you will not understand the lecture on Tuesday.
2. Even though many professors have office hours, very few college students actually seek individual help from professors.
3. We must appreciate the freedoms we have as Americans and exercise your right to vote and protest.
4. Some of the most profound changes in American history are the result of hard work by many who were willing to risk our reputations and lives.
5. Jonathan and Maurice invited many on campus to join their organization to raise awareness about protecting albino pelicans on Egmont Key.
6. Each child must learn the alphabet before you move on to learning numbers.
7. Practice the multiplication tables until you have memorized all the answers, and then the student can move on to division.
8. I always found subtraction easier than division because you can round every number off to a ten.
9. All students must bring their textbooks to class.
10. If everyone shows up on time and brings your scantron, students can leave class at 3:00 pm today.
11. All athletes must meet on the recess field and bring your water bottles.
12. When most runners compete in a 100-meter hurdle, you take three steps between each hurdle.
13. If you hit your knee on the hurdle, runners should keep going without stopping.
14. Because many runners can injure their hamstrings if they compete in multiple events, it is important that they stretch and warm up between events.
15. To go to regionals, everybody must bring two pairs of running shoes and your own spikes.
16. However, you must also hydrate throughout the track meet so that your body does not cramp up.
17. Cross country running usually involves 3.1 mile distances in high school meets, and most runners are able to meet their goals.
18. The 4x100 relays require runners to pass a baton without dropping it, but sometimes you can't grab it while you are running.
19. Anyone who wants to try out for track and field must show up on Wednesday and bring your completed registration form.

Parents at the swim meet are responsible for her child's bathing suit and towel.

PRONOUN PROBLEMS EXERCISE 17.2 D

Correct the various pronoun errors in the following sentences. Label the sentence as "correct" if it contains no pronoun errors:

1. If you drive with caution, most people should expect to avoid traffic tickets.
2. All students need to submit their work on time, and if you don't, please expect a late penalty.
3. Remember to check one's calendar so that you don't miss any deadlines for the project.
4. After buying a house, your taxes can become complicated, so I decided to hire an accountant so they could tell me if you're penalized when you file a tax deadline extension.
5. Sandra is old enough to remember when you would have to return VHS tapes to video rental stores on time or else they would assess a late fee.
6. If you want to retire early, it is best if you start investing wisely as young as you can.
7. I've always thought it's best to take multivitamins because they say it's good for you.
8. Someone left their phone in the men's locker room.
9. Jeff was upset that the interior of his car was soaking wet, but that's what happens when you leave your windows open on a rainy day.
10. Most people should expect the job search to be arduous; it almost always is if you aren't incredibly lucky.
11. The fact that he was such a good tennis player no one could beat him.
12. The selection of the committee was chosen by the principal.
13. Television is a great way to relax.
14. A quatrain is when you have a verse of four lines.
15. The reason she was fired was because she was always late to work.
16. Just because I made the cookies doesn't mean you should eat them.
17. Although you paid me $10.00 doesn't mean we are even.
18. He never has and never will sing on key.
19. He is concerned and interested in helping the poor.
20. An applicant who knows the company's needs is more likely to get the job.
21. I hired the dancers before the director.
22. The trip was fun, but I liked New York more than my father.
23. He is as smart, if not smarter than, my brother.
24. Tampa is more populated than any city in Hillsborough County.
25. On his vacation, all he wants to do is sleep, read his book and sailing.
26. Quickly, urgently, and without making a sound, the mice scampered away.
27. Thinking logically, organizing well, and expressing ideas clearly are three requirements of good writing.
28. You are either late or I am early.
29. Just because you have to work doesn't mean that you can't go to the party.
30. Even though you need a haircut doesn't mean you will look funny in the photograph.

Pronoun Problems Exercise 17.2E

Underline the pronoun and circle the antecedent. Then mark correct or incorrect. If incorrect, make the pronoun and antecedent agree in number.

1. Everybody wants to attend the concert on Friday, but they must purchase tickets before Wednesday night to reserve their seats.
2. To pass the philosophy exam, a student must understand Descartes' philosophical idea "Cogito, ergo sum," translated in English to mean "I think; therefore, I am," and they must know the meaning of nihilism as Nietzsche defines it.
3. Jose and Mellinia volunteered to help the fundraisers by bringing everybody coffee and fresh fruit during their morning shift.
4. Even though Tropical Storm Alberto appears to be headed toward Alabama and not Florida, Governor Scott has ordered a state of emergency for all counties in Florida. To find out if school is canceled, everyone should keep an eye out for a text alert on their cell phones.
5. Every photo of an agitated cat somersaulting off a piece of furniture will be considered for the book, but they must be received by email attachment before the deadline.
6. Be sure to back up on your computer all photos that are entered for submission in case the editors need more information about it.
7. Despite the long wait, neither the coach nor the children want his place on the track schedule to be changed.
8. Each of the contestants on *The Voice* must be prepared to work with one of the judges and adapt their personal styles.
9. Filing a tax return on time or filing for an extension is every citizen's responsibility. If they fail to file, they are subject to late penalties or loss of tax refund.
10. Ricki gave her class notes to Janis who let someone else copy them too.

Pronoun Problems Exercise 17.2F

Correct the paragraph to make pronouns consistent throughout.

Before playing a complicated piano piece such as *Moonlight Sonata* for a jury of judges, piano students should spend twenty minutes on drills to warm up their fingers. Drills help you learn different techniques and finger positions. Without this practice, a piano student is more likely to make mistakes and to lack flexibility in his fingers. Initially, *Moonlight Sonata* seems simple because the piece is repetitive and slow. However, you must also pay close attention to symbols, such as the decrescendo and the slur, to build emotion in your performance. Practicing the piece over and over is the only way you can master a piece as complex as *Moonlight Sonata.* The memorization of any piece of music depends not only on the brain but also on the hands to recall each note and symbol. When you can play the piece without the sheet music, piano students are ready to perform before three faculty judges. If you freeze before the judges and cannot recall the piece, begin the piece again. If the piano student cannot recall the lines, it is best to wait for the judges to excuse you than to run off stage embarrassed.

17.3 RUN-ON/FUSED SENTENCES

Run-on sentences are common writing errors. In popular usage, the term **run-on sentence** refers imprecisely to any overlong, rambling sentence. In the academic world, however, **this usage is incorrect**. A run-on sentence can be long or short, and it can even be narrowly focused. Consider this run-on sentence:

Incorrect: I love my job I find the work to be rewarding.

The above sentence has only eleven words and makes a precise point, but it is nevertheless a run-on sentence. Why? The sentence contains two independent clauses improperly joined. To put it another way, the sentence is actually two sentences stuck together incorrectly:

I love my job.   *And*   I find the work to be rewarding.

While it may be tempting to correct the above example simply by adding a comma, this creates a different (but related) error.

Incorrect: I love my job, I find the work to be rewarding.

The above example contains a **comma splice**, which is a specific type of comma error. A comma splice results when two independent clauses are improperly joined (i.e., without a conjunction). This writing error is discussed in Ch. 17.4.

Here are some correct versions with commentary related to each:

Correct: I love my job. I find the work to be rewarding.

Correcting a run-on sentence or comma splices by using a period is a legitimate way to correct these errors. Use caution, however, because the result may be a series of short sentences close together—technically correct, but stylistically awkward.

Correct: I love my job; I find the work to be rewarding.

Note the use of the semicolon, which implies that the two independent clauses it connects are closely related.

Correct: I love my job because the work is rewarding.

Consider revising the sentence entirely, as above, which may at times be your best option.

MORE EXAMPLES OF RUN-ONS AND HOW TO CORRECT THEM

Incorrect: Alicia was concerned for her health she made an appointment with her doctor.

Correct: Alicia was concerned for her health, so she made an appointment with her doctor.

Correct: Alicia was concerned for her health; therefore, she made an appointment with her doctor.

Correct: Alicia was concerned for her health until she made an appointment with her doctor.

Correct: Because Alicia was concerned for her health, she made an appointment with her doctor.

Incorrect: Some people believe that good cooking requires expensive equipment it doesn't.

Correct: Some people believe that good cooking requires expensive equipment; it doesn't.

Correct: Some people believe that good cooking requires expensive equipment, but it doesn't.

Correct: Although some people believe that good cooking requires expensive equipment, it doesn't.

Incorrect: Nikki bought a new pillow it was too soft.

Correct: Nikki bought a new pillow, but it was too soft.

Correct: Nikki bought a new pillow; unfortunately, it was too soft.

Incorrect: I fell for an Internet scam what a mistake!

Correct: I fell for an Internet scam. What a mistake!

Incorrect: My husband doesn't like barbeque food do you?

Correct: My husband doesn't like barbeque food. Do you?

A NOTE ON TERMINOLOGY:

Some grammar guides use the term **fused sentence** to refer to a run-on sentence. Sometimes the term **run-on sentence** is a wide category that also includes comma splices (discussed later). These terms are all related in one significant way: They are all the result of two independent clauses (i.e., sentences) being joined improperly.

For more information about independent and dependent clauses, see Chapter 15.

Exercises

Run-ons/ Fused Sentences Exercise 17.3A

Most of these examples are run-on sentences. Identify the **three** examples that are already correct, and revise the **seven** others that are run-ons. Remember that run-on sentences can be revised using one of many methods.

1. The meeting is at noon I feel prepared.

2. Our projects never take too long when we have clear goals.

3. A short break can be a great way to clear one's mind this can result in superior work.

4. The history of cinema is rich and varied movies can be deep and meaningful.

5. Some people enjoy working in a garden others find the work to be dreadful.

6. Simple inventions can change the world can you think of some examples?

7. I want to do volunteer work because I feel it is my duty to give back to the community.

8. I always like to visit my parents sometimes my hometown can be boring, however.

9. Safety should always be a priority it is our highest ethical responsibility.

10. Sometimes new opportunities have arisen for me at the times that I have least expected them.

Run-ons/Fused Sentences Exercise 17.3B

Revise the following sentences.

1. The deadline was fast approaching the book wasn't ready yet.

2. Sarah worried about her car breaking down leaving her stranded on the side of the road.

3. John enjoyed the break from the routine he spent his days reading at the beach.

4. She really needed a break to eat some lunch her lunch break wasn't long enough to leave the building and grab better food.

5. Barney wanted to meet someone who could mend his broken heart he had just broken up with his longtime girlfriend.

17.4 COMMA SPLICES

For a better understanding of the punctuation error known as the **comma splice**, it is best to first understand **run-on sentences**, which are discussed in Chapter 17.3.

Like a run-on sentence, a comma splice is the result of two independent clauses being improperly joined. You can think of a comma splice as being two sentences stuck together with nothing but a comma to separate them. Here is an example:

> **Incorrect:** I have not yet chosen a definite career path, it is exciting to have so many options.

Note that the above sentence is actually two sentences joined with a comma. This is an incorrect way to structure a sentence. Because a comma splice is an error, writers are at times tempted to simply remove the offending comma. However, this results in a **run-on sentence**:

> **Incorrect:** I have not yet chosen a definite career path it is exciting to have so many options.

Note that the above example contains two sentences joined together without any punctuation or conjunction at all.

A. FIVE WAYS TO REVISE A COMMA SPLICE

Correcting a comma splice is much like correcting a run-on sentence. You have many options to consider.

1. ADD A PERIOD.

One way to fix a comma splice is to add a period between the two sentences (independent clauses).

> **Correct:** I have not yet chosen a definite career path. It is exciting to have so many options.

In the above example, the two sentences are now separated with a period. This method is a legitimate way to correct comma splices and run-on sentences—just be careful not to have two short, choppy sentences back-to-back, which may be grammatically correct but stylistically weak.

2. ADD A COORDINATING CONJUNCTION.

Another way to fix this error is to add a coordinating conjunction (FANBOYS). Consider the nuanced difference between these two revisions:

> **Correct:** I have not yet chosen a definite career path, **and** it is exciting to have so many options.
> **Correct:** I have not yet chosen a definite career path, **but** it is exciting to have so many options.

In each of the above examples, a **coordinating conjunction** has been added (see chapter 14.7 for a list of conjunctions). A comma can indeed be used to combine two independent clauses but only if it comes before a coordinating conjunction, which functions to provide the reader with the relationship that exists between the two independent clauses: "and" indicating addition and "but" indicating contrast.

Some readers may detect a subtle difference in tone in the above two examples, depending on whether "and" (addition) or "but" (contrast) is used.

3. USE A SEMICOLON.

If the clauses are closely related, a semicolon may be used to link the two independent clauses.

> **Correct:** I have not yet chosen a definite career path; it is exciting to have so many options.

The semicolon implies that the two independent clauses are closely related.

You may also use a relationship word followed by a comma to introduce the second independent clause linked by a semicolon. You may use a transitional expression or a conjunctive adverb (see Ch. 10.3 for more information).

> **Correct:** I have not yet chosen a definite career path; however, it is exciting to have so many options.

4. THINK ABOUT A COLON.

If the clauses mean exactly the same thing, a colon may be used to link the two independent clauses.

> **Correct:** I have chosen a definite career path: I want to be a forensic pathologist.

If an independent clause follows a colon, you have the option to begin it with a capital letter or not but be consistent.

5. REWORD THE SENTENCE.

Perhaps you can change one of the independent clauses into a dependent clause (see Ch. 15.3 Coordination and Subordination for more information).

> **Correct:** My future is filled with so many options that I have not yet chosen a definite career path.

Always consider completely revising problematic sentences. Sometimes—though not always—a radical reworking is your best option.

"Rule of Thumb" for comma splices: If you think you might have a comma splice, put your thumb over the suspect comma and read the words to the right of your thumb and to the left of your thumb. If the words to the right sound like a complete, stand-alone sentence (a subject and a verb without being introduced by a subordinating word) that you could say to someone and the words to the left do also, you probably have a comma splice and need to correct it.

EXERCISES

COMMA SPLICES EXERCISE 17.4A

Most of these examples contain comma splices. Identify the **three** examples that are already correct, and revise the **seven** others that contain comma splices. Remember that comma splices can be revised using one of many methods.

1. I love to sing, karaoke is a fun way to spend an evening.
2. I watched a documentary about dangerous jobs, it made me respect the brave souls who can do that work.
3. Music used to be sold primarily on vinyl records, today, music distribution is very different.
4. I used to be a fan of that athlete, but his history of cheating has made me reconsider his merits.
5. Although I have never played sports professionally, I look forward to helping kids learn about wellness and exercise.
6. Some people love to camp, others prefer expensive hotels.
7. I believe that watches have not been particularly fashionable since the rise in popularity of smartphones.
8. My car won't start, would you mind helping me diagnose the problem?
9. I was once unable to do a single push-up, today, I have exceeded all my expectations.
10. My brother retired three years early, I hope I can be as fortunate as he is.

COMMA SPLICES EXERCISE 17.4B

Correct the comma splices in the following sentences. Not all sentences have comma splices; label those sentences as "Correct." Hint: Be careful not to use a semicolon (or other punctuation) in those cases in which a comma would have been correct.

1. My boyfriend came from a military family, they used to travel frequently.
2. Although I should have gone to bed earlier last night, I felt compelled to read a few more chapters of my new novel.
3. Working out at the gym wasn't his favorite activity, but he was determined to lose weight.
4. I've never been a home repair expert, a professional should perform dangerous electrical work.
5. The man fell asleep on the bus, I wondered if he was going to miss his stop.
6. Roberta's mother decided to cancel the family's cable TV subscription, the amount of money they saved was impressive.
7. By the time I finally arrived at the theater after having driven in the worst rush hour traffic jam of the year, the movie had already started, and I was deeply frustrated and disappointed.
8. The small island relies on tourism as the main driving force of its economy, like many islands do.
9. Even though the night was mostly quiet, we could hear a chorus of chirping crickets.
10. My roommate has many unusual habits, for example, whenever she places a book on a table, she makes sure that the cover is face-down, and she insists on spraying her frying pans with two different brands of canola oil every time she cooks dinner.

17.5 Sentence Fragments

A sentence fragment is a sentence that is incomplete. In order to be complete, a sentence must have a subject and a verb. Someone or something must be doing something. Sentence fragments are missing one of these two elements: a subject or a verb. They often leave the reader hanging, waiting for the rest of the information.

A. Missing Subject: Verb alone fragment

Incorrect: Discovered in the depths of the African jungle.,

Identify the verb. Does the sentence have one? The verb is "Discovered." Ask yourself "who" or "what" was discovered to find the subject. In this group of words, there is no subject, so it is a fragment.

Correct: The ancient temple was discovered in the depths of the African jungle.

B. Missing Verb: Subject alone fragment

Incorrect: The picture I found in the garage.

What about the picture? What did it do? What happened to it? This sentence leaves the reader hanging, waiting for more information. It is a fragment. (There is an implied "that" making the subject "I" and the verb "found" into a dependent clause and not providing a verb for the subject "picture.")

Correct: The picture I found in the garage was a masterpiece worth millions.

A Note on Sentence Length

Sentence fragments have nothing to do with the number of words in the sentence. Really short sentences can be complete. Really long sentences can be fragments. It doesn't matter how many words you have—it matters what those words are doing in the sentence.

Example: The picture I found in the garage of the night sky with dark blues and swirling gold stars covering the entire canvas in nearly a half-inch of ancient paint.

There are a lot of words here, and even more details, but this is still not a complete sentence. This fragment is missing a verb. What did this painting do? What happened to it?

Correct: The picture I found in the garage of the night sky with dark blues and swirling gold stars covering the entire canvas in nearly a half-inch of ancient paint was actually created by Vincent Van Gogh, a famous artist.

C. Fragment Phrases

1. Prepositional phrase fragment
Sentence fragments may also be the result of a prepositional phrase (see Ch. 14.5 Prepositions) that is missing the rest of the information.

> **Example:** By mixing the ingredients together.

This has some action, but it definitely leaves the reader hanging. What happened after mixing the ingredients together?

> **Correct:** By mixing the ingredients together, we made a homemade cake.

2. Gerund phrase fragment
A gerund is a verb ending in "-ing" and may function as a noun (Running is fun. This is not a fragment.) or as a verb requiring a helping verb.

> **Example:** Hoping to catch the bus.
> **Correct:** Hoping to catch the bus, I ran to the bus stop.

3. Appositive phrase fragment or appositional fragment
An appositive is an explanation of the noun preceding it. It can be removed from the sentence without changing the meaning of the sentence, but it is not a sentence on its own.

> **Example:** A cat who loves to catch fish.
> **Correct:** Sam, a cat who loves to catch fish, could not be left alone in the family room with the aquarium.

4. Adjective phrase fragment
This describes the noun in the main clause and usually uses "who," "which," or "that."

> **Example:** Which is a Rhodesian Ridgeback.
> **Correct:** My daughter has a dog that is a Rhodesian Ridgeback.

5. Participial phrase fragment
A participle is a verb used as an adjective and can end in –ing, -ed, or other past tense verb forms used with a helping verb. (See Ch. 14.2 Verbs)
> **Example:** Dissatisfied with my grade.
> **Correct:** Dissatisfied with my grade, I went to talk to my instructor.

6. Noun phrase fragment
A noun phrase includes a noun and its modifier.

> **Example:** The antique collectible plate.
> **Correct:** The antique collectible plate was chipped.

7. Infinitive phrase fragment
An infinitive phrase includes the infinitive form of the verb (to + main verb).

> **Example:** To sing in the rain.
> **Correct:** My favorite part of a storm is the chance to sing in the rain.

D. DEPENDENT CLAUSES

These types of clauses are particularly difficult to identify as fragments if you don't stop at the period (or end mark of punctuation) and continue reading into the next sentence.

Fragments can also occur if the subject and verb are preceded by a subordinating conjunction, resulting in a dependent clause (see Ch. 14.7 Conjunctions). Dependent clauses are sentences with subjects and verbs, but they also have an extra word that makes them dependent on more words—usually an independent clause.

Example: Though I scoured the flea market for hours.

There is a subject here—**I**—and a verb—**scoured**--so this appears complete at first glance. But this sentence has "**though**" at the start, suggesting that there is more to come that is missing.

Correct: Though I scoured the flea market for hours, I was not able to find the booth with the fancy soaps.

Example: When there is lightning and thunder.
Correct: When there is lightning and thunder, I like to watch the storm from my front porch.

Example: Because Hephzibah loved Ife art.
Correct: Because Hephzibah loved Ife art, she collected Ife beads and the life size bronzes.

Or, you could omit the subordinating word.

Correct: Hephzibah loved Ife art.

E. BREAKING THE RULES

There are also acceptable incomplete sentences; however, these are not used in formal academic writing.

1. Imperative mood or command: Close the door! (This has a you-understood subject.)
2. Bullets in a resume: Delivered blueprints.
3. Answer to a question: Yes.
4. Sentences without verbs: Right?
5. An elliptical response: With pleasure.
6. Performative effect: Good evening.
7. Advertisements: Kiwi fruit 4 for $!

For more information about dependent and independent clauses, see chapter 15.

EXERCISES

SENTENCE FRAGMENTS EXERCISE 17.5A

Revise the following sentence fragments.

    Evelyn playing on her tablet for four consecutive hours.

1. Certain that every light would be red on the drive there.
2. Becky waiting for her friend to arrive.
3. Because I could not stop in time.
4. The most beautiful girl in the entire school.
5. Eager to check my phone for messages.
6. Falling asleep during the three-hour long night class.
7. That time in band camp when we played that new song.
8. Wanting to sing along but not knowing the words.
9. Joe, my new next-door neighbor with the Porsche and the jet-ski parked on his lawn.

SENTENCE FRAGMENTS EXERCISE 17.5B

Revise the following sentences.

1. Jessica's new baby home from the hospital.
2. Lex acting so excited to meet his baby sister.
3. Standing on the bed jumping up and down in excitement.
4. The shouting that woke up the sleeping newborn baby.
5. Managing to nap for the brief moments that both children are asleep.
6. Everything being worth it when she looks at her new daughter.
7. Why they waited so long to have another baby is obvious.
8. Her first pregnancy was very dangerous she nearly died in labor.
9. Understandably nervous about the new baby and his beloved wife.
10. That moment when the baby is asleep and the house is quiet.

17.6 MIXED SENTENCES

A mixed sentence is the general term used to describe a sentence that is grammatically incorrect because it has started with one sentence structure in mind and ended with a different structure that does not match up. Mixed sentences can be fragments or run-ons.

A. PREPOSITIONAL PHRASES

A common mixed sentence begins with a prepositional phrase (see Ch. 14.5 Prepositions).

Incorrect: By standing on her feet for eight hours makes her tired.

By standing on her feet for eight hours is a prepositional phrase. Prepositional phrases cannot be subjects of sentences, so this sentence needs a new subject. It can keep this prepositional phrase, but it needs more words in order to be complete.

Correct: Standing on her feet for eight hours makes her tired.
Correct: By standing on her feet for eight hours, she makes a living as a server.

Incorrect: For those who want to donate to the charity should attend the silent auction at the convention center tonight.
Correct: Those who want to donate to the charity should attend the silent auction at the convention center tonight.

B. WRONG WORD FORMAT

Another mixed sentence may have the wrong form of the word.

Incorrect: Swimmers, an Olympic sport, requires years of practice.
Swimmers doesn't require practice—swimming does.
Correct: Swimming, an Olympic sport, requires years of practice.
Correct: Swimmers who participate in the Olympics often spend years in practice.

C. IS WHEN, IS WHERE, REASON IS BECAUSE

Mixed constructions often use is when, is where and the reason… is because. These phrases are inaccurate because the subject usually is not a time or place. The reason is because is redundant. Instead of using is when and is where, follow the word is with a noun or adjective.

Incorrect: A selfie **is when** someone takes a picture of him or herself with a cell phone.
Correct: A selfie is a photo that someone takes of him or herself with a cell phone.

Incorrect: A great feeling **is where** all of your friends show up to support you.
Correct: A great feeling happens when all of your friends show up to support you.

Incorrect: The **reason** the team lost **is because** the soccer field was wet from the morning downpour.
Correct: The team lost because the soccer field was wet from the morning downpour.

D. FAULTY PREDICTION

Faulty predication occurs when the subject and the predicate are not clearly connected.

Incorrect: The invention of social media has helped many people across the world stay connected.

Was it the <u>invention</u> of social media that helped people? Or social media itself?

Correct: Social media has helped many people across the world stay connected.

E. DIFFERENT GRAMMATICAL CONSTRUCTIONS

Mixed construction can occur when the grammatical structure of the sentence seems to be going in one direction but does not continue. For instance, a sentence that begins with an introductory element and is followed by an independent clause would have a mixed construction.

Incorrect: After a cat has kittens <u>is time for rest.</u>

The word "after" signals an introductory element, and readers expect an independent clause to follow, but it's missing here.

Correct: After a cat has kittens, she is ready for rest.

Incorrect: Although the pilot was prepared for a crash landing, <u>so travelers were busy on their cell phones.</u>

Does this leave you confused? What exactly is happening? The "so" is misleading here.

Correct: Although the pilot was prepared for a crash landing, the travelers were still busy on their cell phones.

When you begin a sentence, you must maintain the grammatical structure to the end.

EXERCISES

MIXED SENTENCES EXERCISE 17.6A

Revise the following sentences.

1. Wanting to do the right thing was his goal in life.
2. With an expectation of passing with an A to take the class seriously.
3. The $5 meal box at Taco Bell includes two tacos was a great deal.
4. Singing the new song in the car drove to work went by fast.
5. Molly Hatchett the best band ever opening the show on Saturday night.
6. By handing him the textbook signaling it was time to focus on studying.
7. Teaching, those noble pursuers of knowledge, spend a lot of time in school.
8. Writing the next bestseller needs to focus on writing every single day.
9. By organizing the uprising was the reason for his arrest.
10. Stranded in the middle of snow-encrusted mountains the house sighed.

MIXED SENTENCES EXERCISE 17.6B

Revise the following sentences.

1. A rebel is when you fight against those in power happens.
2. Protests are where people rally together to bring attention to a cause such as women's rights.
3. The Women's March in 2017 was when people all across the world protested against not only women's rights but also LBGT rights and immigration reform.
4. Many claim the reason the president was elected was because of widespread voter fraud.
5. Success is when people achieve the personal goals they set for themselves such as graduating from high school, learning to budget money, or joining the dive team.
6. Adopting a kitten from the Humane Society is where a person can help those rescue animals find a home.
7. The reason the debate team won was because the captain of the team knew the rules for rebuttal.
8. Helping to cleanup after a hurricane is where everyone in a neighborhood gets together to pick up debris in the street and pull trash away from the storm drains.
9. Being an astronaut is when you travel into space on a space shuttle.
10. The reason the students left the auditorium is because the fog machine malfunctioned and smoke began filling the room.

MIXED SENTENCES EXERCISE 17.6C
Revise the following sentences.

1. The increasing number of those who get the flu vaccine each year have the best protection against the flu.

2. At the racetrack is this box for your guests you will find.

3. The soprano's raspy voice was due to falling confetti onto the stage.

4. The holding of opera glasses to better see the baritone's fury helps the audience experience his deep regret.

5. Harry Potter's backstory tries to explain to the audience that he is not a Muggle.

6. Most of you arriving to the party heading out to the farm will be extremely challenging in these conditions.

7. The use of the word "muggle" has been taken out of context recently and used to refer to any group that is marginalized.

8. The doctor's suggestion for treatment is the only known cure for the rare virus.

9. Because of the new soccer rule, the uniforms worn by players who are currently on the roster must pay twice as much.

10. The volcano in Guatemala will help survivors get away from the lava streams.

REVIEW EXERCISES

COMMON ERRORS REVIEW EXERCISE: RUN-ONS/ FUSED SENTENCES, COMMA SPLICES, AND SENTENCE FRAGMENTS 17A

Identify and revise the sentence fragments, comma splices, and fused sentences below. Some sentences are correct.

1. Spoken word performances entertain audiences on college campuses, students who attend the events usually enjoy the live impromptu gatherings.

2. In fact, some students become so energized by those performing that they also share their own original works. Afterwards, those students are more likely to perform again.

3. Among contemporary poets, Maya Angelou is probably the most recognized she is however best known for her novel *I Know Why the Caged Bird Sings*.

4. Although performing seems awkward at first.

5. Some writers value the poem as a platform to raise awareness about everything from world peace to women's rights Angelou's poetry emphasizes many social and global issues.

6. Poets reading out loud to small groups of listeners.

7. Playing soccer teaches players the importance of team building. In addition, players learn the value of competitiveness, perseverance, and good sportsmanship.

8. The lessons that athletes learn on a team are relevant in many other endeavors as well, for instance, college courses require commitment, motivation, and determination.

9. Cross country running requires that runners pace themselves and stay focused on the trail. Otherwise, they could injure themselves and tire quickly.

10. While participating in multiple events at a track meet, runners must hydrate between heats, icing sore ankles and shins may also be required.

Identify and revise the sentence fragments, comma splices, and fused sentences below. Some sentences are correct.

1. The mountain climber that left the trail along the river.

2. Martha and George rode the train until they arrived in Florence, Martha's mother met them at the train station.

3. During the summer and winter months, thousands of people visit the Salvador Dali Museum at sunrise visitors begin lining up outside the museum.

4. To prepare for hurricane season, Florida residents should purchase plenty of water and a portable phone charger, mapping out an escape route is also advised.

5. Plastic bags are used by fewer shoppers today because they are harmful to the environment. Tote bags of all different sizes are preferred.

6. Hybrid cars are a good way to save money and the environment, however many consumers still do not believe that these cars are dependable on the highway.

7. The *Pieta*, the famous sculpture of Mary holding the body of Jesus, sits in St. Peter's Basilica the draping of Mary's gown is carved in Carrara marble and appears so realistic.

8. Since the recession of 2008, construction workers have been very busy new home and commercial construction has been on the rise.

9. No one imagined eight years ago that the Dow Jones would climb above 20,000 investors are relieved to see the stock market improve.

10. Fishing for trout, bass, and snook in Tampa Bay is better today than ever. The effort over the last fifteen years to restore the bay has been very effective.

11. Michelangelo's famous sculpture *David* can be seen at the Galleria dell' Accademia in Florence, Italy this Renaissance piece stands under a dome of light at the end of a short hallway.

12. Juan Felipe Herrera has been Poet Laureate of the United States for two years, he is a performer and a teacher.

13. Recycling plastic, glass, and paper is a responsibility that all Florida residents should take seriously without citizen involvement, the environment has little chance of improving.

14. Future generations depend on us to care for our clean bays and rivers, alligators, herons, water moccasins, and deer must be protected.

15. When George returned from Washington, he went right to work on building a city co-op. Cherry tomatoes, yellow squash, and green peppers began sprouting immediately.

17.7 COMMONLY CONFUSED WORDS

The following are words that are commonly confused and misused. Some of these words are homonyms, words that sound similar but have different meanings. Study the words in this list and learn how to use them correctly.

Accent – stress in speech or writing
Ascent – act of going up
Assent – consent, to accept or agree

Accept – to agree to something or receive something willingly
Except – to omit or exclude, not including

Adapt – to adjust, to make fitting or appropriate
Adept – proficient
Adopt – to choose as one's own, to accept

Affect – to influence, to pretend
Affect – feeling
Effect – result of an action
Effect – to accomplish or to produce a result

All ready – completely prepared
Already – even now; before the given time

Any way – in whatever manner
Anyway – regardless

Appraise – to set a value on
Apprise – to inform
Bibliography – list of writings on a particular topic
Biography – written history of a person's life

Bizarre – odd
Bazaar – market, fair

Coarse – rough, crude
Course – route, progression

Costume – special way of dressing
Custom – usual practice or habit

Decent – proper
Descent – fall, coming down
Dissent – disagreement, to disagree

Definite – clearly defined; absolute (for sure, for certain)
Defiant – open disregard for authority
Desert – arid region
Desert – to abandon
Dessert – sweet course served at the end of a meal

Device – a contrivance
Devise – to plan

Elusive – hard to catch or understand
Illusive – misleading, unreal

Emigrate – to leave a country and take up residence elsewhere
Immigrate – to enter a country to take up residence

Farther – more distant (refers to space)
Further – additional (refers to time, quantity, or degree)

Flair – natural ability, knack for style
Flare – to flame, to erupt, a blaze of light

Good – an adjective
Well – an adverb

In to – part of a verb phrase (He went back in to the house)

Into – preposition meaning the inside or interior of

Its – possessive form of it
It's – contraction for it is

Lay – to set something down or place something
Lie – to rest or recline, to tell untruths

Lead (n) – a heavy bluish-gray metal; the kind of graphite used in pencils
Lead (v) – to go before, as in a leader
Led – past tense of "lead"
Leaded – containing the chemical properties of lead (n)

Lose – to misplace
Loose – hanging, not fitting tightly, free

Moral – lesson, relating to right and wrong
Morale – mental state of confidence, enthusiasm

Or – a coordinating conjunction
Ore – a metal-bearing rock or mineral
Our – plural possessive pronoun for of "we"
Err – as in to err, to make a mistake or error

On to – an idiomatic expression for a movement from one location to another
Onto – to a position upon something: the book onto the desk

Passed – past tense of pass
Past – to go beyond a location or time
Personal – private
Personnel – a body of people, usually employed in an organization

Precede – to go before
Proceed – to advance, to continue
Pre·sent' – to introduce to another; to show
Pres'·ent – a gift from one to another

Profit – to gain earnings, financial gain on investments
Prophet – predictor, fortune-teller

Quiet – not noisy, a sense of calm
Quit – to stop
Quite – very
Step – footfall, to move the foot as in walking
Steppe – large, treeless plain

Team – group of people working together on a project
Teem – to swarm or abound

Thorough – complete
Through – from beginning to end, in one side and out the other
Throw – the act of tossing or propelling forward
Threw – past tense of throw: tossed or propelled forward

Than – word used in comparison
Then – at that time, next in order of time

To – a preposition or infinitive marker
Too – an adverb – suggests extremes or in addition to (an alternative to also)
Two – the number following one

EXERCISES

COMMONLY CONFUSED WORDS EXERCISE 17.7A

Choose the correct word in the parentheses.

1. The puppy (laid, lied, lay, layed, lain) by my side and whimpered.
2. She (laid, lied, lay, layed, lain) the baby in his crib.
3. I have (laid, lied, lay, layed, lain) on this bed for over an hour.
4. (Lay, Lie) the book on the table please.
5. The paper (laid, lied, lay, layed, lain) on the counter yesterday.
6. He has (laid, lied, lay, layed, lain) the baby in his crib.
7. I don't (accept, except) your apology.
8. He gave her his (advice, advise).
9. Will the score on this test (affect, effect) my grade?
10. Everyone was invited (accept, except) Bob.
11. She (adviced, advised) him not to marry her.
12. The (affect, effect) of this test on your final grade will be minimal.
13. John Milton's (allusion, illusion) to the Old Testament is obvious in *Paradise Lost*.
14. She certainly brushed her hair (alot, a lot).
15. His stories about his winning the lottery are just an (allusion, illusion).
16. She divided the work (among, between) the three boys.
17. The (amount, number) of people who are absent today is twelve.
18. He answered politely (as, like) a proper young man should.
19. The (amount, number) of stars in the sky is infinite.
20. The picture looks (as if, like) a three-year-old child painted it.

COMMONLY CONFUSED WORDS EXERCISE 17.7B

Choose the correct word in the parentheses.

1. He felt (bad, badly) about losing the game.
2. I put the magazine (beside, besides) me on the couch.
3. The Devil Rays played so (bad, badly) this year that they are not in the playoffs.
4. I like him, (but, but yet) he doesn't like me.
5. (Can, May) I stay out until midnight, Mother?
6. She (complemented, complimented) me on my dress.
7. Her (conscience, conscious) bothered her because she told a lie.
8. I (could of, could have) listened to him sing for hours.
9. My one (criterion, criteria) for buying a car is price.
10. Her shoes (complemented, complimented) her outfit.
11. He is different (from, than) the rest of the boys.
12. There are (fewer, less) flowers on the bush this year.
13. My house is (farther, further) from the park than his.
14. Golda Meir (emigrated, immigrated) to Israel and became a great leader.
15. She sings (good, well), but she can't play the piano.
16. The thief was (hanged, hung) for his crime.
17. Mrs. Gaysinski (emigrated, immigrated) from Poland in 1952.
18. He feels (good, well) {healthy} since his surgery.
19. Do you mean to (imply, infer) that he is married?
20. I will vote for you (irregardless, regardless) of your age.
21. (It's, Its) a shame that he can't go.
22. I don't wish to discuss this with you any (farther, further).
23. The puppy wagged (it's, its) tail.
24. He stabbed me with his pencil (led, lead).
25. He (led, lead) his troops to victory.

COMMONLY CONFUSED WORDS EXERCISE 17.7C

Choose the correct word in the parentheses.

1. I got the (led, lead) in the school play.
2. My pants are too (loose, lose, loss).
3. My (principal, principle) reason for leaving is the low salary.
4. Try not to (loose, lose, loss) your temper.
5. The (principal, principle) never paddles the students.
6. He is a man of high (principals, principles).
7. I have paid off some of the interest but none of the (principal, principle).
8. The (principal, principle) of gravity is not hard to understand.
9. She is a (real, really) pretty girl.
10. She has (raised, risen) an interesting point.
11. The boxes (sat, set) on the floor until the movers arrived.
12. We remained (stationary, stationery) while the mourners passed.
13. I wrote to her on my prettiest (stationary, stationery).
14. She (use, used) to be my friend.
15. I am not (suppose, supposed) to answer that question.
16. They are richer (than, then) we are.
17. Students (that, who) study hard will pass this quiz.
18. They gave (theirself, themself, themselves) a pat on the back.
19. (There, Their) are many reasons for my response.
20. They gave (there, their) uncle a gift.
21. He is (to, too) smart for his own good.
22. I paid for the tickets (to, too).
23. Please (try and, try to) be on time.
24. He is a (unique, very unique, truly unique) individual.
25. (Whose, Who's) ten dollar bill is this?
26. They gave the envelope to the man (whose, who's) sitting in that corner.
27. (Your, You're) the reason I am living.
28. I love (your, you're) new house.
29. The dishes (laid, lay, lied) in the sink all week.
30. He is (laying, lying) on the floor.
31. He has (laid, lied, lay, layed, lain) beneath that tree for an hour.
32. (Lay, Lie) down beside me and talk to me.
33. (Lay, Lie) the money on the counter and leave.

Chapter 18

STYLE

When we speak about style in writing, we are usually referring to several things, but it ultimately boils down to the words you have used in your writing.

Writing is sometimes viewed as a difficult task because there are so many things to pay attention to at one time. One must pay attention to the logic of an argument, to documentation of ideas, to movement of thought, to correctness of grammar, to the need of the audience—and this is where the conversation of style becomes most relevant. (However, please know that writing always gets easier with practice. Anything you do well involves a lot of practice.)

When your instructors speak about style, they are speaking about your method of communication, and depending on your audience, your method will vary. Research papers, for example, because they are written for an academic community, should take a formal tone and approach. A narrative essay, on the other hand, might take a more casual approach. Your style will always depend on your audience and your purpose. There is the old adage to writing: know your audience.

Certain things that fall under the rubric of style always deserve your attention:

- Person
- Voice
- Diction
- Clarity and Conciseness
- Tone

18.1 Person

Person and point of view refer to a special grouping of pronouns. Point of view is divided into three voices or persons, or three groups of pronouns known as 1st, 2nd, and 3rd person. The most skilled writers pay attention to point of view because they know it is a key element in writing style. As a general rule, it is best to write an entire paper in the same person because switching the point of view throughout the paper can confuse the reader.

Point of View	List of Pronouns	Typical Writing Occasions
1st Person (Typically where students use their "Spoken Voice"; in most academic writing, 1st person should be avoided)	I, me, mine, myself, we, us, ours, ourselves	-A personal narrative -It can be appropriate in a formal academic essay ONLY WHEN giving *a specific personal experience* as a form of argumentative evidence
2nd Person (This is rarely appropriate in the formal academic essay)	You, yours, yourself, yourselves	-A letter or email -A written speech or public address -Directions (pamphlets, etc.)
3rd Person (Typically where students use their "Written Voice"; this IS appropriate)	he, she, it, him, her, his, hers, himself, herself, itself, they, them theirs, themselves	-Formal academic writing, including: • Argumentative • Summary/Response • Compare/Contrast • Expository Essays • Descriptive Narrative • Research

Often many college professors will expect their students to write papers in third person as most research and academic writing is written in third person. Academic writing emphasizes third person because of the objective nature it provides (or at least it sounds like it). When something is written in first person, using pronouns such as "I" or "me" allows a reader to dismiss those ideas as subjective and personal rather than objective and scholarly.

Some students struggle to write in third person because they are not used to it. While it may seem challenging at first, with a little practice, all writing can be rewritten into third person. Two areas students should watch carefully in their writing are the introduction and the conclusion. In these paragraphs, many students are tempted to speak directly to the reader by using second person (you, your, etc.) as they are unaware of the unintentional effect using second person has on readers. When reading a second person pronoun such as you, readers sometimes can assume the writer is directly questioning or accusing them of something they may not have said or done. Moreover, it often shifts the focus from the topic to the reader.

Read the first and second-person examples below and the suggestions on how to rewrite them into third person.

A. Writing in Third Person

Example 1:

> I believe that students often accrue thousands of dollars of school debt without considering the long-term consequences.

Rewritten into third person:

> Students often accrue thousands of dollars of school debt without considering the long-term consequences.

Often if one of these phrases—I believe that, I think that, I feel that, etc.—begins a sentence, students can simply remove that phrase and continue with the rest of the sentence. If the remaining part of the sentence uses some first or second person, then the sentence will require more rewriting.

Example 2:

> Do you ever wonder why college athletes are not paid for playing sports for the school?
>
> OR
>
> Do you believe college athletes should be paid for playing school sports?

Rewritten into third person:

> Why are college athletes not paid for playing sports for the school? OR Should college athletes be paid for playing school sports?

Be careful writing questions. It is natural to want to direct your words to the reader personally, through the use of second person, when writing a question. However, by doing this, readers may feel completely alienated or uninterested if they do not agree with the writer's line of thinking.

Example 3:

> Even if you have not taken a student loan, you can see why this issue is becoming a crisis.

Rewritten into third person:

> Despite students' personal experience with taking loans, most students understand why this issue is becoming a crisis.

Instead of using the second-person pronoun "you," think about who the intended audience or group is—students, athletes, shoppers, lawmakers, children, parents, etc. If the audience is very broad and general, then consider using a word like people, one, or everyone. (Make sure to pay attention, however, to whether or not the word is singular or plural, especially when using other pronouns later on in the writing to refer to this word.)

At times, anecdotal writing can be appropriate for academic essays; however, sometimes you might have a professor who prefers you write the anecdotal information in third person. The following example shows how to do that.

Example 4:

> My sister, who is a teacher at Jackson Elementary, told me that each year the amount of time that her students admit to playing on electronics outside of school increases.

Rewritten into third person:

Ms. Murr, a 5th grade teacher at Jackson Elementary, shared that each year the amount of time that her students admit to playing on electronics outside of school increases.

When trying to change first-hand stories or information into third person, use the person's name instead of the relationship they have to you. For instance, instead of saying "my sister" say "Ms. Murr" as shown in the example. Again, in many academic papers, the focus is the subject being discussed, not you; therefore, it is best to emphasize what about that person (job, physical condition, experience) makes his or her story pertinent to the topic at hand.

EXERCISE

PERSON EXERCISE 18.1A

Please change this first person paragraph into third person. You can can use your own name or any other name you want to use.

I sat on the living room couch and stared out the sliding glass door. The afternoon sun lit up the trees, turning their leaves a beautiful shade of light green, and beyond them I could faintly see the outline of a mountain. This was the first time I had ever left the South and I had never seen scenery like that before. My father and I were spending the summer visiting my cousin, Cathy, out in Colorado Springs. So far, the trip had been pleasant, but we had only arrived a couple of days previously. My father and Cathy were both avid hikers who enjoyed the outdoors; I preferred being indoors and reading or playing video games. It's safe to say that I was not very prepared for this trip; I would come to find out that I truly had no idea what was in store for me that day.

(Jessica Oswald, "Past The Limits," Ch. 12.1)

18.2 VOICE

Voice is the term for verbs' ability to show whether a subject acts or receives the action named by a verb. Two voices exist in English, the active and the passive. In active voice, the subject performs the action, while in passive voice, the subject is acted upon.

You should generally avoid passive voice as it tends to create a style in which the reader may not immediately see the action or meaning that you are trying to convey.

A. RECOGNIZING ACTIVE AND PASSIVE VOICE

Transitive verbs, those that can take direct objects, usually appear in the active voice. In the active voice, the subject performs the action and a direct object receives the action.

Example: The early *bird* sometimes *catches the early worm*.

This sentence may be transformed into the passive voice, with the subject receiving the action instead:

The early worm is sometimes *caught* by the early bird.

What was once the direct object (*the early worm*) has become the subject in the passive-voice transformation, and the original subject appears in a prepositional phrase beginning with *by*.

Note: the *by* phrase is frequently omitted in passive-voice constructions.

The early worm is sometimes caught.

Verbs in the passive voice can be identified by their form alone. The main verb is always a past participle, such as *caught*, preceded by a form of *be* (*be, am, is, are, was, were, being, been*): *is caught*. Sometimes adverbs intervene (*is* sometimes *caught*).

The <u>active</u> voice of the verb: *Regular form of the verb*	The <u>passive</u> voice of the verb: *Was, were* + past participle
The assistant *measured* the solution.	The solution *was measured* by the assistant.
My brother *prepared* a great lunch.	A great lunch *was prepared* by my brother.
Jane *will cook* dinner tonight.	Dinner *will be cooked* by Jane tonight.

B. EMPLOYING PASSIVE VOICE APPROPRIATELY

The passive voice is appropriate if you wish to emphasize the receiver of the action or to minimize the importance of the doer. For example, observe how this sentence was written in the passive voice:

As the time for the harvest approaches, the tobacco plants *are sprayed* with a chemical to inhibit the growth of suckers.

The writer wished to focus on the tobacco plants, not on the people spraying them.

Sometimes, we may choose to use the passive voice because we are **not interested,** or **less interested,** in who or what did the action, only that the action was **done.**

Active voice	Passive voice
Jones *did* the blood test; James was innocent!	The blood test *was done*; James was innocent!
Fifty-five percent *elected* the President.	The President *was elected* by fifty-five percent.

We may use the passive voice to conceal **who** did the action, either intentionally (to shield the guilty) or because we do not yet know.

Active voice	Passive voice
I *broke* the expensive glass vase.	The expensive glass vase *was broken*. (by whom?)
Saturday night, someone *murdered* Smith.	Saturday night, Mr. Smith *was murdered*.

EXERCISES

VOICE EXERCISE 18.2A

Identify the voice used in each sentence. Label active voice sentences "active," and label passive voice sentences "passive."

1. Pennies are often thrown into the fountain by tourists.
2. Little attention is being paid to cheap, nutritious foods by the average shopper.
3. It is greatly feared by the citizens that the judge will have too harsh a sentence for the defendant.
4. The plot is arranged in a series of scenes designed to capture the reader's attention.
5. Jenner's work on vaccination was published in 1796.
6. All doors in this building will be locked by 6:00.
7. While conducting these experiments, the chickens were seen to panic every time a hawk flew over.
8. Questioned by the authorities, the churlish villain then plotted his next move.
9. Britain was defeated by the United States in the War of 1812.
10. Many were stricken with yellow fever.
11. One very important quality developed by an individual during a first job is self-reliance.

VOICE EXERCISE 18.2B

Revise the following sentences.

1. The award for Best News Article was given to Max Hernandez by the high school newspaper editor.
2. The flooding from Hurricane Harvey was endured for eight weeks by Houstonians who lived near the interstate.
3. Despite days of preparation, many who attended the Tampa Bay Rays' game were soaking wet by the end of the third inning .
4. The black bear that escaped previous hunters was finally shot by sixteen-year-old Miranda Chevalerie, the most experienced bear hunter in Gatlinburg, Tennessee.
5. A parking permit is given by the receptionist to hotel guests so they can park their cars in the hotel parking lot.
6. Secretaries receive an end-of-year bonus from their bosses at the company holiday party.
7. The bright red frisbee thrown by Leonard, the dog's owner, sailed over the park fence.
8. The pancakes were smothered in hot syrup by the cooks in the back of the kitchen.
9. Pounds and pounds of gulf shrimp were caught in huge nets by Forrest Gump and Lieutenant Dan aboard the boat named Jenny.
10. The clown with the sad eyes and big crooked smile terrified the children at the Barnum and Bailey circus.

VOICE EXERCISE 18.2C

Rewrite the following sentences from passive to active voice.

1. The moody *Moonlight Sonata,* one of his most famous piano compositions, was composed by Beethoven in 1801.
2. As the 2016 presidential election was unfolding, Facebook users were being influenced by misleading campaign ads.
3. The free speech campus policies protecting students' right to protest and to sponsor rallies were revised by a few concerned administrators.
4. When the opposing racquetball team comes to Austin for the state tournament, they will be met by the University of Texas coaches at the university gym.
5. My personal email account was hacked by cyber attackers who sent fake emails phishing for my social security number, address, and phone number.
6. The Dali Museum fundraiser, which each year raises money for local charities such as Hope Children's Home and Ronald McDonald House, was attended by three hundred local CEO's.
7. After the professor left the classroom, his notes on the board were photographed by three students.
8. The history notes for Chapter 13 on General Grant and General Lee were shared among the study group.

18.3 DICTION

"This above all: to thine ownself be true, And it must follow as the night the day, Thou canst not then be false to any man."

"Most importantly, be true to yourself, son, and then you shouldn't get into any trouble with anyone else."

Consider these two very different ways of saying the same thing. The first version comes from Shakespeare's *Hamlet*: this is Polonius' advice to his son Laertes as the son heads back to school in France (I iii). The second version is what a father might say to a child leaving home for college.

The first version uses formal diction, with the words chosen to fit the seriousness of the occasion. The second version uses informal diction, with a touch of the colloquial in the phrase "get into any trouble." As in these two examples, your word choice is likely to depend on your purpose and audience.

A. TYPES OF DICTION

Most frequently, "diction" simply means word choice. One could equate one's diction with one's vocabulary. It may be helpful to think of diction in terms of clothing: a person can dress in a tuxedo or ballgown, khakis and a polo, or shorts and flipflops. Similarly, diction can be categorized into formal, informal, and colloquial language.

- Formal diction is academic and professional.
  - In the academic environment, formal diction would be appropriate in essays, research papers, and scholarly journals.
  - In the business environment, formal diction would be found in job descriptions, business plans, financial reports, and other legal documents.

- Informal diction uses words correctly and grammatically but in more casual situations. For example, formal medical diction may use the term myocardial infarction while informal diction would simply say heart attack.
  - In the academic environment, you may encounter informal diction in a creative writing class or certain class discussions.
  - Beyond academics, informal diction may appear in popular publications such as magazines and tabloids.

- Colloquial diction reflects the everyday use of words. It includes slang, text language, local expressions, and even profanity.
  - In the academic and professional environments, colloquialisms are generally avoided.
  - In other environments, colloquialisms are common among friends and family through text messages and social media.
  - Creative writers who want to write realistic dialogue can study colloquialisms carefully and reflect that language in their writing.

B. Denotation/Connotation

Denotations refer to the dictionary definition of a term. Connotations are the associations that people make with that term. The diction you choose reflects more than the denotative meaning; the words also prompt an emotional response in readers and that response reflects a connotative meaning.

Think about the difference between the following examples: fragrance, odor, perfume, smell, stink, aroma, whiff, waft, reek, stench. Each of these may denote a scent in the surrounding air, but the connotations for each term will vary among your readers. Always consider what your readers will associate with your diction and how that will affect their response to your ideas.

C. Things to Avoid

Writers may use idioms, cliches, slang, and jargon when writing informally, but these should be used sparingly, if at all, in formal writing. Always remember your purpose and audience when considering diction.

- Idioms are figures of speech that express ideas that differ from their literal meanings. Specific cultural interpretations may confuse readers.
  - **Idiom-filled:** You don't want to <u>put your foot in your mouth</u> and make your readers <u>scratch their heads</u> or, even worse, <u>get hot under the collar</u>. <u>Bend over backwards</u> and <u>give writing clearly your best shot</u>.
  - **Idiom-free**: You don't want to say the wrong thing and leave readers confused or, even worse, angry. Try your very best to write clearly.

- Clichés are well-known expressions that have become part of everyday conversation (e.g. "You don't know what you've got til' it's gone"). Original writing is generally more interesting for readers to enjoy.
- Slang is informal or colloquial language that changes rapidly (e.g. groovy, sweet, cool, GOAT, dope, sick, lit, awesome).
- Jargon refers to the specialized terminology understood by members of a specific community. Consider whether your audience will contain members who are not familiar with the technical language of your topic.
  - **Jargon-filled**: Michael Bolton turned in his third copy of the TPS reports to Bill Lumbergh confirming the quarter's NPS and P&L.
  - **Jargon-free:** Michael Bolton gave his boss Bill Lumbergh a report of the quarter's net promoter score as well as profit and loss figures.

- Over-the-top language refers to exaggerated diction.
  - **Too much**: Florida has the most beautiful, miraculous, life-affirming beaches that are superior to any beach anywhere else in the world. (This is too good to be true.)
  - Just right: Florida has beautiful beaches comparable to other world-class beaches.

- Absolutes are words such as every, everyone, all, never, and always that can be proven false by a single example to the contrary. Instead, writers can use qualifiers like often, most, nearly, or rarely because they allow other possibilities that the absolutes don't.
  - **Absolute:** Everyone knows that smoking is dangerous to human health.
  - **Qualifiers**: Most adults know that smoking is dangerous to human health.

D. A Comparison of Diction

Review the following four examples of effective diction:

"The City upon the Hill"

This sermon by John Winthrop was delivered in 1630 on the *Arbella* as the Pilgrims were approaching landfall off Massachusetts Bay.

John Winthrop—*July 2, 1630 on board the ship Arbella while en route to the Massachusetts Bay Colony*

The Lord will be our God, and delight to dwell among us, as his oune people, and will command a blessing upon us in all our wayes. Soe that wee shall see much more of his wisdome, power, goodness and truthe, than formerly wee haue been acquainted with. Wee shall finde that the God of Israell is among us, when ten of us shall be able to resist a thousand of our enemies; when hee shall make us a prayse and glory that men shall say of succeeding plantations, "the Lord make it likely that of New England." For wee must consider that wee shall be as a citty upon a hill. The eies of all people are uppon us. Soe that if wee shall deale falsely with our God in this worke wee haue undertaken, and soe cause him to withdrawe his present help from us, wee shall be made a story and a by-word through the world.

Note that the spelling is 17th Century style, but if you accept what looks like a "u" as sometimes a "v," it is not hard to read. And if you read this carefully, in the context of the Pilgrims first coming to the new land they call "New England," you recognize that they arrived on the shore in search of freedom from the oppression of the British Crown and the Roman Catholic James I.

Centuries later, President Ronald Reagan ended his second term with a farewell address referencing John Winthrop's vision of "The City upon the Hill":

President Ronald Reagan—*January 11, 1989, "Farewell Address to the Nation"*

And that's about all I have to say tonight, except for one thing. The past few days when I've been at that window upstairs, I've thought a bit of the "shining city upon a hill." The phrase comes from John Winthrop, who wrote it to describe the America he imagined. What he imagined was important because he was an early Pilgrim, an early freedom man. He journeyed here on what today we'd call a little wooden boat; and like the other Pilgrims, he was looking for a home that would be free.

I've spoken of the shining city all my political life, but I don't know if I ever quite communicated what I saw when I said it. But in my mind, it was a tall, proud city built on rocks stronger than oceans, windswept, God-blessed, and teeming with people of all kinds living in harmony and peace; a city with free ports that hummed with commerce and creativity. And if there had to be city walls, the walls had doors and the doors were open to anyone with the will and the heart to get here. That's how I saw it and see it still.

And how stands the city on this winter night? More prosperous, more secure, and happier than it was 8 years ago. But more than that: After 200 years, two centuries, she still stands strong and true on the granite ridge, and her glow has held steady no matter what storm. And she's still a beacon, still a magnet for all who must have freedom, for all the pilgrims from all the lost places who are hurtling through the darkness, toward home.

Note the imagery—the pictures created by the words—that Reagan uses. His diction differs from that of Winthrop but is no less formal; in fact, many might view Reagan's words as more formal because of the context in which he wrote this speech (presidential farewell). Reagan also uses the religious images of the city built on rocks "stronger than oceans, windswept, God-blessed, and teeming with people of all kinds living in harmony," imagery that reflects the vision shared by both Winthrop and Reagan.

"Four score, five score"

In 1863, President Abraham Lincoln gave one of the most famous speeches in American history:

President Abraham Lincoln—*November 19, 1863, Dedication of the Cemetery at Gettysburg, Pennsylvania*

Four score and seven years ago our fathers brought forth on this continent, a new nation, conceived in Liberty, and dedicated to the proposition that all men are created equal.

Now we are engaged in a great civil war, testing whether that nation, or any nation so conceived and so dedicated, can long endure. We are met on a great battle-field of that war. We have come to dedicate a portion of that field, as a final resting place for those who here gave their lives that that nation might live. It is altogether fitting and proper that we should do this.

But, in a larger sense, we cannot dedicate—we cannot consecrate—we cannot hallow—this ground.

You may recognize this passage as the introduction to the "Gettysburg Address" by President Abraham Lincoln. A century later, Dr. Martin Luther King, Jr. would echo some of Lincoln's language as he delivered another one of the most revered speeches in American history.

Note the similarity between Lincoln's opening line and Dr. King's opening line below ("score years ago"). Dr. King uses additional repetition, such as "one hundred years later," which emphasizes the time between the signing of the Emancipation Proclamation (1863) to Dr. King's speech about jobs and freedom and equality (1963).

Dr. Martin Luther King, Jr. *August 23, 1963, in front of the Lincoln Memorial on the occasion of the "March on Washington for Jobs and Freedom"*

Five score years ago, a great American, in whose symbolic shadow we stand today, signed the Emancipation Proclamation. This momentous decree came as a great beacon light of hope to millions of Negro slaves who had been seared in the flames of withering injustice. It came as a joyous daybreak to end the long night of their captivity.

But one hundred years later, the Negro still is not free; one hundred years later, the life of the Negro is still sadly crippled by the manacles of segregation and the chains of discrimination; one hundred years later, the Negro lives on a lonely island of poverty in the midst of a vast ocean of material prosperity; one hundred years later, the Negro is still languished in the corners of American society and finds himself in exile in his own land.

This example of formal diction, like the example of Lincoln's use of repetition, helps create both denotative clarity and connotative imagery for the reader (and listener).

EXERCISE

DICTION EXERCISE 18.3A
Revise the following sentences for diction issues.

1. I effected a transaction to facilitate my transportation needs.

2. I was like OMG when he busted out that swagger.

3. The prepubescent child perfected her culinary skills with her maternal unit.

4. The dude had totally had too much to drink that night.

5. The kid was way over the line with his behavior last night.

18.4 CLARITY AND CONCISENESS

No matter what type of text you are writing, clarity is going to be essential.

Clarity is somewhat of an umbrella term that focuses on several practices. The first and most obvious of these is avoiding wordiness.

One way a writer can create wordiness, staleness, and informality in his or her prose is by using too many clichés. We've heard these trite expressions many times before: She is as slow as a snail; it happened in the nick of time; she ran like the speed of light; it lasted an eternity.

Stale expressions such as these suggest a lack of ingenuity in the writer. The following example illustrates this point:

> She was as slow as a snail getting ready. She took her time to put things one by one in the suitcase and worked with the speed of a sloth folding and refolding and folding again.

The sentence takes far too long to get to where it needs to get to and because of the clichés, it is boring and pedestrian.

A revision of the sentence might read as such:

> She worked slowly getting ready, putting things one by one in the suitcase and folding and refolding everything.

The second sentence is much tighter, neater, and gets to the point without too many distractions. Writers almost always want to try to avoid using clichés. Although they are a part of everyday speech, they have been used so often that to most readers, they sound stale and bland. Clichés are also shortcuts to ideas, and good writing provides specifics and details. You want your writing to be fresh and interesting. You want your writing to explain with precision, and clichés do neither of these. If you find yourself using a cliché, try to replace it with language that is fresh and specific.

While you want to be creative with your word choice, try not to overdo it. Writing too many complex words/phrases often obscures meaning. Growing up, you may have heard the directive "Use your words." The problem with that directive is that it is too easy to go overboard with words. In an attempt to "sound smart," you might employ fancy words to state a simple point. While this CAN work sometimes, most times, you risk confusing your audience. The point of communication is that OTHERS understand what you're saying. Doing that as directly as possible is the best way to achieve success.

Consider the following sentence:

> Prior to the convening of my collective knowledge-procurement experience, I leisurely perambulated around the institution of higher learning.

What on earth does that mean? If you're scratching your head, you're not alone. The above sentence is pseudo-intellectualism at its best (or its worst).

Revised for clarity and concision:

> I strolled around the college until class started.

Which sentence was easier to understand? The second sentence, right? That's because it is clear and to the point. It retains the exact meaning of the first sentence, but the second sentence makes (A LOT) more sense. In your writing, respect your readers' time by carefully selecting the most effective words, as well as the fewest words, possible to make your point.

A. Avoiding Generalizations

College writing (or academic writing in general) requires that you speak specifically and with precision. For that reason, you want to be particularly careful of language that lumps groups of people together, resorts to stereotyping, or assumes that a part functions the same as the whole. You also want to avoid indulgences (i.e., those literary flourishes that might have served you well in high school). Academic writing requires specificity and often avoids words such as "always" and "never," simply because words such as these leave little room for difference or exceptions.

In order to tighten your writing and to avoid generalizations, you will find it helpful to make sure you never take any belief system for granted. Be sure to verify all your assumptions before delivering them as fact. For example, before telling your reader that 19th century women were housewives and were not allowed to work, you might want to do little bit of reading about 19th century women before making such claims. After a little reading, you might find that despite the commonly held assumption that these women were extensions of their husbands only, many women (who were not part of the planter class) worked to help support the home.

Other techniques to avoid generalizations involve avoiding the assertion that your belief is held by all. Never assume that your reader holds the same values you do. Try to keep an open mind as you write and engage with the conversations of those with whom you might disagree or who might disagree with you.

College writing or academic writing requires that you speak specifically and with precision. For that reason, you want to pay particularly careful attention to language that lumps groups of people together, resorts to stereotyping, or assumes that a part functions the same as a whole.

Example:
    a. Moviegoers should always read the reviews of a film before viewing. (Always is a strong word, and there probably is no good reason why people "always" need to read reviews.)
    b. All adults should rigorously exercise at least five times a week. (All adults are not able to do this.)
    c. Women love to wear makeup. (Not all women love to wear makeup.)

Revision:
    a. Reading reviews before watching a film might help viewers in understanding the popular attraction to certain movies.
    b. Health professionals have suggested that capable adults should exercise at least five times a week.
    c. Many women enjoy wearing makeup.

EXERCISES

CLARITY AND CONCISENESS EXERCISE 18.4A
Look over an essay that you have written. Revise for both clarity and conciseness. Rewrite any generalizations you have as well.

18.5 Tone

Tone refers to the way you are perceived by your readers. In academic writing, there is an expectation of more formal writing. This does not need you need to use every fancy word in the dictionary, but it does mean that you should refrain from slang or jargon if possible. Always consider your audience—what do you want them to think about the way you discuss the topic?

Ask yourself to whom you are speaking and how you want to be received. If you want readers to consider your perspective, you must consider your readers' feelings. But you don't want to lecture your readers or push them away.

What is your reaction to this argument?

> If you really care about your children and their future, you should make sure that you save enough money for them to attend college, instead of spending your money foolishly.

What is your reaction to this argument?

> Parents who want their children to attend college should consider contributing part of their earnings into a college fund.

The first argument has an accusatory tone and makes assumptions about the readers. The use of the second-person "you" also creates distance between the writer and reader because the use of "you" doesn't include the writer. In fact, it includes everyone but the writer.

A. Avoid Ranting and Preaching

Perhaps this concept speaks for itself. This style of writing is unacceptable for an academic paper. Academic arguments are never an unorganized stream of consciousness. They are never reflections of personal absorptions or indulgences in one's opinion. Academic arguments convince or persuade through objective reasoning, which is reasoning derived from evidence, logic, and fact. This reasoning differs from the subjective reasoning that derives from personal feelings, individual experience, and beliefs.

Writers can avoid ranting and preaching by taking time to think about how they want to organize the argument and how the argument might be perceived by those who do not see things the same way. You can also avoid this by staying clear of the first person point of view and phrases such as "people should" do this or do that. Planning, reading about your subject, knowing the various sides of an argument, and speaking objectively will certainly help to avoid those easy traps of self-indulgent writing.

B. Inclusive Language

It is important to use inclusive language in academic and professional writing. The Modern Language Association defines inclusive language as language which "aims to be respectful to others by treating language describing individual and group identity with sensitivity and by avoiding bias that could make some people feel excluded" (134).

When considering your audience, strive to avoid language that is insensitive to race and ethnicity, economic or social status, sexual orientation, gender, age, and ability. Using inclusive language will enhance your credibility as a writer and affirm each audience member's dignity. A good rule of thumb is to remember that any individual whom you are trying to describe is first and foremost a *person*, who is not defined or limited by a particular characteristic. Review the common examples below.

Ability or Ailment

> Preferred: *persons with disabilities, persons with mental illness*

> Avoid: *disabled person, handicapped person, retarded, challenged, crazy*

Race and Ethnicity

Preferred: *African American, Asian-American, person of Asian descent, people of color, Latinx*

Avoid: *black people, negroes, colored people, Orientals, Asians, Chinese people, Spanish people*

Sexual Orientation

Preferred: *person of homosexual orientation, people who identify as homosexual, those who identify as heterosexual*

Avoid: *gays, queers, straight people*

(Note: Although the term *LGBTQ+* is now commonly used to discuss LGBTQ+ theory, most critics deem a self-referential use of a term as acceptable, such as in "*Queer* Theory.")

Gender-Inclusive Language

Preferred: *humankind, mail carrier, waste collector*

Avoid: *mankind, mailman, garbage man*

On the note of gender, when choosing personal and possessive pronouns, if the gender of the individual is obvious or self-identified information, use the corresponding gender-specific personal pronoun. For example, use pronouns like "she" and "her" for an article written by Stephanie Smith. However, if you are unsure of someone's gender, if the individual's gender is irrelevant, or if the individual uses "they" as their pronoun, it is acceptable to use the singular "they." For example, if an author's first name is Peyton, the author may identify as male, female, or non-binary. It is fine to research the author to see how they identify; if in doubt, simply use "they" as a generic third-person singular pronoun.

Works Cited

MLA. *MLA Handbook.* 9th edition, The Modern Language Association of America, 2021.

EXERCISES

TONE EXERCISE 18.5 A

Make each of these sentences more professional by revising for tone:

1. If you had read the instructions more carefully, you wouldn't have caused so many problems with the system.

2. You will no doubt be excited by my qualifications.

3. I can't offer you this internship because you are obviously not qualified.

4. You were apparently too busy to read the progress report carefully, so I'll be happy to send it to you again.

5. I need you to send me a status update by the close of business today.

6. I can't believe you scoundrels sold us defective equipment!

7. You claimed that our previous fiscal year had been profitable, but I beg to differ.

8. I urge you to consider me for this prestigious job at your outstanding organization.

9. You're going to have to fix the underlying budget problem if you expect us to complete this project on time.

10. This promotion would offer me many opportunities for my professional growth, and I would love to make so much more money than what I'm making now.

TONE EXERCISE 18.5B

Choose an iconic painting by a famous artist. Describe it using an authoritative tone. Then, in a new paragraph, consider what it means in a reflective tone. Finally, discuss the effect of the image in an uncertain tone. Think of your word choice as your write in each tone.

Chapter 19

REFERENCE

Although following the rules for numbers, abbreviations, and capitalization can seem daunting, knowing and understanding the rules is the first step to your success.

- Numbers
- Abbreviations
- Capitalization

19.1 NUMBERS

The rules for formatting numbers depend on the style guide (MLA, APA, Chicago, etc.) your discipline requires. MLA format will be used for the following examples, but be sure to confirm which style guide your instructor has designated for your assignment.

A. GENERAL NUMBER USAGE

1. Numbers may be written with numerals (87) or words (eighty-seven). In academic writing, it is customary to spell out numbers and fractions that can be written in one or two words (thirty-one, fifty-seven, one-half). You should, however, use numerals for one-word numbers if they appear in a series with at least one three-word number.

> **Example**: The new video game Jan designed has 101 cats, 71 mice, and 1 debutante trapped in an Escher-designed house.

2. You should use numerals for any number that requires more than two words (use 375, not three hundred seventy-five).

> **Examples:**
> We sold 221 gift bags last month.
> There are 331 million people in the USA.

3. Additionally, if you must use a number at the beginning of a sentence, spell it out.

> **Example:** Twenty-six cats are hiding behind the bushes.

Note: If a three-word or more number appears at the beginning of a sentence, rather than write it out, try flipping the sentence so that the number is not the first word in the sentence to avoid awkwardness.

> **Incorrect:** 327 people responded to the survey.
> **Awkward:** Three hundred twenty-seven people responded to the survey.
> **Correct:** The survey received 327 responses.

4. Remember to separate numbers when used next to other numbers to avoid confusion by using numerals and figures.

> **Unclear:** Yesterday, 20 6-year-olds came to Jan's birthday party.
> **Clear:** Yesterday, twenty 6-year-olds came to Jan's birthday party.

5. For larger numerals, commas are used between the third and fourth numbers from the right (and sixth and seventh, etc.) but should not be used in page and line numbers, street addresses, or in four-digit years.

> **Examples**:
> The bookstore ordered 5,243 copies of the textbook for the 2021-2022 academic year.
> Over 25,000 people attended Superbowl LV at Raymond James Stadium located at 4201 North Dale Mabry, Tampa, Florida 33607.

B. ABBREVIATIONS

When abbreviations for words are used, such as lbs. for pounds, then it is acceptable to use the numeral instead of spelling out the word. Either format is fine, but consistency is important, so pick a style and follow it throughout your writing.

> **Examples**:
> The box weighs over 6 lbs.
> The box weighs over six pounds.

C. Addresses

Location numbers in addresses are usually not written out, while street names can be, but if in doubt, refer to the USPS or local authority for the official format.

Examples:
The SouthShore campus of HCC is located at 551 24th Street Northeast, Ruskin, Florida, 33570.
She considered moving into the apartment at 6266 Tenth Street or 245 East 78th Street.

D. Dates

The day and year usually use numerals, but again, consistency in the order of elements is crucial. In the United States, it is common practice for the month to precede the day (March 6 or 3/6) while in other locations, the day will precede the month (6 March or 6/3). This can cause confusion, so be aware of your audience's expectations.

Examples:
My nephew's birthday is 18 May 2018.
May 18, 2018 is my nephew's birthday.

An important date in English history is AD 1066 (or 1066 CE).
An important date in Roman history is 43 BC (or 43 BCE).

Note: AD precedes the year while CE/BC/BCE follows it. MLA prefers the abbreviation for the year notation.

Synthesizers became popular in the music of the eighties
Synthesizers became popular in the music of the '80s.
Synthesizers became popular in the music of the 1980s.

E. Other Number Uses

Follow the models below that illustrate how to use decimals, percentages, identification numbers, money, parts of a written work, ratios, statistics, and time.

Decimals and percentages: 12.42 percent (in non-scientific contexts)
66% (in scientific contexts)

Identification numbers: Channel 1009
Interstate 75
Henry VIII

Money: $4.55 for exact but uneven amounts
Four dollars for even dollar numbers or $4.00
$0.60 or 60 cents or sixty cents
$1 million or one million dollars

Parts of a written work: in volume 2, act 3
in act 3, scene 2
in Act III, Scene ii
page 9 or chapter 17

Ratios: 10:1 or 10 to 1

Statistics: use numerals

Time: Generally, use noon instead of 12:00 p.m. and midnight for 12:00 a.m.
Other times, use numerals or words:
6:22 AM or a.m.
8:00 AM or eight o'clock in the morning
4:30 PM or p.m. or half-past four in the afternoon

EXERCISE

NUMBERS EXERCISE 19.1A

Please revise the following sentences as needed:

1. According to his contract, Isaac would make eighteen dollars and twenty-four cents at his new job.

2. Of all the expressions my mother used to say, I remember 1 the most: A bird in the hand is worth 2 in the bush.

3. Profits increased by two point three percent last year.

4. $60,000 was the asking price for the new luxury car.

5. Cameron noted that the hole in the wall was only 6 cm wide, and he was confident he could repair it for about $5.

6. After the camera crew had shot the 37th take, Victor knew it was going to be a long night.

7. Most 6-year-olds can't solve the puzzle, but Brayden found the solution in exactly 38.4 seconds.

8. After 139 days, Hailey reached her fitness goal: She had lost twenty-five pounds.

9. *Pulp Fiction* is Henry's favorite movie of the 1990's.

10. Nora's insurance company sent her a check for one thousand, four hundred and sixty-three dollars and sixty-one cents.

19.2 ABBREVIATIONS

An abbreviation is a shortened form of a longer word or phrase. Review customary abbreviations below.

A. TITLES

Abbreviate and capitalize first letters of titles when they appear before a specific name. When titles appear after a name, spell out as common noun (use only one form at a time).

Dr. Anthony Fauci or Anthony Fauci, MD

Rev. Jones (for reverend)

St. Francis (for saint)

Mr. James Smyth (the plural of Mr. is Messrs.)

Mrs. Jane Smyth (the plural of Mrs. is Mmes.)

Ms. Amy Smyth

Note: Writers typically refer to a man as Mr. and a woman as Ms. unless the woman specifically requests Mrs. However, Mr. and Ms. both denote gender and not marital status as Mrs. does. Miss indicates an unmarried woman and does not have a period at end because it is not an abbreviation. If gender is unknown, then use the person's full name without a title.

Some abbreviations follow names: Jr., Sr., MD, PhD, DDs

Tom Arnold, Jr.

Jim Joneston, Sr.

Benjamin Barrett, PhD

Matthew Hunter, DDS

B. ACRONYMS AND INITIALISMS

Acronyms use the first letters of a group of words that are put together and pronounced as a word.

NASA (National Aeronautics and Space Association)

NATO (North Atlantic Treaty Organization)

laser (light amplification by stimulated emission of radiation)

scuba (self-contained underwater breathing apparatus)

AIDS (acquired immunodeficiency syndrome)

Initialisms are made up of the first initials of groups of words and are pronounced as letters.

NFL (National Football League)

CD (compact disc)

ATM (automatic teller machine)

FBI (Federal Bureau of Investigation)

CIA (Central Intelligence Agency)

AFL-CIO (American Federation and Congress of Industrial Organizations)

HIV (human immunodeficiency virus)

If you are going to frequently use a group of words in your writing, you may create your own abbreviation; for example, write out "operating room (OR)" the first time, and then use the "OR" for the rest of the paper.

If you don't know what an acronym stands for, or if you think your readers won't, look it up and write out all the words. Just as you would do with forming your own abbreviation, follow the name with the abbreviation in parentheses and then use the abbreviation after that first use: Hillsborough Community College (HCC).

Please note that not all words that go into making an abbreviation are capitalized unless they are proper nouns. Also note that not all abbreviations use periods. Acronyms and initialisms frequently do not. The preferred form for academic abbreviations is not to use periods.

Note: Please remember that HCC could stand for many other words: Honolulu Community College, Houston Community College, Hispanic Contractors of Colorado, Highland Community College, etc., so you should think about your audience (classroom, local community, global) or be safe and write out the proper name (Hillsborough Community College) followed by (HCC).

C. Time abbreviations

AM or a.m. (ante meridiem) means before noon
PM or p.m. (post meridiem) means after noon
BC (before Christ)—200 BC
BCE (before the common era)—200 BCE
AD (anno domini)—AD 1066 (AD is placed BEFORE the year)
CE (common era)—1066 CE

Designate year by either BC/AD designation or BCE/CE designation; do not interchange them. In formal academic writing, do not abbreviate days of the week or seasons of the year.

D. Latin terms

Abbreviate common Latin terms.

etc. (and so forth)
i.e. (that is)
e.g. (for example)
et al. (and others)

E. Style Guide

Follow the abbreviation rules of the documentation system you are using. For example, the names of months may be abbreviated in headings, footnotes, or bibliographies, but not in the body of a paper. When asked to write a research paper, be sure to ask your instructor what style sheet to use. Examples of a few style sheet abbreviations:

AAA (American Anthropological Association)
ACS (American Chemical Society)
AP (Associated Press)
APA (American Psychological Association)
APSA (American Political Science Association)
ASME (American Society of Mechanical Engineers)
CMOS (Chicago Manual of Style, usually referred to as Chicago)
MLA (Modern Language Association)

Most educational areas of specialization have a specific style sheet with specialized uses of abbreviations, numbers, page format, and other features.

EXERCISES

ABBREVIATIONS EXERCISE 19.2A

In the following sentences, correct all abbreviation errors. Some sentences may contain multiple errors. If a sentence is already correct, write "Correct."

1. Alden was looking forward to starting his internship with NASA in FL but knew it would be challenging.
2. Roberto was looking thru his closet for the perfect T-shirt to wear to the R&B concert.
3. When Jeannie was 16 yrs old when she knew that her future would be in the US Navy.
4. Noah wanted to become an MD so he could research new treatments for HIV.
5. Lee enjoys exercising early in the a.m., whereas his wife prefers to go to the gym after she gets out of work at 6:15 p.m.
6. The CEO was excited that profits had been increased by 15 million USD.
7. Maria was worried that her son had a temp of 101°F.
8. A single night at the hotel cost $450 and was clearly out of the family's budget.
9. Emma decided to buy a 4 oz. bottle of the new herbal supplement even though it wasn't approved by the FDA.
10. Olivia was grateful that Dr. Rodriguez was able to diagnose her condition.

ABBREVIATIONS EXERCISE 19.2B

In the following sentences, correct all abbreviation errors. Some sentences may contain multiple errors. If a sentence is already correct, write "Correct."

1. The PSA claimed that it would take only one min to update one's information online.
2. Earning a PHD requires hard work and dedication.
3. Only people with the highest IQ's could become members of the elite club for intellectuals.
4. Laim's favorite author was Kurt Vonnegut, Jr. and finished reading all of his books last Feb.
5. Barbara first learned HTML when she was a USF student in the nineties.
6. Aiden nearly collided with the tree but missed it by 7 cm's.
7. To repair her PC, Sophia watched a step-by-step guide on YouTube.
8. Although she knew she would miss her family, Emily decided to move to the Pacific NW.
9. Working for the CIA was Owen's lifelong goal.
10. Jacob was amazed by many 20th Century inventions: RADAR, SCUBA, LASERs, and etc.

19.3 Capitalization

Capitalization is an important aspect of English grammar. The key to understanding capitalization is knowing when to capitalize a particular word. Review the rules for capitalization below.

1. Capitalize the pronoun I and the first word of every sentence.

> **Example:** My mother and I have been watching *Breaking Bad* on Netflix.

2. Capitalize proper nouns (names of specific people, places, and things).

> **Example:** The Sunshine Skyway Bridge is a famous landmark in Tampa Bay.

3. Capitalize certain adjectives derived from proper nouns, particularly the names of places and people. However, there are exceptions to this rule. For example, do not capitalize "french" in french fries. Consult a dictionary to verify whether an adjective should be capitalized.

> **Example:** We read "Harlem Dancer," the Shakespearean Sonnet by Claude McKay, in my English class.

4. Capitalize company and brand names but not the common noun that follows. If in doubt, research the popular capitalization of the term.

> **Example:** Henry packed Crest toothpaste for his trip to the Apple conference to learn about iPhones.

5. Capitalize family relationships when used as proper names, but not when used with a possessive pronoun.

> **Examples:**
> Evelyn loves going to the park to feed the ducks with Aunt Mary.
> I enjoy spending time with my favorite aunt, Jeanette.
> After school, Mom wants to take us shopping.
> Do you want to stay here with your dad?

6. Capitalize titles before a person's name, but do not capitalize occupations before names.

> **Examples:**
> My professor said that President Abraham Lincoln is often misunderstood.
> My favorite movie is *E.T. the Extra-Terrestrial* from director Stephen Spielberg.

7. Capitalize important words in a title. For more information on titles, please review Ch. 24 and Ch. 25.

> **Examples:**
> Damon Salvatore's favorite book is *Gone with the Wind*. (MLA)
> He was intrigued by the book *Hillbilly elegy: A memoir of a family and culture in crisis.* (APA)

8. Capitalize geographic locations but not compass directions.

> **Example:** I lived in the Midwest. You can get there if you head north on I-75.

9. Capitalize the official names of courses but not the subject itself.

> **Example:** I'm taking Introduction to Anthropology, but my husband is taking a history class.

10. Capitalize seasons when they are part of an official title.

> **Example:** During the Spring 2020 semester, many classes moved online, but things were still uncertain for the summer session.

When in doubt, look up the word or phrase in question. Capitalization can depend on style guides and industry standards as well as purpose and audience.

EXERCISES

CAPITALIZATION EXERCISE 19.3A

Correct all capitalization errors in the following sentences. Some sentences have multiple errors. Assume these are all in an academic context, and adhere to MLA's capitalization rules. If a sentence is correct, write "Correct."

1. In your email, you stated that your Dad purchased a used iPad on eBay.
2. My favorite Teacher at high school inspired me to love english.
3. The best leaders in our Government will sometimes have to make tough decisions.
4. Unfortunately, the results of this Science experiment are unreliable.
5. Isn't it true that my favorite fast food restaurant, taco bell, used to be owned by PepsiCo?
6. People who practice polytheistic religions worship multiple gods.
7. My Psychotherapist, Dr. D'Elia, got her degree from a University in my home state.
8. Sometimes PowerPoint presentations are boring, but today's lecture was fascinating.
9. Being an Independent voter with no party affiliation, I can't vote in Florida's Primaries.
10. I'm old enough to remember when caller id was a somewhat expensive novelty.

CAPITALIZATION EXERCISE 19.3B

Correct all capitalization errors in the following sentences.

1. Ashley learned about the history of radar when she was in the Military.
2. After he passed out in the cafeteria, Bryan was transported from Sarasota High School to a nearby Hospital, but now he's doing fine.
3. Bill loves working at the department of defense and plans to stay in Washington, D.C. after he retires.
4. Although he wasn't jewish, reverend Stevenson enjoyed discussing god with his best friend, a rabbi.
5. Every halloween, mom used to pass out fruit instead of candy to trick-or-treaters.
6. Nguyen's doctor measured her glucose levels, prescribed her claritin for her allergies, and told her to stop taking so much aspirin.
7. *The Simpsons* was arguably the best television program that Twentieth Century Fox produced during the Twentieth Century.
8. Clara asked her lawyer, "should i proceed with the lawsuit as planned?"
9. Because he was always fascinated with literature and religion, Juan enjoyed studying The Bible in his English class at The University of South Florida.
10. Rosa wanted to learn about Archaeology though she chose Accounting as her career.

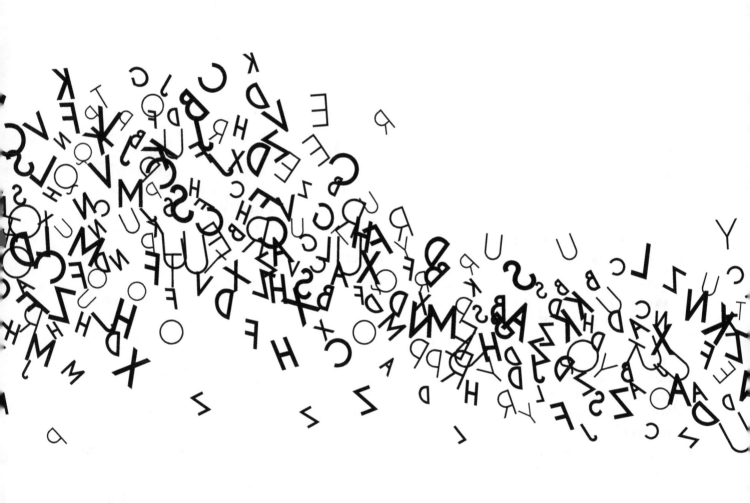

PART FIVE

Research

A few things to know before beginning:

- Research is a long process, but it doesn't need to be overly complicated.

- Yes, we know that Google is the default search method; that said, don't forget that you have access to the HCC library databases. You have solid sources available at the touch of button.

A note on the structure of this section:

- Part Five begins with a discussion of plagiarism.

- Next, we have an overview for the research process, followed by a look at finding sources and integrating them into your paper.

- The final sections cover both MLA and APA format.

Chapter 20

PLAGIARISM

Plagiarism is one of the most serious ethical violations that can be committed in an academic or professional setting. Although precise definitions of plagiarism vary depending on context, the act involves an attempt to fool your reader into believing that words or ideas that you took from somewhere else are actually your own. In the academic world, plagiarism can result in an automatic "F" for the project in which it is committed, an "F" for the entire course, or even dismissal from the institution.

A particularly blatant form of plagiarism occurs when a student copies an existing essay instead of writing his or her own. However, plagiarism can occur in ways that are less obvious. If a student copies even a single sentence or significant phrase and doesn't provide proper attribution, that student has committed plagiarism. If a student takes somebody's unique ideas and fails to give that person credit, plagiarism has been committed. Take plagiarism seriously and remember that the consequences can be severe.

Keep in mind that in a composition course, instructors want to help their students become better writers. If a student submits work that isn't original, that instructor is unable to provide the guidance that will allow that student to improve the work. Plagiarism isn't just an unethical act—it also wastes time.

Some acts of plagiarism are unintentional. Sometimes a student will simply forget to provide attribution. However, all acts of plagiarism are taken seriously, and it is always the student's responsibility to check the draft before submitting it for feedback or evaluation.

A NOTE ON TERMINOLOGY

Be careful not to confuse the idea of plagiarism with the idea of copyright infringement. Although the terms overlap, they are not interchangeable. Plagiarism is a specific ethical concept, while infringement is a legal one. For example, while selling a bootlegged DVD of a popular movie is illegal in the United States (and almost certainly unethical), it is not properly called plagiarism if the seller isn't claiming to have created the movie. (Remember, pretending to be the author of someone else's words or ideas is key to the definition of plagiarism.) Likewise, publishing a copy of Shakespeare's *Hamlet* and listing yourself as the author is clearly plagiarism, but because the play is so old, it is arguable that no laws have been violated as long as a public domain edition of the play was used.

EXERCISES

PLAGIARISM EXERCISE 20A

Florence Nightingale is regarded as the founder of modern nursing. Her book *Notes on Nursing: What It Is and What It Is Not* was first published in 1859 and is old enough to be in the public domain. Therefore, people are welcome to download and read—entirely for free—online editions such as the one found on the Project Gutenberg website (www.gutenberg.org/files/17366/17366-h/17366-h.htm). However, even if her work is no longer under copyright, all researchers (included students) who use it in their own research are obligated ethically to identify the original source and to distinguish their own words and ideas from those of Nightingale.

First, consider this passage from book mentioned above. It concerns the idea that nurses are responsible not only for treating diseases but for keeping patients comfortable and healthy:

> In watching disease, both in private houses and in public hospitals, the thing which strikes the experienced observer most forcibly is this, that the symptoms or the sufferings generally considered to be inevitable and incident to the disease are very often not symptoms of the disease at all, but of something quite different—of the want of fresh air, or of light, or of warmth, or of quiet, or of cleanliness, or of punctuality and care in the administration of diet, of each or of all of these. And this quite as much in private as in hospital nursing.

Second, read each of the following passages from student essays and answer the following questions: Does each passage include any instances of plagiarism? Explain your reasoning. If it does include plagiarism, what would a writer need to revise to maintain academic honesty?

1. What is the responsibility of a nurse? Some people believe that a nurse needs to treat the disease, but more accurately, a nurse needs to treat the patient. All too often, patients don't get enough fresh air, light, warmth, quiet, cleanliness, and healthy food.

2. Florence Nightingale, the founder of modern nursing, believed that nurses have an ethical responsibility to keep every patient healthy and comfortable. She even suggested that a patient's suffering is often caused by conditions that have nothing to do with the actual disease. For example, sometimes a patient might be in need of fresh air, or of light, or of warmth, or of quiet, or even of cleanliness. It is the role of a nurse, according to Nightingale, to take care of the patient, not just the disease.

3. Florence Nightingale, the founder of modern nursing, believed that nurses have an ethical responsibility to keep every patient healthy and comfortable. She even suggested that a patient's suffering is often caused by conditions that have nothing to do with the actual disease. For example, sometimes a patient might be in need of fresh air, light, warmth, quiet, or cleanliness. It is the role of a nurse, according to Nightingale, to take care of the patient, not just the disease.

4. Florence Nightingale, the founder of modern nursing, believed that nurses have an ethical responsibility to keep every patient healthy and comfortable. The suffering of a patient, she argued, is often caused not by the disease itself but by a lack "of fresh air, or of light, or of warmth, or of quiet, or of cleanliness, or of punctuality and care in the administration of diet."

5. Florence Nightingale, the founder of modern nursing, believed that nurses have an ethical responsibility to keep every patient healthy and comfortable. All too often, she argued, the suffering of a patient is caused not by the disease itself but by the environment in which the patient was recovering. To get healthy, patients need appropriate medical care, which involves cleanliness, a healthy diet, and comfort.

6. Florence Nightingale believed that in watching disease, both in private houses and in public hospitals, the thing which strikes the experienced observer most forcibly is this, that the symptoms or the sufferings generally considered to be inevitable and incident to the disease are very often not symptoms of the disease at all, but of something quite different—of the want of fresh air, or of light, or of warmth, or of quiet, or of cleanliness, or of punctuality and care in the administration of diet, of each or of all of these. She also noted that this quite as much in private as in hospital nursing.

7. Florence Nightingale believed that one can observe a medical setting and conclude that the symptoms or the sufferings generally considered to be inevitable and incident to the disease are very often not symptoms of the disease at all, but of something quite different. All too often, she argued, patients are denied fresh air, light, warmth, quiet, and cleanliness. Sometimes medical professionals are remiss in the punctuality and care in the administration of a healthy diet. Unfortunately, this can happen as much in private nursing as in hospital nursing, and therefore, simply moving the patient from one environment to another will not necessarily solve the problem.

PLAGIARISM EXERCISE 20B

Read the following paragraph, and then check each sentence for exact words, correct paraphrasing, and proper in-text citation to determine whether a sentence is correct or plagiarized. If the sentence is plagiarized, explain why. The source is identified under the passage.

Like many other professors, he no longer sees traditional term papers as a valid index of student competence. To get an accurate, Internet-free reading of how much students have learned, he gives them written assignments in class -- where they can be watched.

These kinds of precautions are no longer unusual in the college world. As Trip Gabriel pointed out in *The Times* recently, more than half the colleges in the country have retained services that check student papers for material lifted from the Internet and elsewhere. Many schools now require incoming students to take online tutorials that explain what plagiarism is and how to avoid it.

Nationally, discussions about plagiarism tend to focus on questions of ethics. But as David Pritchard, a physics professor at the Massachusetts Institute of Technology, told me recently: "The big sleeping dog here is not the moral issue. The problem is that kids don't learn if they don't do the work." Prof. Pritchard and his colleagues illustrated the point in a study of cheating behavior by M.I.T. students who used an online system to complete homework. The students who were found to have copied the most answers from others started out with the same math and physics skills as their harder-working classmates. But by skipping the actual work in homework, they fell behind in understanding and became significantly more likely to fail.

The Pritchard axiom -- that repetitive cheating undermines learning -- has ominous implications for a world in which even junior high school students cut and paste from the Internet instead of producing their own writing. If we look closely at plagiarism as practiced by youngsters, we can see that they have a different relationship to the printed word than did the generations before them. When many young people think of writing, they don't think of fashioning original sentences into a sustained thought. They think of making something like a collage of found passages and ideas from the Internet.

They become like rap musicians who construct what they describe as new works by "sampling" (which is to say, cutting and pasting) beats and refrains from the works of others.

Staples, Brent. "Cutting and Pasting: A Senior Thesis by (Insert Name)." *New York Times*, 13 July 2010, p. A24(L). Academic OneFile, http://link.galegroup.com. db11.linccweb. org/apps/doc/57055882. Accessed 27 May 2018.

1. Plagiarism is common in today's college classroom, so more than half the colleges in the country have retained services that check student papers for material lifted from the Internet and elsewhere (Staples).
2. To check for plagiarism, many universities now use anti-plagiarism software to be sure students have not used material from outside sources, according to Brent Staples.
3. Young students today approach writing differently than students in the past who wrote and revised original ideas that extended into full essays of their own making (Staples).
4. Today's students view a writing assignment "like a collage of found passages and ideas from the Internet" (Staples).
5. While most acknowledge plagiarism is a form of cheating, some argue the bigger issue is that students who cheat don't learn and they are significantly more likely to fail. Repetitive cheating undermines learning.
6. Many students today do not understand the intellectual value of developing their own ideas and choose instead to compose written essays like rap musicians who construct what they describe as new works by "sampling" (which is to say, cutting and pasting) beats and refrains from the works of others (Staples).
7. Staples claims that producing their own writing is the only way students learn the critical thinking and communication skills to be successful.
8. College writing is challenging so it is understandable why many college writers knowingly plagiarize.
9. But as David Pritchard, a physics professor at the Massachusetts Institute of Technology, told me recently: "The big sleeping dog here is not the moral issue. The problem is that kids don't learn if they don't do the work."

PLAGIARISM EXERCISE 20C

Read the following paragraph.

Before playing a complicated piano piece such as Beethoven's *Moonlight Sonata* for a jury of judges, piano students should spend forty-five minutes on drills to warm up their fingers. Drills help students learn different techniques and finger positions. Without this practice, piano students are more likely to make mistakes and lack flexibility in their fingers as they attempt complex classical pieces. After playing *Moonlight Sonata* for the first time, music majors think the piece will be easy to learn because it is repetitive and slow. However, as they pay close attention to the placement of symbols, such as decrescendos and the slurs, they realize the piece is complex and it will take time to learn how to build emotion into the performance. Practicing the piece over and over is the only way to learn to control the depth and mood of this moving sonata.

Memorization of any piece of music depends not only on the brain but also on the hands to recall each note and symbol. When students can play the piece without the sheet music, they are ready to perform before three faculty judges. Their professors will prepare them for the experience by walking them through a simulation of a juried performance. They also explain to students that if they freeze on the bench before the jury and cannot recall the piece that they must not speak or look away. Instead, they should begin the piece again. If they cannot recall the lines, it is best for them to wait for the judges to excuse them than to run off stage embarrassed.

Original source:

Isperindo, Jaspar. "The Art of the Juried Performance." *Journal of Music Theory Pedagogy,* vol. 33, no.1, Fall 2012, pp. 36 -52. *Oxford Music Online*, doi: 10.333/SR. 12.1345. (The paragraphs above can be found on pages 39 -40.)

Analyze the sentences below for correct use of a source. If the sentence is plagiarized, rewrite it correctly.

1. Isperindo explains that many music majors think *Moonlight Sonata* will be easy to learn because it is repetitive and slow (39).

2. One of the most important steps before performing before a faculty jury is for students to "spend forty-five minutes on drills to warm up their fingers" (Isperindo).

3. In order to learn a variety of skills needed for piano, practice drills are necessary.

4. Initially students do not realize how complex *Moonlight Sonata* is, but as they practice, they come to understand it will take playing it over and over to learn to control the depth and mood of Beethoven's piece (Isperindo 39).

5. It is only when a student has memorized the piece that he or she is ready to perform it before a jury of faculty (Isperindo).

6. Memorizing any piece of music "depends not only on the brain but also the hands" where many believe "each note and symbol" is actually stored (40).

7. Before the juried performance, professors help students by setting up a similar model in the classroom to help students feel prepared to be judged (Isperindo 40).

8. Professors encourage students to remain seated at the piano and try the piece again should they be unable to complete their performance (Isperindo 40).

9. "If they cannot recall the lines, it is best for them to wait for the judges to excuse them than to run off stage embarrassed."

Chapter 21

THE RESEARCH PROCESS

In order to begin to approach the task of writing a research paper, you have to first understand what research is. Depending on one's scholarly discipline, the definition of research will vary slightly. For composition purposes, think about research as the process of discovering new knowledge, engaging with the ideas of others, and participating in a public discourse from an informed perspective.

College writing is academic writing; in other words, academic writing is done by scholars for scholars; and although you might not yet consider yourself scholar, you will be engaging with the ideas of other scholars as you practice, yourself, to become one. (After all, brilliance needs to begin somewhere.)

Academic writing focuses on topics that are relevant and appropriate to an academic community, so this kind of writing is not usually a personal first-person casual run-of the mill discussion about one's individual feelings. Academic writing is quite the opposite. It is informed argumentation. In other words, it is a presentation of an issue through logical systematic and engaged presentation. And really, there's only one way to achieve this: You must read. In order to present yourself as someone who is credible and informed, your paper must demonstrate a thoroughness of the issue. You must understand what other people are saying about the issue, and you must engage with those conversations throughout your paper.

You may do this in several ways: You may agree with what other people have said; you may disagree with what other people have said; you may build on what other people have said. The one important thing to remember about academic papers is that they do not simply *tell* your reader that you have read, nor do they simply *summarize* what you've read. The purpose of an academic research paper is to present an argument that is plausible, logical, reasonable, and informed. The way to achieve this is by reading the ideas of others and using those ideas to help you move your own theories and ideas forward.

Here are a few steps that might help you along the way:

1. CHOOSE A TOPIC

Once you settle into the idea of research, the first and most logical thing to do is to settle on a topic. Your topic should probably be something that has serious interest for you; otherwise, you will get bored with the topic and your paper will reflect your boredom. Try to engage in a topic that you want to learn something about, or engage with a topic that has some interest or relevance for you. Take the series *The Walking Dead*, for example. If you think it's a brilliant TV series for many reasons, you might settle on that for your research paper.

2. REFLECTION MOMENT

You now have a topic and one that you probably will enjoy. Your first task is to find out what you know about the topic, and you need to think beyond just the obvious. You know it is a TV show. You probably enjoy the main characters. You know it is about zombies. These ideas are all obvious and don't give you anything to write about that pushes the boundaries of knowledge and thought.

You will need to ask yourself some difficult questions that will help you move beyond that first-person stream of consciousness about your love for the show:

- What do zombies represent?

- Why have we become so fascinated by zombies and all their depictions?

- What does this fascination say about us?

3. RESEARCH TIME

At this point, you will have a decent hold on what might be relevant to an academic community. You now need to start doing some reading. You might begin with a very vague or general search on zombies. As you begin your search, and as you begin reading, you'll find that you have the tools to help narrow down the topic because you are now so much more informed. You know your research topic needs to be narrow in focus and that the topic of zombies is just that—it is a *topic*, not a focus.

- This means that you'll need to figure out what specifically you want to say about zombies that might have some interest for others. You'll need to ask yourself an important question: What is one specific argument that I can elaborate on and sustain throughout my paper?

As you begin your reading, and as you learn about the concept of the post-human, you may begin to think that this concept might be an interesting way to frame a discussion about *The Walking Dead.* From your readings, perhaps you've learned about the post-human culture and how zombies are often looked at as an allegory for the evils of humanity. You could build on this idea and look at the characters from *The Walking Dead*—might the "real" zombies be the true definition of post-human?

4. DRAFTING

You now have your idea, which has been appropriately narrowed down so that your argument extends beyond the obvious fact that the series is about zombies. You have decided that your paper will focus on Daryl as the king of the post-humans. You are ready to begin your writing.

Begin your writing with the thesis—a working thesis, if you will, which will be subject to change depending on where you go with this paper.

5. SYNTHESIS

As you begin writing, you will begin asking yourself questions, and as you do this, you will realize that there is still so much more research to be done. This is one of the hazards of research. It seems to never stop. The more you know, the more you want to know, the more questions you have, the more you must investigate. But alas, your paper has a deadline, and that means that at some point you'll need to stop reading and begin to synthesize the information you have learned. So you plug on and continue asking yourself the following questions:

- How can I justify that claim?

- Why is this valid or relevant?

- What are the connections between this idea and others?

- Why did I say that?

- How can I prove that?

As you find the core connections between your readings and your ideas, and as you answer the questions in your head, your paper becomes a little bit more clear, a little bit more defined, and a little bit more substantive, and of course, a little more ready for the academic community.

EXERCISES

RESEARCH PAPER WRITING EXERCISE 21A

Smoking marijuana, reading pornography, engaging the services of a prostitute (male or female)—these have been referred to as "victimless crimes." Present your position on the legalization of any one of these "crimes."

RESEARCH PAPER WRITING EXERCISE 21B

Henry David Thoreau wrote: "Under a government which imprisons any unjustly, the true place for a just man [or woman] is in prison." In reference to civil disobedience, defend or dispute the morality of breaking the law.

RESEARCH PAPER WRITING EXERCISE 21C

A favorite cousin, who is 14, comes to you as the older, wiser mentor that you are. The question that is pondered is: how does one have "safe sex"? (Phrase your answer in a 500-word essay.)

RESEARCH PAPER WRITING EXERCISE 21D

Americans are obsessed with dieting. Discuss the effects of this obsession on the way Americans live.

RESEARCH PAPER WRITING EXERCISE 21E

Compare children's toys (activities) at the beginning of the 21st century to the toys (activities) at the beginning of the 20th century.

RESEARCH PAPER WRITING EXERCISE 21F

Discuss the methods of treating clinical depression in the 1890s compared to the methods implemented today.

Chapter 22

FINDING SOURCES

You are fortunate to be living in the Information Age. Research that was once accessible only to people who lived in cities with libraries is now available to anybody with internet access. However, traditional libraries continue to play a vital role in the research process. As valuable as the internet may be, students should not dismiss the physical resources available at college and community libraries. Likewise, students who prefer brick-and-mortar libraries should not be intimidated by the vast resources available online. Remember, too, that librarians are experts in finding research sources, and often they can guide you in finding materials—both electronic and in print—for your academic projects.

Be aware that even with electronic sources, simply having internet access is not always enough. Many specialized academic journals are published online but are not free, and the full text of these articles will not be found through a simple Google or Yahoo search. However, by being a student at a college with a good library system, you can download many of these articles free of charge. To access these valuable resources (which are made by professionals, for professionals), always start not with a general search engine but with your library's website. The library professionals at your campus can guide you through online databases that will allow you to read articles that the general public would be able to access only after paying expensive subscription fees. These scholarly journals are considered to be top-of-the-line in the academic world, so use them for your research projects whenever you can.

Many students new to academic research are often intimidated by the task of what seems like a monumental academic chore. One fact of life can't be avoided: Research is a difficult process. Its difficulty, however, does not come from its unmanageability. It comes from the patience that it takes to create a good final product.

A. Annotated Bibliography

An annotated bibliography is a list of the sources consulted for a research project with an explanation beneath each entry.

For each item or source, **cite** your source in MLA style. If the citation goes to a second line, indent the second line one tab—or, even better, use the automatic "hanging indent" option in your word processing program. In Microsoft Word, this option is found under the "Paragraph" menu.

- The items should be **alphabetized** by last name of author or editor (or organization). Follow the citation with your **notes on the source.** These notes are called the **annotations.**

- The annotations should **describe and evaluate** each item or source. That description should **describe** its scope, authority/credibility, relevance, usefulness, etc. Your annotations can also **evaluate** the source, giving your judgment on its credibility, usefulness, and value for your paper.

- Your annotation should generally be between five and ten lines for each item. Some of your annotations may be longer. They should not be shorter than four or five lines, except for a standard reference work like the *OED*.

- Your annotations should be **indented** one tab from the margin.

(1)   Sample Ann. Bib. entry for a book:

Author. *Book Title.* **Publisher, Year.**

Richardson, Alan. *Genesis 1-11: The Creation Stories and the Modern World View.*
    SCM 1953.
    Though somewhat dated, this introductory commentary on Genesis 1-11 in the
    SCM Torch series still retains its freshness. Richardson deals profoundly with the
    difficult problems of interpretation that Genesis presents. He writes from a liberal
    standpoint, but conservative readers would also find much insight in his
    comments. His comprehensive introduction looks at Jewish and Christian
    interpretation, the character of J and P, the "parables" of Genesis, and questions of
    science and Genesis. His writing is always helpful, as are his detailed, verse by
    verse comments.

(2)   Sample Ann. Bib. entry for a journal article.

Author. "Article title." *Journal title,* **vol. #, no. #, Year, pp. # - #.**

Ullrich, David W. "Reconstructing Fitzgerald's "Twice-Told Tales": Intertextuality in *This
    Side of Paradise* and *Tender is the Night.*" *The F. Scott Fitzgerald Review,* vol.3,
    2004, pp. 43-71.
    A thought-provoking article in which Ullrich shows the extent to which Fitzgerald
    is rewriting *This Side of Paradise* in *Tender is the Night,* and returning to similar
    themes, metaphors, and tropes in his later work. He is helpful particularly in his
    discussion of "Geneva," water symbolism, and the parallelism between major
    characters and events in *Paradise* and *Tender.* He includes parallels with *The
    Great Gatsby.* He also links his discussion nicely with larger issues of
    determinism, free will, and the writer's craft, when he says "[t]hus the conflict
    between determinism and free will that informs Fitzgerald's best protagonists also
    finds expression in his own lifelong struggle as a writer between mere repetition
    […] and the genius of his best short fiction and novels, wherein he asserts himself
    as a"writerly" personage, rededicating himself to his recombinant literary
    imagination" (67). This is certainly a useful article in interpreting Fitzgerald.

Callout annotations:

Name is given as **Last Name, First Name**

Your **annotation** follows the citation and is indented. It is both a **description** and also an **evaluation** (a value judgment). It is a kind of mini **book review** or book report.

Citation in MLA format. For an article, give the **inclusive page numbers** with pp.

Second (and third) line of citation is **indented.** Then the annotation follows, on a new line, also **indented.**

Your annotation follows the citation. If you want to, you can **quote** from your source (with page number).

Remember, your Annotated Bibliography – like a list of Works Cited – should be arranged **alphabetically** (A-Z) by the **last name** of the **author** (or by the name of the **corporate** body. So Richardson (R) will be listed before Ullrich (U).

Raymond M. Vince, © April 9, 2013
Revised July 2014 and 1 Sep 2016 (MLA 8ᵗʰ)

EXERCISE

FINDING SOURCES EXERCISE 22A

Use the HCC library for the following research assignment. Be sure to provide the information and a full MLA citation for each entry. This is a research and citation assignment; please provide complete information for all entries.

1. Locate and cite a single biography of a former U.S President.

2. Using the Oxford English Dictionary (OED), locate the definition and etymology of the terms "style" and "culture."

3. Using the electronic Occupational Outlook Handbook (OOH), or the hard copy, locate the necessary training and education for two professions of your choice (include earnings, anticipated job prospects, and working conditions).

4. Locate an article on "academic writing" and provide a citation.

5. Using the Google Book Search, find a book on the subject of "investing wisely" and provide a citation.

6. Using the HCC Library, locate and cite: (a) a book on the subject of "hypertension," (b) a book by Stephen King, (c) a book about Ronald Reagan, and (d) a book about the "World War 2," published 2016/2017

7. Using the same resource, locate and list all books in the HCC collection by author Tillie Olsen.

8. Using the keyword "economic stimulus" and searching "all community colleges," cite two of the most relevant search result(s).

INTEGRATING SOURCES

Proper documentation is essential to scholarly research.

In writing a scholarly paper and incorporating the ideas of others, it is important to attribute the ideas that you've used in your paper to their corresponding authors. If you don't do that, you are guilty of plagiarism, a serious ethical violation. Please remember that you cite because you need to give credit to your sources, but documentation also provides a trail for other scholars for where you have been. This way, if your readers find your ideas interesting, they have a way to pursue their interests and build on your ideas.

Any idea taken from someone else must be documented. It does not matter whether the material is verbatim (word for word) or paraphrased; in either case, the words or the ideas must be documented. There are multiple ways to document research, depending on the field of study, but this chapter uses MLA format in the examples. (The wonderful thing about knowing one documentation format is that it makes it very easy to apply other documentation formats. You simply go to that documentation source and apply the guidelines just as you would with MLA format.)

A. INTEGRATING QUOTATIONS

In MLA, periods and commas always go inside the quotation marks unless you have documentation behind your quotation.

For example, the following sentence concerns a literary analysis of a Hemingway short story:

Jig mentions that all they "ever do is drink and travel."

Consider the thought process a writer might have regarding the above sentence:

I don't have any documentation behind this quotation because I'm not writing a research paper. I'm writing a paper of analysis and there are no other sources to confuse where these quotes come from. I also have not documented here because I've taken the text from the Internet, and there are no page numbers, so there's really nothing here to document.

However, the writer is incorrect. Instead, this sentence should use parenthetical documentation:

Jig mentions that all they "ever do is drink and travel" (Hemingway 23).

I've documented here because I've used a specific printed source, so I have a page number. I have also documented because I am writing a research paper and am using several different sources in the text. In order not to confuse one source from the other, I document so that my primary and secondary sources remain separate in the mind of my reader.

Now the writer has successfully thought through the process and has properly integrated the source with documentation.

As illustrated above, documenting a paper requires a specific format. Here are a few other concepts to remember:

1. The end punctuation goes at the end of the documentation, not at the end of the quote.
2. In MLA, document with the author's last name and page number, if available. In APA, document with the author's last name, the year the work was published, and the page number, if available.
3. The punctuation mark goes inside the quotation if there is no documentation to follow. (For our purposes here, punctuation refers only to commas and periods. All other punctuation marks go behind the quotation marks. Question marks, exclamation marks, and other punctuation marks do not go inside quotation unless it is part of the quote.)
4. Please know that long quotes (block quotes) are documented differently than short quotes. A long quote is defined as a quote that takes up more than four lines of text. Long quotes are indented one inch. They do not use quotation marks, and end punctuation will go at the end of the sentence, before the end documentation.

To review:

When you document, you will be using the author's last name and page number. You will document immediately behind your quote or right after the idea taken from your source. Many students are surprised by how simple this process can be.

Assume this paragraph supports your discussion that Shakespeare's *Hamlet* is actually a type of play that was common at the time, a "revenge tragedy":

> The blood-revenge of the protagonist distinguishes the pure type of Kydian "tragedy of revenge." This revenge constitutes the main action of the play in the sense that the audience is chiefly interested in the events which lead to the necessary revenge for murder, and then in the revenger's actions in accordance his vow. The revenge must be the cause of the catastrophe, and its start must not be delayed beyond the crisis. "Revenge tragedy" customarily (but by no means necessarily) portrays the ghosts of the murdered urging revenge, a hesitation on the part of the avenger, a delay in proceeding to his vengeance, and his feigned or actual madness. The antagonist's counter-intrigue against the revenger may occupy a prominent position in the plot. (63-64)

Bowers, Fredson. *Elizabethan Revenge Tragedy* 1587-1642, Princeton UP, 1966.

When integrating quotations into your own argument, you will generally do three things: **introduce the material**, **provide the quotation**, and **comment on it**. Never drop a quotation into the paper as its own sentence or paragraph. Here's an example of a quotation that is properly integrated into an essay. Please keep in mind, this example is a block quote (a full paragraph); therefore, it is formatted according to MLA block quote standards.

> Perhaps the most concise outline of the "revenge tragedy," of which *Hamlet* is the most famous example, comes from Fredson Bowers:
>
> > The blood-revenge of the protagonist distinguishes the pure type of Kydian "tragedy of revenge." This revenge constitutes the main action of the play in the sense that the audience is chiefly interested in the events which lead to the necessary revenge for murder, and then in the revenger's actions in accordance his vow. The revenge must be the cause of the catastrophe, and its start must not be delayed beyond the crisis. "Revenge tragedy" customarily (but by no means necessarily) portrays the ghosts of the murdered urging revenge, a hesitation on the part of the avenger, a delay in proceeding to his vengeance, and his feigned or actual madness. The antagonist's counter-intrigue against the revenger may occupy a prominent position in the plot. (63-64)
>
> Clearly, all of the major points of *Hamlet* correspond to this pattern. Hamlet's revenge on Claudius will lead to the deaths of all the major characters. The ghost of Hamlet's father does urge him to action. Hamlet does hesitate (most obviously when he fails to kill the praying Claudius). Hamlet does pretend to be mad, and Claudius does attempt to kill Hamlet in various ways.

Notice the three parts here. This example begins with introducing the work and the author (**introducing the material**). Then, it **provides the quotation**. Lastly, there is a brief **comment on the quotation**.
There are three ways to incorporate a quote into a sentence:

1. Work it into the grammar of your own sentence:

Readers "have to identify thousands of little marks on paper" (Vonnegut 67).
(The writer wrote the subject; the verb is Vonnegut's words.)

2. Add a colon after your own complete sentence:

Readers have a tough job: "They have to identify thousands of little marks on paper" (Vonnegut 67).

3. Add a source phrase and a comma, and identify the source:

Best-selling 20th-century satirical novelist and essayist Kurt Vonnegut writes, "They have to identify thousands of little marks on paper" (67).

Unless the source is well known to your audience, using a source phrase (method #3) is tricky because it means you have to identify that source so that your readers know why they should pay attention to what that source has to say. Notice that identifying the source in example #3 requires about half of the sentence! If the essay's point is that writers need to consider their audiences, spending half of the sentence telling them about Kurt Vonnegut is inefficient. Will the audience care, or will they want the essay to stay on topic and get to its points? (By the way, Vonnegut was pretty well known. Imagine if the source were someone whom the audience had never heard of. That would require even more words.)

Instead of using a source phrase like "Vonnegut writes," keep the emphasis on the point by working the quote into the sentence in one of the other two ways. Look back at all three examples above. Notice how the first two stick closer to the topic.

It can seem difficult to write a sentence like example #1 or #2 for writers who have gotten into the habit of using the #3 format for all quotes, so here are a few tips:

- Start your sentence with a transition word ("Moreover," "Meanwhile," "Likewise," and other adverbs) or prepositional phrase (like "For example," or "In addition,") followed by a comma; then follow that with the complete-sentence quote.

    ○   Here are examples:
    - Furthermore, "[t]hey have to identify thousands of little marks on paper" (Vonnegut 67).
    - For instance, "[t]hey have to identify thousands of little marks on paper" (Vonnegut 67).

- You do not have to quote a complete sentence. Write your own subject (noun or pronoun) and use only the predicate of the original sentence (the verb and any adverbs, phrases, and clauses that modify it) like example #1 above.

- Write a complete sentence of your own making a point, but instead of a period, end it with a colon (:) followed by the quote giving an example of the point you just made like example #2 above.

These are not the only ways to use methods #1 and #2, but they are some of the easiest and may help.

B. Modifying a Quoted Passage

Usually, undergraduate essays do not include block quotes (though graduate school will expect them). Instead, you may remove portions of long quotes or adapt their syntax to fit your writing more effectively.

1. Removing Part of a Direct Quote

When you want to leave out a part of the quotation to make the passage more direct, you will use ellipses (. . .) to account for the missing material. When replacing text with ellipses, be sure to retain the original meaning of the source.

> One critic comments that "'revenge tragedy' customarily . . . portrays the ghosts of the murdered urging revenge, a hesitation on the part of the avenger, a delay in proceeding to his vengeance, and his feigned or actual madness. The antagonist's counter-intrigue against the revenger may occupy a prominent position in the plot" (Bowers 63-64). With these criteria in mind, one can immediately see that *Hamlet* is not by any means a unique play, but that it does work within the conventions of the genre.

2. Adding to or Changing Part of a Direct Quote

Another situation you may encounter is one in which you must "adapt" the syntax of the quoted material so that it blends with the syntax of your own sentence. In this case, you will use brackets [ ] to indicate that you have added or changed material:

> Bowers writes, "This revenge constitutes the main action of the play . . . [and it] must be the cause of the catastrophe" (63).

3. Errors within the Direct Quote [sic]

Including [sic] after a quotation shows that an error appearing inside the quotation is the original source's mistake, not yours:

> George Bernard Shaw is famous for writing, "Nothing can extinguish my interest in Shakespear [sic]" (22).

C. Two Other Options: Paraphrasing and Summarizing

1. Paraphrasing

Instead of using a direct quotation, you may paraphrase, which means to restate a passage in approximately the same number of words. This technique is helpful if you need either to make complex language simpler or to make a passage more professional. Also, you can paraphrase to maintain a consistent tone in your writing.

> Perhaps the most concise outline of the "revenge tragedy," of which *Hamlet* is the most famous example, comes from Fredson Bowers. He explains that the main character's "blood-revenge" demonstrates a "Kydian 'tragedy of revenge'" (63). This type of revenge accounts for the majority of the play, which provides the audience with the events that reveal the reason and purpose for revenge along with the steps the character takes. Bowers also details that in a revenge tragedy the revenge is a result of a larger calamity. Bowers continues by examining how a revenge tragedy, like with Hamlet, often uses ghosts as a way to encourage the murder(s). Of course, the use of ghosts is not required for the work to be a revenge tragedy. This type of tragedy typically includes the avenger unsure about the revenge resulting in the postponement of his actions. In the end, as Bower explains, the character appears to be or is actually brought to insanity. Still, the overall plot of the revenge tragedy will include not only the plot for revenge but also the "antagonist's counter-intrigue against the revenger" (64).

Even though the underlined portion is a paraphrase, you still need to introduce the material and provide comments after it. Plus, since the ideas are not yours, you must credit the author to avoid plagiarism. However, since it is not a direct quote, you will not format it as a quote.

2. Summarizing

In summarizing, you are condensing the information contained in the passage, omitting the detail but keeping the main idea. For example, an entire article may be summarized in a full paragraph whereas a paragraph in an article may require only a sentence or two.

> Perhaps the most concise outline of the "revenge tragedy," of which *Hamlet* is the most famous example, comes from Fredson Bowers. He explains the typical parts of a revenge tragedy: murdered ghosts encouraging retribution, revenger delaying because of uncertainty, a postponement of avengers actions, and his appearance of or actually insanity. As Bowers details, throughout the revenge tragedy, viewers understand the need for revenge based on the events, and the viewers not only see the plot for revenge but also the "antagonist's counter-intrigue against the revenger" (64).

Like the paraphrase, the summary is still taking someone else's ideas and using them as your own. Therefore, you still need to cite those ideas and provide credit to the original author.

EXERCISES

INTEGRATING SOURCES EXERCISE 23A

Find creative ways to integrate each quote in your sentences. Be sure to follow the guidelines in the brackets.

> **Example:** "Fourscore and seven years ago." [Integrate this phrase into a sentence about Abraham Lincoln's Gettysburg Address]

In his Gettysburg Address, President Lincoln began with what would become one of the most famous phrases in American history: "Fourscore and seven years ago."

1. "You miss 100% of the shots you don't take." [Integrate this into a sentence about legendary hockey player Wayne Gretzky.]

2. "No man is an island." [Integrate this into a sentence in which you also mention an inspirational person in your life.]

3. "The content of their character." [Integrate this fragment of a quote by Dr. Martin Luther King, Jr. into a sentence about racial prejudice.]

4. "You might as well give up." [Integrate this discouraging sentiment into a sentence in which you disagree with the idea this is expressing.]

5. "When you first moved to Florida, didn't the weather surprise you?" [Integrate this line of dialogue, spoken by a close family member of your choice, into a sentence.]

6. "Is everybody ready to begin the exam?" [Integrate this line of dialogue, spoken by a cheerful middle school teacher, into a sentence.]

7. "You cannot deduct contributions to a Roth IRA." [Integrate this rule, mentioned on irs.gov, about Individual Retirement Accounts into a sentence about saving for the future.]

8. "Happy birthday!" [Integrate this exclamation into a sentence that describes at least one attendee at a young child's birthday party.]

9. "Absence makes the heart grow fonder." [Integrate this saying into a sentence about long-distance relationships.]

10. "You may now kiss the bride." [Integrate this line into a sentence about a wedding.]

INTEGRATING SOURCES EXERCISE 23B

Read the following sentences and arrange them in a clear and meaningful discussion. Please use your own transitional phrases and/or whole sentences to create a fluid and coherent paragraph.

Questions to consider:

- Which of the statements below makes the best topic sentence?
- What sequence seems most logical?
- How can these ideas best connect to one another with transitional phrases?
- What signal phrases are most appropriate to introduce the given quotes and paraphrases?

1. The majority of jobs held by minorities and people from poor backgrounds offer few opportunities for influencing the system.
2. The healthcare system today perpetuates the racist and sexist stereotypes that exist in society.
3. "Women of color, immigrant women and poor women as well as lesbians are at a significant disadvantage as long as the delivery system is controlled by individuals whose backgrounds are so different from [theirs]." Author: Handy Sherman. Article Title: Healthcare in the 21st Century. Journal: *The New England Journal of Medicine*. This quote is on page 232.
4. By keeping people from oppressed communities out of health care, the healthcare system keeps them from being healthy and thus from having the same chances as affluent non-minorities.
5. Most doctors and hospital administrators are white males, and most nurses are females.
6. Women and minorities have no real voice in the healthcare system.
7. "The healthcare system does not merely mirror the power and privilege structures of the larger society; it maintains them." Author: Handy Sherman. Same article and journal as above. This quote is on page 235.

INTEGRATING SOURCES EXERCISE 23C

Write two brief paragraphs on the topics provided; select and incorporate a brief quote from a different source into each paragraph to support your topic. Be sure to include the in-text citation.

1. Draft a paragraph on the process of **buying a car** or **eating out** and add a quote from a source with **one author** to support your position. Follow the text guidelines for citing the borrowed material (Ch. 24 MLA Formatting).

2. Draft a paragraph expressing your position on **freedom of speech** and include a quote from the United States Constitution (not the Bill of Rights). Follow your text MLA citation guidelines.

Here is a link to the U.S. Constitution: https://www.archives.gov/founding-docs/constitution-transcript

INTEGRATING SOURCES EXERCISE 23D

Now find an article on a topic that interests you. Write a paragraph and integrate two quotes and one paraphrase from the article to support your points.

Chapter 24

MLA Format

When formatting your papers, it is important to follow the guidelines. Just like one airplane out of place in an airshow can cause a catastrophe, you need to stay on target and adhere to the accepted rules for your papers to avoid problems.

MLA format breaks down into three categories:

- Page Layout
- In-Text Citations
- Works Cited Page

24.1 MLA FORMAT: PAGE LAYOUT

As with any style, you need to adhere to the formatting rules of that style when writing a paper. MLA stands for Modern Language Association, and this organization has created general formatting and citation rules for papers. The disciplines using MLA primarily belong to English, foreign languages, and other humanities; however, on occasion, other disciplines will use them. In addition, sometimes your instructor will let you decide which documentation style (such as MLA, APA, Chicago, etc.) to use.

The following general rules apply for creating any document in MLA format:

- Set up your paper with a 1" margin on all sides.

- Select a font that is easily readable (such as Times New Roman). Also, make sure the regular and bold version of the font differ enough that a reader can tell the difference. Use the 12-point size of whatever font you select.

- The paper should be aligned to the left except for the titles.

- Double-space the entire paper, including the heading and title on the first page and the Works Cited page. Do not include extra space between paragraphs.

- Indent each paragraph, including the first one, one half inch from the left margin. This half-inch indent can be created by hitting the Tab key once or the spacebar eight times.

- Use only one space after a period.

- If you have any block quotes (quotes of four or more lines with prose and three or more lines with poetry), indent those quotes also one half inch from the left margin. Do **not** use quotation marks around it, and place any in-text citation at the end **after** the final punctuation. (see Ch. 23 Integrating Sources)

- MLA formatting does not have a title page, so you should not include one unless your instructor specifically asks for it. Instead of a title page, the first page has a special four-line heading. These four lines should be double-spaced, and the lines should include this information in this order: your name, instructor name, course name and/or number, and date. Remember the date should be written as day month year.
  ◦ Example: 1 January 2021

- Position the title of the paper on the next line after the four-line heading (still maintaining the double spacing).
  ◦ It should be written in the same type and size font as the rest of the document. In addition, do not underline or bold the title, nor place it in italics or quotation marks.
  ◦ Make sure it is centered.
  ◦ All major words of the title should be capitalized.

- Always capitalize the first word of the title and subtitle (if you have one).

- Always capitalize the last word of the title.

- Unless they are the first word of the title or subtitle, do not capitalize prepositions (Ch. 14.5 Prepositions), articles (a, an, the), coordinating conjunctions (Ch. 14.7 Conjunctions), and the "to" in an infinitive phrase (Ch. 14.2 Verbs).

- MLA also requires a running header, which should be placed in the upper right-hand corner of each page, one half inch from the top. The running header should include the student's last name and the page number (no p. or pg.). See sample.
  ◦ Example: Smith 1
  ◦ Make sure it is in the header, not in the body of your paper, and make sure to select the page number option and not simply type in the number.

- If you have cited sources in the paper, then you must include a Works Cited page. This page should include the full bibliographic information for each source cited in the paper. In addition, this page should be found at the end of the paper, and it should be on its own page.

EXAMPLE OF FIRST PAGE IN MLA

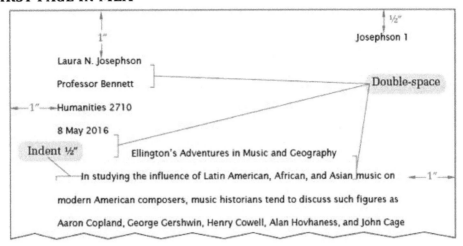

EXAMPLE OF WORKS CITED PAGE

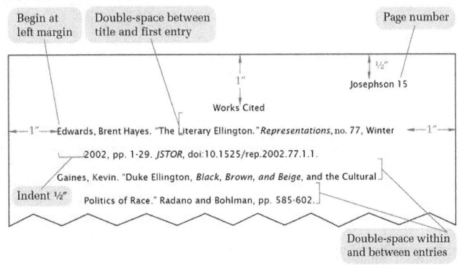

MLA Format: Visuals created by Michelle Sanders
Note: MLA 9th edition requires that "winter" be lowercase (not capitalized as in the image)

Some tips for writing an essay in MLA format:

When submitting a college essay, a formal, academic tone should be employed. Consider the following as strong academic practice:

- Include a title that reflects the topic. Capitalize appropriately as detailed earlier in the chapter.
- Spell out contractions (don't = do not).
- Do not use exclamation marks (!), slang, or any conversational tone that addresses the reader as if in a conversation. Also, avoid racist or sexist language. Try to stay away from generalizations or overly biased opinions (See Ch. 18.5 Tone).
- Write the essay from the third person perspective. In a narrative essay, it is permissible to use the first person.
- Maintain a strong thesis that is stated clearly in the introduction and rephrased for the conclusion (See Ch. 7 Thesis Statements).
- Proofread closely to avoid simple typos, as well as grammar, punctuation, format, and proofreading errors.

Differences Between APA and MLA format: Page Layout

Component of Format	MLA	APA
Title Page	Does not require title page (unless indicated by instructor)	Requires title page (this will be the first page)
First Page	Right-aligned in top margin · Header (last name page number) Left-aligned in body · Four-line heading o Your name o Instructor's name o Course name or number o Date (written in Day-Month-Year format) Centered in body · Title of your paper	Title page Left-aligned in margin · Running head Note: The use of "Running head: TITLE" (quotation marks used here only for emphasis) only appears on the title page Centered one-third of a way down the page · Title of your paper · Your name · Name of your institution
Running head	Right-aligned in top margin · Your last name · Page number	Left-aligned in top margin · Abbreviated essay title · The entire abbreviated essay title is capitalized Right-aligned in top margin · Page number
Abstract	Does not require abstract	Not always required, especially not for shorter papers (check with instructor)
Page on which body of paper begins	Begins on first page	Without abstract: Begins on page after title page With abstract: Begins on page after abstract Includes · Running head Centered at top of first body page · Page number
Throughout the rest of the paper	Header	Running head May contain headings and subheadings

EXERCISE

MLA FORMAT: PAGE LAYOUT EXERCISE 24.1A

Look at this next page (which demonstrates correct MLA formatting) and compare it with the page after it (which has incorrect MLA formatting). Make note of all the differences you find.

Asma Abdallah

Professor Ortiz

ENC 1101

1 November 2020

Why the Japanese Education System is the Most Successful

Nelson Mandela once said, "Education is the most powerful weapon which you can use to change the world" (Strauss). Every country has its unique methods of teaching and raising children, Japan is no different. Japan is one of the most creative and innovative societies in the world. It's no doubt that Japan has gained attention worldwide with its modernized yet traditional education. The Japanese educational system is well-known for its moral education and emphasis on student collaboration that is attributable to its success of a 99% literacy rate and other outcomes that make the students highly competitive in the modern world (Hussain and Salfi 4). In contrast, America's education system lacks many elements such as the stagnant spending on school funds and little to no innovation concerning teaching methods that ultimately contribute to the failing system. Although Japan has a high youth suicide rate and their students lack creativity, Japan's education system is more efficient and successful than many other countries, such as America, because of its emphasis on discipline and cultural values, its considerate and thoughtful lessons by qualified teachers, and the promotion of equality in education.

In comparison to America's education system, one reason behind the successes of the Japanese educational system is the significance of morality and cultural learning that is stressed at a young age. Japanese people approach education in a different sense: the development of a student in social skills and character is

Professor Ortiz
ENC 1101
1 November 2020

<u>why the japanese education system is the most successful</u>

Nelson Mandela once said, "Education is the most powerful weapon which you can use to change the world" (Strauss). Every country has its unique methods of teaching and raising children, JAPAN is no different. JAPAN is one of the most creative and innovative societies in the world. It's no doubt that JAPAN has gained attention worldwide with its modernized yet traditional education. The JAPANese educational system is well-known for its moral education and emphasis on student collaboration that is attributable to its success of a **99%** literacy rate and other outcomes that make the students highly competitive in the modern world (Hussain and Salfi 4). In contrast, **AMERICA'S** education system lacks many elements such as the stagnant spending on school funds and little to no innovation concerning teaching methods that ultimately contribute to the failing system. Although JAPAN has a high youth suicide rate and their students lack creativity, JAPAN's education system is more efficient and successful than many other countries, such as **AMERICA**, because of its emphasis on discipline and cultural values, its considerate and THOUGHTFUL LESSONS BY QUALIFIED TEACHERS, and the promotion of EQUALITY IN EDUCATION.

In comparison to **AMERICA'S** education system, one reason behind the successes of the JAPANese educational system is the significance of morality and cultural learning that is stressed

24.2 MLA Format: In-Text Citations

In-text citations are found in the essay or writing itself. These in-text citations should be used to indicate any ideas that are not your own original ideas and give credit to the original author or source. Thus, any ideas that you quote, paraphrase, or summarize must include a citation at the end of the sentence. This helps avoid plagiarism.

In MLA documentation, as a general rule, these in-text citations place the author's last name and the page number(s) of the ideas you are citing in parentheses at the end of sentence. There is no comma between the author's last name and the page number(s). If it is an online source, you can omit the page number. If you wish, or your instructor requests it, you may include the paragraph source with a "par." in front of the paragraph number.

Since the in-text citations provide brief source documentation, they must match the first word(s) on your Works Cited, which is where your reader(s) will look to find the more detailed documentation of that source.

A. Standard MLA citation examples

1. Author not mentioned in sentence

The main character, Samantha, tells her mom, "You can't just judge people by their skin color! What if they just judged you by your weight?" (Harris 238).

2. Author mentioned in sentence

In the short story, "Through a Colorful Lens," Azsha Harris creates a complex character Samantha who tries to help her mom see her own hypocrisy with these words: "You can't just judge people by their skin color! What if they just judged you by your weight?" (238).

3. Two authors

Animals communicate through a combined use of sounds, body position, and fur signals (Blankenship and Tollifer 167-8).
According to Suzanne Blankenship and Travis Tollifer, Animals communicate through a combined use of sounds, body position, and fur signals (167-8).

4. Three or more authors

When a source has three or more authors, you only use the first author's name. After that name, you use "et al." (Latin abbreviation for "and others") to indicate there are more authors, but you do not actually list the other authors. This applies for the in-text citations as well as the Works Cited page entry.

In order to live a balanced life, a person must take inventory of how much time she devotes to the activities in her life (Douglass et al. 48).

5. Indirect Source

Occasionally your source will continue a quote or citation said by someone other than the author of the source. This is called an indirect source. To properly cite this source, you should acknowledge the name of who said it in the sentence itself, and then in the in-text citation use the words "qtd. in" (which stand for quoted in) before the author's last name.

According to the famous cartoon artist Lucy Lilac, "cartoonists should always begin in pencil" (qtd. in Peabody and Sherman 85).

6. No author

When an author is not given, you should use the title of the work or a shortened version of the title of the work. Remember the in-text citation should match the first words of your Works Cited page, so a reader can easily locate the documentation information. In the in-text citation, you should place the title in quotation marks or italics as it is on the Works Cited page.

a. Example of a website page with no author

For international students wishing to enroll at Hillsborough Community College, they must begin by completing an application and showing proof of high school graduation and English proficiency ("How to Become").

If your instructor requires a paragraph number, you would indicate that as follows:

International students wishing to enroll at Hillsborough Community College must begin by completing an application and showing proof of high school graduation and English proficiency ("How to Become," par. 8).

7. TIME-BASED MEDIA (SUCH AS VIDEO CLIPS OR FILMS)

a. Example of a movie

In his quest to remember that day, Julius interviewed Emmett, his former coach, inquiring about how his teammate died (*The Lost Day* 1:40-43).

b. Example of a YouTube clip

Despite popular belief, simply covering your windows in tape will not protect them from hurricane-speed winds. (ABC News 1:28-48).

8. TWO SOURCES BY THE SAME AUTHOR

When you have two sources by the same author (as there is with Terrance Jones on the Sample Works Cited at the end of this section), you should include the author's last name along with the title of the work and the page number. Place a comma between the author's last name and the title of the work.

Although successful players will take the initiative to practice on their own, the instruction and encouragement a baseball player receives from an excellent coach can help a player flourish in a competitive, overfilled sport (Jones, "The Power of a Great" 66).

9. CORPORATE AUTHORS

For concision, when a corporate author (i.e. an organization) is named in a parenthetical citation, shorten the name to the shortest noun phrase. For example, the American Historical Association consists entirely of a noun phrase, so you would write out the name in its entirety. By contrast, the Modern Language Association of America can be shortened to its initial noun phrase, Modern Language Association (excluding "of America," which is a prepositional phrase). If possible, give the first noun and any preceding adjectives, while excluding any initial article (i.e. a, an, the).

The updated user agreement explains the new privacy settings (Facebook Privacy).

10. GOVERNMENT AUTHORS

If more than one entry for different administrative units of the same organization or government author appears on the Works Cited page, in the parenthetical citation, give only as much of the name as is needed to locate the entry.

The newest research reveals the side effects only occurred in one in every 7 million recipients (Report on Adverse 22).

The full name of the source is Report on Adverse Effects from ZT122 Update.

Additional research into the unintended side effects of the ZT122 Update revealed that the instances of adverse reactions were very low (Report on Unintended 35).

The full name of the source is Report on Unintended Side Effects of ZT122 Update.

DIFFERENCES BETWEEN MLA AND APA FORMAT: IN-TEXT CITATIONS

In the body of the paper, all in-text citations are contained within parentheses.

Component of Format	MLA	APA
Citing author not mentioned in sentence	Author's last name and page number Example: (Smith 22)	Author's last name (comma) year of publication, and page number (only if using a direct quote. Paraphrase or summary only require Last Name (comma) and year of publication. Example: Direct quote: (Smith, 2019, p.22) Paraphrase or Summary: (Smith, 2019)
Author mentioned in sentence	Only the page number of cited material at the end of the sentence Example: (22).	Year of publication directly after author's name Example: Smith (2019)
Two authors not mentioned in sentence	Both last names (separated by "and") and page number Example: (Hawk and Hill 22)	Both last names separated by "and" (comma) year of publication Example: (Hawk and Hill, 2021)
Three or more authors not mentioned in sentence	First author's last name, "et al." and page number Example: (Johnson et al. 22)	First mention of source with Three-Five Authors Each author's last name (comma) year of publication Example: (Johnson, Hamilton, and Sheets, 1999) Each subsequent mention: (Johnson et al., 1999)
No author	Shortened version of title of work (In either italics or quotation marks, depending on type of source) Example: ("How to Become")	Shortened version of title of work (In either italics or quotation marks, depending on type of source) (comma) and year of publication Example: ("How to Become," 2019)

EXERCISE

MLA FORMAT: IN-TEXT CITATIONS EXERCISE 24.2A

Fix the following parenthetical citation errors.

1. Faulkner's gothic influence can be found "in the darkness under the cedars where he [examines] the tombstones in the Sutpen family cemetery, symbols of Sutpen's megalomania (Kerr 48)."

2. When salt was "scarce and expensive," it influenced where and how people lived. (MacGregor 50)"

3. One study shows that the population of China around 1990 was increasing by more than fifteen million annually. (Natl. Research Council 21).

4. All four authors researched the "complexity of empathy." (Janis et al. 611)."

5. In 1923, Bessie Smith, one of the most famous blues artists of the time, said, "I'ma do what I'ma do". (Shaw 96)

24.3 MLA Format: Works Cited Page

The Works Cited page is a page at the end of the paper that includes the complete bibliographic information for the sources cited in the paper. This complete bibliographic information allows a reader to locate a source more easily. Just as we do not write descriptors such as the words "street number" and "name" on envelopes (we just write the street number and name, like 39 Columbia Drive), the same is true for MLA documentation. We do not write descriptors to tell the reader this is the author or source title; instead, we just write them. Thus, it is critical for writers and readers to be familiar with the information included in a Works Cited entry, as well as the order the information appears. This way, just like when you view an address on an envelope and know what each piece of information tells, you will know what each piece of information on a Works Cited page is telling you if you are familiar with the type and order of the elements in an entry.

A. General Features of the Works Cited Page

A few general things to know about the Works Cited page:

- It begins on its own page after the final page of the essay (even if your last page of writing only fills the first two or three lines of that page). In addition, the page should continue with the 1" margins on all sides as well as the running header.
- It includes the title Works Cited. Both words are capitalized. That title should be in the same font and size as the rest of the paper. Do not place the words in bold font or underline them. In addition, do not place them in quotation marks or italics, and do not put a colon after them. A word of caution: Some templates are **wrong** and do not obey these rules (and others).
- It continues the running header already in the paper.
- It continues the double spacing already in the paper.
- Do **not** skip lines between entries; instead, create a hanging indent for this page. That means the second line (as well as any subsequent lines) of the entry will be indented ½ an inch. You create this hanging indent by locating the "paragraph" tab in Word and then locating the "special" drop-down box. For additional directions on how to create a hanging indent, you can visit this website: http://asklibrary.com.edu/faq/57140.
- The entries are listed alphabetically. If you have more than one source by the same author, list them in alphabetical order by the title. You may also use ---. in your list to signify the same author as above.
- Remember that all entries should end with a period.
- Do **not** list any sources on this page that are not cited in the paper itself.

In April 2021, MLA updated the citation format to be simpler and more consistent. This new edition is called MLA 9th edition. While several modifications have been made from the 8th edition, here is a highlight of a few key changes:

- In English-language titles, spell out numbers that would be spelled out in text, but follow the source for numbers in foreign language titles.
- If the name of an academic press contains the words *University* and *Press* or a foreign language equivalent, use the abbreviation *UP* or the equivalent in the publisher's name. If the word *University* or a foreign language equivalent does not appear in the name of the press but the word *Press* does, spell out *Press*.
- For concision, when a title is needed in a parenthetical citation, shorten the title if it is longer than a noun phrase. Use only the beginning words of the title up to at least the first noun and any preceding adjectives, while excluding any initial article (a, an, the).
- A DOI (digital object identifiers) is a string of numbers and letters that typically begins with the number 10. If the DOI is not preceded by http:// or https:// in your source, precede the DOI in your entry with the following: https://doi.org.
- Doing so will allow others to call up the source in a browser window. (p.110)
- Lowercase seasons of the year when they are part of the publication date in the Works Cited, just as you would in prose.
- Since online works typically can be changed or removed at any time, the date on which you accessed online material is often an important indicator of the version you consulted. The date of access is especially crucial if the source provides no date specifying when it was produced or published.
- For more detailed changes, please consult the MLA website: style.mla.org
- Instead of needing to check the format for each type of source, the format contains the same nine core elements for every source.

Note: Page numbers in this list refer to the MLA Handbook.

B. THE NINE CORE ELEMENTS

The nine core elements are listed in the graphic on the right. They should always be listed in that order and include the punctuation shown after each element, provided you are using that element. If your source does not have information for that core element, do not include a placeholder, such as n.d. for no date; instead, skip that element and continue on with the next element for which you have information. If information in a core element is repeated in another core element, list it only the first time.

Here is an overview of each core element in order to better understand what constitutes that element:

1. AUTHOR

This is what it sounds like. The author is the person, people, or organization (including corporate and government authors) that created the source. Like before, the author's last name is listed first (for the first author only—if there is more than one). Pseudonyms and handles can be used.

1 Author.

2 Title of source.

3 Title of container,

4 Contributor,

5 Version,

6 Number,

7 Publisher,

8 Publication date,

9 Location.

Examples

- Harris, Azsha
- Blankenship, Suzanne and Travis Tollifer
- Douglass, Teresa, et al.
- @WSJ
- ABC News
- U. S. Department of Education

2. TITLE OF SOURCE

The FULL title of the specific source you are using. In many things (websites, textbooks, TV shows, newspapers, YouTube, etc.) today, this is often the name of that smaller, specific piece (such as the web page, chapter title, episode title, article title, *YouTube* clip name).

Examples

- "Through A Colorful Lens"
- "The Language of Animals"
- "MLA 9th edition updates"
- *Living a Balanced Life*
- *The Lost Day*

3. TITLE OF CONTAINER

This is the name of a larger whole that contains the specific source (websites, textbooks, TV shows, newspapers, *YouTube*, etc.). The container titles belong in italics. If it is a standalone book, then the source and title container are the same, so you only list the title once.

Examples

- *Introduction to Literature*
- *Veterinary Science*
- *Living a Balanced Life*
- *The Lost Day YouTube*

4. CONTRIBUTOR

People, groups, and organizations can contribute to a work while not being its primary creator. This may be the case for works that have a primary author, whether specified or anonymous, and for ensemble works that are the product of many contributors but not of a single, primary creator. Key contributors should always be listed in your entry. Other kinds of contributors should be listed on a case-by-case basis in the Contributor element. Whenever you list a contributor, include a label describing the role played.

Examples

- edited by Kelly Postle and Rogier Sanders
- directed by Stephen Spielberg
- translated by William Grunion

5. VERSION

The version means the form of the source used when there is more than one form. If no specific version is mentioned, then omit this part. You can also use the version element to specify that you have used an e-book version of a printed book. (An e-book is defined here as a digital book that lacks a URL and that you use software to read on a personal electronic device.)

Examples

- 4th ed.
- rev. ed.
- director's cut ed.
- e-book ed.

6. NUMBER

If the source is given a number (such as volume and issue number for a journal or season and episode number for a TV show), then you include the number with a brief descriptor. For volume, use vol. abbreviation, and for issue or number, use no. For other descriptors, write them out.

Examples

- vol. 12, no. 4
- season 7, episode 14
- no. 8

7. PUBLISHER

The publisher refers to the organization, company, or group that sponsors or produces the source. For websites, you can often look at the bottom of the home page (or look for the copyright symbol) to find the publisher. The city of publication is no longer required. If the publisher and the container are the same, it is acceptable to omit this.

Examples

- Penguin Books
- DreamWorks Studios
- Oxford UP

8. PUBLICATION DATE

The date the source was publicly published, updated, performed, released, etc. If more than one date is given, often it is best to use the most recent date. The publication date can be as specific as a month, day, and year while other times it may just be a month and a year or just a year of publication. Lowercase seasons of the year when they are part of a publication date on the Works Cited page, just as you would in prose.

Examples

- 2015
- 12 Feb. 2014
- Aug. 2016
- spring 2008

9. LOCATION

In case someone else wishes to locate the information you cited, it is helpful to know the exact location. This means the location is often given as a page number(s), URL, DOI, or performance location. If the doi is not preceded by http:// or https:// in your source, precede the doi in your entry with https://doi.org.

Examples

- p. 238
- pp. 165-171
- www.studentaid.ed.gov/qualifications
- https://doi.org/10.1008/QRZ5423X189

NOTE ON PUNCTUATION

The punctuation on the Works Cited page can be somewhat tedious to remember; however, the changes in MLA 9th edition simplify it. The visual list of the nine core elements provides an overview of the punctuation normally included after each element type. In summary, normally a period is used at the end of the author entry, at the end of the title of the source, and at the end of the location. You should note that if the title of the source is in quotation marks, then then the period belongs *inside* the quotation marks. For the other core elements, generally a comma is used at the end of each one.

In addition, you should note the following punctuation rules for the Works Cited entries:

- A comma is used between an author's last name and first name: Harris, Azsha.
- If there is more than one author, a comma is used after an author's first name as well: Blankenship, Suzanne, and Travis Tollifer.
- If the author is a handle name, you should include the @ symbol, such as @WSJ.
- If there are multiple sources by the same author on the Works Cited page, then every source after the first one would include three hyphens instead of the author's name. This indicates that the source is written by

the same author as the previous source. (Alphabetize them then by the source title.) When creating the in-text citation, however, write the author's last name.
- For the version, edition is abbreviated ed. (with a period after it).
- For the number, volume is abbreviated vol. and issue is abbreviated no. (both have a period after them).
- For location, if you have only one page, abbreviate it as p. (with a period after the p). If you have more than one page, abbreviate it as pp. (with a period after the p).
- For location, if you have a DOI, use a colon after the DOI and before the numbers.
- For location, it is acceptable to break a URL before a slash and continue on the next line; however, do **not** put a hyphen in it.

C. WORKS CITED SAMPLE ENTRY FORMATS

1. BOOK WITH ONE AUTHOR
Author's Last Name, First Name. *Title*. Publisher, Date of publication.

Jones, Terrance. *Making It to the Big Leagues*. Scholastic Inc., 2010.

2. BOOK WITH TWO AUTHORS
Author's Last Name, First Name, and 2nd Author's First and Last Name. *Title*. Publisher, Date of publication.

Peabody, Adam, and Maria Sherman. *Creating Realistic Cartoon Characters*. Penguin Books, 1998.

3. BOOK WITH THREE OR MORE AUTHORS
1st Author's Last Name, First Name, et al. *Title*. Publisher, Date of publication.

Douglass, Teresa, et al. *Living a Balanced Life*. Oxford UP, 2005.

4. BOOK WITH AUTHOR PLUS EDITOR OR TRANSLATOR
Author's Last Name, First Name. *Title*. Role by First and Last Name(s), Publisher, Date of publication.

Peabody, Adam, and Maria Sherman. *Creating Realistic Cartoon Characters*. Translated by William Grunion, Penguin Books, 1998.

5. AN ENTIRE ANTHOLOGY
Last Name, First Name, editor. *Title of Anthology*. Publisher, Date of publication.

Last Name, First Name, and 2nd First and Last Name, editors. *Title of Anthology*. Publisher, Date of publication.

Postle, Kelly, and Rogier Sanders, editors. *Introduction to Literature*. 4th ed., Harper Collins, 2015.

6. WORK IN AN ANTHOLOGY
Author Last Name, First Name. "Title of Work." *Title of Anthology*, edited by First and Last Name(s), Publisher, Date of publication, Pages.

Harris, Azsha. "Through A Colorful Lens." *Introduction to Literature*, 4th ed., edited by Kelly Postle and Rogier Sanders, Harper Collins, 2015, pp. 235-42.

7. MAGAZINE ARTICLE (PRINT)
Author's Last Name, First Name. "Title of Article." *Name of Magazine*, Date of publication, Pages.

Jones, Terrance. "The Power of a Great Little League Coach." *Sports Illustrated*, 24 May 2012, pp. 64-8.

8. MAGAZINE ARTICLE (ONLINE)
Author's Last Name, First Name. "Title of Article." *Name of Magazine*, Date of web publication, Pages (if any), URL. Accessed Day Month Year.

Jones, Terrance. "The Power of a Great Little League Coach." *Sports Illustrated*, 24 May 2012, www.sportsillustrated.com/greatllcoach. Accessed 23 July 2020.

9. NEWSPAPER ARTICLE (PRINT)
Author's Last Name, First Name. "Title of Article." *Name of Newspaper*, Date of publication, Pages.

Jeffers, Tobias. "Tourist Money." *The Orlando Times*, 6 Mar. 2018, B12.

10. Newspaper Article (Online)

Author's Last Name, First Name. "Title of Article." *Name of Newspaper,* Date of web publication, URL. Accessed Day Month Year.

> Jeffers, Tobias. "Tourist Money." *The Orlando Times,* 6 Mar. 2018, www.orlandotimes.com/touristmoney. Accessed 12 Dec. 2019.

11. Article in an Online Database

Author's Last Name, First Name. "Title of Article." *Name of Periodical*, Volume, Issue, Date of publication, Pages. *Name of Database*, DOI or URL. Accessed Day Month Year.

> Blankenship, Suzanne, and Travis Tollifer. "The Language of Animals." *Veterinary Science*, vol. 12, no. 4, 12 Feb. 2014, pp. 165-171. *Science in Context*, https://doi.org/10.1008/ QRZ5423X189. Accessed 15 Feb. 2020.

12. An Entire Website

Title of Website. Publisher, Date of web publication, URL. Accessed Day Month Year.

> *Federal Student Aid.* U. S. Department of Education, 2017, www.studentaid.ed.gov. Accessed 1 Apr. 2019.

13. A Page on a Website

Author Last Name, First Name. "Title of Article." *Title of Website*, Publisher (if any), Date of web publication, URL. Accessed Day Month Year.

> Rivera, Jose. "In These Troubled Times." *American Politics*, 28 Jan. 2017, www.americanpolitics.com/ troubledtimes/2017-01-28. Accessed 20 Feb. 2019.

14. A Page on a Blog

Author Last Name, First Name (or Pseudonym). "Title of Blog Post." *Title of Blog*, Publisher (if any), Date of web publication, URL. Accessed Day Month Year.

> MSanders14 [Michelle Sanders]. "What Is Web 2.0?" *Teaching Through Technology*, WordPress, 12 May 2014, msanders14.wordpress.com/2014/05/12/what-is-web-2-0. Accessed 13 Mar. 2020.

15. A Page on a Website with No Author

"Title of Web Page." *Title of Website*, Publisher (if any), Date of web publication, URL. Accessed Day Month Year.

> "How to Become an International Student." *Hillsborough Community College*, Aug. 2016, www.hccfl.edu/ internationalstudents/instructions. Accessed 17 Feb. 2020.

16. A Movie or Film

Title of Movie or Film. Role by First and Last Name(s). Production Studio, Date produced.

> *The Lost Day.* Directed by Stephen Spielberg, DreamWorks Studios, 2013.

17. A YouTube Video

Author Last Name, First Name (or Pseudonym). "Title of YouTube Video." *YouTube*, Date of web publication, URL. Accessed Day Month Year.

> ABC News. "How to Stay Safe during a Hurricane." *YouTube*, 2 Oct. 2015, www.youtube.com/ watch?v=TSik3jqTTo4. Accessed 10 May 2020.

18. Interview (Personal)

Last Name, First Name (of Interviewee). Personal Interview. Day Month Year.

> Lemke, Dustin. Personal Interview. 30 June 2014.

19. Interview (Broadcasted/Published)

Last Name, First Name (of Interviewee). "Title of Interview." *Title of Program or Publication*, Network or Publisher (if any), Date.

> Obama, Barack. "Surviving the Presidency." *Coffee with Joe*, CNN, 30 Nov. 2016.

NOTE: While CNN can be a container or a publisher, in this example, it's the publisher while *Coffee with Joe* is the container.

20. Sound Recording (i.e. Song) Online

Last Name, First Name (or Group Name). "Title of Song." *Title of Album*, Distributor, Date, *Name of Audio Service*, URL.

> U2. "Sunday Bloody Sunday." *War*, Windmill Lane Studios, 1983, *Spotify,* open.spotify.com/track/0OPEX6Zw5r8728pqr12t.

21. Sound Recording (i.e. Song) CD

Last Name, First Name (or Group Name). "Title of Song." *Title of Album*, Distributor, Date.

> U2. "Sunday Bloody Sunday." *War,* Windmill Lane Studios, 1983.

22. TV Show

"Title of Episode." *Title of TV Show,* role by First and Last Names, season, episode, Network, Day Month Year.

> "The Door." *Game of Thrones*, written by David Benioff and D.B. Weiss, directed by Jack Bender, season 6, episode 5, HBO, 22 May 2016.

Contributor last name, first name, role. "Title of Episode." *Title of TV Show*, season, episode, Network, Day Month Year. *Streaming service*, URL.

> Mei Lin, Jesse, performer. "A Searing Burst of Light." *Shadow and Bone,* season 1, episode 1, Netflix, 14 Apr. 2021. *Netflix*, www.netflix.com/watch/80236160.

23. Tweet

@handle. "Entirety of Tweet." *Twitter,* Date of posting, Time of posting (user's time). Date accessed (if you choose, especially if the tweet is no longer available).

> @strephon. "The Lady's Dressing Room is the Grossest Poem Ever! Thanks Dr. Swift for that image in my brain." *Twitter*, 20 May 2019, 5:42 p.m. Accessed 5 May 2020.

D. Difference between MLA and APA format: Name for list of sources

Component of Format	MLA	APA
Name of List	Centered at top of new page Only one source: Work Cited More than one source: Works Cited	Centered at top of new page Only one source: Reference More than one source: References

MLA Format: Works Cited Page created by Jen Paquette

Works Cited

Blankenship, Suzanne, and Travis Tollifer. "The Language of Animals." *Veterinary*

> *Science*, vol. 12, no. 4, 12 Feb. 2014, pp. 165-171. *Science in Context*, https://doi.

> org/10.1008/QRZ5423X189.

Douglass, Teresa, et al. *Living a Balanced Life*. Oxford UP, 2015.

@EnglishEdUSF. "History of English 1." *YouTube*, 13 Sept. 2019, www.youtube.com/

> watch?v=dQw4w9WgXcQ. Accessed 1 Apr. 2020.

Harris, Azsha. "Through a Colorful Lens." *Introduction to Literature*, 4th ed., edited by

> Kelly Postle and Rogier Sanders, Harper Collins, 2018, pp. 235-42.

"How to Become an International Student." *Hillsborough Community College*, Aug. 2019,

> www.hccfl.edu/internationalstudent/instructions. Accessed 21 Feb. 2020.

Jones, Terrance. *Making It to the Big Leagues*. Scholastic Inc., 2019.

---. "The Power of a Great Little League Coach." *Sports Illustrated*, 24 May 2018, www.

> sportsillustrated.com/greatcoach. Accessed 23 Sept. 2020.

The Lost Day. Directed by Stephen Spielberg, DreamWorks Studios, 2013.

Peabody, Adam, and Maria Sherman. *Creating Realistic Cartoon Characters*, translated by

> William Grunion, Penguin Books, 1998.

"Run Boy Run." *The Umbrella Academy*, season 1, episode 1, Netflix, 15 Feb. 2019. *Netflix*,

> www.netflix.com/watch/80190196.

EXERCISES

MLA FORMAT: WORKS CITED PAGE EXERCISE 24.3A
Revise the following Works Cited Page.

Dean, Cornelia. Executive on a Mission: Saving the Planet "*The New York Times*". 22 May 2007. www.nytimes.com/2007/05/22/science/earth/22ander.html?_r=0. Visited 12 May 2016.

Robert Smith, 2017, "The best article you have ever read in your life". Published on RSmith's

Blog called "My Wonderful Ideas Every Day" www.mywonderfulideas/bestarticle/html Visited 22 May 2017..

An Inconvenient Truth. 2006. Davis Guggenheim, Director. Performances by Al Gore and Billy West, Paramount, 2006.

Shulte Bret. "*Putting a Price on Pollution.*" EBSCO. *US News and World Report*, 14 May 2017, no.

17, vol. 142, p. 37. Access no: 24984616.

MLA Format: Works Cited Page Exercise 24.3B

Arrange the following information into correct entries in a Works Cited list. (Be sure to omit extraneous information that is not supposed to be included in a Works Cited list.)

1. Franz Kafka, "The Hunger Artist"
   Anthology: Literature: Reading, Reacting, Writing
   Editors: Laurie G. Kirzner and Stephen R. Mandell
   Edition: 6th ed.
   Publisher: Thomson Wadsworth
   Place of Publication: Boston
   Year of Publication: 2007
   Pages: 367-374

2. Jonathan Safran Foer, "A Primer for the Punctuation of Heart Disease"
   Periodical: The New Yorker
   Date of Publication: June 10, 2002
   Pages: 43-46

3. J. D. Salinger, "Perfect Day for Bananafish"
   Collection: Nine Stories
   Publisher: Little Brown
   Place of Publication: New York
   Year of Publication: 1953
   Pages: 3-18

4. A non-fiction book entitled Write Away, which was most recently published by Pearson in 1962. The authors are Octavia Jones and C.J. Thompson. The text was published first in Boston and the latest publication was done in London, and there are 320 pages.

5. Inside the Pentagon is an article found on MyPyramid.gov and was produced by the United States Department of Military Defense. There is no publication date, and there is no author provided.

6. Tomcat in Love **and** If I Die in a Combat Zone: Box Me Up and Ship Me Home are **two** books written by Tim O'Brien. The first was published in October 1984 by Bedford in New York. The second was published in New York by Holt in 1999.

7. A short story called "The Lone Ranger and Tonto Fistfight in Heaven" was written by Sherman Alexie and was found in an anthology (2nd edition) entitled Fiction of the Paranoid Indigenous, edited by Tom Timmery and Joe Josephson. Published in 1964 by Bantam in Los Angeles, and can be found on pages 565-71.

8. A poem entitled "Leaves of Glass" on pages 25-42 by Walt Wheatman in a collection of his own poems titled *Poems of a Rip Off Hippie*. The collection was edited by George Herbert and published in 1987 by Wadsworth, in the city of Boston and distributed in New York and Canada.

9. A journal article entitled "The Farmer Boy" published in the 1996 issue of The Library Quarterly by Tod Oppenheimer appears on pages 26-28. Volume 91, Issue 3.

10. "Who is He?" is an interview of Kurt Vonnegut that was conducted on March 3rd 1996 and was found in New Yorker on pages 36-38.

11. An article entitled The Legend of Lampoon written by Dietrich Goebbels was found in a reference book called New Age Propaganda on pages 12-27, edited by Jerome Jackson, and published in Connecticut by Harper Collins in 1974.

12. An article entitled The Rain Below, written by Peter Smith, was found in an online scholarly journal (Web) called Wet and Dry. It was retrieved May 9, 2006 and published on April 9, 2003. The URL is as follows: http://www.ran. org/info-center/products.html. It was found in the 12th volume and was the 2nd issue.

13. The Big Lebowski is a film (DVD) starring John Goodman and Jeff Bridges and directed by Joel Coen distributed by Universal in the United States in 1999.

14. In Praise of the "F" Word is an article written by Mary Sherry was first published in the newspaper The New York Times on the 25th of May in 1991 in the National Edition, page A1+

15. "Motion Picture" is an article found on Encyclopaedia Britannica Online, an encyclopedia on the Internet, and was composed of 3 paragraphs. The article was published by the Encyclopaedia Britannica in March of 1992 and retrieved on August 12th of 1997. The URL is as follows: http://www.eb.com/:220

MLA Format: Works Cited Page 24.3C
Practice finding resources using the HCC databases.

- Pick a topic.
- Use HCC databases only for research: Academic Search Complete and New York Times. Search only magazine and newspapers published in the US. Do not use academic journals.
- Compile selected direct quotations and note if the source is a magazine or newspaper.
- Copy and paste the MLA work cited underneath the quote. Be sure to correctly format.
- Create a Works Cited page.

First step:
Choose one of the following topics. Sometimes it is best to do a little searching on databases before deciding on THE topic. Your goal is to educate your reader, so be sure to select information that helps your reader learn about:

- Easter or Passover – Easter bunny and dyed eggs or the actual origin; meaning; rituals, and traditions of Easter
- Passover -- origin, meaning, tradition
- Zombies – origin; who/what are they? Change of zombie characterization over time; films that show difference in characterization
- Effects of laughter
- Two most iconic female athletes

Second step:
After you have chosen your topic, begin the research. Choose the best information and the best four sources. Be selective. Copy and paste selected quotations, and copy and paste MLA citations underneath each. See the example below:

Example: Research on Frankenstein by Mary Shelley
First source: magazine article

"The creature struggles to understand who he is, why he was made, and where and with whom he belongs. He considers what it means to be human even as he concludes that he is a singular creature, not created in the image and likeness of God but in the image and likeness of Victor Frankenstein. Too bad that Victor's moral blindness prevents him from becoming fully human himself. Instead, he flounders in his own pride to the detriment of his own existence. And the creature? He floats away on an ice raft in the Arctic, vowing to seek rest in death" (36).

"Mary Shelley, just 19 when she penned the first draft of Frankenstein, was writing before the scientific revolution of the later 19th century, with its body-snatching industry that supplied medical schools with freshly dead specimens for their surgical theatres in the stated interest of advancing science and medicine" (34).
Rose, Michael S. "Literature MATTERS." New Oxford Review, vol. 86, no. 6, July 2019, pp. 33–36. EBSCOhost, search.ebscohost.com/login.aspx?direct=true&db=a9h&AN= 138131908& authtype=shib&site=ehost-live.

Second source: magazine article

"Mary Shelley's Frankenstein is one of the most adaptable and adapted novels of all time, countless renditions in film, television, comic books, cartoons, and other products of popular culture. About 50,000 copies of the book are

still sold each year in the United States. According to the Open Syllabus Project, it is the most commonly taught literary text in college courses" (59).

BAILEY, RONALD. "Victor Frankenstein Is the Real Monster." Reason, vol. 49, no. 11, Apr. 2018, pp. 56–62. EBSCOhost, search.ebscohost.com/login.aspx?direct=true& db=a9h&AN=128081701& authtype=shib&site=ehost-live.

Third source: magazine article

"It originated in Ovid's Metamorphoses, where Prometheus is described as making human beings out of clay and bringing them to life. There is no fire in Ovid's story. It is in later, that Prometheus steals fire from heaven to introduce a spark of life (the soul) into his creatures. Victor Frankenstein, in Mary's story, is a modern Prometheus because he makes a human being out of dead matter and brings it to life with a spark, the spark of electricity" (65).

Wootton, David. "Frankenstein between Two Worlds." History Today, vol. 70, no. 9, Sept. 2020, pp. 65–73. EBSCOhost, search.ebscohost.com/login.aspx?direct=true& AuthType= shib&db=khh&AN=145123530&site=eds-live.

Fourth source: newspaper article

"From the old Dracula and Frankenstein films to the slasher exploits of contemporary ghouls such as Freddy Krueger, movie horror has become synonymous with cheap thrills and cobwebbed cliches. Monsters get no respect. But this month, the living dead attempt to refurbish their dignity on the Hollywood screen as two Gothic blockbusters square off at the box office: Mary Shelley's Frankenstein and (Anne Rice's) Interview with the Vampire."

Johnson, Brian D. "Mary Shelley's Frankenstein." Maclean's, vol. 107, no. 46, 14 Nov. 1994, p. 112+. Gale General OneFile, https://link.gale.com/apps/doc/ A15876848/ITOF? u= lincclin_hcc&sid=ITOF&xid=7b3ab660. Accessed 25 Oct. 2020.

Works Cited

BAILEY, RONALD. "Victor Frankenstein Is the Real Monster." Reason, vol. 49, no. 11, Apr. 2018, pp. 56–62. EBSCOhost, search.ebscohost.com/login.aspx?direct=true& db=a9h&AN=128081701& authtype=shib&site=ehost-live.

Johnson, Brian D. "Mary Shelley's Frankenstein." Maclean's, vol. 107, no. 46, 14 Nov. 1994, p. 112+. Gale General OneFile, https://link.gale.com/apps/doc/ A15876848/ITOF? u= lincclin_hcc&sid=ITOF&xid=7b3ab660. Accessed 25 Oct. 2020.

Rose, Michael S. "Literature MATTERS." New Oxford Review, vol. 86, no. 6, July 2019, pp. 33–36. EBSCOhost, search.ebscohost.com/login.aspx?direct=true&db=a9h&AN= 138131908& authtype=shib&site=ehost-live.

Wootton, David. "Frankenstein between Two Worlds." History Today, vol. 70, no. 9, Sept. 2020, pp. 65–73. EBSCOhost, search.ebscohost.com/login.aspx?direct=true& AuthType= shib&db=khh&AN=145123530&site=eds-live.

STUDENT SAMPLE

All student samples have been preserved in the form in which they were submitted in class; thus, they contain some errors. After all, papers are never truly done; they are just due.

SAMPLE MLA ESSAY: RESEARCH PAPER

Asma Abdallah
Professor Ortiz
ENC 1101
1 November 2020

Why the Japanese Education System is the Most Successful

Nelson Mandela once said, "Education is the most powerful weapon which you can use to change the world" (Strauss). Every country has its unique methods of teaching and raising children, Japan is no different. Japan is one of the most creative and innovative societies in the world. It's no doubt that Japan has gained attention worldwide with its modernized yet traditional education. The Japanese educational system is well-known for its moral education and emphasis on student collaboration that is attributable to its success of a 99% literacy rate and other outcomes that make the students highly competitive in the modern world (Hussain and Salfi 4). In contrast, America's education system lacks many elements such as the stagnant spending on school funds and little to no innovation concerning teaching methods that ultimately contribute to the failing system. Although Japan has a high youth suicide rate and their students lack creativity, Japan's education system is more efficient and successful than many other countries, such as America, because of its emphasis on discipline and cultural values, its considerate and thoughtful lessons by qualified teachers, and the promotion of equality in education.

In comparison to America's education system, one reason behind the successes of the Japanese educational system is the significance of morality and cultural learning that is stressed at a young age. Japanese people approach education in a different sense: the development of a student in social skills and character is equally as important as their academic excellence. For example, the study conducted by several researchers indicated that "Japanese participants considered it more appropriate to report minor transgressions than American participants did" (Loke et al. 1524). The findings of the study further disclose the prominence of morality within Japan in contrast to America because Japanese children conveyed social responsibility and empathy to a greater extent than American children did. Besides, Japan upholds cleanliness as a necessity in every aspect of their lives. The streets have almost no litter and very few garbage bins. Because the country lacks natural resources, Japan minimizes waste and encourages citizens to sort out trash properly and save water. According to "Japanese and American Children's Moral Evaluations of Reporting on Transgressions," people in the U.S. are "more likely to have an 'independent' view of themselves" whereas people in Japan "are more likely to have an 'interdependent' view" (1525). This further proves how prominent morals and ethics are in a Japanese school setting. For example, the first three years of schooling for a pupil are focused on establishing good manners and etiquette. They are taught to respect others, to be empathetic, and to treat nature and animals with kindness and reverence. More so, most Japanese schools do not hire custodians or janitors. Students have to clean and take care of the school by dividing up the tasks to keep the school tidy and clean. Japanese pupils are required to wear indoor shoes. They are also taught at a young age to stand and greet their teachers at the beginning and end of class as a sign of respect.

In "Young Children's Beliefs about School Learning in Japan and the United States: Cultural and Socioeconomic Comparisons," Yamamoto notes that Japanese children's willingness and diligence in learning stems from the bonds formed with their parents so that they may internalize social norms (26). Parental involvement and cultural values have caused Japanese students to be more academically motivated. Japan's fostering of child growth through a moral education illustrates the remarkability of their system.

Secondly, the reasoning behind the success of the Japanese education system in contrast to America's is the virtuous teachers who are dedicated to delivering qualitative lessons to their students. The teaching culture is vastly different in Japan. Japanese teachers urge classmates to be loyal to one another and assume leadership roles by delegating responsibilities and decision-making to everyone. Teachers cultivate individuality, how to speak politely, nutrition, personal hygiene and sleep, and other various skills that'll aid them in their personal lives and public (Wieczorek 107). Japanese teachers stress perseverance, engage students, build strong classroom relationships, and unify the class (107). Additionally, "Japanese mathematics' teachers' lesson plans are more complex than their U.S. counterparts" (107). This conveys how passionate the teachers are in developing a curriculum that is the utmost beneficial for their pupils. Japanese students are explicitly taught problem-solving and critical thinking, rather than rote memorization. Furthermore, Staples references "The Teaching Gap" which demonstrates strategies used by teachers when revising lessons, reflecting the success of schools there because of intensive teacher development (A22). Japan boasts teachers who collaborate for the sake of making quality lessons to improve their methods, a process known as "lesson study" (A22). "Lesson study" is a model that utilizes bottom-up learning, with teachers and students collaborating to formulate projects and ideas to meet learning objectives and gives teachers the autonomy to identify school-wide issues and how to resolve them. The study model receives praise in literature and has been implemented in the UK. In addition to the method of "lesson study," there are research groups in Japan who solely focus on improving and strengthening the curriculum, such as integrating hands-on or interactive learning during the early primary years. In America, however, novice teachers are expected to deliver lessons competently (A22). Teacher unions infrequently strive to encourage good behavior as a citizen but rather look for personal advancements in their financial welfare or their "use of power to promote their own special interests" over the interests of children. Teacher unions' political power is used to "stifle progress" and to stagnate reform in public education as seen by the 41% graduation rate in urban areas like Philadelphia and Los Angeles (Moe 11). There is a lack of teacher education innovation because teaching methods are outdated and do not reflect the ongoing demands of the classroom. Japan takes pride in its education system because its teachers' approaches to learning and knowledge have allowed its pupils to outperform their counterparts around the world.

Thirdly, Japan differs from America in that it promotes equality in education as it aims to benefit all students. As stated in "Japan: A Story of Sustained Excellence," Japanese teachers and principals are "often reassigned to different schools" to "make sure that the distribution of the most capable teachers among schools is fair and equitable." The Japanese government ensures that areas with underprivileged students receive better teachers and resources (qtd. in OECD). The United States is among many of the countries where a student's economic background determines the standard of the education they receive. In Japan, however, the country ranks highly in providing equal educational opportunities to all students and economic stances (qtd. in OECD). Japan's educational equity is additionally a matter of how the funds are allocated. The Japanese educational system is carefully planned and designed so that there is equal opportunity nationwide to learn. The gifted programs in U.S. schools are distinguishable from the classroom settings in Japan where better students are expected to help the struggling ones. More so, America doesn't have a coherent, national curriculum with a variety of standards in each state which makes it disadvantageous to improve educational outcomes for all students and backgrounds. In "Why the United States Should Look to Japan for Better Schools," America's low performance is a result of politicians and businesses neglecting the poor education system and instead, prioritizing how to profit from the field of education (Staples A22). For example, "at least 15 states are providing less funding per student to local school districts in the new school year than they provided a year ago" (Leachman and Mai). School spending in America has become stagnant, even as the economy improves, resulting in a growing achievement gap. This is contrary to the Japanese education system because America allows for the best students to excel, leaving the financially unstable students to fend for themselves. After all, in the eyes of politicians and the government, education is nothing but a monopoly rather than a means for schoolers to intellectually grow as a person.

Some may argue that schools in Japan discourage individuality and place extreme stress onto their pupils causing suicide to be at an all-time high. For example, a professor at Hokkaido University reports that in Japan 1 in 12 primary school students and 1 in 4 secondary school students suffer from depression, which causes many of them to commit suicide (Lu). Recent curriculum changes, however, have evolved in an attempt to address these issues. The Japanese education system does indeed have its flaws, but so do other education systems around the world. The Japanese education system may be far from perfect, but on average, it is undoubtedly better than the United States of America because of its strong curriculum, education equity, and teacher training. Not only is the scholastic performance high, but criminal violence is a lot less common than in the U.S. Japan remains one of the world's least violent societies as it has "consistently logged fewer than one-tenth the number of homicides" (Kaplan). Contrary to popular belief, the education system in Japan is not directly at fault for the suicide rate there. Claims by academics of how the Japanese system compromises interests and abilities is ideologically based and does not discredit the effective results of the system.

In conclusion, it is strikingly apparent how excellent and exceptional the Japanese educational system is in contrast to America's curriculum, because of the components that comprise the Japanese education system. The successes behind Japanese education is its emphasis on moral education in the early years of the pupil, the quality teachers, and curriculum, as well as the focus on equity. Despite the critiques, Japan's approaches to learning have prompted extraordinarily low illiteracy and other impressive results that have made Japanese students highly competitive in the globalized world.

Works Cited

Hussain, Ashiq, and Naseer Ahmad Salfi. "Literacy Improvement Efforts in Pakistan: Comparison with South Asian Countries." *International Journal of the Book*, vol. 8, no. 2, June 2011, pp. 1-13. *EBSCOhost*, search.ebscohost.com/login.aspx?direct=true &AuthType=shib&db=hus&AN=656 47645&site=eds-live.

Kaplan, David E. "More Stressed, but Still Safer." *U.S. News and World Report*, no. 11, 2007. *EBSCOhost*, search.ebscohost.com/login.aspx?direct=true&AuthType=shib&db=edsgao &AN=edsgcl.160725805&si.

Leachman, Michael, and Chris Mai. "Most States Funding Schools Less Than Before the Recession." *Center on Budget and Policy Priorities*, 11 Oct. 2017, www.cbpp.org/research/ most-states-funding-schools-less-than-before-the-recession.

Loke, Ivy, et al. "Japanese and American Children's Moral Evaluations of Reporting on Transgressions." *Developmental Psychology*, vol. 50, no. 5, May 2014, pp. 1520-1531. *APA PsycArticles*, https:// doi.org/10.1037/a0035993.

Lu, Stephanie. "The Mystery Behind Japan's High Suicide Rates among Kids." *The Wilson\Quarterly*, Woodrow Wilson International Center for Scholars, Oct. 2015. *Wilson Quarterly*, wilsonquarterly. com/stories/the-mystery-behind-japans-high-suicide-rates- among-kids/.

Moe, Terry M. "Special Interest: Teachers Unions and America's Public Schools." Brookings Institution Press, 2011. *JSTOR*, www.jstor.org/stable/10.7864/j.cttl2616v.

OECD. *Lessons from PISA for the United States*: *Strong Performers, and Successful Reformers in Education. OECDilibrary*, OECD Publishing, 2011, https://doi.org/10.1787/97892606.

Staples, Brent. "Why the United States Should Look to Japan for Better Schools." *New York Times*, vol. 155, no. 53405, 21 Nov. 2005, p. A22. *EBSCOhost*, search.ebscohost.com/login.aspx?direct =true&db=a9h&AN=20327388&authtype=shib&site=ehost-live.

Strauss, Valerie. "Nelson Mandela on the Power of Education." *The Washington Post*, WP Company, 22 Apr. 2019, www.washingtonpost.com/news/answer-sheet/wp/2013/12/05/ nelson-mandelas-famous-quote-on-education/.

Wieczorek, Craig C. "Comparative Analysis of Educational Systems of American and Japanese Schools: Views and Visions." *Educational Horizons*, vol. 86, no. 2, 2008, pp. 99-111. *JSTOR*, www. jstor.org/stable/42923715. Accessed 19 Oct. 2020.

Yamamoto, Yoko. "Young Children's Beliefs about School Learning in Japan and the United States: Cultural and Socioeconomic Comparisons." *Early Childhood Research Quarterly*, vol. 50, no. 2, Jan. 2020, pp. 25-37. *EBSCOhost*, https://doi.org/10.1016/j.ecresq.06.013.

REVIEW EXERCISE

PLEASE CORRECT ALL ERRORS IN THE FOLLOWING EXAMPLE.

According to the article "Ybor City," the United States "in an attempt to raise revenue ...put a high tariff on Cuban cigars" in 1857. (White 189). To avoid the additional expense, some Cuban cigar factory owners, like Vincente Martinez Ybor, came to Florida in 1885 and "obtained 40 acres of land" (White) and began to build what became known as Ybor City. From 1885 until the death of Vincente Ybor in 1910, the small community thrived. Many cigar companies were established and employed thousands of workers who hand-rolled cigars. Both men and women "worked side-by-side in the factories, and most lived within walking distance". Soon stores, restaurants, housing, and activity centers were built. The Columbia Restaurant still remains in Ybor City today. However, over time, "the combination of the Depression, increasing automation, and the boom in the popularity of cigarettes" left Ybor City "a shell of its former self." (White and Pennington-Gray 129).

While the Ybor City of today is very different from the Ybor City of 1929, there are still many remnants of the original cigar capital of the world. According to an article, Ybor City was established by Cuban immigrants who found local "entrepreneurs [who] leased land and loaned money to [them] for the construction of company towns and cigar factories and tenement housing for skilled Cuban and Spanish cigar makers." Key West was actually the "center of the United States-Cuban cigar industry from the late 1870s" until Vincente Ybor established cigar factories in Ybor City (393).

During its peak years, the number of cigars that came out of Ybor City was enormous. "More than 200 cigar factories fueled by an immigrant-population put out some eight million hand-rolled cigars a week" ("Florida Melting Pot").

Work Cited

White, Erin E., and Lori Pennington-Gray. "Ybor City." Parks and Recreation, vol. 36, no. 9, Sept. 2001, p. 129. EBSCOhost, search.ebscohost.com/login.aspx?direct=true&db= a9h&AN= 5192912& authtype= shib&site=ehost-live.

Bronstein, Daniel. "La Cubana City: A Cuban Cigar Manufacturing Community Near Thomasville, Georgia, During the 1890s." Georgia Historical Quarterly, vol. 90, no. 3, Fall 2006, pp. 391–417. EBSCOhost, search.ebscohost.com/login.aspx?direct=true&db=a9h&AN= 22341494& authtype=shib&site=ehost-live.

Rothman, HeathCliff. "Florida Melting Pot." National Geographic Traveler, vol. 23, no. 8, Nov. 2006, pp. 222–226. EBSCOhost, search.ebscohost.com/login.aspx?direct=true&db=a9h& AN=23043273& authtype= shib&site=ehost-live.

Chapter 25

APA FORMAT

The following is based on the Sixth Edition of the APA manual and updates available on the APA website (www.apastyle.org).

If you write an assignment for a course in psychology, education, anthropology, sociology, economics or any other behavioral or social science, you will most likely use APA (American Psychological Association) Style to document your sources. Your instructor will specify which documentation style you should use.

APA format breaks down into:

- Page Layout
- In-Text Citations
- Reference Page

25.1 APA Format: Page Layout
A. General APA Information and Formatting Guidelines

- Employ 1" margins and double-spacing throughout the entire paper.

- Each paragraph should be indented.

- Paragraphs must be at least two sentences but not longer than a full page.

- In the running head, the whole of the condensed title is capitalized. For student papers, only use a running head if your institution requests it.

B. Title Page

- APA has slightly different formats for the title page of student papers and professional papers (those for conferences or publication).

- Both should include the title of your paper, your name, and the name of your institution.
  - For a student paper, include the course name and number, instructor name, and the assignment due date, but not a complete running head–only the page number aligned right.
  - For a professional paper, include an author note.

- The title of your paper, your name, and the name of your institution should be centered and begin roughly one-third down the title page.

- The title of the paper should not exceed 12 words.

- Running head should be a condensed version of the title. It should retain the key points of the title.

- The use of "Running head: TITLE" only appears on the title page.

- Pagination begins on the title page.

C. Abstract

- Not all instructors will require an abstract, especially for shorter essays. Check with your instructor and the specifications of your assignment to see if it is required.

- An abstract summarizes the key points of your paper in 150-250 words. It also contains keywords that allow researchers/readers to quickly ascertain whether your paper relates to their topic of interest. This is a non-database version of a keyword search.

D. Body

- The body of the paper begins with the full title centered at the top of the page.

- There are different headings in APA Style. Your instructor may ask you to separate your paper with headings and subheadings.

- Headings and subheadings separate the Who? What? When? Where? Why? How? So What? and Now What? of your paper.

- There are five levels of headings and subheadings. Each level has a different format and should be used in order. That is, always start with level one before proceeding to level two, then three, and so on.

Sample APA Layout

HCC Presents a Brief Guide to APA Style

Abstract

An abstract summarizes the key points of a paper in 150-250 words. If your paper was about a study you conducted, you would include a brief description of the importance of conducting your study, the methodology you used, general information about the participants involved in the study, and a short explanation of your findings. If your paper contains headings and subheadings, you could provide a sentence or two that summarizes each main idea presented in those sections. Reading dozens of articles that might not be entirely related to your research topic is time-consuming. Abstracts grant you a sneak peek into a paper's content. Since they are short, you can read dozens of abstracts before deciding which papers you should read in their entirety. An abstract should also list keywords that allow researchers/readers to quickly ascertain whether a paper relates to their topic of interest. This is a non-database version of a keyword search.

Keywords: writing abstracts, APA format

HCC Presents a Brief Guide to APA Formatting

This is where the body of your paper will start. If you write an assignment for a course in psychology, education, anthropology, sociology, economics or any other behavioral or social science, you will most likely use APA (American Psychological Association) Style to document your sources.

Exercise

APA Format: Page Layout Exercise 25.1A

Review a paper you have written in APA format. Revise for page layout issues.

25.2 APA Format: In-Text Citations

In-text citations allow readers to distinguish your words and ideas from those of your sources. As such, properly documenting your sources is crucial to avoiding plagiarism.

APA format is similar to MLA format because both styles use parenthetical citation for in-text citations. The difference is in what information goes inside the parentheses. In MLA, you add the author's last name and the page number. For APA, you add the author's last name, the year of publication, and then the page number—but only if you have a direct quote. If you have paraphrased or summarized an idea, you only include the author's last name and the year.

> **Example**: In her stunning new work, Jones has "outdone all of her years of service" (Smith, 2019, p. 22).

> **Example**: In her stunning new work, Jones has gone above and beyond anything else she has done in all of her years in this position (Smith, 2019).

A. Standard APA in-text citation examples

1. Author not mentioned in sentence

For the most effective and injury-free leg day, it is important to activate the leg muscles with a comprehensive warm-up (Eastman, 2021).

2. Author mentioned in sentence

Eastman (2021) pointed out that the most effective and injury-free leg days begin with a comprehensive warm-up.

3. Two authors

Hawk and Hill (2016) focused on how media depictions of higher education influenced student enrollment at community colleges, not how students were affected by those portrayals.

To some extent, media depictions of higher education influence student enrollment at community colleges (Hawk and Hill, 2016).

4. Three to Five Authors

When a work has three to five authors, include each author's last name when you first cite the source. After that, only include the first author's last name followed by "et al." In all citations, include the year of publication.

First mention:

Johnson, Hamilton, and Sheets (1999) studied motives concerning student involvement in drinking games. Students are drawn to drinking games for a variety of reasons (Johnson, Hamilton, and Sheets, 1999).

Subsequent mentions:

Johnson et al. (1999) studied motives concerning student involvement in drinking games. Students are drawn to drinking games for a variety of reasons (Johnson et al., 1999).

5. No author

A work with no author follows a similar rule as MLA Style. Use a shortened version of the title followed by a comma and the year of publication.

Parenthetical citation: ("How to Become," 2016)

EXERCISE

APA FORMAT: IN-TEXT CITATIONS EXERCISE 25.2A

Fix the following parenthetical citation errors so they reflect APA format guidelines.

1. Faulkner's gothic influence can be found "in the darkness under the cedars where he [examines] the tombstones in the Sutpen family cemetery, symbols of Sutpen's megalomania (Kerr, 2005, 48)."

2. When salt was "scarce and expensive," it influenced where and how people lived. (MacGregor page 50, 2016)"

3. One study shows that the population of China around 1990 was increasing by more than fifteen million annually. (2006 Natl. Research Council 21).

4. All four authors researched the "complexity of empathy." (Janis, Jones, Smith, Grimes et al. 2016, pg. 611)."

5. In 1923, Bessie Smith, one of the most famous blues artists of the time, said, "I'ma do what I'ma do". (Shaw, 1955, 96)

25.3 APA Format: References Page

In an APA Style research paper, your sources will appear in two places: within in-text citations and on a reference list at the end of your document.

- Your reference list is an alphabetized record of all the works you cite within your document. This page shows readers where you found your information and gives them a starting point to find more information about your topic, gain a better understanding of your claims, or verify the claims you support in your assignment.

- You will notice that many words in the titles on the sample reference list are not capitalized. Here are a few capitalization rules:
  - Capitalize the first letter of titles and subtitles.
  - Proper nouns should always remain capitalized.

- You will also notice that some titles are italicized and others are not. Here are a few italicization rules:
  - Italicize titles of complete, standalone works (e.g., books, plays, television series, collected volumes, journals, website).
  - DO NOT italicize titles of shorter works (e.g., a chapter in a book, a single episode, a single poem in a collection of poetry, an article in a journal, webpage).
  - Italicize volume numbers of periodicals. Do not italicize issue numbers.

- Though the examples below are single-spaced, all entries on a reference list should be double-spaced.

- Reference list begins on a new page and is titled "References" (without quotations).

- The first line of each entry is flush left. Subsequent lines of the same entry are indented.

- APA 7th edition lists the URL, but you can add "Retrieved date from URL" if the page is likely to change.

Note: "Initials" refers to initials of first and, when available, middle names.

A. References Page Sample Entry Examples

1. Work with One Author

a. Book (Print)

Author's Last Name, Initials. (Year of Publication). *Title of book*. Publisher.

> Schwarz, D. R. (2016). *How to succeed in college and beyond: the art of learning*. Wiley Blackwell.

b. Journal Article (Print)

Author's Last Name, Initials. (Year of Publication). Title of article. *Name of Journal. Volume*(Issue), page numbers.

> Baker, T. (2003). Boredom in the first-year composition classroom. Teaching English in the Two Year College, 30(4), 404-415.

2. WORK WITH TWO AUTHORS

List authors in the same order as they appear in the given work. A comma (,) a space and ampersand (and) separates each name after the first author. The format of all other information remains the same as a work for one author.

> Hawk, J. L., and Hill, L. H. (2016). "Hipster freshman": popular culture's portrayal of community college students. *Community College Enterprise, 22*(1), 28-42.

3. WORK WITH THREE TO FIVE AUTHORS

A comma (,) a space and ampersand (and) separates each name after the first author. The format for all other information remains the same as a work for one author.

> Johnson, T. J., Hamilton, S., and Sheets, V. L. (1999). College students' self-reported reasons for playing drinking games. *Addictive Behaviors, 24*(2), 279-286.

4. WORK WITH NO AUTHOR

Italicize longer/standalone/collected works. Use quotation marks for shorter works. Refer to italicization rules for examples of longer and shorter works.

> "How to Become an International Student." (2019, August). https://www.hccfl.edu/intern/

5. WORK WITH TRANSLATOR

Add (Initials. Last name, Trans.) after the title of the work. End the entry with (Original work published in Year).

> Hedayat, S. (1958). *The Blind Owl* (D.P. Costello, Trans.). Grove Press.
> (Original work published in 1936).

6. DOCTORAL DISSERTATION

> Vanderlinden, M. E. (2011). *Associating with occupational depictions: How African American college women are influenced by the portrayals of women in professional careers on television* (Publication no. 8675309). [Doctoral Dissertation, University of South Florida].ProQuest Dissertation Publishing.

7. REPRINTED CHAPTER OR ARTICLE IN BOOK

> Heath, S.B. (2005). Questioning at home and at school: A comparative study. In J.L. Paul (Ed.), *Introduction to the philosophies of research and criticism in education and the social sciences* (pp. 135-151). Pearson. (Reprinted from *Doing the ethnography of schooling: Education anthropology in action*, by G. Spindler, Ed., 1982, Waveland Press)

8. AN ENTIRE ANTHOLOGY

> Mays, K.J. (Ed.) (2016). *Norton Introduction to Literature* (Shorter 12th ed). Norton.

9. WORK IN AN ANTHOLOGY

> Hansberry, L. (1959). *A raisin in the sun*. In K.J. Mays (Ed.) *Norton Introduction to Literature* (Shorter 12th ed) (pp.1456-1520). Norton.

10. MAGAZINE ARTICLE (PRINT)

> Frey, R. (2017, Summer). Movement mechanics. *Muscle and Fitness Hers. 18*(3), 32-33.

11. MAGAZINE ARTICLE (ONLINE)

> Witt, K. (2014, February 11). Love me Tinder. *GQ*. https://www.gq.com/love-me

12. NEWSPAPER ARTICLE (PRINT)

If the article appears on multiple pages, place pp. before you list the page numbers.

> Phillips, D. (2017, May 27). Infantry's first women shoulder heavy gear and weight of history. *New York Times*. p. A12.

13. NEWSPAPER ARTICLE (ONLINE)

Phillips, D. (2017, May 26). For army infantry's 1ˢᵗ, heavy packs and the weight of history. *New York Times.* https://www.nytimes.com/army-infantry

14. ARTICLE IN AN ONLINE DATABASE

Ignelzi, M. (2000, Summer). Meaning-making in the learning and teaching process. *New Directions for Teaching and Learning, 82,* 5-14. https://doi.org/10.1002/tl.8201

15. SHORT WORK FROM A WEBSITE

Eastman, H. (2017, May 11). How The Rock starts his leg day. *Bodybuilding.* https://www.bodybuilding.com/the-rock

16. BLOG POST

Peloquin, A. (2020, 5 May). Vacations are truly magical. *Breaking Muscle.* https://breakingmuscle.com/fitness/vacations-are-truly-magical

17. VIDEO BLOG POST (E.G., YOUTUBE)

Murphy, C. [Charles Murphy]. (2017, January 14). *APA format in Word—in 4 minutes* [Video]. YouTube. https://www.youtube.com/watch?v=_ODakMMqvIs

18. PERSONAL COMMUNICATIONS

(e.g., your own unpublished letters, digital correspondence, interviews). Since readers cannot readily access your unpublished personal communications, such sources do not appear on the reference page. Cite personal communications within the body of the paper (see entry in "In-text Citations" section).

19. TED TALK

Nelson, P.R. (2019, December 10). *Larry Lives Longer* [Video]. TED. https://www.ted.com/talks/larry-lives-longer

20. A MOVIE OR FILM

Marvin, N. (Producer) and Darabont, F. (Director). (1994). *Shawshank Redemption* [Film]. Castle Rock Entertainment.

21. SOUND RECORDING (I.E. SONG)

Place format of recording in brackets following the title of the album. The songwriter should be listed as the author. If the writer is someone other than the performer, follow the song title with a space and, in brackets, [Recorded by Initial. Last Name].

Hill, L. (1998). Ex-Factor. On *The Miseducation of Lauryn Hill* [Album]. Ruffhouse Records.

22. EPISODE OF TELEVISION SHOW

Lloyd, C. (Writer), and MacKenzie, P.C. (Director). (1995). Fool me once, shame on you, fool me Twice (Season 2, Episode 7). In D. Angel (Producer), *Frasier.* Paramount Studios.

23. TELEVISION SERIES

Harmon, D. (Producer). (2009). *Community* [TV series]. National Broadcasting Company.

References

Baker, T. (2003). Boredom in the first-year composition classroom. *Teaching English in the Two Year College, 30*(4), 404-415.

Eastman, H. (2017, May 11). How The Rock starts his leg day. *Bodybuilding.* https://www.bodybuilding.com/the-rock

Hansberry, L. (1959). *A raisin in the sun.* In K.J. Mays (Ed.) *Norton Introduction to Literature* (Shorter 12th ed) (pp.1456-1520). W.W. Norton.

"How to Become an International Student." (2019, August). https://www.hccfl.edu/intern/

Ignelzi, M. (2000, Summer). Meaning-making in the learning and teaching process. *New Directions for Teaching and Learning, 82,* 5-14. https://doi.org/10.1002/tl.8201

Lloyd, C. (Writer), & MacKenzie, P.C. (Director). (1995). Fool me once, shame on you, fool me Twice (Season 2, Episode 7). In D. Angel (Producer), *Frasier.* Paramount Studios.

Peloquin, A. (2020, 5 May). Vacations are truly magical. *Breaking Muscle.* https://breakingmuscle.com/fitness/vacations-are-truly-magical

Schwarz, D. R. (2016). *How to succeed in college and beyond: the art of learning.* Wiley Blackwell.

EXERCISE

APA FORMAT: REFERENCES PAGE EXERCISE 25.3A

Put the following sources into the proper format for a References Page. (Some entries give more information than is needed for your citation.)

1. Franz Kafka, "The Hunger Artist"

    Anthology: Literature: Reading, Reacting, Writing

    Editors: Laurie G. Kirzner and Stephen R. Mandell

    Edition: 6th ed.

    Publisher: Thomson Wadsworth

    Place of Publication: Boston

    Year of Publication: 2007

    Pages: 367-374

2. Jonathan Safran Foer, "A Primer for the Punctuation of Heart Disease"

    Periodical: The New Yorker

    Date of Publication: June 10, 2002

    Pages: 43-46

3. J. D. Salinger, "Perfect Day for Bananafish"

    Collection: Nine Stories

    Publisher: Little Brown

    Place of Publication: New York

    Year of Publication: 1953

    Pages: 3-18

4. A non-fiction book entitled Write Away, which was most recently published by Pearson in 1962. The authors are Octavia Jones and C.J. Thompson. The text was published first in Boston and the latest publication was done in London, and there are 320 pages.

5. Inside the Pentagon is an article found on MyPyramid.gov and was produced by the United States Department of Military Defense. There is no publication date, and there is no author provided.

6. Tomcat in Love **and** If I Die in a Combat Zone: Box Me Up and Ship Me Home are **two** books written by Tim O'Brien. The first was published in October 1984 by Bedford in New York. The second was published in New York by Holt in 1999.

7. A short story called "The Lone Ranger and Tonto Fistfight in Heaven" was written by Sherman Alexie and was found in an anthology (2nd edition) entitled Fiction of the Paranoid Indigenous, edited by Tom Timmery and Joe Josephson. Published in 1964 by Bantam in Los Angeles, and can be found on pages 565-71.

8. A poem entitled "Leaves of Glass" on pages 25-42 by Walt Wheatman in a collection of his own poems titled *Poems of a Rip Off Hippie*. The collection was edited by George Herbert and published in 1987 by Wadsworth, in the city of Boston and distributed in New York and Canada.

9. A journal article entitled "The Farmer Boy" published in the 1996 issue of The Library Quarterly by Tod Oppenheimer appears on pages 26-28. Volume 91, Issue 3.

10. "Who is He?" is an interview of Kurt Vonnegut that was conducted on March 3rd 1996 and was found in New Yorker on pages 36-38.

11. An article entitled The Legend of Lampoon written by Dietrich Goebbels was found in a reference book called New Age Propaganda on pages 12-27, edited by Jerome Jackson, and published in Connecticut by Harper Collins in 1974.

12. An article entitled The Rain Below, written by Peter Smith, was found in an online scholarly journal (Web) called Wet and Dry. It was retrieved May 9, 2006 and published on April 9, 2003. The URL is as follows: http://www.ran.org/info-center/products.html. It was found in the 12th volume and was the 2nd issue.

13. The Big Lebowski is a film (DVD) starring John Goodman and Jeff Bridges and directed by Joel Coen distributed by Universal in the United States in 1999.

14. In Praise of the "F" Word is an article written by Mary Sherry was first published in the newspaper The New York Times on the 25th of May in 1991 in the National Edition, page A1+

15. "Motion Picture" is an article found on Encyclopaedia Britannica Online, an encyclopedia on the Internet, and was composed of 3 paragraphs. The article was published by the Encyclopaedia Britannica in March of 1992 and retrieved on August 12th of 1997. The URL is as follows: http://www.eb.com/:220

Editing Symbols

ab	faulty abbreviation	19.2
ad	misused adjective/adverb	14.3/14.4
agr	error in subject verb agreement	17.1
ap	apostrophe misuse	16.5
APA	APA format issue	15
appr	inappropriate language	18.3
arg	faulty argument	12.9
awk	awkward sentence construction	15
cap	use capital letter	19.3
case	error in verb case	14.2/17.1
cit	citation error	22/23/24/25
coh	lacking coherence	18.4
con	be more concise	18.4
coord	coordination issue	15.3
crit	critical thinking issue	4.2
cs	comma splice	17.4
d	ineffective diction	18.3d
dm	dangling modifier	15.4
frag	sentence fragment	17.5
fs	fused sentence	17.3
gram	error in grammar	Part 4
hyph	hyphen use error	16.6
ital	use italics	16.9
lc	use lowercase	19.3
mixed	mixed sentence construction	17.6
MLA	MLA format issue	24
mm	misplaced modifier	15.4
mng	meaning unclear	15.4/18.4
no cap	incorrect capital letter	19.3
num	number use error	19.1
p	punctuation use error	16
pass	ineffective passive voice	18.2
pn agr	pronoun agreement error	17.2
ref	pronoun reference error	17.2
rep	unnecessary repetition	18.4
rev	revise/proofread	11
run-on	run-on sentence	17.3
sp	misspelled word	17.7
sub	subordination error	15.3
trans	transition needed	10.3
var	vary sentence structure	15.2
ww	wrong word	17.7

Symbol	Meaning	Example
	delete	Hamlet said, "To be or not to be be."
	insert period	I ran the race
	insert comma	I like cake but I don't like ice cream.
	insert colon	My gripe people who don't use coasters.
	insert semicolon	I like cake I don't like ice cream.
	insert question mark	Which one
	insert exclamation mark	Hurray
	insert hyphen	The well known actor won an award.
	insert apostrophe	My mothers dog is hungry.
	insert quotation marks	Hamlet said, To be or not to be.
	insert single quotation marks	She said, "The song Let it Be is great."
	insert en dash	Read Chapters 1 2
	insert em dash	My husband like his father is very nice.
	insert space	Iran the race.
	close up/delete space	I ran the r ace.
	begin new paragraph	Therefore, my thesis is true. Furthermore…
	indent	Another reason my thesis is true is…
	transpose (in text)	Hamlet said, "To be or to not be."
	transpose (in margin)	Hamlet said, "To be or to not be."
	spell out	Please don't use contractions.
	use italics (in text)	Have you read The Invisible Man?
	use italics (in margin)	Have you read The Invisible Man?
	capitalize	Elizabeth gaskell is a masterful writer.
	use lower case	Elizabeth Gaskell is a masterful Writer.
	let it stand	Hamlet said, "To be or not to be."

Printed in the USA
CPSIA information can be obtained
at www.ICGtesting.com
LVHW081609160823
755429LV00009B/398

9 781644 505960